PASS THE 6 ™

A PLAIN ENGLISH EXPLANATION TO HELP YOU PASS THE SERIES 6 EXAM

ROBERT M. WALKER

PASS THE 6™ - A PLAIN ENGLISH EXPLANATION TO HELP YOU PASS THE SERIES 6 EXAM

By Robert M. Walker

Revised Edition – January, 2017 – 3rd Edition

NASAA Statements of Policy and Model Rules reprinted with permission.

FINRA rules and definitions from the FINRA manual reprinted with permission from FINRA; ©2017 Financial Industry Regulatory Authority (FINRA).

MSRB General Rules reprinted with permission from MSRB.

www.examzone.com

Pass the 6™, 2nd Edition ISBN-13 978-0-692-61290-3

Library of Congress Control Number (LCCN) 2016900472

Publisher: Sure Fire Publications, LLC.® Chicago, IL (Acquired by Examzone, Inc. August 2016)

Printed in the U.S.A.

Table of Contents

How to Use This Book

We're happy you chose Examzone to help you pass the Series 6 exam. Our Pass the 6 Textbook is written in Plain English so you can learn concepts and memorize the material quickly and easily. We hope you take advantage of our full **Series 6 Success Program™**, complete with test prep materials for each step of the learning process.

The Learning Components of the **Series 6 Success Program™** can be found at http://www.examzone.com/series6 and include:

- Pass the 6™ Textbook
- Pass the 6™ DVD Lesson Set
- Pass the 6™ Online Training Videos
- Pass the 6™ Test-Taking Strategies Videos
- Pass the 6™ Practice Exam Question Bank
- Pass the 6™ Go/No Go Exams

Our research has shown that students who follow the entire **Series 6 Success Program™** have considerably higher pass rates than those who use only one or two of the Learning Components.

Our Success Program integrates each of the Learning Components on a chapter-by-chapter basis. The sequence starts with each textbook chapter, followed by the requisite Practice Exams and finishes with the videos and DVDs for that chapter. You can see this sequence outlined on the next page in the Study Plan for the **Series 6 Success Program™**.

Additionally, our Pass the 6™ Go/No Go Exams are designed to test your readiness for the Series 6 exam. We recommend you take the Go/No Go at least two weeks prior to your scheduled test date. If you score an 80% or above, we think you're ready to take the Series 6 exam.

All of the Success Program materials mentioned above are available for purchase at http://www.examzone.com/series6 Email us at support@examzone.com or call us toll free at 1-855-EXAM-CARE – 1 (855) 392-6227 with any questions.

Thanks for studying with Examzone, and good luck!

 examzone

Pass the 6™ Study Plan

Estimated Time Commitments:

- 4-6 weeks of study (60-80 hours)
- 3-5 days per week
- 2-4 hours per day

Weekly Study Plan:

WEEK 1 Goals:	<ul><li>Finish textbook through Chapter 1</li><li>Take Chapter 1 Review Quiz in Online Practice Question Bank</li><li>Listen to DVD and/or Online Streaming Video Session 1</li></ul>
WEEK 2 & WEEK 3 Goals:	<ul><li>Finish textbook through Chapter 2</li><li>Take Chapter 2 Review Quiz in Online Practice Question Bank</li><li>Listen to DVD and/or Online Streaming Video Sessions 2 & 3</li></ul>
WEEK 4 Goals:	<ul><li>Finish textbook through Chapter 3</li><li>Take Chapter 3 Review Quiz in Online Practice Question Bank</li><li>Listen to DVD and/or Online Streaming Video Session 4</li></ul>
WEEK 5 Goals:	<ul><li>Finish textbook through Chapter 4</li><li>Take Chapter 4 Review Quiz in Online Practice Question Bank</li><li>Listen to DVD and/or Online Streaming Video Session 5</li></ul>
WEEK 6 Goals:	<ul><li>Take all 6 Practice Exams in the Online Practice Question Bank</li><li>Review textbook, DVD and Streaming Video materials</li><li>Take the Go / No Go exams and proceed according to recommendation</li></ul>

Introduction

The Series 6 exam outline is organized according to the critical job functions performed by a registered representative with a Series 6 registration. I have laid out the book in four chapters to match these four critical job functions indicated by the FINRA outline. I've made an alteration only to the order in which the four sections appear so that it moves like this: opening a customer account, determining suitable recommendations, processing orders, and then knowing the important industry rules and regulations. FINRA starts out with the rules and regulations, which isn't surprising, since they write and enforce most of them. You, on the other hand, are trying to learn a lot of information in a short space of time, so I didn't want to introduce you to rules and regulations before I first explained who and what is being ruled and regulated.

If you skim the Table of Contents, you'll see that, as on the Series 6 Exam, Chapter 2 is much longer than the other three sections. The material from this section makes up 47 of the 100 questions on the Series 6 Exam. That is why the chapter is relatively longer than the other three and why we suggest you spend two weeks getting through it compared to just one week for the others.

What should you do at this point? Start reading this book, one chapter at a time. After finishing a chapter, take the online review exercises in our Pass The 6™ Online Practice Question Bank. After a break, come back and take the chapter review quiz online. If you have our training videos, watch the lesson or lessons that correspond, as indicated in our study schedule.

Above all, remember that concepts are what we're after here—not memorization of bullet points.

And, if you put in the work, it's likely you will pass the Series 6 in one attempt. But, please, don't put too much pressure on yourself. This is a test; this is only a test. Just give yourself enough time to complete the process.

Ready?

Excellent. Let's get started.

CHAPTER 1:
Opens, Maintains, Transfers and Closes Accounts and Retains Appropriate Account Records

Bank deposits are backed by the federal government's **FDIC** insurance, so the money one puts in a savings or checking account with a bank is not at risk. The money one places with a **broker-dealer,** on the other hand, is not backed by any arm of the federal government. Broker-dealers help their clients invest in **securities** including stocks, bonds, and mutual funds. Unlike money in the bank, money in the securities markets is always at risk. No matter how suitable a stock, bond, or mutual fund investment might be, investors can and do lose money by investing in securities, unlike when they put money in a bank.

So, it's not surprising that the process of opening an investment account for a customer of a broker-dealer is highly regulated.

OPENING AN ACCOUNT

Every business has "books," showing their financial transactions and results of those transactions. Not long ago, a company's books would have been on paper, but these days most books and records are kept electronically. My own company uses accounting software, so our books are also electronic, allowing us to easily back things up, as well as generate all kinds of reports for our CPA and various tax collection agencies. Luckily, our books and records are simple, like our textbooks.

On the other hand, broker-dealers have some of the most complicated books of any business, as reflected in their balance sheet, trial balance sheet, income statement, etc. The records required are detailed and numerous. Imagine all the correspondence and other communications happening between the broker-dealer and their customers, all the buy and sell orders executed through the firm, and all the deposits and withdrawals of cash and securities happening through that office.

These transactions all require records to be kept, as stipulated by the **Securities Exchange Act of 1934,** the rules under that Act, and various FINRA rules. Most records are required to be retained by FINRA member firms for a period of three years, and when no time is specified, the records are to be kept for a period of six years.

Now, chances are you just highlighted the "three years" and the "six years." That is fine; just don't expect test questions to focus on such easily memorized trivia. Both could be testable points, but your test is not based on memorized numbers. Your test forces you to think through unfamiliar situations quickly and knowledgably, which is why I'm taking my time explaining what things mean and how they fit together.

Regardless of how long they are kept, the records are to be maintained and made available upon request by FINRA staff members examining the firm for compliance. Records may be produced or reproduced on micrographic media or electronic storage media. Micrographic media includes the stuff I once used at the university library when researching old newspaper or magazine articles. I'm thinking most firms would be using a CD-ROM, DVD, magnetic tape, or USB storage device these days, which would fall, of course, under "electronic storage media." The main thing here is that whichever electronic storage media the firm uses itself or through a third-party vendor, the system or device must:

- Preserve the records in a non-erasable, non-rewritable format
- Verify automatically the quality and accuracy of the storage media recording process
- Serialize the original and, if applicable, duplicate units of storage media, and time-date the information for the required period of retention
- Have the capacity to readily download indexes and records on the electronic storage media to other media as required by the Commission or the self-regulatory organizations of which the firm is a member

For firms using the micrographic media (microfiche/microfilm) there must be devices for viewing/projecting the media available to visiting regulators, and if the regulators request an enlargement/print-out of specific sections, these must be made available as well.

So, FINRA has some common-sense rules regarding electronic storage and the reproduction of records—make sure the records are accurate and easily accessible to the SEC or FINRA staff members.

One of the most important areas of record keeping for broker-dealers involves customer account records. FINRA requires broker-dealers to obtain and maintain the following on file concerning a customer account:

- Customer name and residence
- Determination of legal age
- Name of the registered representative responsible for the account
- Signature of the principal (supervisor) approving the account
- If customer is business entity, names of those with authority to transact business
- For discretionary accounts, record of dated manual signature of each individual with authority to exercise discretion

Broker-dealers must also make a reasonable effort to determine and maintain the following information:

- TIN (taxpayer identification number), meaning SS # or business tax ID #
- Customer occupation and employer name and address
- Whether customer is associated with a FINRA member

- Information to determine suitability: objectives, financial info, etc.

If a customer refuses to supply any of the last four bullet points, the firm should document that an effort was made and that the customer refused to provide it. The four bullet points immediately preceding those are required for all accounts except institutional accounts and retail accounts that are limited to open-end funds not recommended by the broker-dealer. We'll talk more about open-end funds in Chapter 2.

For purposes of this rule an "institutional account" is an account for a bank, savings and loan association, insurance company, registered investment company, an investment adviser, and any other person (individual or entity) with assets of at least $50 million. As usual, the regulators provide more protection for retail investors than for large financial institutions or even individuals with $50 million to invest. The SEC provides investor protection, but also wants to foster capital formation and market efficiency.

FINRA provides a template that member firms can use when designing and updating their customer account applications at http://www.finra.org/sites/default/files/Industry/p125981.pdf.

Once all the required customer information has been obtained, the customer must be sent a copy of it and must provide verification that the information is accurate. The firm also asks the customer if she would like interest and dividend checks distributed to her or credited to her account. Customers often choose to have all mutual fund distributions reinvested into more shares of the fund. There are also many issuers who allow shareholders to reinvest dividends into fractional shares of common stocks, especially the blue-chip companies that pay regular dividends. These are sometimes called DRIP programs (Dividend Reinvestment Programs).

Customer information must be verified and/or updated regularly by the customer so the firm can see if the investment profile has changed due to an increase or decrease of income, educational funding needs, reaching a higher tax rate, or getting married or divorced, etc. The name on a customer's account, or the type of account, cannot be changed without a principal/supervisor approving of that action. So, suitability information can be handled by the registered representative and the customer, but to change the name or the type of account, always get a principal's approval. As you might expect, customer information is confidential, meaning you only provide information on your customers to others if the customer gives permission or if a legal action (such as a subpoena from FINRA, the courts, or a state securities regulator) requires it.

Also, broker-dealers and agents make recommendations to customers, but they may not invest or spend the customer's money without the customer's knowledge and consent. That's why FINRA has a rule on negotiable instruments drawn from a customer's account designed to protect customers from honest and not-so-honest mistakes over a few hundred thousand dollars maybe. Member firms "may not obtain from a customer or submit for payment a check, draft, or other negotiable paper drawn on a customer's checking, savings or similar account without that person's express written authorization." To document that express written authorization, the firm can either have the customer sign the negotiable instrument itself or sign a separate authorization form, of which they would be required to maintain a copy. If the customer signs the check, draft, etc., there is no need for the firm to keep a copy of that.

A member firm is not allowed to carry an account for a customer under any sort of bogus name, but, surprisingly, the account could be identified by a number or symbol (**numbered account**), provided the firm obtained and maintained evidence in writing signed by the customer attesting that the customer owns that account identified by only a number or a symbol. Perhaps the client is a celebrity who doesn't want everyone at the firm looking at her financial affairs, let alone selling stories to the tabloids based on her trading activity or frequent withdrawals from a dwindling account.

Customers frequently transfer assets held at one broker-dealer to another, and FINRA requires that both firms expedite this process by using the system known as **ACATS** (Automated Customer Account Transfer Service). The customer may want to transfer all the cash and securities from her account to another account, or, perhaps, just perform a partial transfer of assets. Either way, these are FINRA's concerns and requirements:

- When the member receives a customer transfer instruction form (TIF) to receive securities account assets from the carrying member firm, the receiving member must immediately submit the instructions to the carrying member in the ACATS system.
- Carrying member within one business day must validate or take exception to the transfer instructions (sent by the other firm, or the customer directly) and attach a list of customer account assets.
- Carrying and receiving members must promptly resolve any exceptions taken to the transfer instructions.

There are, unfortunately, some assets that are not ready to be transferred. For these situations the firms must promptly notify the customer and explain the situation. For example, stocks or bonds in a bankrupt company, or limited partnership interests that have no secondary market are not assets that can be easily transferred. On the other hand, customers can easily transfer their cash, their stocks, and their bonds from one firm to the other without having to liquidate everything, paying commissions and maybe capital gains taxes, and then paying more commissions to turn the cash back into securities within the new account at the new firm. So, ACATS is a good thing for customers and a good thing for broker-dealers who use it correctly.

Still, FINRA has concerns surrounding the fact that some member firms may recruit registered representatives away from other members and then encourage the agent's existing customers to make the switch as well. FINRA "is concerned that former customers may not be aware of other important factors to consider in making a decision whether to transfer assets to the recruiting firm, including directs costs that may be incurred."

Therefore, when this situation occurs FINRA rules require delivery of an educational communication by the recruiting firm that highlights key considerations in transferring assets to the recruiting firm, and the direct and indirect impacts of such a transfer on those assets. This communication, put out by FINRA, encourages customers to make further inquiries of the registered rep, the new member and the existing brokerage firm holding his assets. The educational material must be delivered to the customer whether he was contacted by the registered representative or the recruiting firm, or even if he just transferred assets to an account assigned to the newly hired/recruited agent.

A former customer is defined here as any retail customer who had a securities account assigned to the registered person at the representative's previous firm.

As FINRA explains:

> *The educational communication would highlight the following potential implications of transferring assets to the recruiting firm: (1) Whether financial incentives received by the representative may create a conflict of interest; (2) that some assets may not be directly transferrable to the recruiting firm and as a result the customer may incur costs to liquidate and move those assets or account maintenance fees to leave them with his or her current firm; (3) potential costs related to transferring assets to the recruiting firm, including differences in the pricing structure and fees imposed by the customer's current firm and the recruiting firm; and (4) differences in products and services between the customer's current firm and the recruiting firm.*

Without this FINRA rule customers could end up being hit with surrender charges or other liquidation fees and even tax penalties simply because they trusted their registered representative without looking at any of the details.

FINRA requires that [most] member firms provide "education and protection" to customers by complying with the following requirement:

> *Each member shall once every calendar year provide in writing (which may be electronic) to each customer the following items of information:*
>
> *(1) FINRA BrokerCheck Hotline Number;*
>
> *(2) FINRA Web site address; and*
>
> *(3) A statement as to the availability to the customer of an investor brochure that includes information describing FINRA BrokerCheck.*

As we'll explore elsewhere, FINRA's **BrokerCheck** provides registration and disclosure information on broker-dealers, principals, and agents. Whenever an agent, principal, or member firm is disciplined by FINRA, such information goes into BrokerCheck. So, be on your best behavior, since you will be searchable by name and/or CRD (**Central Registration Depository**) number indefinitely after you associate with your employing broker-dealer.

FINRA now requires member firms to provide a prominent reference to BrokerCheck and a hyperlink to the site on the initial landing page intended for retail investors and on any other page that profiles investment professionals who conduct business with retail investors. Typically, an employing member firm publishes a website that profiles each registered representative. A photograph, a career summary, and a list of securities licenses obtained are typically provided for each representative. FINRA requires that a reference to BrokerCheck and the URL to the site also be provided, encouraging investors to check the background of their prospective and current agents, as well as the member firms they represent.

All **customer written complaints** must be acted upon, with the correspondence kept on file by the broker-dealer. As FINRA rules indicate:

> *Each member shall keep and preserve in each office of supervisory jurisdiction either a separate file of all written customer complaints that relate to that office (including complaints that relate to activities supervised from that office) and action taken by the member, if any, or a separate record of such complaints and a clear reference to the files in that office containing the correspondence connected with such complaints. Rather than keep and preserve the customer complaint records required under this Rule at the office of supervisory jurisdiction, the member may choose to make them promptly available at that office, upon request of FINRA. Customer complaint records shall be preserved for a period of at least four years.*

How does FINRA define a "customer complaint"? Like this:

> *any grievance by a customer or any person authorized to act on behalf of the customer involving the activities of the member or a person associated with the member in connection with the solicitation or execution of any transaction or the disposition of securities or funds of that customer.*

FINRA is the **SRO (Self-Regulatory Organization)** that regulates your firm, your principals, and you. FINRA, in turn, is registered with and overseen by the SEC or **Securities and Exchange Commission** under the **Securities Exchange Act of 1934**. I've noticed that many tutoring clients seem to be skimming if not skipping over any reference to federal securities law when studying, and I'm here to tell you—cut it out. You don't need a deep understanding of the federal securities acts, but you also don't need to miss a handful of rather easy questions, either. So, the Securities Exchange Act of 1934 is the one that empowered the SEC to oversee broad aspects of the securities markets, including the authority to register the exchanges and national securities associations, e.g., NYSE, and NASD (now FINRA). Here is how the SEC—the federal government—explains themselves at www.sec.gov:

> The mission of the U.S. Securities and Exchange Commission is to protect investors, maintain fair, orderly, and efficient markets, and facilitate capital formation.

> As more and more first-time investors turn to the markets to help secure their futures, pay for homes, and send children to college, our investor protection mission is more compelling than ever.
>
> As our nation's securities exchanges mature into global for-profit competitors, there is even greater need for sound market regulation.
>
> And the common interest of all Americans in a growing economy that produces jobs, improves our standard of living, and protects the value of our savings means that all the SEC's actions must be taken with an eye toward promoting the capital formation that is necessary to sustain economic growth.

That's the SEC's mission statement.

This is what they say about the Securities Exchange Act of 1934:

> With this Act, Congress created the Securities and Exchange Commission. The Act empowers the SEC with broad authority over all aspects of the securities industry. This includes the power to register, regulate, and oversee brokerage firms, transfer agents, and clearing agencies as well as the nation's securities self-regulatory organizations (SROs). The various stock exchanges, such as the New York Stock Exchange, and American Stock Exchange are SROs. The Financial Industry Regulatory Authority, which operates the NASDAQ system, is also an SRO.
>
> The Act also identifies and prohibits certain types of conduct in the markets and provides the Commission with disciplinary powers over regulated entities and persons associated with them.
>
> The Act also empowers the SEC to require periodic reporting of information by companies with publicly traded securities.

Sections of this Act and the Rules the SEC writes pursuant to the Act guide the brokerage industry that you are now entering. Even a quick reading of SEC rules or the federal acts that gave them their authority shows us what is considered essential to this regulatory body:

- Full and fair disclosure
- Meticulous record keeping
- A fair and level marketplace

So, if any activity explained on the exam shows someone trying to deceive or mislead investors by making misstatements of material facts about an investment, you know there's no way that's okay. Not everything has to be written down in triplicate at a broker-dealer, but you also have to assume that correspondence with customers regarding recommendations or complaints with the handling of their accounts would be items for which the regulators would require records. Then again, assumptions can only take you so far on this exam, so let's see what the SEC requires in terms of record keeping for the brokerage industry under the Securities Exchange Act of 1934. Heads up—this is one detailed list:

1. Blotters (or other records of original entry) containing an itemized daily record of all purchases and sales of securities, all receipts and deliveries of securities (including certificate numbers), all receipts and disbursements of cash and all other debits and credits. Such records shall show the account for which each such transaction was effected, the name and amount of securities, the unit and aggregate purchase or sale price (if any), the trade date, and the name or other designation of the person from whom purchased or received or to whom sold or delivered.

2. Ledgers (or other records) reflecting all assets and liabilities, income and expense and capital accounts.

3. Ledger accounts (or other records) itemizing separately as to each cash and margin account of every customer and of such member, broker or dealer and partners thereof, all purchases, sales, receipts and deliveries of securities and commodities for such account and all other debits and credits to such account.

4. Ledgers reflecting: securities in transfer, dividends and interest received, securities loaned and borrowed, moneys loaned and borrowed, securities failed to receive and failed to deliver

5. Ledger or securities record showing each security held "long" or "short" for the firm or any customer account

6. Memorandum of each brokerage order. "The memorandum shall show the terms and conditions of the order or instructions and of any modification or cancellation thereof; the account for which entered; the time the order was received; the time of entry; the price at which executed; the identity of each associated person, if any, responsible for the account; the identity of any other person who entered or accepted the order on behalf of the customer or, if a customer entered the order on an electronic system, a notation of that entry; and, to the extent feasible, the time of execution or cancellation."

7. Memorandum of each order for the member itself showing price and time of execution. And, if the transaction is with a person other than a broker or dealer (retail customer) more details are required.

8. Copies of confirmations of all purchases and sales of securities, including all repurchase and reverse repurchase agreements, and copies of notices of all other debits and credits for securities, cash and other items for the account of customers and partners of such member, broker or dealer.

9. Record in respect of each cash and margin account with such member, broker or dealer indicating a record in respect of each cash and margin account with such member, broker or dealer indicating and whether or not the beneficial owner of securities registered in the name of such members, brokers or dealers, or a registered clearing agency or its nominee objects to disclosure of his or her identity, address and securities positions to issuers, and for margin accounts the signature of each owner.

10. A record of all puts, calls, spreads, straddles and other options in which such member, broker or dealer has any direct or indirect interest or which such members, broker or dealer has granted or guaranteed, containing, at least, an identification of the security and the number of units involved.

11. A record of the proof of money balances of all ledger accounts in the form of trial balances, and a record of the computation of aggregate indebtedness and net capital, as of the trial balance date.

12. A questionnaire or application for employment executed by each "associated person" (as defined in paragraph (h)(4) of this section) of the member, broker or dealer, which questionnaire or application shall be approved in writing by an authorized representative of the member, broker or dealer

13. For each account for a natural person: An account record including the customer's or owner's name, tax identification number, address, telephone number, date of birth, employment status (including occupation and whether the customer is an associated person of a member, broker or dealer), annual income, net worth (excluding value of primary residence), and the account's investment objectives. In the case of a joint account, the account record must include personal information for each joint owner who is a natural person; however, financial information for the individual joint owners may be combined. The account record shall indicate whether it has been signed by the associated person responsible for the account, if any, and approved or accepted by a principal of the member, broker or dealer. The record or alternative document sent to the customer should prominently alert the customer to mark any corrections and return the document and to notify the firm of any changes/updates in the future.

14. For the records above: the firm must keep a record showing it has furnished the information to the customer within **30** days of opening the account and no less frequently than every **36** months thereafter. And, for each change of name or address, the firm has furnished the customer and associated person over the account of notification within **30** days—to the customer's old address, and, if applicable, to the address of each owner of a joint account.

15. For changes in investment objectives the firm must confirm the changes within **30** days or with the next account statement.

16. All guarantees of accounts and all powers of attorney and other evidence of the granting of any discretionary authority given in respect of any account, and copies of resolutions empowering an agent to act on behalf of a corporation.

A "sales blotter" is a record of original entry showing "an itemized daily record of all purchases and sales of securities, all receipts and deliveries of securities (including certificate numbers), all receipts and disbursements of cash and all other debits and credits." The blotter shows all movements of cash and securities that the broker-dealer is responsible for during the business day. It's an important record to keep, and, of course, if FINRA were investigating a member firm and found that one of the principals had been trying to alter such records chances are at least one person would be in trouble very quickly.

The word "ledger" is a more precise term used for "record." The SEC requires that broker-dealers keep detailed "ledgers" or "records" of assets vs. liabilities of the firm, and their income vs. expenses. Records of all movements of cash and securities within each customer account carried by the member firm must be meticulously kept, as well. We don't discuss margin accounts a lot on this exam, but you'll need to know that they are watched more closely than cash accounts because the customer is investing borrowed money in a margin account and can end up losing more than he puts down initially. Therefore, the SEC requires the signature of any margin customer so the firm can show some evidence that the customer knows she's in such an account.

Violations of SEC rules are frequently handled by FINRA, but the SEC also has administrative hearings, and neither process would be good for a financial services career, of course. Also, whenever an agent gets in trouble under FINRA disciplinary procedures, his state securities Administrator can take action as well. For those who have no hope of hanging onto their career, the state securities administrative action is often not a big deal. Many individuals, in fact, refuse to cooperate with FINRA, which is at least two violations in one—it violates a specific FINRA rule that says oh-yes-you-do-have-to-cooperate, and the general provision that all members must "maintain high standards of commercial honor." Refusing to cooperate with FINRA might not be the worst thing an agent can do, but it is one of the surest ways of getting kicked out of the industry.

On the other hand, for the agents who are merely being suspended by FINRA for a few weeks or months there is plenty of incentive to deal with the state Administrator as well as FINRA to keep the job and career alive. The downside here is that a state-level administrative hearing would likely add nasty legal bills to whatever the disciplined agent already spent during the FINRA hearing process.

In other words, knowing the rules that we discuss in this textbook is not just important for your exam; it's important for your career survival as well. Agents often start cutting corners and get into trouble because they're in financial dire straits, so right when FINRA and the state securities regulators start taking disciplinary action, the agent needs but doesn't have, say, $25,000 to pay for adequate legal counsel. A respondent can represent himself **pro se,** though that seems about as bright as doing so in civil or criminal court from any lawyer's perspective. Then again, I have attended one hearing at a state administrator's office where the former agent did exactly this, and, frankly, things turned out just fine for him. But, I still don't like facing regulators without an attorney speaking for me and—maybe more importantly—telling me when not to speak.

TYPES OF ACCOUNT OWNERSHIP

INDIVIDUAL ACCOUNTS

An account opened by an individual is called an **individual account** for obvious reasons. If an individual opens an account, the firm must only accept purchase and sell orders or instructions to move assets from that individual.

A **Transfer on Death** (TOD) account allows the account to pass directly to the **beneficiary** or beneficiaries, bypassing **probate** court. That means that these assets do not have to be transferred subject to the court's record or approval, keeping things private. Only the assets that are in the account pass to the beneficiary, and this account has no effect on estate taxes. It just makes the transfer faster and simpler.

To establish an individual account as a TOD account, the account owner signs a Transfer on Death Beneficiary Agreement with the broker-dealer. In this agreement the customer can indicate primary and contingent beneficiaries, and can indicate more than one of either type, indicating a % that each one is to receive. A "contingent beneficiary" is named in case the primary beneficiary dies or disclaims the inheritance. But, an individual might want to name his two children as primary beneficiaries, each receiving 50%, with maybe a niece and nephew named as contingent beneficiaries, with the stated percentage each is to receive in case the primary beneficiaries don't end up inheriting the assets.

Now, since nothing is ever simple in this business, there is a way that you could accept orders from someone other than the customer. That is if your customer grants the other person **trading authorization**. Limited trading authorization means the other person can give buy and sell orders but can't withdraw cash or securities. Full trading authorization means he can do all the above. Trading authorization can also be referred to as "power of attorney." When you grant **power of attorney** to someone, you give them the power power to to make important decisions on your behalf—the represent you.

JOINT ACCOUNTS

Two or more people can open a **joint account**. If two (or more) individuals want to share an account, they will open it either as JTWROS or JTIC. JTWROS stands for **joint tenants with rights of survivorship**. The phrase "rights of survivorship" means that the survivor gets the assets if the other party dies. They go straight to the surviving owner(s), again, bypassing probate if it's spouse-to-spouse.

A JTIC (**Joint Tenants in Common**) account is a little different. In these accounts, the assets do not transfer to the other account owner upon death. Instead, they pass to the deceased individual's **estate**. The account owners would list the percentage each party owns in the account on the joint account agreement, and that percentage would pass to the deceased's estate upon death.

If it's a joint account, orders will be accepted from any party listed on the account. Account statements and related documents can be sent to either party. But if we are talking about cutting a check or transferring securities, the check or transfer must be made to all names on the account, exactly as the account is titled. In other words, we don't cut a check to Barbara and tell her to settle with Sheila and Suzanne next time the three have lunch. If the account is titled Barbara Benson, Sheila Stevens, and Suzanne Somerville, as Joint Tenants in Common, then that is how the check will be drawn up.

FIDUCIARY ACCOUNTS

➢ UGMA/UTMA

Minor children are not legal persons, which means they can't open investment accounts no matter how smart they are. An adult must open a **custodial account** on behalf of a minor if the kid is going to beneficially own securities. That makes the adult the **nominal owner** and the child the **beneficial owner** of the account. Everything in the account is to be done for the benefit of the minor child.

When the child becomes an adult, the assets will be re-registered in his name, but until then we'll have an adult custodian handle the account. If a donor wants to donate money for the benefit of a minor, all she must do is set the account up as either an **UGMA** (Uniform Gifts to Minors Act) or **UTMA** (Uniform Transfers to Minors Act) account, which doesn't require any supporting documentation in either case—it's just an account type. The registered representative opens it as either UGMA or UTMA, depending on the state of residence, making sure there's just one adult custodian and one minor child per account. If you see "Jim and Judy Smith as custodians for…" stop right there. You can't have two adults as custodians. And you can't have more than one minor child per account.

Also, the gifts cannot be taken back once given, nor can they be treated as a loan. The legal phrase is the gifts are all "irrevocable and indefeasible."

We put the minor child's social security number on the account because these accounts are taxable if a certain amount is earned per year. Typically, the income earned escapes taxation, and because of the special tax treatment, a custodian could get himself in trouble if he used a child's UTMA account as sort of a revolving line of credit to keep various businesses afloat. Any use of the assets must be only for the benefit of the minor child. Using funds to send the child to music camp would be just fine. Borrowing money that the custodian fully intends to repay someday—not so much. Also, parents may not charge their kids room and board and consider that a benefit to the child. So, withdrawals going to parents for providing basic child support would be a violation of the tax code, as well.

> Trust Accounts

With an UGMA/UTMA account a 21-year-old could suddenly have full ownership of a large investment account. For most "kids" at that age, a **trust** account would be more prudent. In a trust account, the **grantor**—the one funding the trust with a grant of assets—can specify in the **trust agreement** all kinds of things, such as how much money can be withdrawn per year, what types of investments are considered appropriate/allowed, etc.

If you open a trust account for a customer, you'll need a copy of the trust agreement so that you can verify that the trustee has the authority to manage the account on behalf of the beneficiary and you can see what is and is not allowed. Maybe the person who established the trust, the grantor, got burned in the stock market and wrote a provision that no stocks shall be purchased unless the company is earning a profit or maybe no more than 10% of trust assets shall be invested in equities, what have you. A trust document can be written to guide the actions and inclinations of the trust long after the grantor is dead and gone. We said that an UTMA/UGMA account requires no supporting documentation. A trust account must be supported by the trust agreement, at least.

> Estate Accounts

Not to bring up a sore subject, but let's say that this summer your grandmother passes away. You discover that her **will** named you as the **executor**. Had Grandma died without a will, a **probate court** must appoint an "administrator" of the estate. In either case, an executor or administrator of an estate can open an investment account in the name of the estate. Estate accounts require all kinds of supporting documentation. We need the estate's **tax identification number** as issued by the federal government, a death certificate, and court documents showing that this person is, in fact, empowered to act as the executor/administrator of the estate. The exam could call these documents a "court appointment" or "letters of office," and these documents must be no more than 60 days old. An estate is a legal entity that holds the assets of a deceased person: real estate, farmland, stocks, bonds, checking, savings, CDs, etc. The estate typically closes out in six months, sometimes in two years. Either way, the investment recommendations would be based on a very short time horizon.

> Discretionary Accounts

As a registered representative, you typically only recommend investments to your customers. But, believe it or not, if a customer trusted you, she could let you make investment decisions for her— while also paying yourself a commission. That means if you want to buy 1,000 shares of MSFT for her account, you can do so without even bothering to call her. Of course, the purchase must be suitable for the account, but if you think today is a good day to buy her some MSFT or SBUX common stock, go ahead and buy it with the money in her account, pocketing a commission for you and your firm in the process.

Before the first trade pursuant to your discretion she must sign a **discretionary authorization** form, and the account would be reviewed more frequently. But, from then on, you could choose which securities to buy or sell and how many shares/units to buy or sell. You could, for example, buy 100 shares of MSFT or put $5,000 of her un-invested cash into a mutual fund without even bothering to call her first. On the other hand, without discretionary authority a registered representative can never determine which securities are bought or sold or how many shares/units. Unless the account is a **discretionary account,** the only thing a representative can determine is the time or price at which to execute a transaction. So, if a client calls and says, "Buy some consumer staple stocks today," do you need discretionary authority before you buy 100 shares of Procter & Gamble?

Yes. If you choose the investment vehicle, that constitutes discretion.

If a client says, "Buy as much Procter & Gamble as you think I should buy today," you would also not be able to take that order as-is, not until the client okays the number of shares you're going to purchase.

But, if a client tells you to "Buy 1,000 shares of Procter & Gamble for me today," do you need discretionary authorization over the account to accept that order?

No, your client has chosen the asset (PG) and the amount (1,000 shares). Only thing left for you to decide is the best time and price to do it, and time/price decisions do not require written discretionary authorization Note, however, that the order to buy 1,000 shares of PG does must be entered that day; if not, it goes away. And, even though you wouldn't need anything signed by the customer, as a registered representative, you would indicate that you have "time and price discretion" on the order ticket.

Now, if I gave you discretion over my account and was clearly an income investor with a low risk tolerance and a short time horizon, the exam might say that if you use your discretion to purchase aggressive growth funds, you have made an **unauthorized transaction.** Even though Series 6 licensees don't execute orders for individual shares of stock, you might run into the same situation if a client just wants to cut a check for, say, $25,000 to the investment company and let you and your supervisor decide how to allocate it. Without discretion over the account, you would not be able to take it from there. Rather, you would be required to help the customer determine specifically how much should go into each fund.

FINRA rules require that firms review any discretionary accounts carefully, as we see here:

> *The member or the person duly designated shall approve promptly in writing each discretionary order entered and shall review all discretionary accounts at frequent intervals to detect and prevent transactions which are excessive in size or frequency in view of the financial resources and character of the account.*

A **guardian account** is established for a minor when the parents are ruled mentally incompetent or the child is orphaned. Or, sometimes such an account is established when an adult is determined to be mentally incompetent. In other words, somebody must look out for the financial affairs of another person, acting as that person's guardian. As with an estate account, we would need to see the court order appointing the guardian, and it would need to be no more than 60 days old. A "receiver" is a party placed in charge of the assets of a company in bankruptcy. We would be required to see the court papers putting this party in charge of the assets of a struggling company.

BUSINESS ACCOUNTS

A corporation or partnership can open an investment account, too. If your client is a corporation or partnership, you'll be required to look at the documents that govern these entities. You'll need a copy of the corporate resolution for a corporation. For a partnership, you'll need a copy of the partnership agreement. These documents tell you who has authority to trade on behalf of the corporation or partnership. Even though mutual funds cannot be purchased "on margin," the term "margin" might show up on the Series 6. Buying "on margin" means to use money borrowed through your broker-dealer, backed up by the stock's current market value as collateral.

If a corporation wants to trade on margin, the registered representative needs a copy of the corporate charter to make sure those documents say it's okay. If a partnership wants to trade on margin, the rep must make sure the partnership agreement says it's okay.

An investment adviser is a firm that provides investment advice for compensation. They often have discretion over their clients' accounts and place trades through your broker-dealer. Therefore, you would be required to see documentation that the adviser does have authority to place trades on behalf of its customers.

So, we've looked at various types of customer accounts. Now, let's look at all kinds of important procedures and regulations connected to opening, maintaining, and closing customer accounts.

ANTI–MONEY LAUNDERING

Broker-dealers are businesses that like to make as much profit as possible. Any effort they are required to expend that doesn't lead to profit is a burden. Sometimes it's their SRO (Self-Regulatory Organization) called FINRA that is requiring them to cooperate, sometimes the SEC, and sometimes other parts of the U.S. Government, including the Department of the U.S. Treasury.

Anti–Money Laundering (AML) programs are a requirement of broker-dealers, along with all the other compliance requirements we look at in this textbook. As FINRA rules make clear to member firms:

> *Each member shall develop and implement a written anti-money laundering program reasonably designed to achieve and monitor the member's compliance with the requirements of the Bank Secrecy*

The **Bank Secrecy Act** (BSA) authorizes the U.S. Treasury Department to require financial institutions such as banks and broker-dealers to maintain records of personal financial transactions that "have a high degree of usefulness in criminal, tax and regulatory investigations and proceedings." It also authorizes the Treasury Department to require any financial institution to report any "suspicious transaction relevant to a possible violation of law or regulation." These reports, called **Suspicious Activity Reports**, are filed with the Treasury Department's Financial Crimes Enforcement Network ("FinCEN").

FINRA rules state that at a minimum member broker-dealers must implement an AML program that:

- Establishes and implements policies and procedures that can be reasonably expected to detect and cause the reporting of transactions required under [the BSA].
- Provides for an annual (calendar-based) independent testing for compliance to be conducted by member personnel or by a qualified outside party.
- Designates and identifies to FINRA an individual or individuals responsible for implementing and monitoring the day-to-day operations and internal controls of the program. And promptly notify FINRA of any changes.
- Provides ongoing training.

The U.S. Treasury Department under the Bank Secrecy Act (BSA) requires that for wire transmittals of funds of $3,000 or more, broker-dealers are required to obtain and keep certain specified information concerning the parties sending and receiving those funds. In addition, broker-dealers must include this information on the actual transmittal order. Also, any <u>cash</u> transactions over $10,000 require the same type of record keeping. For these, broker-dealers must file a **Currency Transaction Report** with FinCEN.

Why? Because terrorist and other criminal organizations thrive through **money laundering**. Since broker-dealers are financial institutions, they're lumped in with banks and required to do all kinds of record keeping to help the government prevent these operations. What is money laundering? It's the process of turning "dirty" money "clean." Without it, organized crime and terrorist organizations could not function. The goal of money laundering is to hide proceeds derived from illegal sources and to make them appear legitimate. For example, if a mobster can take profits made from loan sharking and turn them into shares of stock, soon it appears he has a legitimate source of income.

As fans of the TV series Breaking Bad know, there are three stages of money laundering. **Placement** is the stage when funds are moved into the system. **Layering** is the stage when a confusing set of transactions is conducted to make it unclear where these funds originated. **Integration** is the stage when the funds are invested in legitimate enterprises or investment vehicles.

With the passage of the **USA Patriot Act**, broker-dealers and other financial institutions must help the government monitor suspicious activity that could be tied to money laundering.

Broker-dealers now must report any transaction that involves at least $5,000 if the broker-dealer knows, suspects, or has reason to suspect that it doesn't pass the smell test. FINRA spells out four specific characteristics that would make a broker-dealer file a suspicious activity report (SAR-SF). An SAR-SF report would be filed if the transaction falls within one of four classes:

- the transaction involves funds derived from illegal activity or is intended or conducted to hide or disguise funds or assets derived from illegal activity;
- the transaction is designed to evade the requirements of the Bank Secrecy Act;
- the transaction appears to serve no business or apparent lawful purpose or is not the sort of transaction in which the specific customer would be expected to engage and for which the broker/dealer knows of no reasonable explanation after examining the available facts; or
- the transaction involves the use of the broker/dealer to facilitate criminal activity.

Notice that broker-dealers must look not just at individual transactions but at patterns of transactions that, taken together, appear suspicious.

Confidentiality when complying with all this is required by federal law—as FINRA explains:

The rule also requires that the filing of a Form SAR-SF report must remain confidential. The person involved in the transaction that is subject of the report must not be notified of the Form SAR-SF. In other words, if subpoenaed, the broker/dealer must refuse to provide the information and notify FinCEN of the request, unless the disclosure is required by FinCEN, the SEC, an SRO or other law enforcement authority. Where two or more broker/dealers are filing one Form SAR-SF, the confidentiality provisions apply equally to each broker/dealer participating in a transaction, and not only the broker/dealer that filed the Form SAR-SF.

An exam question might ask what the agent or firm should do after filing an SAR-SF form—does that relieve them of their reporting obligations? Not necessarily. If the activity involves terrorist financing, for example, or ongoing money laundering schemes, the member firm must notify the appropriate law enforcement agency and/or call FinCEN's hotline if the activity appears to be related to terrorism. As with everything else, broker-dealers must keep records connected to any SAR-SF reports, which they maintain for 5 years, making them available to FINRA staff upon request.

Broker-dealers now must have a **customer identification program (CIP)** whereby they require more information to open an account. If the customer is not a U.S. citizen, the firm will need:

- taxpayer ID number
- passport number and country of issuance
- alien ID card
- other current (not expired) government-issued photo ID card

Even the U.S. citizen may be required to show a photo ID, just as you do when you go take your Series 6 exam. The CIP program requires agents and their firms to take reasonable steps to verify the identity of anyone opening an account, to maintain the records used to verify the person's identity, and to consult a list of known and suspected terrorists to prevent opening an account for anyone on that list.

The federal government now maintains an **Office of Foreign Asset Control** (OFAC) designed to protect against the threat of terrorism. This office maintains a list of individuals and organizations viewed as a threat to the U.S. These suspected threats are called "Specially Designated Nationals" or SDNs. Broker-dealers and other financial institutions now must make sure they aren't setting up accounts for these folks, or—if they are—they must block/freeze the assets. A compliance officer must be designated to handle this responsibility.

SECURITY OF CUSTOMER INFORMATION

Sharing customer information with law enforcement officials is one thing. Providing it to telemarketers and identity thieves is quite another. To fight identity theft and to protect customers from having too much of their information shared with people they've never met, the SEC enacted **Regulation S-P** to put into place a requirement from the Gramm-Leach-Bliley Act. Basically:

> a financial institution must provide its customers with a notice of its privacy policies and practices, and must not disclose nonpublic personal information about a consumer to nonaffiliated third parties unless the institution provides certain information to the consumer and the consumer has not elected to opt out of the disclosure.

A "**consumer**" is basically a prospect, someone interested in establishing some type of account. A "**customer**" is someone who has now opened a financial relationship with the firm. Broker-dealers and investment advisers must deliver initial and annual notices to customers explaining their privacy policies and practices, the types of information they share and with whom, and about the opportunity and methods to opt out of their institution's sharing of their nonpublic personal information with nonaffiliated third parties. The initial notice must be provided no later than when the firm establishes a customer relationship with the individual.

For some purposes the difference between the terms consumer and customer is important. In terms of limiting the information that is shared for certain purposes we will just refer to "consumers." Consumers (and customers) can only limit certain types of information sharing between a financial institution and another party. The other party is either an affiliate or a non-affiliate, as defined in the financial institution's privacy statement. Consumers can limit the sharing of information with an affiliate for their everyday business purposes that involves the consumer's creditworthiness. The consumer can also limit the information shared to both affiliates and non-affiliates for the purpose of marketing to the consumer. Consumers do not have the right under federal law to limit the sharing of information that the financial institution engages in for the following purposes:

- the financial institution's marketing purposes

- joint marketing with other financial companies
- affiliates' everyday business purposes involving transactions and experiences

Broker-dealers and investment advisers also must have written supervisory procedures dealing with the disposal of consumer credit report information. Since firms typically look at a consumer's credit history before opening accounts—especially margin accounts—selling annuities, or providing financial planning services, the firms must safely dispose of the information rather than just setting it all in a big box out back.

Broker-dealers often must respond to requests for documents under disciplinary investigations. When providing such information through a portable media device (DVD, CD-ROM, flash drive), FINRA requires that the information be encrypted. As FINRA states:

> the data must be encoded into a form in which meaning cannot be assigned without the use of a confidential process or key. To help ensure that encrypted information is secure, persons providing encrypted information to FINRA via a portable media device are required to use an encryption method that meets industry standards for strong encryption and to provide FINRA staff with the confidential process or key regarding the encryption in a communication separate from the encrypted information itself (e.g., a separate email, fax or letter).

Beyond responding to the regulators' requests, customer emails also must be encrypted, and registered representatives should not go around sharing customer information with anyone who doesn't need to know it.

The **FACT Act** is short for the **Fair and Accurate Credit Transactions Act.** Under this federal legislation the three major credit reporting agencies, in cooperation with the Federal Trade Commission (FTC) set up a website at www.AnnualCreditReport.com that allows consumers to monitor their credit reports. This Act also attempts to reduce identify theft by requiring firms who collect information on individuals to safely dispose of it and by allowing individuals to place alerts on their credit history if they suspect fraudulent transactions. Broker-dealers gather information from consumers through various sales and marketing efforts. The FACT Act requires that they don't simply toss thousands of post cards or computer hard drives containing personal and financial information about consumers out in a dumpster behind the branch office. For example.

The FACT Act requires the various agencies charged with its implementation to "identify patterns, practices, and specific forms of activity that indicate the possible existence of **identity theft**." The guidelines must be updated as often as necessary and cannot be inconsistent with the requirement to verify a customer's identity when opening an account. Right? See how we have competing concerns there? On the one hand, we want to shield customers from unauthorized access to their identities; on the other hand, we can't be so secretive that we don't know who's who on our customer list.

The Federal Trade Commission (FTC) has implemented a red flags rule that requires broker-dealers and other financial institutions to create written "Identity Theft Protection Programs" or "ITPPs" designed to identify, detect, and respond to warning signs (red flags) that could indicate identity theft. The four elements of a firm's ITPP (Identity Theft Protection Program) require broker dealers and other financial institutions to:

- <u>identify</u> relevant red flags for the covered accounts that the firm offers or maintains, and incorporate those red flags into its ITPP;
- detect red flags that have been incorporated into the ITPP of the financial institution or creditor;
- respond appropriately to any red flags that are detected to prevent and mitigate identity theft; and
- update the ITPP and its red flags periodically to reflect changes in identity theft risks to customers and the firm.

Broker-dealers must design their Identity Theft Protection Program and have it approved by the Board of Directors of the firm or a designated member of senior management. The principals who approve the program must be involved in its oversight, development, implementation and administration. The firm must train staff to implement the ITPP. If the broker-dealer utilizes any third-party providers to help them with their responsibilities under the red flag rules, the firm must oversee those arrangements carefully.

WORKING WITH CUSTOMERS

Before a registered representative starts making recommendations, he must get to know the important facts about a customer's financial situation.

KNOW YOUR CUSTOMER

Under FINRA's **Know Your Customer** rule agents and their firms must "use reasonable diligence, in regard to the opening and maintenance of every account, to know (and retain) the essential facts concerning every customer and concerning the authority of each person acting on behalf of such customer." FINRA says that the *essential facts* involved with *knowing the customer* "are those required to (a) effectively service the customer's account, (b) act in accordance with any special handling instructions for the account, (c) understand the authority of each person acting on behalf of the customer, and (d) comply with applicable laws, regulations, and rules."

A FINRA Notice to Members explains that requesting the information from the customer is usually considered using reasonable diligence. But—as always—there are buts. FINRA follows up that statement with this one: when customer information is unavailable despite a firm's reasonable diligence, however, the firm must carefully consider whether it has a sufficient understanding of the customer to properly evaluate the suitability of the recommendation.

So, as usual, FINRA tells its members and their associated persons what their obligations are and gives them some guidance. But, ultimately, it's up to the member firms, their principals, and their agents to get it right. Similarly, we'll see that to follow suitability rules, you'll need to obtain the customer's investment profile, but not all that information will be relevant in all cases. Therefore, firms must use their judgment as to whether a specific document or response from a customer is necessary to know the customer well enough to recommend securities or strategies. And, as always, they must obtain and retain the records connected to gathering all this required information.

FORWARDING INVESTOR COMMUNICATIONS

FINRA Rules require broker-dealers to forward certain communications from securities issuers to their stock- or bondholders if the firm is holding the customer's securities on their behalf. In other words, some investors are now directly registered as the owners of shares of stock, but most title them in the name of the broker-dealer for the beneficial ownership of themselves. This common practice of letting your broker-dealer hold title of your securities on your behalf is called registering the securities in **street name,** by the way. Annual and special shareholder meetings involve routine and/or critical shareholder votes on matters affecting the company. In connection with these shareholder votes a **proxy statement** is sent to shareholders by the issuer, and since broker-dealers usually hold the shares on behalf of the customer, they must be sure their customer—the shareholder—receives them promptly.

Issuers also send out quarterly and annual reports (10Q and 10K reports) that broker-dealers forward to their customers, and issuers of corporate bonds also send out communications to their bondholders, which also must be promptly forwarded to the firm's customers. Later, we'll see that your customers will hold shares of mutual funds as opposed to holding shares of, say, Starbucks or McDonald's. If you get your Series 7 license in the future, many of your customers will hold shares of stock or individual bond issues, and they will be receiving communications directly from those issuing corporations.

In addition to communications from issuers, broker-dealers send customers **trade confirmations** for every purchase or sale of securities and **account statements** to verify the positions of securities and cash currently in the account.

With all this mail coming to the customer's mailing address, what happens if the customer is going to be traveling or living at another address for an extended period? The FINRA rule says that the broker-dealer can hold back customer mail provided the following requirements are met:

- The member receives written instructions from the customer that include the time period during which the member is requested to hold the customer's mail.
- If the time period is for > three consecutive months, the customer's instructions must include an acceptable reason for the request (e.g., safety or security concerns). Convenience is not an acceptable reason for holding mail longer than three months.
- The member informs the customer in writing of any alternate methods, such as email or access through the member's website, that the customer may use to receive or monitor account activity and information and obtains the customer's confirmation of the receipt of such information.
- The member verifies at reasonable intervals that the customer's instructions still apply.
- During the time that a member is holding mail for a customer, the member must be able to communicate with the customer in a timely manner to provide important account information (e.g., privacy notices, the SIPC information disclosures), as necessary.

And, above all, the rule requires that "A member holding a customer's mail pursuant to this Rule must take actions reasonably designed to ensure that the customer's mail is not tampered with, held without the customer's consent, or used by an associated person of the member in any manner that would violate FINRA rules or the federal securities laws." Why would the regulators be concerned with any of that? Maybe the customer's registered representative has been executing unauthorized transactions that he would prefer she not see in an account statement or trade confirmation. Or, maybe a family member has been gaining unauthorized access to the customer's account and—like the agent— doesn't want her to see what's been going on. I still remember a case where a "friend of the family" was able to perform switches on variable annuities and conceal the heavy surrender charges by having the paperwork sent to a PO Box that he controlled. For these reasons and more, it is important to be sure the customer is requesting the firm to hold back her mail and that the customer has a legitimate reason for asking the firm to hold back the delivery of account statements, trade confirmations, etc.

FINANCIAL EXPLOITATION

FINRA has proposed rules designed to protect certain investors from caregivers or family members who might try to exploit their assets held by a broker-dealer. If adopted, the rule will apply both to senior investors and any adult with a physical or mental impairment that renders him unable to protect his own interests. New rules will require member firms to make reasonable efforts to obtain the name and contact information for a trusted contact person upon opening a customer's account. Then, if the firm ever suspects that financial exploitation could be occurring, they will notify the customer's trusted contact. Although firms will not be required to spot potential exploitation and prevent it, they will be granted safe harbor for putting a temporary hold on an account if they suspect financial exploitation is going on.

Rather than discuss the details of a rule that had not been finalized at the time of this writing, let's talk about what FINRA is already doing to protect such investors. As their website explains, "On April 20, 2015, FINRA launched a toll-free senior hotline – 1-844-57-HELPS – to provide older investors with a supportive place to get assistance from knowledgeable FINRA staff related to concerns they have with their brokerage accounts and investments. To date, FINRA has received over 1500 calls on issues including how to find information on their brokers, calls from children of deceased parents trying to locate assets or having difficulty moving assets from a brokerage firm, concerns from seniors ranging from routine poor service complaints to routine sales practice issues at firms, and fraud raised by a senior and/or child on behalf of senior investors."

NOW WHAT?

We no longer print quizzes in the textbook, where our customers' activities cannot be checked and analyzed. Also, too many people wanted to judge their readiness based on doing 10, when they needed to spend hours working with hundreds and hundreds of practice questions.

Our practice questions are all online now, within our Online Practice Question Bank. You will find online review exercises, chapter review quizzes, and practice exams covering all the material at once. First, though, let's discuss how Series 6 exam questions might look, and how you'll need to approach them to achieve the success you're going for.

Your job involves opening accounts, gathering documentation, transferring accounts, and so on. Therefore, the Series 6 exam will see if you know what to do when various situations arise, like this one:

This morning you receive a phone call from a young man who introduces himself as the executor of one of your elderly customer's estates. Your customer has died, the executor informs you, and he would like you to "go to cash" with her account, from which he would like to receive one cashier's check. What should you do?
   A. Carefully follow the executor's instructions
   B. File a Currency Transaction Report
   C. Freeze the account and await proper documentation
   D. Liquidate the securities positions and hold them in cash

EXPLANATION: anyone can call and claim that an elderly customer has died and that he is the executor or trustee. Not good enough—the executor must provide your firm with a death certificate and "letters of office" showing he is, in fact, the executor and that the customer is, in fact, dead. We can eliminate Choice A, since it's too soon to follow the executor's instructions. Choice B has to do with cash transactions over $10,000, which has nothing to do with this question. Eliminate Choice B. Choice D is another version of Choice A, and we aren't going to be executing any trades at this point. Eliminate Choice D, leaving us with

ANSWER: C

Notice that I didn't look for the correct answer right away. Rather, I used what I know to eliminate the three wrong answers. That is the approach you'll need to use at the testing center because the right answer is often not something you've seen before. The right answer is often just the answer choice that could not be eliminated.

Let's try another one.

Exercising discretion over a customer account is a big deal. Normally, if a registered representative entered a transaction without talking to the customer, we would be looking at a career ending violation known as an unauthorized transaction. There are also cases where the customer gives the registered representative some information but not enough to count as a decision. "Buy some oil company stocks," is not enough for a registered representative to turn into an order, unless he has discretion over the account. As we saw, choosing the stock or the number of shares requires the registered representative and the member firm to have discretionary authorization over the account. Time and price, of course, do not require this authority. If the customer says to "buy 300 shares of MSFT today," provided the order is entered that day it can be entered whenever the registered representative decides to do so. Therefore, you might get a question like this:

At 10 AM this morning one of your customers tells you to sell 500 shares of ABC at the close of the day's trading session. ABC is a thinly traded stock, and when you go to sell the shares at the close, there is only buying interest for 300 shares. Therefore, you should
   A. Cancel the order
   B. Sell the 300 shares

C. Sell the 300 shares to the market and purchase the other 200 for the firm's trading account
D. Change the order to "at the open" and enter it electronically for tomorrow's trading session

EXPLANATION: questions like this are not easy. I don't see an answer that looks crazy enough to eliminate right away. Maybe you should sell whatever you can sell. Or, maybe you're not supposed to change the number of shares, so your firm should just buy the difference? This order is either executed at the close or not—you can't execute it tomorrow. Eliminate Choice D. The question doesn't say you have discretion, so you can't alter the number of shares, no matter how tempting Choices B and C might be. Eliminate them both. Cancel the order, leaving us with

ANSWER: A

It's time to do take the Chapter 1 Review Quiz in our Online Practice Question Bank. Then, watch the lesson in the training videos and move onto the next chapter in the textbook.

CHAPTER 2:
Evaluates Customers' Financial Information, Identifies Investment Objectives, Provides Information on Investment Products, and Makes Suitable Recommendations

When you open a new customer account at your broker-dealer, you must gather important facts to understand the customer's **investment profile**. It's important to know your customer because all your investment recommendations to him must make sense given his needs, goals, holding period, risk tolerance, etc. Your recommendations of mutual funds and variable annuity subaccounts will not always turn out to be profitable, but they all must be **suitable**. The only way to make a suitable recommendation is to first get to know the essential facts about the customer.

FINRA: SUITABILITY RULES

FINRA is the **Self-Regulatory Organization (SRO)** formed when the NASD and NYSE regulators merged several years ago. SROs (Self-Regulatory Organizations) including FINRA register with the SEC under the Securities Exchange Act of 1934. The NYSE had a "know your customer" rule, while the NASD had a "suitability" rule. FINRA has taken elements of each while also adding some new requirements to assure that registered representatives and their firms do their due diligence when getting to know the customer and when making recommendations to buy, sell, or hold securities.

As we saw in Chapter 1, FINRA's "know your customer rule" requires firms to use "reasonable diligence" when opening and maintaining customer accounts. It requires firms to know the "essential facts" on every customer, as well. Essential facts are defined as:

> *those required to (a) effectively service the customer's account, (b) act in accordance with any special handling instructions for the account, (c) understand the authority of each person acting on behalf of the customer, and (d) comply with applicable laws, regulations, and rules.*

The "know your customer" obligation starts at the beginning of the broker-dealer and customer relationship, even before any investment recommendations have been made to that customer. FINRA's new suitability rule requires that agents/registered representatives have:

> *a reasonable basis to believe that a recommended transaction or investment strategy involving a security or securities is suitable for the customer, based on the information obtained through the reasonable diligence of the member or associated person to ascertain the customer's investment profile.*

This is how FINRA defines an *investment profile*:

> *a customer's investment profile includes, but is not limited to, the customer's age, other investments, financial situation and needs, tax status, investment objectives, investment experience, investment time horizon, liquidity needs, risk tolerance, and any other information the customer may disclose to the member or associated person in connection with such recommendation.*

Suitability requirements for the agent and his broker-dealer are triggered only when there is an investment **recommendation** made to the client. As usual, defining the term "recommendation" is more complicated than one would like. FINRA is straightforward in one of their regulatory notices concerning the new suitability rules, so let's allow them to tell us:

> *For instance, a communication's content, context and presentation are important aspects of the inquiry. The determination of whether a "recommendation" has been made, moreover, is an objective rather than subjective inquiry. An important factor in this regard is whether—given its content, context and manner of presentation—a specific communication from a firm or associated person to a customer reasonably would be viewed as a suggestion that the customer take action or refrain from taking action regarding a security or investment strategy. In addition, the more individually tailored the communication is to a specific customer or customers about a specific security or investment strategy, the more likely the communication will be viewed as a recommendation. Furthermore, a series of actions that may not constitute recommendations when viewed individually may amount to a recommendation when considered in the aggregate. It also makes no difference whether the communication was initiated by a person or a computer software program. These guiding principles, together with numerous litigated decisions and the facts and circumstances of any specific case, inform the determination of whether the communication is a recommendation for purposes of FINRA's suitability rule.*

The suitability rule mentions securities and strategies. As soon as an agent recommends that a customer do—or not do—something in relation to a security or investment strategy, he has made a recommendation for purposes of the suitability rule. And, he will be much better off if he knows what he's talking about. On the other hand, if the agent or broker-dealer put out purely educational material that <u>explains</u> investment strategies without recommending any specific security or strategy, then those materials are exempt from the suitability rule. However, if the agent/firm is recommending that customers consider using margin or liquefied home equity to purchase securities, that is covered by the suitability rule. Even if it doesn't mention specific securities, and even if it doesn't lead to a transaction, a recommended strategy must be suitable. And, guess what, margin accounts and liquefied home equity are not suitable for most investors.

So, the margin handbook or margin disclosure brochure simply explains how margin works—that is educational material and must be provided to customers before they open margin accounts. On the other hand, any brochure that recommends or implies that a customer ought to open a margin account and buy securities on credit would be considered a recommended strategy. If you, therefore, send it to my 87-year-old Aunt Bessie, living on social security and the kindness of fellow church members, well…that wouldn't be suitable.

By the way, an explicit recommendation to *hold* a security is just as much a recommendation as a recommendation to buy or sell a security. As FINRA states:

> *The rule recognizes that customers may rely on firms' and associated persons' investment expertise and knowledge, and it is thus appropriate to hold firms and associated persons responsible for the recommendations that they make to customers, regardless of whether those recommendations result in transactions or generate transaction-based compensation.*

However, an agent would have to specifically tell a client not to sell a security—or not to sell securities in general—before he has made an explicit recommendation to hold. The fact that the agent did not tell the customer to sell is not a recommendation to hold. Right? FINRA adds:

> *That is true regardless of whether the associated person previously recommended the purchase of the securities, the customer purchased them without a recommendation, or the customer transferred them into the account from another firm where the same or a different associated person had handled the account.*

There are now three explicit suitability obligations spelled out in the rule:

1. Reasonable-basis suitability: the agent must use reasonable diligence to understand the potential risks and rewards associated with the recommended security or strategy and have a reasonable basis to believe the recommendation is suitable for at least some investors.

2. Customer-specific suitability: the agent must have a reasonable basis to believe that a recommendation is suitable for a specific

customer based on his/her profile. The profile now adds new items to the existing list (age, investment experience, time horizon, liquidity needs and risk tolerance).

3. Quantitative suitability: an agent with control over an account must make sure that a series of transactions that might make sense in isolation are not unsuitable based on an excessive number of transactions given the customer's investment profile. This would not apply to unsolicited transactions initiated by the customer.

For the three requirements above, understand that Number 1 and Number 3 apply equally to retail and **institutional investors**. However, Number 2 is applied differently for the two types of customer. Above, we see how **retail investors** are to be handled. But, if the investor is an "institutional account," the firm can meet their "customer-specific suitability" requirement by having a reasonable basis to believe the customer is able to evaluate investment risks independently and by having the institutional customer acknowledge in writing that it is exercising independent judgment—unlike the typical retail investor, who relies on what her stockbroker tells her in most cases.

So, if an agent or member firm tries to provide evidence that they had a reasonable basis to believe that a recommendation is suitable to at least some investors, one would think that having documentation would be important. That depends. As FINRA states in a member notice, the suitability rule:

> *does not include any explicit documentation requirements. The suitability rule allows firms to take a risk-based approach with respect to documenting suitability determinations. For example, the recommendation of a large-cap, value-oriented equity security generally would not require written documentation as to the recommendation. In all cases, the suitability rule applies to recommendations, but the extent to which a firm needs to evidence suitability generally depends on the complexity of the security or strategy in structure and performance and/or the risks involved. Compliance with suitability obligations does not necessarily turn on documentation of the basis for the recommendation. However, firms should understand that, to the degree that the basis for suitability is not evident from the recommendation itself, FINRA examination and enforcement concerns will rise with the lack of documentary evidence for the recommendation. In addition, documentation by itself does not cure an otherwise unsuitable recommendation.*

In other words, a recommendation that an equity investor purchase shares of Walmart or a blue-chip equity mutual fund would not require lots of documentation that such an investment might be suitable for at least some investors. However, some of the mortgage-based derivatives that preceded the meltdown in September 2008? Maybe no investor should have been pitched those investments, regardless of the documentation one might try to provide.

If the agent uses reasonable diligence to obtain all the necessary information from a customer, what happens if the customer does not supply all the information requested? In that case the agent and firm must use their best judgment to determine whether they have enough information to make suitable recommendations to that customer. Perhaps the investor refuses to supply her age—what if all other information makes it clear that she should be in short-term bonds and money market mutual funds? Could the agent make those recommendations? Probably. Just keep good case notes. Also, firms can decide that for certain categories of customers the information FINRA requires is not relevant.

For example, a broker-dealer can decide to not ask for the age of customers that are not human beings but merely legal entities or not ask about liquidity needs if the firm is only going to recommend liquid securities in the first place. As FINRA explains:

> *The significance of specific types of customer information generally will depend on the facts and circumstances of the specific case, including the nature and characteristics of the product or strategy at issue.*

Some firms use product committees to review whether a specific investment product or strategy is suitable for at least some customers. Can an agent simply rely solely on the committee's findings?

No. FINRA clarifies that an agent has a responsibility to assure that he understands the risks and rewards of a specific product or strategy before recommending it to any investor.

FINRA and the SEC have determined that agents must not just make recommendations that make sense. Agents must be sure to "act in their customer's best interests." That means that the agent must never place his own interests ahead of the customer's. Examples of agents violating that rule include an agent recommending one product over another based on the higher commissions he can earn, or an agent asking customers to make loans to him so he can start a business.

Now, an agent does not have to recommend the least expensive investment to a customer. Provided it is suitable, and provided the higher expenses are not related to higher commissions to the agent. In other words, if your broker-dealer only sells three families of mutual funds, then you simply recommend the ones that are suitable from these mutual fund families. The fact that there may be other, less-expensive mutual fund families out there? Not your problem.

Where an agent will be disciplined and, perhaps, barred from the business is when he pushes customers to do things that benefit the agent while potentially harming the customer. A margin account, for example, allows a customer to buy roughly twice as much stock as he otherwise could. That might lead to higher commissions to the agent, but if he puts someone in a margin account for that reason, he's in trouble.

INVESTMENT OBJECTIVES, TIME HORIZON, RISK TOLERANCE

So, getting to know your customer involves digging into his situation enough to determine his investment profile. What is the investor looking for; what are his **investment objectives?** Investment objectives include: capital preservation, income, growth & income, growth, and speculation. If the individual is in his 30s and is setting up a retirement account, he probably needs growth to build up his net worth before reaching retirement age. If he's already in retirement, he probably needs income since by he's no longer working or not working as much as he used to. He might need income almost exclusively, or, to protect his purchasing power, he might also need growth. And, as you might expect, this is where growth & income funds come in handy. But, any blue-chip stock that pays regular dividends would fit that bill, also.

Some firms separate growth from **aggressive growth.** Aggressive growth investments include international funds, sector funds (healthcare, telecommunications, financial services, etc.) and emerging market funds (China, India, Brazil, etc.). For **speculation,** there are options and futures, and most investors should limit their exposure to these derivatives to maybe 5–15% of their portfolio.

If someone is saving up for retirement, that generally means he needs capital appreciation. On the other hand, some investors are already wealthy, and they just want to preserve their capital (**capital preservation**).

INVESTOR'S OBJECTIVE	RECOMMENDATIONS
Capital Preservation, Safety of Principal	U.S. Government/Treasury, Ginnie Mae
Liquidity	Money market funds
Income	Bonds (other than zero coupons)
Tax-Exempt	Municipal bonds/bond funds
High-Yield	Low-rated corporate or municipal bonds/funds
From Stock	Preferred stock, large cap value funds, equity income funds
Growth	Common stock, stock funds
Portfolio Diversification	Add bonds, stock, and money market as needed to diversify investments among different instruments, industries, maturities, etc.
Speculation	Options, high-yield bonds, precious metals funds

Knowing the investor's objective is important, but it must be factored in with the **time horizon** before we start recommending investments. In general, the longer the time horizon the more volatility the investor can withstand. If the investor has a three-year time horizon, he must stay almost completely out of the stock market and invest instead in high-quality bonds with short terms to maturity. If he is in for the long haul, on the other hand, who cares what happens this year? It's what happens over a 20- or 30-year period that matters. With dividends reinvested, the S&P 500 has historically gained about 9% annually on average, which means money would double approximately every 8 years. Sure, the index can drop 30% one year and 20% the next, but we're not keeping score every year. It's where we go over the long haul that counts.

A good way to see the real-world application of risk as it relates to time horizon is to pull out the prospectus for a growth fund and see if you can spot any two- or three-year periods where the bar charts are pointing the wrong way. Then, compare those scary short-term periods to the 10-year return, which is probably decent no matter which growth fund you're looking at. That's why the prospectus reminds investors that they may lose money by investing in the fund and that "the likelihood of loss is greater the shorter the holding period."

See how important time horizon is?

Younger investors saving for retirement have long time horizons, so they can withstand more volatility. On the other hand, when the investor is 69 years old, she probably needs income and maybe not so much volatility. So, the farther from retirement she is, the more likely the investor will be buying stock. The closer she gets to retirement, the less stock she needs and the more bonds/income investments she should be buying.

There are mutual funds that shift the focus from growth to income over time. These are often called **target funds** or **lifecycle funds**. Here, the investor picks a mutual fund with a target date close to her own retirement date. If she's currently in her mid-40s, maybe she picks the Target 2040 Fund. If she's in her mid-50s, maybe it's the Target 2030 Fund. For the Target 2040, we'd see that the fund is invested more in the stock market and less in the bond market than the Target 2030 fund. In other words, the fund automatically changes the allocation from mostly stock to mostly bonds as we get closer and closer to the target date. The same happens with the age-based portfolios in the educational 529 plans—as the child gets closer to college age, the portfolio allocation shifts away from stocks and into short-term bonds and money market securities.

An investor might have the primary objective of growth. He might also have a time horizon of 10+ years. However, if he doesn't have the **risk tolerance** required for the stock market, we keep him out of stocks. Risk tolerance involves not only the financial resources, but also the psychological ability to sustain wide fluctuations in market value, as well as the occasional loss of principal that bothers some people no end. The terms risk-averse, conservative, and low risk tolerance all mean the same thing—these investors will not tolerate big market drops. They invest in safe-money products like fixed annuities, or in U.S. Treasuries or investment-grade corporate bonds. To invest in sector funds or emerging market funds, the investor needs a high risk tolerance. A moderate risk tolerance would likely match up with balanced funds, equity income funds, and conservative bond funds.

Let's put the three factors together: investment objective, time horizon, and risk tolerance. If we know that the investor in the suitability question seeks growth, we then need to know his time horizon and risk tolerance. If he's a 32-year-old in an IRA account, his time horizon is long-term. Unless he can't sleep at night knowing the account balance fluctuates, we would almost have to recommend growth funds. His risk tolerance would tell us whether to use small cap, mid-cap, or large cap growth funds— the higher the risk tolerance the smaller the "cap." If the investor is 60 years old and living on a pension income, she might need to invest in common stock to protect her purchasing power over the next several years. If so, her time horizon is long, but her risk tolerance is probably only moderate or moderate-low. So, we'd probably find a conservative stock fund—maybe a growth & income, equity income, or large cap value fund.

If another investor seeks income primarily, we need to know her time horizon and risk tolerance. We don't buy bonds that mature beyond her anticipated holding period. If she has a 10-year time horizon, we need bonds that mature in 10 years or sooner. Her risk tolerance will tell us if we can maximize her income with high-yield bonds, or if we should buy investment-grade bond funds instead. If she needs tax-exempt income, we put some of her money into municipal bond funds.

For capital preservation nothing beats U.S. Treasury securities. GNMA securities are also safe. Money market mutual funds are safe—though not guaranteed by the U.S. government or anyone else—but they pay low yields. Money market mutual funds are for people who want to not only preserve capital but also make frequent withdrawals from the account. See, even though your money is safer in a 30-year Treasury bond than in a money market mutual fund, the big difference is that the market price of your T-Bond fluctuates (rates up, price down), while the money market mutual fund typically stays at $1 per share.

So, if **liquidity** is a major concern, the money market mutual fund is better than T-Bonds, T-Notes, and even T-Bills, all which must be sold at whatever price.

The questionnaire that the client fills out when opening an account with your firm will try to gauge what is more important—going for large returns or maintaining a stable principal? Earning a return on his money, or getting the return of his money? Does he need to withdraw a large portion of his portfolio at a moment's notice? If so, we put that portion in money market securities and short-term bonds.

AGGRESSIVE VS. DEFENSIVE STRATEGIES

So, if investing is a game, do you prefer playing offense or defense? Do you like to risk it all trying to put serious points on the board (offense), or do you prefer to prevent a bunch of bad stuff (defense) from advancing against you?

If you're an aggressive investor, you must have several things going for you:

- good job
- long time horizon
- good cash flow
- high risk tolerance

The first thing to know is that investing in stocks is inherently riskier than investing in bonds. I was reading my current issue of *Forbes* on the El yesterday and saw an advertisement for a mutual fund. You can see how accepted this stock-is-riskier notion is in the industry from the following line in the advertisement:

Investors should note that the higher a fund's allocation to stocks, the greater the risk.

A more defensive investment strategy would not focus so hard on the potentially bright future but would concentrate more on all the bad news that a company could survive. Companies like Walmart, GE, or Microsoft offer a strong defense against economic downturns that might take out smaller competitors. There are companies that still sell their products and services during a recession. Supermarkets and discount retailers will keep selling food, underwear, and razor blades. On the other hand, companies that sell big-ticket items like automobiles or home appliances could take a hit. So, a defensive investor would buy stock in established companies that will likely sell the following products/services even during a recession:

- Food
- Basic clothing
- Healthcare/pharmaceuticals
- Alcohol
- Tobacco

An aggressive investor is willing to take on more risk. He'll buy stock in companies involved with unproven technologies working in an undeveloped industry. As soon as he reads an article on fuel cells, he wants to buy stock in any company involved with fuel cells. Trouble is, these companies aren't profitable, and nobody knows how long it will take for fuel cells to take off, assuming they ever do. Not to mention, we have no clue which three of the current fifty companies will survive, let alone become profitable. An aggressive investor would be interested in the following:

- Aggressive Growth funds
- Emerging Market funds
- Small Cap funds
- Sector funds
- Growth stocks

CLIENT PROFILES

No matter who your client is, you must gather some information so that you can make suitable recommendations. You must determine the financial status of the client, gathering key information such as:

- Income sources
- Current expenditures (bills, obligations)
- Discretionary income (what's left after paying bills)
- Assets (cash, real estate pension/retirement accounts, life insurance)
- Tax bracket

Probably the most important figure to obtain from a client is known as "discretionary income" or "excess cash flow." This is the money left over after covering all essentials. A personal income statement might look like this:

Monthly Income	
Salary	$7,000
Investment Income	$1,000
Other Income	$500
Total Monthly Income	**$8,500**

Monthly Expenditures	
Taxes	$2,000
Mortgage Payment	$2,000
Living Expenses	$2,000
Insurance Premiums	$300
Loan Payments	$200
Travel/Entertainment	$300
Other Expenses	$200
Total Monthly Expenses	**$7,000**
Monthly Capital for Investing	**$1,500**

So, a customer with the above income statement has excess cash flow or discretionary income of $1,500. An agent should make recommendations that make sense given the fact that he has $1,500 available for investing in a typical month.

If the investor is in a high **marginal tax bracket**, we may want to recommend municipal bonds, which, generally, pay interest that is tax-free at the federal level. This same client probably doesn't want to do a lot of short-term trading, either, since any gain taken within the space of a year will be taxed at the short-term capital gains. He also might want to buy stocks that pay qualified dividends rather than REITs or royalty trusts, which will force him to pay his ordinary income rate on the dividends. Of course, one of the best answers you can give a client is, "Please consult with a qualified tax professional."

A business has both an income (earnings) statement and a balance sheet (statement of financial condition). So do investors. Assets represent what somebody owns, while liabilities represent what he owes. The difference between the two is his net worth. A customer's assets include the value of his home, automobiles, personal possessions, investments, savings, and checking accounts. Liabilities include mortgages and other loans, credit card balances, and, perhaps, debit balances in margin accounts.

A personal balance sheet might look like this:

Assets		
Tangible property:	House	$400,000
	Automobiles	$30,000
	Personal possessions	$15,000
Investments:	Stocks and Bonds	$100,000
	Keogh Plan	$80,000
	IRA	$20,000
Savings:	Checking	$5,000
	Savings Account	$5,000
	Money Market	$5,000
	Total Assets	$660,000
Liabilities		
	Mortgage	$250,000
	Auto Loans	$10,000
	Credit Card Balances	$15,000
	Total Liabilities	$275,000
Net Worth		**$385,000**

This represents total net worth. Since some assets are difficult to liquidate, we could exclude those items (house, limited partnerships, rental property) to calculate liquid net worth. If a client has high total net worth but low liquid net worth, you might try to steer the client toward more liquid investments, like the money market, or at least heavily traded stocks and bonds, as opposed to hedge funds, principal protected funds, or thinly traded securities.

TYPES OF RISK

Saving money is not the same thing as investing money. In a savings account, the only risk is that your money will lose purchasing power. When you invest, on the other hand, you take the risk that you could lose your money. As Jerry Seinfeld said, there are times when we put our money to work and it ends up getting fired. This is called **capital risk**. If you buy U.S. Treasury Bonds, you eliminate capital risk, but if you buy corporate bonds or common stock, you face the risk of losing some or all your capital. Investing in common stock presents significantly more capital risk than investing in corporate bonds, which is why the potential reward is also higher.

One of the best ways to brush up on **investment risks** is to read the first pages of a mutual fund prospectus. I'm looking at the prospectus for a growth fund myself. It states that its investment goal is "growth of capital," and then goes on to say that "dividend income, if any, will be incidental to this goal." In other words, the fund invests in growth stocks, but some companies that are expected to grow also pay dividends, and this fund does not mind cashing their checks. It's just that the dividends have nothing to do with the fund's reasons for investing in the stock. It's the growth or capital appreciation that they're after. The "principal strategy" tells me that the fund focuses on companies with $10 billion or more of market value and uses fundamental analysis to determine which companies show strength in terms of earnings, revenue, profit margins, etc.

➢ Systematic Risk

The next section of the prospectus is called "important risks," and it lists investment risks such as:

```
Stock market risk, or the risk that the price of securities held
by the Fund will fall due to various conditions or circumstances
which may be unpredictable.
```

> Market Risk

Market risk is a type of **systematic risk,** which means it affects securities across the board, as opposed to an **unsystematic risk**, which affects only specific stocks or bonds or specific industry sectors. Market risk is the risk that an investment will lose its value due to an overall market decline. As the prospectus says, the circumstances may be unpredictable. For example, no one can predict the next war or where the next tsunami, hurricane, or nuclear disaster will hit, but when events like that take place, they can have a devastating effect on the overall market. Whether they panic because of war, weather, or whatever, the fact is that when investors panic, stock prices plummet. We might think of stock market risk as the fact that even though the company might be doing ok, our stock investment in that company could drop just because the overall stock market drops due to a panic.

The S&P 500 index is generally used to represent the overall market, so what can an investor do to combat overall market risk? He can make a little side bet against the overall market by purchasing put options on a broad-based index such as the **S&P 500**. Or, he can sell the **ETFs** (**exchange traded funds**) that track a broad-based index short. Now, if the market rises, his stocks make money. If the market drops, his little side bet against the overall market makes money. To bet the other way is called

hedging. **Diversification** does not reduce overall market risk. If the overall market is going down, it doesn't matter how many different stocks an investor owns; they're all going down. That's why he would have to bet against the overall market to protect himself. Or, he would simply have to be prepared for and willing to bear this risk.

Each of the 500 stocks in the S&P 500 has a **beta**. Beta is a risk measurement that indicates how volatile the individual stock is compared to the overall market. For example, if MSFT has a beta of .8, it goes up and down only 80% as much as the overall market as measured by the S&P 500. If the S&P 500 rises 10%, MSFT goes up only 8%, and when the S&P 500 drops 10%, MSFT drops only 8%. If SBUX has a beta of 1.3, it is 30% more volatile than the overall market—or 1.3 times as volatile, whichever clicks for you. If the S&P drops 4%, SBUX drops 5.2%, and so on. A stock with a beta of 1 is in line with the overall market in terms of volatility. Note that a stock with a beta of less than 1 is simply less volatile than the overall stock market. Stocks in general are volatile, so that investment could still scare off many investors.

> Natural Event Risk

Natural event risk refers to the fact that a tsunami, earthquake, hurricane, etc., could have a devastating effect on a country's economy, and possibly the economy of an entire area such as Europe or Southeast Asia. A recent annual report from Starbucks mentions a "global pandemic" as a major risk to the price of the stock, something I would not have thought of. In other words, if disease sweeps the globe or any part of it, public gathering places are going to be shut down, people will be too sick to pick coffee beans, and transportation routes may be closed to prevent the spread of illness. None of that would have anything to do with the taste of Starbucks coffee or the management skills of the company.

Unfortunately, it's not easy to place natural event risk exclusively in the systematic or unsystematic risk category. While a tsunami would have a negative impact on the markets overall, there are many weather-related events that hit certain sectors or issuers in specific, making it an unsystematic risk. For example, food and energy producers are affected by weather events that might not impact other industries. And, there are some industries that do well after a flood or band of thunderstorms—mold remediation, construction, disaster recovery, etc. As always, read the question carefully rather than jumping to any conclusions, and you'll be fine.

> Interest Rate Risk

Unlike with stocks, bond pricing lends itself to the precision of mathematics. The big brains at the firm can calculate the risk of default, the risk of various interest-rate and inflation scenarios over the term to maturity, and come up with an extremely accurate price for any bond. With stock, on the other hand, everything is based on speculation of future profits. Even if the investor is good enough to pick a good company, it's hard to pick the right price at which to buy its stock. Stock investors must be able to handle big fluctuations of value, while bondholders can often go months or years without thinking about their investment's market price.

Then again, there are still risks involved with bond investing, starting with **interest rate risk**. Interest rate risk is the risk that interest rates will rise, knocking down the market price of bonds. The longer the term on the bond, the more volatile its price, too. When rates go up, all bond prices fall, but the long-term bonds suffer the most. And, when rates go down, all bond prices rise, but the long-term bonds go up the most. So, a 30-year government bond has no default risk, but carries more interest rate risk than a 10-year corporate bond.

The reason we see short-term and intermediate-term bond funds is because many investors want to reduce interest rate risk. Maybe they have a shorter time horizon and will need this money in just a few years. Therefore, they can't risk a big drop in market value due to a sudden rise in interest rates. They will probably sacrifice the higher yield offered by a long-term bond fund, but they will sleep better knowing that rising rates won't be as devastating to their investment in short-term bonds.

In a bond fund prospectus, we see that the important risks include:

```
Risk that the value of the securities the Fund holds will fall as
a result of changes in interest rates.
```

That is interest rate risk. Rates up, price down, and it's more severe the longer the term to maturity.

......Duration

Duration measures the interest rate risk of a bond, predicting how a small change in interest rates would affect the bond's market price. The longer/higher a bond's duration, the more sensitive it is to a change in interest rates. So, when interest rates go up, they push the prices of bonds with long/high durations down much harder than those with lower durations.

Another way of talking about duration is to say that at some point all the coupon payments received by an investor will represent what the investor paid for the bond. If you pay par for a 30-year bond paying $50 a year, it would take you 20 years to receive $1,000 in the form of interest/coupon payments, right? So, the duration could be expressed as 20 years. Since a coupon payment of 5% is low and a 30-year maturity long, the bond's duration is high. A bond with a high duration is more susceptible to a rise in interest rates. To express that mathematically, we could see how much the bond's price would decline if rates rose 1%. Just multiply the 20 (duration) by 1% to get an expected 20% decline in the bond's price should rates rise by just 1 point. And if rates shot up 2%, the price decline would be 40%. That's volatile. If the bond paid a higher coupon, you'd get your original investment back sooner, reducing the duration and making the bond's price less sensitive to interest rates.

A common definition used for duration is "the weighted average of a bond's cash flows."

>   Purchasing Power Risk

Purchasing power or **inflation risk** means that if inflation erodes the purchasing power of money, an investor's fixed return can't buy what it used to. Fixed-income investments carry purchasing power or inflation risk, which is why investors often try to beat inflation by investing in common stock. The ride might be a wild one in the stock market, but the reward is that we should be able to grow faster than the rate of inflation, whereas a fixed-income payment is fixed. Retirees living solely on fixed incomes are more susceptible to inflation or purchasing power risk than people still in the workforce, since salaries tend to rise with inflation. The longer the retiree must live on a fixed income, the more susceptible she is to inflation risk.

Unfortunately, common stock is often too volatile for investors with shorter time horizons and high needs for liquidity. The solution is often to put most a retiree's money into short-term bonds and money market instruments with a small percentage in large-cap stock, equity income, or growth & income funds. That way, the dependable income stream from the short-term debt securities will cover the living expenses, while the smaller piece devoted to conservative stock investments will likely provide some protection of purchasing power. Not to mention that blue chip stocks almost by definition pay dividends, and dividends tend to increase over time. So, putting a reasonable percentage of a retiree's money into blue chip stocks is not necessarily risky, as might have been thought in the past.

> ### Call Risk

The bond fund prospectus on my desk also warns of **call risk**, or "the risk that a bond might be called during a period of declining interest rates." Most municipal and corporate bonds are **callable**, meaning that when interest rates drop, corporate and municipal bond issuers will borrow new money at today's lower rate and use it to pay off the current bondholders much sooner than they expected. The problems for the current bondholders are that, first, the bond price stops rising in the secondary market once everyone knows the exact call price that will be received. And, second, what do they do with the money they just received from the issuer? Reinvest it, right? And, where are interest rates now? Down—so they probably take the proceeds from a 9% bond and turn it into a 6% payment going forward. Hmm—you used to get $90 per year; now you can look forward to $60.

Some bonds are non-callable, but they offer a lower yield to investors in return for that safety feature.

> ### Prepayment and Extension Risk

Prepayment risk is the form of call risk that comes with owning a mortgage-backed security. A homeowner with a mortgage will typically take advantage of a sudden drop in interest rates by refinancing. Therefore, if an investor holds **mortgage-backed securities** like those issued by GNMA, FNMA, or FHLMC (Ginnie, Fannie, Freddie), that investor will take a hit if interest rates drop suddenly and all the principal is returned sooner than expected. This is called **prepayment risk**. When the investor receives the principal sooner than expected, she typically ends up reinvesting it into similar mortgage-backed securities and receiving a lower rate of interest going forward, while the homeowners in the pool of mortgages, on the other hand, are enjoying paying lower interest rates going forward.

On the other hand, if interest rates rise, homeowners will take longer than expected to pay off the mortgages. This scenario is called **extension risk.** Notice that most debt securities have stated maturities, while an investment in most mortgage-backed securities comes with an estimate only. Sort of like bonds without maturity dates.

Since GNMA (Ginnie Mae) securities are guaranteed by the U.S. Treasury, their main risk is prepayment—or extension—risk. An investment in FNMA or FHLMC securities would carry that plus credit/default risk.

>   Reinvestment Risk

Bonds paying regular interest force investors to reinvest into new bonds every few months or so. What kind of rates will debt securities be offering when they go to reinvest the coupon payments? Nobody knows, which is why it's a risk, called **reinvestment risk**. It's annoying to take a 9% interest payment and reinvest it at 3%, but it does happen. To avoid reinvestment risk, buy a debt security that gives you nothing to reinvest along the way: zero coupons, i.e., Treasury STRIPS.

>   Currency Exchange Risk

Since most countries use a different currency from the American dollar, **currency exchange risk** is also part of the package when investing in foreign markets, emerging or otherwise. The value of the American dollar relative to foreign currencies, then, is a risk to both international and emerging markets investors. So, even if it's a **developed market**, such as Japan, if you're investing internationally into Japanese stocks, the value of the yen versus the dollar presents foreign exchange or currency risk. If you're investing in China, you have that risk, plus the political risk of investing in companies operating in an immature capitalist system likely to suffer many fits and starts before all the kinks are worked out.

>   Political Risk

The American business climate and financial markets are dependable, especially when compared to, say, Syria. Of course, we might occasionally want to raise the bar a little bit, but you get the point. **Political risk** is part of the package if you want to invest in **emerging markets**. An emerging market is a country or region where the financial markets are immature and unpredictable. They're not fully developed, a little awkward, a bit volatile, basically like teenagers—bright future, but some days you aren't sure if they're going to make it.

If you own stocks and bonds in companies operating and trading in undeveloped economies, what happens if the Chinese government gets tired of capitalism and nationalizes the companies whose shares you used to own? Total loss. Or maybe the transition from communism to capitalism doesn't go so well, and suddenly the whole country is shut down with riots in the streets and government tanks rolling in. When this type of thing happens, emerging market investments naturally are affected, and not in a good way. An investor facing this sort of political risk is also facing currency exchange risk, among all the other risks that may be presented as part of the investment package.

➢   Unsystematic Risk

Unsystematic risk relates to a specific issuer or industry space, as opposed to the overall market. The fact that interest rates could rise affects all bonds regardless of the issuer or industry. On the other hand, the risk that government regulators will increase requirements on the automobile or aerospace industry is not system-wide. Rather, it affects only a few issuers and industries. Diversifying a portfolio reduces these more specific risks by spreading them out among stocks of many different issuers operating in different, unrelated industry sectors. Or, a municipal bond investor might diversify her holdings geographically to avoid the risk that an area of the country could be hit by a weather event or an economic slump. Although municipal bond investors generally seek safety, they can also enhance their yield by purchasing some lower-rated municipal bonds with some percentage of the account assets. After all, even conservative bond funds frequently put 20% or so in junk bonds issued by corporations or municipalities. Municipal bonds come in many flavors, also, so investors might purchase bonds used for many different purposes—some general obligation and some revenue—to avoid being too dependent on just toll roads, for example, or airport revenues. While an individual bond investor could use a registered representative to put together a diversified portfolio, more likely the registered representative would find a mutual fund portfolio already designed to achieve what the investor is looking for.

I happen to pick individual stocks as opposed to buying mutual funds, which is why I face the risks we're about to explore to a much higher degree than do mutual fund investors. A growth fund, value fund, or balanced fund, for example, would invest in many issuers operating in many different industry spaces. That diversification goes a long way toward smoothing out the wild ups and downs of the securities markets from what I've been told.

> Business Risk

Buying stock in any company presents **business risk**. Business risk includes the risk of competition, a labor strike, the release of inferior products, and the risk of **obsolescence**, which is the risk that a company's offerings suddenly become obsolete. In the past shareholders in companies producing telegraph equipment, typewriters, encyclopedias, and 8-track players all felt the sting of obsolescence risk. Nowadays, investing in a bookstore chain carries more risk of obsolescence than investing in a company that manufactures underwear.

The risk of poor management, of better competitors, or of products becoming obsolete are all part of business risk. In other words, stock is only as solid as the businesses who issued it. So, investors also must diversify their portfolios so that it's not all subject to the same type of business risk. Airlines, retailers, and financial services companies, for example, would all face different business risks.

And, this shows how inherently risky stock investing is. Investors can get hurt by the individual companies they invest in, as well as the fact that the stock market overall can drop in value, whether the individual companies do well or not.

> Legislative/Regulatory Risk

Legislative or **regulatory risk** means that if laws change, certain securities could be negatively affected. If the federal government announced that all car makers are required to get 35 mpg for their large SUVs and pickup trucks by the following year, this would probably knock down the value of certain stocks and bonds issued by companies including Ford and GM. Or, what if an investor bought a portfolio of tax-exempt municipal bonds, and then Congress decided to eliminate the exemption for municipal bond interest? Most likely, investors would dump their municipal bonds, forcing the market prices down.

Different industries are subject to different regulatory risks, so diversification will protect the investor from legislative risk somewhat. Therefore, mutual funds focusing on just one industry sector are riskier than the typical fund that is broadly diversified.

> Credit/Default Risk

Credit risk is the risk that the issuer of a bond will be unable to pay interest and/or return principal to the bondholders. U.S. Treasury securities have little or no default risk, but some municipal securities and most corporate bonds carry default/credit risk to some degree. Even if the issuer never misses a payment, if S&P and Moody's downgrade their credit score, the market value of the bonds could also drop.

> Liquidity Risk

Marketability or liquidity is the ability to quickly turn an investment into cash and at a fair price. Money market securities are easy to buy and sell at a fair price; municipal bonds and thinly traded stocks are not. Thinly traded securities have **liquidity risk** compared to securities with more active secondary markets.

> Opportunity Cost

If you pass up an investment opportunity to make 5%, your **opportunity cost** is 5%, and you need to do better than 5% with the opportunity you choose instead. If you could have made 5% and you end up making 7% with another investment, you made 2% better than your opportunity cost.

Finally, separating investment risks into two neat categories is an inexact science. While any resource worth its salt would call inflation a systematic risk and legislative risk unsystematic, it also appears that no two resources agree on where to put all the risks we just discussed. I choose to put anything that is specific to an issuer or an industry group under the unsystematic heading and anything that would affect securities of many different issuers and across all industry groups as systematic.

INVESTMENT RISK	SIGNIFICANCE		NOTES
Systematic	Affect the overall market	"Non-diversifiable"	Diversification won't help; investor must "hedge"
Un-systematic	Affect specific stocks only	Diversifiable	Buy many stocks in many industries
Market	Markets panic due to war, weather events, etc.	Measured by Beta	Hedge with options, futures, ETFs, etc.
Business	How strong is the issuer?	Competition, obsolescence	Diversify your holdings
Political	Emerging markets, e.g., China, Vietnam	Unstable political-economic systems	Don't confuse with "legislative risk"
Legislative/ Regulatory	Changes to laws/regulations	Tax code changes EPA requirements, OSHA mandates	Could have negative effect on stock or bond price
Currency	Value of dollar	ADRs, international and global investing	Weak dollar makes ADR more valuable
Interest Rate	Rates up/Market price down	Long-term bonds most susceptible, measured by "duration"	Preferred stock is rate-sensitive, too

INVESTMENT RISK	SIGNIFICANCE	NOTES	
Credit, Default	Issuer could fail	Downgrade in credit rating lowers value of bond	Low bond values = high-yield
Purchasing Power	Inflation erodes buying power	Fixed-income presents purchasing power risk	Live and die by the CPI
Reinvestment Risk	Investing at varying rates of interest	If rates down, investor goes forward at lower rate	Zero-coupons avoid this risk
Liquidity Risk	Trying to sell when there are few or no buyers	Esoteric securities, partnerships, hedge fund investments are illiquid	Thinly traded stocks less liquid
Opportunity Cost	What you give up to invest elsewhere	If you give up a 5% T-Bond investment, 5% is your opportunity cost	Try to do better than 5%

INVESTMENT VEHICLES

Before investors subject their capital to the investment risks we just looked at, they typically first put down a layer of financial protection. To protect against a sudden loss of income investors buy disability and life insurance. Disability insurance pays some percentage of the individual's income should he become injured, ill, or otherwise unable to perform his job—or, with some policies, any job. Many policies only pay out after 90 days, so keeping several months' worth of living expenses in a savings account usually goes hand in hand with disability insurance.

Life insurance is intended to pay off the mortgage, get the kids through college, and replace the total loss of income experienced when a bread winner dies.

Unfortunately, no matter how wisely they invest, many customers face the risk of outliving their retirement accounts. To protect against this risk individuals often purchase annuities.

ANNUITIES

➢ Types of Annuities

An **annuity** is an investment sold by an insurance company that either promises a minimum rate of return to the investor or allows the investor to allocate payments to various mutual funds that invest in the stock and bond markets. These products offer regular payments for the rest of the annuitant's life, but owners of annuities can instead take money out as lump sums or random withdrawals on the back end. Annuities are part of the retirement plans of many individuals, and they can either be part of the "safe-money" piece or can provide exposure to the stock and bond markets.

The three main types of annuities are fixed, indexed, and variable. That's only two types, since an indexed annuity *is* a fixed annuity, but it has many features that make it completely different from a plain-old fixed annuity.

> Fixed Annuities

A **fixed annuity** promises a minimum rate of return to the investor in exchange for one big payment into the contract or several periodic payments. The **purchase payments** are allocated to the insurance company's own **general account,** so the rate of return is "guaranteed." But, that just means it's backed by the claims-paying ability of the insurance company's general account—so before turning over your hard-earned money to an insurance company, expecting them to pay it back to you slowly, you might want to check their **AM Best** rating and their history of paying claims.

A fixed annuity would be suitable for someone who wants a "safe money" investment that is more dependable than anything in the stock or bond markets, something that promises to make dependable payments for the rest of his life, no matter how long he ends up living. The fixed annuity offers peace of mind if not a high rate of return. What does the investor want—peace of mind or high rate of return? Sorry, this is an either-or thing.

> Indexed Annuities

An interesting type of fixed annuity is the **equity indexed annuity.** With this product, the investor receives a guaranteed minimum rate of return. But, he/she receives a higher rate of return when an index—usually the S&P 500—has a good year. Do they receive the full upside, as if they owned an S&P 500 index fund? No, and that should be made clear by the sales representative. Equity indexed annuities have a **participation rate.** A participation rate of 70% means that the contract only gets credited with 70% of the increase in the S&P 500. If the index goes up 10%, the contract makes only 7%. Except when it doesn't. The contracts also have a **cap** placed on the maximum increase for any year, regardless of what the stock market does. So with a participation rate of 70% and a cap of 12%, what happens if the S&P goes up 30%? Well, 70% of that would be 21%; however, if you're capped at 12%, then 12% is all the contract value will rise that year. As you can see, indexed annuities are all about the downside protection, which is why a securities license is not required to sell fixed annuities, equity-indexed or otherwise.

> Variable Annuities

A **variable annuity** doesn't promise a rate of return, which is where they got the "variable" part. Since investors are investing in little mutual fund–type accounts of their choosing, maybe they'll end up doing much better than the modest rate that the fixed annuity guarantees. In other words, in a variable annuity, the annuitant bears the investment risk rather than having the insurance company promise a certain rate of return. In exchange for bearing the risks we've looked at in the stock and bond markets, the variable annuitant gets the opportunity to do much better than he would have in a fixed annuity.

Could he do worse? Sure, but what does he want? If he wants a guarantee, he buys a fixed annuity where the insurance company guarantees a certain rate of return. Now he lives with "purchasing power risk," because if the annuity promises 2%, that's not going to be sufficient with inflation rising at 4%. If he wants to protect his purchasing power by investing in the stock market, he buys a variable annuity, but now he takes on all the investment risks we've discussed.

Life is full of tough choices. Your job is to help investors make the one that's right for them.

Variable annuities use mutual fund accounts as their investment options, but we don't call variable annuities "mutual funds." We call the investment options that would otherwise be called "mutual funds" **subaccounts.** Salespeople must go out of their way to avoid confusing customers into thinking an annuity *is* a mutual fund. It is not a mutual fund. Mutual funds aren't subject to early withdrawal penalties from the issuer or the IRS. Mutual funds don't offer a death benefit or add expenses to cover it. On the other hand, mutual funds are not tax-deferred accounts. A mutual fund held in a regular old taxable account will subject investors to taxation every year. The dividend and capital gains distributions are taxable, and if the investor redeems some shares for a gain, that's also taxable for the year it occurs. This tax burden reduces the principal in the account each year, which is a major drag on long-term returns. A variable annuity, however, is a retirement plan where you get to keep all the dividends and capital gains in the account, adding to your principal, and compounding your returns forever and ever and ever.

Whoa, sorry. Not forever. You get to defer taxation until you take the money out, which is usually at retirement. Your money grows much faster when it's not being taxed for 10, 20, maybe 30 years, but every dance reaches the point where you are required to pay the fiddler. It's been a fun dance, for sure, but the reality is that you will pay ordinary income tax rates on the earnings you've been shielding from the hungry hands of the IRS all these years. Ordinary income rates, too. If you're in the 35% tax bracket, the gains coming out of your variable annuity are taxed at that rate.

➤ Features of Annuities

Annuities are complicated products. Therefore, the individual generally has at least 10 business days to change his or her mind without losing any money to the insurance/annuity company on a variable annuity. This is called the **free-look period.** Insurance law is state-specific, and the free-look on fixed annuities is the same as what the state uses for insurance policies.

An annuity comes with a **mortality guarantee,** which means that once you go into the pay-out phase, you will receive monthly payments provided you are alive (a mortal). Of course, the fixed annuity tells you what the check will be worth at a minimum, while the variable annuity—well, it varies, people. In the variable annuity, the annuitant will get a check each month, but it could be meager if the markets aren't doing well.

A fixed annuity is an insurance product providing peace of mind and tax deferral. A variable annuity functions like a mutual fund investment that grows tax-deferred and offers some peace of mind. See, whether it's fixed or variable, the insurance company offers a **death benefit** that promises to pay a beneficiary at least the amount of money invested by the annuitant during his life—period.

Insurance companies sell peace of mind. Both the mortality guarantee and the death benefit help a lot of investors sleep better. Tough to put a price tag on that. For maximum peace of mind, individuals should buy a fixed or indexed annuity. For some peace of mind and the chance to invest in the stock and bond markets, individuals should consider a variable annuity. A variable annuity offers the investment choices that you'd get from a family of mutual funds (growth, value, high-yield bonds, etc.), the tax deferral you'd get from an IRA or 401(k) plan, plus a death benefit similar to a life insurance policy. A fixed annuity—or indexed annuity—offers the tax deferral, the death benefit, and a dependable stream of minimum payments, even if you live to 115.

Interestingly, an annuity gives the insurance company a different kind of "mortality risk." In a life insurance policy, their risk is that somebody will put in $10,000 and die the next year, forcing the company to pay out hundreds of thousands, maybe a million. In an annuity, their mortality risk is that the annuitant will end up living to 115. The insurance company makes a mortality guarantee, which promises to pay the annuitant each month for the rest of her life. But, they cover their risk with a fee, called a mortality risk fee. An insurance company has the risk that their expenses will rise. They promise to keep expenses level, but they charge an expense risk fee to cover their risk. In fact, usually the two are combined and referred to as a "mortality and expense risk fee," or "M & E" for those in the real world who love to abbreviate. Variable annuities use mutual fund–type accounts as investment vehicles, but they add charges in excess of what those mutual funds charge investors—all the guarantees offered in the annuity contract can easily add an extra 1% to annual expenses, which can add up over 20 or 30 years.

Just like owners of mutual fund shares, owners of variable annuities get to vote their units on important decisions such as:

- Electing the Board of Managers
- Changing the Investment Objectives, Policies
- Ratifying the Independent Auditor/Accounting Firm

> Deferred and Immediate Annuities

If an individual buys an annuity and plans to wait several years to receive payments, he has purchased a **deferred annuity.** If the individual is ready to retire and/or receive payments immediately, he purchases an **immediate annuity** instead.

While holding a deferred annuity, the individual can **surrender** the contract for its "surrender value." But, watch out here. The first several years typically comprise your **surrender period**. During that time if you decide to cash in the annuity, you will get hit with a **surrender charge**, which is often called a "contingent deferred sales charge" just as we discuss elsewhere in connection with mutual fund B-shares. Yes, many annuities allow people to withdraw 10% of the contract value per year, but anything beyond that is subject to some nasty surrender charges. These surrender charges start out high—say 8% or higher—which is one reason that deferred annuities are long-term investments. Don't be pitching a deferred annuity to a senior citizen, who might need to access a big chunk of her money for an emergency. You must be sure the individual can leave the money alone for at least provided the surrender period.

When the individual purchases the annuity, the following are deducted from the check:

- Sales charge (if they have a front-end load)
- Administrative fee
- State premium tax

Most annuities use the contingent deferred sales charge called the "surrender period," but some are still sold with front-end sales charges. Either way there is a premium tax, and there are administrative fees are taken out of the check.

In a variable annuity the individual then allocates what's left of his **purchase payment** to the various subaccounts, the little mutual fund portfolios. Maybe 20% goes into the conservative income subaccount, 20% into the growth subaccount and 60% to the high-yield long-term bond subaccount. From the money invested there are plenty of fees that will be deducted. We have all the operating expenses we saw for mutual funds: management fee, 12b-1 fee, and other expenses. And, we also have the "mortality & expense risk fee" charged for the annuity features.

What is the maximum that an insurance company can charge for sales charges and expenses? The current regulations just say that the charges and expenses must be "reasonable."

Seriously.

> Bonus Annuities

Think of a "bonus annuity" as an annuity with features added as a bonus to the investor. With a **bonus annuity** the annuity company may offer to enhance the buyer's premium by contributing an additional 1 to 5% of what he/she puts in. Of course, this comes with a price. First, there are fees attached and, second, the surrender period is longer. Third, if the investor surrenders the contract early, the bonus disappears. An investor will be penalized by the annuity company with a "surrender charge" if they pull all their money out early. For "bonus annuities" that period where the investor could get penalized is longer.

Bonus annuities are not suitable for everyone. Variable annuities in general are not good for short-term investment goals, since the surrender charge will be applied during the first 7 years or so. Should you switch a customer into a bonus annuity? Maybe. But, even though the annuitant can avoid taxes through a 1035 exchange, when she exchanges the annuity, her surrender period starts all over again. And, yes, FINRA will bust you if it looks like you did the switch just to make a nice commission, forcing the investor to start the surrender period all over again. In general, investors should maximize their 401(k) and other retirement plans before considering annuities. Annuities are ideal for those who have maxed out those plans, since the annuity allows investors to contribute as much as they would like.

> Purchasing Annuities

The categories of fixed, indexed, and variable annuities refer to the way payments will be calculated on the way out. In terms of buying annuities, the two major types are "immediate" and "deferred." These terms refer to how soon the contract holder wants to begin receiving payments—now, or later? These are retirement plans, so you do need to be 59½ to avoid penalties. Therefore, some customers might want or need to wait 20 or 30 years before receiving payments. If so, they purchase a deferred annuity, because "deferred" means "I'll do it later," the way some readers may have "deferred" their study process a few weeks—or months—before buckling down.

The tax deferral is nice, but if the individual is already, say, 68, she may want to retire now and start receiving payments immediately. As you can probably guess, we call that an immediate annuity.

While there are immediate *variable* annuities, it just makes more sense somehow to buy the fixed *immediate* annuity. Why? Well, the whole point of buying an immediate annuity is to know that—no matter what happens to social security and your 401(k) account—there is a solid insurance company obligated to make a payment of at least X amount for provided you live. An immediate *variable* annuity would work out well only if the investments did—while there would be some minimal payment guaranteed, it would be meager. An immediate fixed annuity does not offer a high rate of return, but it does provide peace of mind to investors in retirement. Many financial planners would suggest that at least some of their clients' retirement money be sitting in a fixed immediate annuity— maybe just enough to provide a monthly payment covering all monthly expenses. Figuring withdrawal rates from retirement accounts is tricky, so having a payment of X amount from a solid insurance company could smooth out the bumps.

Customers can buy annuities either with one big payment or several smaller payments. The first method is called "single premium" or "single payment." The second method is called "periodic payment." If an investor has a large chunk of money, she can put it in an annuity, where it can grow tax-deferred. If she's putting in a big single purchase payment, she can choose either to wait (defer) or to begin receiving annuity payments immediately. She must be 59½ years old to annuitize, but if she's old enough, she can begin the pay-out phase immediately. That's called a **single-payment immediate annuity**. Maybe she's only 42, though, and wants to let the money grow another 20 years before taking it out. That's called a **single-payment deferred annuity** (SPDA).

Many investors put money into the annuity during the accumulation phase (pay-in) gradually, over time. That's called "periodic payment," and if they aren't done paying in yet, you can bet the insurance company isn't going to start paying out. So, if you're talking about a "periodic payment" plan, the only way to do it is through a **periodic *deferred* annuity**. There is no such thing as a "Periodic Immediate Annuity" since no insurance company I'm aware of would let me start sending in $100 a month while they go ahead and start sending me $110.

To review, then, there are three methods of purchasing annuities:

- Single-Payment Deferred Annuity
- Periodic-Payment Deferred Annuity
- Single-Payment Immediate Annuity

Again, understand that variable annuities use mutual funds (called subaccounts) as the investment vehicles in the plan. But, annuities add both features and extra expenses for the investor on top of all the investment-related expenses. Tax deferral is nice. So are the death benefit and the annuity payment that goes on provided the individual lives. But, that stuff also adds maybe 1.0–1.5% per year in expenses to the investor. You can either slide that fact past your investor or fully disclose it. Depends on whether you want your name up on FINRA's website or not.

➢ Receiving Payments (Settlement Options)

Some investors make periodic payments into the contract while others make just one big payment. Either way, when the individual gets ready to annuitize the contract, he tells the insurance company which payout option he's choosing. And, he is not able to change this decision—he makes the decision and lives with it. Or, maybe more accurately, dies with it. Essentially, what's going on at this point in the contract is that the individual is about to make a bet with the insurance company as to how long he will end up living.

If the individual throws the switch to receive payments and chooses **life only** or **straight life,** he'll typically receive the largest monthly payout. Why? Because the insurance company sets those payments and the insurance company knows better than he does when he's going to die. Not the exact day or the exact method, of course, but they can estimate it with amazing precision. Since the insurance/annuity company only must make payments for provided he lives, the payments are typically the largest for a "life only" or "straight life" annuity settlement option. How does the individual win the "bet"? By living a lot longer than the actuarial tables would predict. Not a bad motivation for exercising and eating right, huh?

If this option seems too risky, the individual can choose a "unit refund life annuity." This way he is guaranteed a certain number of payments even if he does get hit by the proverbial bus. If he dies before receiving them, his beneficiary receives the balance of payments.

So, does the annuitant have family or a charity she wants to be sure receives the balance of her payments? If not, why not go with the life only/straight life option? Tell the insurance company to pay her as much as possible for provided she lives. If she dies—well, what does she care if the annuity company comes out ahead? If she does have family, friends, or a charity that she'd like to name as a beneficiary, she can choose a **period certain** settlement option. In that case, the insurance company does what the name implies—make payments for a certain period. To either her or the named beneficiaries. For older investors, this option typically leads to a lower monthly payment, since the insurance company will now be on the hook for several years even if the annuitant expires early.

If it's a 20-year period certain payout, the payments must be made to the beneficiary for the rest of that period, even if the annuitant dies after the first month or two. The annuitant could also choose **life with period certain**, and now we'd have a complicated either-or scenario with the insurance company. With this option the company will make payments for the greater of his life or a certain period, such as 20 years. If he dies after 2 years, the company makes payments to his beneficiary for the rest of the term. And if he lives longer than 20 years, they just keep on making payments until he finally expires.

Finally, the **joint with last survivor** option would typically provide the smallest monthly check because the company is obligated to make payments provided either the annuitant or the survivors are still alive. The contract can be set up to pay the annuitant while he's alive and then pay the beneficiaries until the last beneficiary expires. Or, it can start paying the annuitant and the beneficiary until both have finally, you know. Covering two persons' mortality risks is an expensive proposition to the insurance company, so these monthly checks are typically smaller than either period certain or life-only settlement options.

➤ Variable Annuities: Accumulation and Annuity Units

There are only two phases of an annuity—the **accumulation period** and the **annuity period**. An individual making periodic payments into the contract, or one who made one big payment and is now just deferring the payout phase, is in the accumulation phase, holding **accumulation units.** When he throws the switch to start receiving payments, the insurance company converts those accumulation units to **annuity units.** In a fixed annuity the annuitant knows the minimum monthly payment he can expect. A variable annuity, on the other hand, pays out the fluctuating value of those annuity units.

And, although the value of annuity units fluctuates in a variable annuity during the payout phase, the number of those annuity units is fixed. To calculate the first payment for a variable annuity, the insurance company uses the following:

- Age of the annuitant
- Account value
- Gender
- Settlement option

Health is not a factor. This is also why an annuity cannot suddenly be turned into a life insurance policy, even though it can work in the other direction, as we'll discuss elsewhere.

> AIR and Annuity Units

Once the number of annuity units has been determined, we say that the number of annuity units is fixed. So, for example, maybe every month he'll be paid the value of 100 annuity units.

Trouble is, he has no idea how big that monthly check is going to be, since nobody knows what 100 annuity units will be worth month-to-month, just like nobody knows what mutual fund shares will be worth month-to-month.

So, how much is an annuity unit worth every month? All depends on the investment performance of the separate account compared to the expectations of its performance.

Seriously. If the separate account returns are better than the assumed rate, the units increase in value. If the account returns are exactly as expected, the unit value stays the same. And if the account returns are lower than expected, the unit value drops from the month before. It's all based on the **Assumed Interest Rate (AIR)** that the annuitant and annuity company agree to use. If the **AIR** is 5%, that means the separate account investments are expected to grow each month at an annualized rate of 5%. If the account gets a 6% annualized rate of return one month, the individual's check gets bigger. If the account gets the anticipated 5% return next month, that's the same as AIR and the check will stay the same. And if the account gets only a 4% return the following month, the check will go down.

If the AIR is 5%, here is how it would work:

Actual Return:	5%	7%	6%	5%	4%
Check:	$1,020	$1,035	$1,045	$1,045	$1,030

When the account gets a 7% return, the account gets much bigger. So, when it gets only a 6% return the following month, that's 6% of a bigger account, and is 1% more than we expected to get. So, just compare the actual return with the AIR. If the actual return is bigger, so is the monthly check. If it's smaller, so is the monthly check. If the actual return is the same as the AIR, the check stays the same.

An insurance company is one of the finest business models ever constructed. See, no one person can take the risk of dying at age 32 and leaving the family with an unpaid mortgage, a bunch of other bills, and a sudden loss of income, not to mention the maybe $15,000 it takes just for a funeral these days. But, an insurance company can take the risk that a certain number of individuals will die prematurely by insuring a huge number of individuals and then using the precise laws of probability over large numbers that tell them how many individuals will die each year with only a small margin of error. Once they've taken the insurance premiums that individuals pay, they then invest what's left after covering expenses and invest it wisely in the real estate, fixed-income, and stock markets. They have just as much data on these markets, so they can use the laws of probability again to figure out that if they take this much risk here, they can count on earning this much return over here within only a small margin of error.

And, of course, insurance companies are conservative investors. That's what allows them to crunch a bunch of numbers and know with reasonable certainty that they will never have to pay so many death benefits in one year that their investments are totally wiped out. This conservative investment account that guarantees the payout on whole life, term life, and fixed annuities is called the **general account**. In other words, the general account is for the insurance company's investments.

They then created an account that is separate from the general account and decided to name it the **separate account**. It's a mutual fund family that offers tax deferral, but we don't call it a mutual fund, even though it's also covered by and registered under the same Investment Company Act of 1940. The Investment Company Act of 1940 defines a separate account like so:

> "Separate account" means an account established and maintained by an insurance company pursuant to the laws of any State or territory of the United States, or of Canada or any province thereof, under which income, gains and losses, whether or not realized, from assets allocated to such account, are, in accordance with the applicable contract, credited to or charged against such account without regard to other income, gains, or losses of the insurance company.

When purchase payments are invested into the general account, the investor is guaranteed a certain rate of return—whole life, fixed annuity. When purchase payments are invested into the separate account, welcome to the stock and bond markets, where anything can happen.

From the perspective of the nice couple sitting across from you at the table, it all looks much the same. You were talking about the Platinum Equity Income Fund a few minutes ago—now that you've switched to your variable annuity spiel, we're still seeing the same Platinum Equity Income Fund. What's up with that? It's the same darned fund, but if you buy it within a variable annuity contract, we call it a subaccount, just to keep everything nice and simple.

Actually, there is a good reason to avoid calling subaccounts "mutual funds." If the investor thinks he's in a "mutual fund," he might think he can take out his money whenever he wants. He also might not realize that he's paying an extra 1.0–1.5% a year to place the annuity wrapper around the "mutual fund" investments. So, be careful with the language out there once you get licensed, people.

LIFE INSURANCE

I've always felt that it would be rude of me to die without insurance and leave family and friends footing the bill for my funeral. That's why I basically "rent" insurance coverage through something called **term life insurance**. It's cheap, but it's only good for a certain term. The individual pays premiums in exchange for a guaranteed **death benefit** payable to a **beneficiary** if **the insured** dies during that period. If the insured does not die during that period, the policy expires. If the **policyholder** wants to renew, he can, but he's older now and costlier to insure. In other words, his premiums will go up, even though the death benefit will stay the same, because he's older and more likely to have some medical condition that raises his rates, too, or even that prevents him from being offered the insurance at all. So, as with all products, there are pluses and minuses. Term insurance is cheap and offers protection, but it does not build any cash value and typically must be renewed at higher and higher rates, just like renting an apartment.

Let's note the language used in insurance:

- **Policyholder**: the owner of the policy, responsible for paying premiums
- **Insured**: the person whose life is insured by the policy, usually the policyholder
- **Beneficiary**: the party that receives the death benefit upon death of the insured
- **Death benefit**: the amount payable to the beneficiary upon death of the insured, minus any unpaid premiums or loan balances
- **Cash value**: a value in the policy account that can be partially withdrawn or borrowed against

So, let's say that Joe Smith buys an insurance policy with a $100,000 death benefit payable to his wife. He's the policyholder and the insured. If he dies, the death benefit of $100,000 is paid to the beneficiary, his wife. As we'll see, most insurance also builds up cash value, which can be withdrawn or borrowed while Joe is still alive (term insurance does not build up this cash value, which is also why it's relatively cheap insurance).

➤ Permanent vs. Temporary Insurance

As with housing, some people prefer to rent insurance for a term, and some prefer to buy it. Some feel that if you're going to be putting money aside, you might as well end up with something to show for it, so they purchase permanent insurance. The most common type of permanent insurance is called **whole life insurance**. The premiums are much higher than on the term insurance you sort of "rent," but insurance companies will guarantee a minimum **cash value**, and you can also hope for an even better cash value than that. This way it works to protect your beneficiaries if you die unexpectedly and acts as a savings vehicle where the cash value grows tax-deferred. Maybe at age 55 you decide to borrow $50,000 of the cash value for whatever reason. Could come in handy, yes?

One other thing to remember: to renew a term policy usually means you pay a higher premium. Premiums are "level" in a whole life policy, meaning they don't go up. You lock in your rate for your whole life.

So, term is "cheap," but after a few years you have no cash value. And, to keep it going, you typically pay more for the same benefit. Reminds me of how I spent five years paying rent to a landlord. It was lower than a mortgage payment would have been on a similar-sized house, but at the end of this 5-

year term I had forked over 40 g's to the landlord and was left with nothing but the opportunity to renew my lease at a higher rate. I covered myself with a roof for five years, and at the end of the five years I owned absolutely no part of that roof.

Whole life insurance is more like buying the house, which is exactly what I did after five years of renting. I had to come up with a down payment, and my monthly mortgage was $200 more per month than my rent was. The upside is that at the end of five years, I had some equity in the house that I could tap into for a loan maybe (much like cash value in an insurance policy that I can borrow against some day). Just like with a whole life policy, I'll be getting at least something back for all those payments I've made over the years. And the time will come when the full value is all paid up.

So, whole life insurance involves premiums that are higher than those for term life insurance, but you end up with something even if you stop paying into the policy. There is a guaranteed cash value, whereas term leaves you with nothing. The death benefit is guaranteed (as it is on a term policy), too, so whole life insurance is a popular product for people who want to protect their families and use the policy as a savings vehicle, where all that increase in cash value grows tax-deferred.

If the exam asks which type of client should purchase term insurance, I would look for a young, single parent, maybe, or someone who absolutely must protect the kids from a sudden loss of income and wants to do it as cheaply as possible.

Nothing is simple in either the securities or insurance industry. Since some clients crave flexibility, the industry bent over backwards to come up with a flexible form of permanent insurance called **universal life insurance**. Think "flexibility" when you see the words "universal life insurance." The death benefit and, therefore, the premiums can be adjusted by the client. They can be increased to buy more coverage or decreased to back off on the coverage and save some money. If the cash value is sufficient, premiums can stop being paid by the client and start being covered by the cash value. The cash value grows at a minimum, guaranteed rate, just like on traditional whole life policies, and if the general account does well, the cash value goes up from there. As mentioned, at some point the policyholder may decide to withdraw part of the cash value, or may usually borrow up to 90% of it.

➢ Variable Policies

So, whether it's term, traditional whole life, or universal life insurance, we're talking strictly about insurance products. Death benefits and cash values (term has no cash value) are guaranteed by the insurance company, who invests the net premiums (what's left after deducting expenses, taxes, etc.) into their general account. Once you start attaching cash value and death benefits to the ups and downs of a separate account, however, you have created a new product that is both an insurance policy and a security. Opens a whole new market for the company, but it also means that those who sell them need both an insurance and a securities license.

Whole life and term life insurance policies tell clients exactly how much they will pay out upon death. So, in term and whole life policies, the insurance company bears all investment risk through their general account.

With variable insurance products, the death benefit—as well as the cash value—fluctuates just like it does in a variable annuity. That's what they mean by "variable." It all varies, based on the investment performance of the separate account. The separate account, as we discussed under variable annuities, is made up of subaccounts. The investor chooses from these quasi-mutual funds that are trying to meet different investment objectives: growth, long-term bonds, short-term Treasuries, etc. He can even choose to invest some of the premiums into a fixed account, just to play it safe, and he can switch between the subaccounts as his investment needs change without a tax problem.

The cash value is tied to account performance, period. So, if the test question says that the separate account grew, it doesn't matter by how much. The cash value increases when the separate account increases. But death benefit is tied to actual performance versus AIR, just like an annuity unit in a variable annuity. If the AIR is 6% and the account gets a 4% return, the cash value will increase due to the positive return, but the death benefit will decrease since the account returned less than AIR.

Variable Life Insurance (VLI) policies pay out the cash value/surrender value whenever the policyholder decides to cash in the policy. Now, there's no way to know what the value might be at the time of surrender. If the subaccounts have performed well, the cash value might be better than expected. But if the market has been brutal, the cash value could go all the way down to zero. Probably not going to happen, but it could.

A minimum or fixed death benefit is guaranteed, however. Some refer to it as the "floor." No matter what the market does, the insurance company guarantees a minimum death benefit that could only be reduced or depleted by failure to pay premiums or taking out loans against the policy. Any guaranteed payments are covered by the insurance company's general account. So, the minimum death benefit is guaranteed, and the policyholder also has the chance of enjoying an increased death benefit, depending on how well the little subaccounts (inside the separate account) do.

As we said, that's tied to AIR, so if the market is kind, the death benefit increases, but if the market is unkind, it could, theoretically, drag the death benefit all the way down to the floor.

As with variable annuities, after the money's been allocated to the little subaccounts of the separate account, the insurance company charges regular fees, just like they do in variable annuities:

- mortality risk fee
- expense risk fee
- investment management fees

The value of the subaccounts and, therefore, the cash value are calculated daily. The death benefit is calculated annually. If the separate account has several below-AIR months, it will take several above-AIR months after that before the customer's death benefit starts to increase.

Remember that flexibility we discussed that separates traditional whole life from universal life? Well, it probably isn't too surprising that somebody eventually married that benefit to variable life to get **Variable Universal Life Insurance**. With VUL we have the death benefit and cash value tied to the separate account (variable), plus we have the flexible premium thing (universal) going on. Regular old variable life is called "scheduled premium." That means the insurance company puts your premium payments on a schedule, and you better stick to it. Variable Universal or Universal Variable Life policies are funded as "flexible premium." That means the client may or may not have to send in a check. With a VUL policy, the customer must maintain enough cash value and death benefit to keep the policy in force. If the separate account rocks, no money has to roll in from the customer. If the separate account rolls over and dies, look out. Since that's a little scary, some VULs come with minimum guaranteed death benefits.

Variable Universal Life can get to be a sort of complicated product, and as with anything you sell, before you do so, make sure you understand all the ins and outs. And talking to a firm specialist or old-timer might not hurt, either, on this or any other product that's new to you. A good question is always, "Worst-case scenario, what could go wrong?"

The advantages of variable life over whole life insurance include the ability to invest some of the premiums into the stock market, which has historically enjoyed relatively high average returns and done well at beating inflation. A robust investment market can increase the cash value and death benefit, often faster than the rate of inflation. A traditional whole life policy, on the other hand, that promised to pay $50,000 when it was purchased in 1964 represented a lot of money then. But if it pays that $50,000 out in 2014, the $50,000 doesn't go far, due to inflation.

> Policy Loans

Variable policies make 75% of the cash value available to the customer as a loan after three years. Of course, they charge interest on that loan, just as they do on a whole life policy. If the loan is not repaid, that reduces both the cash value and the death benefit of the policy. And, if the customer takes out a big loan and then the separate account tanks, he'll have to put some money back in to bring the cash value back to a sufficient level, or risk having the policy lapse. Don't worry, though. Some people take out a loan with absolutely no intention of repaying it. They simply don't need as much death benefit at this point, so why not have some fun with the money right now? The test might point out that whole life insurance policies allow the policyholder to borrow a higher percentage of cash value, while VLI, on the other hand, being backed up by the subaccounts only lets the policyholder borrow up to 75% of cash value.

> Settlement Options for Insurance Policies

The policyholder can choose from many options concerning the method of payment to the beneficiary. These are called "settlement options." The "lump-sum" method is self-explanatory. "Fixed-period" means that the insurance company will invest the proceeds of the policy into an interest-bearing account and then make equal payments at regular intervals for a fixed period. The payments include principal and interest. How much are the payments? That depends on the size of the principal, the interest rate earned by the insurance company, and the length of time involved in this fixed period.

The "fixed-amount" settlement option has the insurance company invest the proceeds from the policy and pay the beneficiary a fixed amount of money at regular intervals until both the principal and interest are gone. The amount received is fixed, but the period over which the beneficiary receives payments varies.

So, for "fixed-period" versus "fixed-amount," the decision comes down to this: do you want to receive an uncertain amount of money for a fixed period, or do you want to receive a fixed amount of money for an uncertain period? In other words, do you want to be paid something like $25,000 for exactly three years (fixed-period)? Or, would you prefer being paid exactly $25,000 for about three years (fixed-amount)?

In a "life-income" settlement option, the proceeds are annuitized. That means the insurance company provides the beneficiary with a guaranteed income for the rest of his/her life. Just like with annuities, the beneficiary's age expectancy is taken into account to determine the monthly payout, along with the size of the death benefit and the type of payout selected.

There is also an "interest-only" settlement option, whereby the insurance company keeps the proceeds from the policy and invests them, promising the beneficiary a guaranteed minimum rate of interest. The beneficiary might get more than the minimum, or not, and may receive the payments annually, semiannually, quarterly, or monthly. He/she also has the right to withdraw all the principal if he/she gets antsy, or to change settlement options.

> Exchanges

Since these variable policies are a little confusing to some, the company must give the policyholder at least two years (24 months) to switch back to traditional whole life without having to provide proof of insurability. The new whole life policy will have the same issue date as the original variable policy.

If I buy a variable life policy, I have the opportunity to exchange it for a different policy even if issued by a different company. I don't have to pay taxes since I would not be taking the cash value out. I would just cash in one policy and exchange it, tax-free, for another insurance policy. Or, I can even exchange a life policy for an annuity. It is not possible to exchange an annuity for a life insurance policy, though.

However I do it, this tax-free exchange is called a **1035 exchange** under the Internal Revenue Code.

When selling variable insurance policies, the representative must remember that these are insurance policies first and foremost. You can discuss the benefits of investing in the subaccounts, but you can't present these insurance policies primarily as investment vehicles. Primarily, they're to be sold for the death benefit. They also offer the opportunity to invest in the separate account's little subaccounts, but they're not to be pitched primarily as investment vehicles.

Four federal acts are involved with variable life insurance and variable annuities. The Securities Act of 1933 covers variable life insurance (and annuities). These products must be registered with the SEC and sold with a prospectus. Even though the company that issues these contracts is an insurance company, the subdivision that sells the securities products must be a broker-dealer registered under the Securities Exchange Act of 1934. The separate account is defined as an investment company under the Investment Company Act of 1940 and is either registered as a UIT or an Open-End Fund as defined under that act. The "money manager" or "investment adviser" must register under the Investment Advisers Act of 1940.

And, at the state level, both securities and insurance regulators are watching these products and those who sell them, too.

DEBT SECURITIES

Once they have secured enough protection for themselves and their loved ones, investors may decide it's time to put some money to work and at some risk. **Fixed-income** securities offer such investors a stated and steady stream of income with a relatively low chance of investment loss. Still, while the chance of loss is low compared to an investment in common stock, fixed-income securities are neither insurance policies nor bank accounts. Investors can and do lose money on fixed-income securities, especially when an issuer goes bankrupt. Luckily, bankruptcies and defaults are extremely rare among corporations that issue **debt securities**.

The most common name for debt securities is **bonds**, which represent loans from investors to the corporation or government entity issuing them. Investors buy the bonds, and the issuer then pays them interest on the loan and promises to return the principal amount at the end of the term. Unfortunately, the issuer takes all the money upfront, paying only the interest payments going forward, until the very last payment comes due. Only then would a purchaser of $1 million worth of bonds see the $1 million of principal again.

A bond has a specific value known as either the "par" or the "principal" amount printed on the face of the certificate. Bonds typically have a **par value** of $1,000. This is the amount an investor will receive along with the last interest payment from the issuer, on what is known as the **maturity date**. A mortgage will eventually be paid off and so will a bond. We call the day that the last interest and principal payments are made "maturity." At maturity, the bond is all paid up.

So, the bond certificate has the par value printed on the face, along with the interest rate the issuer will pay the investor every year. This interest rate could be referred to as the **coupon rate** or the **nominal yield**. If a bond pays 8% of the par value, that's $80 in interest income each year per $1,000. When it's all over, the bondholder gets the par value or principal amount back. Not terribly exciting, but it is satisfying to watch your money earning money while you attend to other matters.

Companies who raise capital by issuing bonds are using **leverage**. These companies are more susceptible to rises in interest rates than those who issue only common stock. Typically, bonds are issued by mature companies with predictable cash flow. Common stock, on the other hand, is better suited for immature but promising companies. That's because shareholders can wait for any upside to their investment without the issuer having to pay out any cash to them. Bonds, on the other hand, are loans requiring the interest to be paid on time, with all the principal returned on a stated maturity date as well.

Now, many of us are used to being on the borrowing end of a debt. We owe the mortgage company, the automobile financing company, or the credit card company, etc. So, we understand what it's like to be a borrower—we always want to pay the lowest rates of interest possible. Well, when a corporation issues bonds, it is simply borrowing money, which is why it likes to pay the lowest rates of interest possible, also. When you apply for a mortgage, the rate you pay is determined by your credit history, your budget, your earnings, and the length of time you want to borrow the money for. Same thing for a corporation. If it has a solid credit history and solid cash flow, it gets to borrow at a lower rate. Time is also a factor, as the issuing company pays more to borrow for 10 years than to borrow for 3 months, just like you'd pay more for a 30-year mortgage than a 15-year. If the issuer pledges collateral, that can reduce the interest rate paid, too, just like your mortgage is offered at a much lower rate than the unsecured borrowing you do through a credit card.

So, it's easy to relate to a borrower. Borrowers want to pay low rates of interest. The corporations that issue bonds are borrowers trying to borrow at the lowest possible interest rate.

Who's lending them the money? Bond investors. If you buy their bonds, you are loaning the corporation money. Now, what type of interest rate are you hoping to see? The highest one possible, right? Suddenly, you're like the mortgage company. Somebody owes you money, and the higher the rate of interest, the more money you make. If rates are high, bond issuers will pay high rates. Heck, bond rates *are* interest rates, so that's sort of redundant. If you issue a bond, you borrow money. The rate of interest you pay will be in line with other interest rates in the economy.

➤ Interest Rates and Bond Yields

So, interest rates represent what new bonds have to pay to attract new investors. If a bond pays a fixed 8% rate of interest, whenever interest rates change, they will change the bond's market price. When rates go up above 8%, the bond's price will go down, since new bonds would be issued with higher rates. Investors like high coupon rates. They won't pay as much for an 8% coupon as they will for a 10% coupon. Wouldn't you put your money into the bank CD paying 10% over the one offering 8%?

On the other hand, when rates go down, the bond's price will go up, since new bonds would be issued with lower rates.

It's all relative. What is 8% worth? Depends on interest rates. When new debt pays more than 8%, an 8% bond looks bad. But, when new debt pays only 6%, suddenly that same old 8% bond looks terrific. It's all relative—relative to interest rates. You'll need to be able to explain this concept to the investors who buy bond mutual funds from you. "How the heck could my account be down 15% that fast—they're all Government bonds!" someone might politely scream at you one morning.

Interest rates, sir. Just like we talked about. Rates up, price down. Even though a bond may have a par value of $1,000, we don't necessarily expect the bond to trade at $1,000 in the open market. As with a stock, a bond's price fluctuates. Why?

Interest rates.

If a bondholder has a bond that pays a nominal yield or "coupon rate" of 8%, what is the bond worth when interest rates in general climb to 10%? Not as much, right? If you had something that paid you 8%, when you knew you could be receiving more like 10%, how would you feel about the bond?

Not too good.

But, when interest rates fall to 6%, suddenly that 8% bond looks good, right? When we take a bond's price into consideration, we're looking at a concept known as **current yield** (CY). Current yield just takes the annual interest paid by the bond to an investor and divides it by what an investor must pay for the bond. If the bond will pay you $80 a year, would you rather put down $1,000 or $800? You'd probably rather only put down $800, leaving you with $200 to invest elsewhere.

It's just how much you get compared to what you put down to get it. In fact, it's the same formula we use for dividend yield, only bonds make interest payments while stocks pay dividends.

So, why are interest rates rising in our example above? Must be an inflationary period—as we'll see this happens when the economy expands and the "Fed" steps in to hike interest rates. As interest rates rise, bond prices drop. The nominal yield of 8% means that investors keep receiving $80 per year in income. But if the bond price drops on the secondary market to $800, the current yield rises to 10%. $80/$800 gives us a current yield of 10%, right? So when interest rates on new bonds are rising, the yields on existing bonds rise, too. How can that happen? They begin trading at lower prices. Rates up—price down. A bond trading below the par value is called a **discount bond.** On paper, the investor is now losing, which we can express either as a lower price *or* a higher yield on the bond he is holding.

Of course, whatever can go up can also go down. What happens when interest rates fall? Bond prices rise. If you owned this 8% bond and saw that interest rates have just fallen to 6%, how would you feel about your bond?

Pretty good, right? After all, it pays 2% more than new debt is paying.

Do you want to sell it? No. But you might sell it to me if I paid you a premium. If I paid you $1,200 for the $1,000 par value bond, you might be willing to sell it. From my perspective, I see that new debt is only going to pay 6%, which is too low for my needs. Even though I pay more than par for your 8% bond, it will all work out if I can get all those interest payments at a higher-than-prevailing rate.

So, we've just pushed the price of the bond up as interest rates went down. Dividing our $80 of annual interest by the $1,200 I put down for the bond gives me a current yield of only 6.7%. That's lower than the coupon rate, and whenever you see a current yield that is lower than the nominal/coupon rate, you know you're looking at a **premium bond**. The coupon rate doesn't change. Therefore, the only way to get the yield lower than the coupon is for somebody to pay more than par for the bond. Just like the only way to get the yield higher than the coupon is to pay less than par for the bond on the secondary market.

So, if the exam says the coupon or nominal yield is 5%, and the current yield is higher than that—it's a discount bond. Rates went up, knocking the price of this bond down to make the yield go up. If the exam says the coupon or nominal yield is 5% and the current yield is less than that—it's a premium

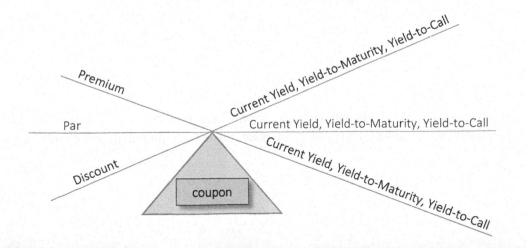

bond. Rates dropped, pushing the price of this bond up on the secondary market to make the yield go down in line with the current low-interest rate-environment.

Choosing a bond investment comes down to this question for the investor—how much of a yield do you want, and how much risk are you willing to take to get it? Your customers would generally prefer no-risk, high-yield bonds. Sorry, doesn't work that way. If you buy a safe bond, you get a lower return. If you go for a higher return, you buy a bond from an issuer with a shaky credit score. Maybe you compromise by purchasing bonds rated right at the cutoff between **investment grade** and **high yield**.

For S&P, the highest rating is AAA, and the lowest investment-grade rating is BBB. Anything below that is attached to a high-yield or "junk" bond. For Moody's, the highest rating is Aaa, with the cut-off called Baa. Anything below either "BBB" from S&P, then, or "Baa" from Moody's, would be issued by a company or municipality with shaky finances. You want to go for a high yield by purchasing a bond on the cheap? Okay, but also ask yourself why that guy was so willing to sell you a bond with "$1,000 par value" printed on it for just $300.

To help with the bond rating, and to make sure the principal can be returned at maturity, corporations and municipalities often establish a **sinking fund**, which is an escrow account earning safe little rates of interest. A sinking fund would be invested in guaranteed U.S. Treasury securities primarily, since putting it in the stock market would be stupid.

When we talk about suitability and clients in more detail we'll mention that many mutual funds would put, say, 80% of their assets into investment-grade bonds and limit their high-yield forays to 20%. That would be conservative. If it were a "High Yield" or "High Income" bond fund, they would focus primarily on bonds rated below BBB/Baa, and they would warn you of the inherent risks there, on top of the interest rate, reinvestment, and other risks we already discussed.

CREDIT RISK	
Standard & Poor's	Moody's
AAA	AAA
AA	AA
A	A
BBB	BAA
NON-INVESTMENT GRADE, HIGH-YIELD, SPECULATIVE	
BB	BA
etc.	etc.

➤ Types of Corporate Bonds

Which interest rate would be lower: the rate you pay for your home equity line of credit, or the rate you pay for a cash advance on your credit card? Obviously, the home equity loan will charge you a lower rate of interest. Why? Because if you don't pay it back, they'll take your house. What's backing up your cash advance from the credit card company? Nothing but your good name and your credit score. Since there is no collateral on that loan, the interest rate you pay is much higher.

In the world of corporate bonds, we have **secured bonds** that are backed up by specific assets, collateral. This way, if the borrowing corporation can't pay the interest and principal, the bondholders can make a claim on the assets. An equipment trust certificate is backed up by airplanes or railroad cars. A mortgage bond is backed up by real estate. A collateral trust certificate is backed up by a portfolio of securities. In all cases, these bonds would offer a lower interest rate compared to the issuer's same bonds that have no specific assets backing them up.

If we buy a bond backed simply by the full faith and credit of an issuer, we are buying a **debenture**. Debenture holders are general creditors. If the company is forced into liquidation, debenture holders have a claim that is lower than that of secured bondholders. Therefore, debentures pay a higher coupon/nominal yield than secured bonds, since they carry more risk.

"Sub-" means "below," as in "submarine" for "below the water," or "subterranean" for "below the ground." **Subordinated debentures** have a claim on corporate assets that is below that of regular ol' debentures when it comes to liquidating a company and paying out money to the bondholders. Since these bonds are riskier, they pay a higher coupon than debentures or secured bonds. Perhaps you've heard of an "80/20" mortgage? The lender uses 80% of the appraised value of your house to get you a decent interest rate, but when they make the second loan using the final 20% of market value, the rate jumps up considerably. If you're maxing out your borrowing, you pay a higher interest rate on that second loan that stretches your budget. Since the lender is taking on more risk, they demand a higher yield.

By the way, what about stockholders? Well, if the company goes into bankruptcy and must be liquidated, stockholders are below all three types of bondholders. Preferred is ahead of common, but behind all the creditors.

If a company becomes unable to pay its suppliers, employees, bondholders, etc., it files a petition for bankruptcy protection either under "Chapter 7" or "Chapter 11" of the federal bankruptcy laws. Under Chapter 11 the company could convince creditors to write off some of the debt or extend the terms of the debt they are currently unable to service. Or, in some cases the entity is completely re-organized under Chapter 11 and former creditors will typically become shareholders of the newly reorganized entity. The business entity often keeps functioning to the best of its abilities and is placed under a trusteeship as a company that is now a "debtor in possession." While the entity struggles along, the U.S. trustee oversees things, demanding that the debtor in possession file regular reports on the operations of the business. The U.S. trustee also appoints a creditors' committee whose role involves consulting with the debtor in possession on administration of the case, investigating the debtor's conduct and operation of the business, and participating in formulating a plan of reorganization. The creditors' committee ordinarily consists of unsecured creditors who hold the seven largest unsecured claims against the debtor.

Under Chapter 7 assets of the company are liquidated by a court-appointed trustee and paid out according to the priority of claims. A liquidation under Chapter 7 is done according to the "absolute priority rule." When the court-appointed trustee liquidates assets, the parties who are owed money would be paid according to the following order or priority:

1. Administrative expenses of the bankruptcy itself
2. Taxes, rents, wages, and benefits
3. Unsecured creditors, including suppliers and bondholders/lenders
4. Equity investors: preferred stock, common stock

As we saw, secured bondholders have a claim on specific assets, so they are outside the priority ordering. They can seize the assets or their value based on the indenture for their secured bonds. For this reason a secured bondholder often gets paid, even when other creditors receive nothing. If secured creditors receive collateral that is insufficient to satisfy their claim, their excess claim becomes another claim by unsecured creditors.

Also, an **income bond** only pays income if the company has income. It's usually issued by a company coming out of bankruptcy and usually offers a high coupon to compensate for the uncertainty of the interest payment. The idea here is that the re-organized company will get some breathing room from the creditors and maybe this breathing room will help it get its act together and start paying interest on its "income" or "adjustment" bonds." A potential trick question could try to confuse you into thinking that an "income investor" with a low risk tolerance should buy an "income bond."

No—only a bond investor with a high appetite for risk and little need for liquidity should do so.

Then, there are **convertible** bonds, which can be converted into a certain number of shares of the issuer's common stock. If the bond has a par value of $1,000, the investor applies the $1,000 of par value toward purchasing the company's stock at a pre-set price. When a convertible bond is issued, it is given a conversion price. If the conversion price is $40, this means that the bond is convertible into common stock at $40. In other words, the investor can use the par value of her bond towards the purchase of the company's common stock at a set price of $40.

If she applies that $1,000 toward the purchase of stock at $40 per share, how many shares would she be able to buy? 25 shares, right? $1,000 of par value divided by $40 per share of stock tells us that each bond can be converted into 25 shares of common stock. In other words, the two securities trade at a 25:1 relationship, since the big one (bond) can be turned into 25 of the little ones (stock). The company sets the conversion price; they have no control over where their common stock trades on the open market, right? If the price goes up, the value of the convertible bonds goes up. Just like if the price goes down, that drags down the market value of the bonds.

So how much is this bond worth at any given moment? Whatever 25 shares of the common stock are worth. Just take par and divide it by the conversion price to find out how many shares of common stock the bond could be converted into. In this case, it's 25 shares, since $1,000 would go exactly that far when purchasing stock priced at $40 a share.

So how much is the bond worth?

Depends. How much are 25 shares of the common stock worth? Since the bond could always be converted into 25 shares, it generally must be worth whatever 25 shares of the common stock are worth. If the common stock price goes up, so does the price of the bond. If the common stock falls, so does the price of the bond. We call this relationship "parity," which is just a fancy word for "same" or "equal." Since one's price depends on the other, the two should have a price that is at "parity."

So, if a bond is convertible into 25 shares of IXR common stock, and IXR is trading @50, what is the bond's price at parity?

$$25 \times \$50 = \$1,250.$$

And if the common stock went up to $60 a share, the bond should be worth 25 times that number, right?

$$25 \times \$60 = \$1,500.$$

Tying the value of the bond to the company's stock makes its price less sensitive to interest rates. I mean, I don't care how high rates are going; if I can turn my bond into 10 shares of Google, with Google common stock trading at $750 a share, I'm good.

➢ U.S. Treasury Securities

 If an investor buys a bill, note, or bond from the United States Treasury, he does not need to worry about credit/default risk. He is going to get the interest checks on time, and he is going to get the principal back at maturity. He just isn't going to get rich in the process. In fact, one usually needs to be rich already to get excited about U.S. Government debt, since they are for capital preservation.

U.S. Government securities are issued with various terms to maturity. There are **T-Bills**, **T-Notes**, **T-Bonds**, and **Treasury STRIPS**, depending on the investor's time horizon. If he has a short time horizon, he buys the T-Bills, which mature in one year or less. Currently, the three- and the six-month T-Bills are what most investors purchase, but that could change whenever the Treasury Department decides to change it, just as they stopped issuing 30-year T-Bonds a while back and then started up again.

T-Bills pay the face amount, and investors try to buy them for the steepest discount possible. If the T-Bill pays out $1,000, we would rather get it for $950 than $965, right? In the first case, we make $50 interest; in the second case, only $35. So, as always, as interest rates rise, the price of T-Bills falls, and vice versa. In a low-interest rate-environment, the price we pay for a T-Bill would be close to the face amount received in three or six months. The minimum denomination for a T-Bill, T-Note, or T-Bond is $100.

If the question says your investor is primarily concerned with interest rate risk, that Treasuries all have no default risk, but do carry various levels of interest rate risk. T-Bills, being extremely short-term, are the best place for this investor. But, if you don't pay attention to time horizon, you could end up causing an investor to lose money on U.S. Treasuries when she goes to liquidate and ends up losing several hundred dollars per bond due to a rise in interest rates

If the investor has a longer time horizon, there are T-Notes available with 2- to 10-year maturities. Unlike the T-Bill which simply puts back more money into the investor's bank account than it took out three or six months earlier, T-Notes pay interest every six months (semi-annually), returning the principal with the last interest check. T-Bonds have maturities up to 30 years.

Treasury STRIPS don't make interest payments to investors. Instead, the investor buys at a deep discount of, say, $650. Eleven years later the STRIP pays out $1,000. The difference of $350 is treated as interest income, but we don't receive it until maturity. Since it makes zero coupon payments, the creative types named this category of bonds "zero coupon bonds." Rather than make interest payments, zero coupon bonds pay out a higher face amount than the investor paid several years earlier.

➤ Non-Marketable Government Securities

> EE Savings Bonds

Series EE bonds are purchased at a discount and redeemed at their much higher face value at maturity. The denominations are as low as $50 and as high as $10,000. The tax on the accrued interest can be paid annually or deferred until maturity. For those who like to avoid tax, the EE bonds can be turned into HH bonds at maturity, allowing the tax to be deferred a little longer.

> HH Savings Bonds

Series HH bonds can be purchased only by trading in Series EE bonds at maturity. These things pay semi-annual interest rather than being issued at a deep discount. The maturity is 10 years, but the investor can redeem them at face value at any time. When things are no longer issued, they are not removed from the investing world all at once. So, the exam may want you to know a little bit about savings bonds, since people may have questions about them when they meet with you.

> I-bonds

An **I-bond** is issued by the U.S. Treasury, which means it's safe and exempt from state and local income taxes. An I-bond pays a guaranteed rate that is fixed but also pays more interest income when inflation rises. The semiannual inflation rate announced in May is the change between the CPI (inflation) figures from the preceding September and March; the inflation rate announced in November is the change between the CPI figures from the preceding March and September. So, since they adjust the interest income to levels of inflation, there's no default risk and no real purchasing power risk, either. There are also tax advantages. First, the interest isn't paid out; it's added to the value of the bond. The owner can, therefore, defer the taxes until cashing in the bond. And, if he uses the proceeds for qualified education costs in the same calendar year that he redeems the bonds, the interest is tax-free. The investor does not even have to declare that the I-bonds will be used for educational purposes when she buys them. Provided she uses the proceeds in the same year she redeems the bonds—and meets the other requirements of the Education Savings Bond Program—the interest is tax-free.

EE, HH, and I-bonds are "non-marketable," which means they cannot be traded. They are savings bonds. T-Bills, T-Notes, T-Bonds, and Treasury STRIPS are all negotiable, which means they have a liquid secondary market.

➢ Municipal Bonds

A "municipality" is any state or local government, including school districts, sewer districts, park districts, sports facilities authorities, what have you. States and local governments borrow money to build roads, schools, and convention centers. Borrowing money is accomplished by issuing bonds to investors. Since municipal authorities issue these bonds, we call them **municipal bonds**. Municipal bonds pay interest that is tax-free to investors. Since the interest income you receive on your municipal bond is tax-free, the city or state issuer can pay you less interest than a corporation must offer—and you can still come out ahead. Yes, a 5% yield on a municipal bond would be much higher than a 7% corporate or U.S. Treasury yield for someone in the 30% tax bracket. We get taxed at our ordinary income rate on corporate bond interest. For municipal securities, the federal government generally does not tax the interest paid to the investor.

What about the states and local governments—can they tax me?

Yes, they can. If you live in Kansas but buy a bond issued by an out-of-state government, Kansas can tax you. If you bought a municipal security issued by the state of Kansas or any local government within the state, the state of Kansas won't tax that interest. Same for the local government—if you live in Topeka and buy a bond issued by Wichita, the federal government won't tax the municipal security interest, the state of Kansas won't tax the interest since both cities are in that state, but the city of Topeka could tax the bond interest since you didn't do them any favors. So, to receive interest checks exempt from federal, state, and local government taxation, a resident of Topeka, Kansas, could buy a municipal bond issued by Topeka, Kansas.

SITUATION	FEDERAL	STATE	LOCAL
Resident of Topeka, KS, buys a Toledo, Ohio, municipal bond	EXEMPT	TAXABLE	TAXABLE
Resident of Topeka, KS, buys a Wichita, KS, municipal bond	EXEMPT	EXEMPT	TAXABLE
Resident of Topeka, KS, buys a Topeka, KS, municipal bond	EXEMPT	EXEMPT	EXEMPT

> Municipal Yields vs. Taxable Yields

If there are two A-rated bonds, both with 10-year maturities, should the investor buy the municipal bond paying 5% or the corporate bond paying a 7% nominal yield? The answer depends on the investor's marginal tax bracket. To compare a taxable yield to a municipal yield, take the taxable bond yield and multiply it by the percentage the investor keeps after tax (100% minus tax bracket). If the investor is in the 30% bracket, he keeps 70% of the bond interest paid to him. If the corporate bond pays 10%, he keeps 70% of that, or 7% as his **after-tax yield**. Bond pays $100; Uncle Sam takes $30 and lets him keep 70% after-tax.

That's the investor's "after-tax yield" or "tax-free equivalent" yield, meaning that the 10% corporate (taxable) yield is equivalent to a hypothetical 7% municipal security yield for this investor.

If they give you the municipal security yield and want you to figure the **tax-equivalent yield**, divide by the same 100% minus the investor's tax bracket. To compare an 8% tax-free bond to a taxable bond, we would take 8% and divide it by 100% minus the investor's tax bracket. If she's in a 25% bracket, we divide .08 by .75. The corporate or Treasury bond would only be equivalent to this 8% municipal security yield if the taxable bond were yielding 10.67%. That's the municipal security's tax-equivalent yield, meaning it's equal to a taxable bond yielding 10.67%.

If the customer is thinking about a corporate bond that's similar in quality to this municipal security, the corporate bond must pay at least 10.67%; otherwise, we recommend the municipal security.

Municipal securities backed by the issuer's "full faith and credit" are called **general obligation bonds**. They require voter approval before getting issued, because they are backed by taxes that voters pay to the municipal government/taxing authority. The bonds that are just backed up by the revenues generated from the toll road or convention center being built with the proceeds…guess what we call them? **Revenue bonds**. The test might call the revenue used to pay bondholders **user fees** or **user charges**. Either way these are not backed by the full faith and credit of the issuer and sometimes there is no revenue to pay the bondholders back.

That's why revenue bonds usually yield more than general obligation bonds. Both, however, are municipal bonds that pay tax-exempt interest at the federal level. Notice how we said nothing about capital gains? If you sell a municipal bond for more than you bought it, first, congratulations, and, second, don't forget your pals and mine at the IRS. The interest income may be tax-exempt, but capital gains are still taxable as—get this—capital gains. That's why a municipal bond mutual fund usually pays dividends that are tax-exempt at the federal level but capital gains distributions that are taxable at capital gains rates.

Don't worry, we'll go over the taxation again before this book is over. **Industrial Development Revenue (IDR)** bonds fund facilities that are then leased long-term to a corporation. The interest and principal are only as dependable as the corporation leasing the facility from the municipality, so it's their credit rating that S&P/Moody's focus on. Then again, if the municipality is the City of Detroit, that may be a good thing. Also, these bonds might not get the favorable tax-exempt treatment most municipal bonds offer, just to keep things nice and simple.

➤ Mortgage-Backed Securities

If a company has, say, $100 million in accounts receivable owed by customers and would rather get most of that money right now in cash, maybe they'll sell those receivables for $85 million and let someone else worry about collecting the full $100 million, keeping the difference for their trouble and risk. Debt securities can be backed up by accounts receivable, inventory, student loans, credit card receivables, artist royalties, etc. And, they can be backed up by mortgages.

To create a **mortgage-backed security**, mortgages are pooled together, packaged, and sold to investors, who then receive interest and principal payments from that pool of mortgages. Interest comes in regularly, since every month mortgage holders pay their mortgage. Principal is returned gradually until, all a sudden, it's paid off in full. When interest rates drop, homeowners refinance and suddenly return the principal all at once. This is not great for the investor, who usually reinvests at a lower interest rate. The exam may call this risk **prepayment risk**.

If the investor buys a GNMA (**Government National Mortgage Association**) **pass-through certificate**, she buys a mortgage-backed security with mortgages all guaranteed by the United States Treasury. If she buys an **FNMA** or **FHLMC mortgage-backed security**, she must understand that the U.S. Treasury probably would—but does not have to—bail out those two quasi-agencies if necessary.

GNMAs would typically yield more than Treasuries, and are considered safe, income-producing securities. We used to say much the same about FNMA and FHLMC, but, well, things change.

➢ CMO

A CMO, or **collateralized mortgage obligation**, is a complicated debt security that gets its value from underlying mortgages or mortgage-backed securities. The key word for a CMO is "**tranche**." Investors purchase certain tranches, which receive interest regularly as mortgage payments are made from homeowners. Principal is returned to just one tranche at a time, so the earliest maturing tranches are up for receiving all their principal first. The exam could say that the early tranches have the most "prepayment risk." That's the risk that interest rates will drop and homeowners will refinance, returning the principal suddenly and without warning. Basic facts on CMOs include:

- PAC stands for "planned amortization class"
- PACs are protected from prepayment risk and extension risk
- TAC stands for "targeted amortization class"
- TACs present more extension risk (the risk that principal will be paid back too slowly)
- TACs generally yield more than PACs

➢ REMIC

The abbreviation "REMIC" stands for "Real Estate Mortgage Investment Conduit." A **REMIC** is another type of mortgage-backed pass-through vehicle. What separates it from a CMO is that REMICs offer mortgage pools separated into different risk classes, not just different maturity classes.

➢ Money Market Securities

The money market refers to debt securities maturing in one year or less. Safe, liquid instruments. If the investor has a short time horizon because she's about to buy a house in the next 6–9 months, we put her down payment in the money market. She'll get back what she put in, plus a little interest income along the way. Money market funds pay whatever short-term interest rates happen to be. Whatever the rates are on T-Bills and bank CDs, that's about what we get in the money market, since T-Bills and CDs are both **money market instruments**.

Municipal securities pay tax-exempt interest, so a tax-exempt money market fund would be buying short-term debt securities issued by municipalities. When cities and school districts borrow long-term, we call those things "bonds." When they borrow short-term, we call the instruments "anticipation notes." There are **TANs**, BANs, RANs, and TRANs (**tax anticipation notes**, bond anticipation notes, revenue anticipation notes, tax and revenue anticipation notes). If the city is about to collect taxes in a few months, why wait? Why not issue a Tax Anticipation Note and get the money right now?

When corporations borrow short-term, we call what they issue **commercial paper**. Commercial paper is probably the main ingredient of most money market mutual funds. It's just a short-term corporate IOU. Spot us $99 million today, and we'll give you back $100 million in 270 days.

The CDs that we buy at the bank are just longer-term deposits that pay a higher rate than a savings account. We can't sell a CD deposit to somebody else, and if we take the money out early, we will typically lose interest income as a penalty. Well, **negotiable CDs** or "Jumbos" are purchased in denominations from $250,000 to several million. These are negotiable, meaning we can sell them to somebody else. But, they're not fully insured by the FDIC. Why would we want a CD not fully insured by the FDIC—wouldn't that be riskier?

Exactly—which is why it would pay a higher yield.

> Brokered CDs

As opposed to just walking into a local bank and accepting the yields they're currently offering on their certificates of deposit, investors who purchase **brokered CDs** open their portfolio up to yields offered by banks across the country. A brokered CD account would also provide liquidity for the investor since he could ask the broker/registered representative to sell the CD on the secondary market as opposed to taking an early withdrawal penalty from a bank. Assuming the CDs are all FDIC insured (up to $250,000), investors can put a substantial amount of money into brokered CD accounts and receive FDIC insurance on each individual certificate of deposit in the portfolio. All without opening accounts at dozens of different banks to avoid exceeding the $250,000 FDIC coverage. Of course, there are fees. These products work like brokered mortgages, where the interest rate we receive is less favorable after the broker takes his cut.

Although most CDs are short-term, there are also long-term certificates of deposit with maturities provided perhaps 20 years. Although brokered CDs can be a great option for many investors, some investors have been shafted by brokers who put them into 20-year CDs which then led to large losses when the investors needed their cash. As one might imagine, these long-term CDs may have limited or even no liquidity and investors can lose money by selling these things on the secondary market. Also, the interest payments on long-term CDs are often complex and explained in fine print few investors understand. Broker-dealers and registered representatives selling these long-term CDs must be sure that investors understand how these products differ from traditional bank CDs and must disclose all potential risks. Higher yields on the one hand, but the secondary market for the products might not be as liquid as one would hope—suddenly, rather than sacrificing the interest on a bank CD, the individual could lose principal. I don't know about you, but "losing money" and "CDs" don't go together in my mind. The regulators tend to have similar difficulty squaring the two concepts.

Finally, a **banker's acceptance** (BA) facilitates foreign trade. Somebody imported $50 million worth of rice but didn't pay for it upfront, so their bank issued a letter of credit to the other side letting them know that the bank guarantees payment. Now, the loan becomes a security purchased at a discount, where the investor then receives the higher face amount, usually in no more than 270 days.

So, when issuers borrow long-term, we call that the "capital market." When they borrow for one year or less, we just call it what it is—the money market.

EQUITY SECURITIES

Pretend you own a car wash. You're convinced you could turn it into a regional chain of car washes if you only had $500,000 to use for expansion. Trouble is, you don't seem to have an extra half-million dollars lying around. However, you do have a friend with some extra money. You ask if you can borrow the $500,000, but your friend has a better idea. Rather than borrow money from him, why not let him buy into your company as an owner? This way you print up a stock certificate and sell this piece of paper to him for $500,000, which you will use to grow your business. He'll use the paper as evidence that he has equity or ownership in your company, and now if the company does well, so do you and so does he. If his equity stake represents 20% of your company's profits, as your profits grow, so does the value of his 20% ownership. Maybe someday you'll have such a large profit that you'll start cutting him a check every three months and call it a "dividend."

Or not. Investors who buy equity securities don't get interest payments, because they aren't lenders. They're just investors who like the company's chances of making a profit. The money invested in equities should only be an amount the investor could afford to lose, and even if things work out the time horizon needs to be a long one.

➤ Common Stock

We'll look at preferred stock in a few pages. Common stock, unlike preferred, is all about the perceived profitability of the company, with a potentially unlimited gain by the investor. As the profits of the issuing company grow, so does the value of the common stock. It's just that no one can ever know how much the issuer's profits will or won't grow, and how the stock price will react. Both the market value and the income associated with common stock are unpredictable.

> Advantages

Owners of common stock enjoy several important advantages. The first advantage is called **limited liability**, and it means exactly what you'd expect: your liability as an investor is limited to the amount you invest. In other words, the creditors of the corporation can't come after you if the company goes into bankruptcy, and you're also shielded from any lawsuits brought against the corporation. So, the bad news is that you can lose all the money you invest in the company's stock. The good news is you can lose only the money you invest in the company's stock.

Shareholders also have the right to transfer their shares to others, by selling them, giving them away, or leaving them to others through a will. A bank or other company keeps a list of all the shareholders and deals with all the transfers of ownership, and we call this entity the **transfer agent**, for obvious reasons. If somebody loses a certificate, or if the certificate is destroyed, the transfer agent can issue new certificates—for a fee, of course. Another entity, usually a bank, audits/oversees the transfer agent to make sure the numbers all add up right. We call this entity the **registrar**.

Shareholders have the right to inspect certain books and records of the company, such as the list of shareholders and the minutes of shareholder meetings. Under the Securities Exchange Act of 1934 public companies must file quarterly and annual reports with the SEC; therefore, shareholders can view these reports to see how their money is being used by the corporation. That's how I know that Starbucks made a profit of about $2 billion recently—I looked it up in their annual 10K report. Starbucks is a public company, which means they must disclose all information to the public that an investor might find relevant.

Public investors finance these public companies by purchasing stock with their hard-earned money, so the companies must disclose things to the public they'd probably rather keep private. There is no law that forces companies to go public. The deal is if an issuer wants to raise money from public investors, they must disclose all the good and bad news to the public from then on. If they don't think they can handle that level of scrutiny, they will keep the company and its affairs private.

Whether the securities are issued by a private or public company, owners of common stock have the right to vote for any major issue that could affect their status as a proportional owner of the corporation. Stock splits, mergers & acquisitions, board of director elections, the authorization of more shares, and changes in business objectives all require shareholder approval. Shareholders do not vote for dividends. Like parents setting their children's allowances, only the Board of Directors can declare a dividend and determine how much it will be.

> Dividends

Some stocks pay **dividends**, but only if the Board of Directors declares them. That's right, if a corporation's Board of Directors doesn't declare a dividend, the dividend doesn't get paid.

End of story. But, if it does declare a dividend, common stockholders have a "claim" on those dividends. Here's how it works. The day that the Board declares the dividend is known as the **declaration date**. The board wonders who should receive this dividend—how about investors who own the stock as of a certain date? We call that the **record date** because an investor must be the owner "of record" by that date if he wants to receive the dividend. The board decides when it will pay the dividend, too, and we call that the **payable date**.

Now, since an investor must be the owner of record on or before the record date to receive the dividend, there will come a day when it's too late for investors to buy the stock and get the dividend.

Why? Because stock transactions don't "settle" until the third business day following the trade date. Settlement means that payment has been made to the seller and stock has been transferred to the buyer officially on the books. So, if a stock is sold on a Tuesday, the trade doesn't settle until Friday, the third business day after the trade. This is known as **regular way settlement**, or "T + 3." The "T" stands for "Trade Date," so just count forward three business days to find the settlement date.

So, if an investor must be the owner of record on the record date, and it takes three business days for the trade to settle, wouldn't she need to buy the stock at least three business days prior to the record date?

This means that if she buys it just two business days before the record date, her trade won't settle in time. We call that day the **ex-date** or **ex-dividend date**, because starting on that day investors who buy the stock will not receive the dividend. On the ex-date, it's too late. Why? Because the trades won't settle in time, and the purchasers won't be the owners of record (with the transfer agent) on or before the record date.

The exchange where the security trades sets the ex-date, as a function of "regular way" or "T + 3" settlement. The ex-date is two business days before the record date.

So, remember DERP. Declaration, Ex-Date, Record Date, Payable Date. The board sets all them except the Ex-Date, which is set by FINRA. If the test question gives you the record date, go back two *business* days to find the ex-date. Don't count weekends or holidays, either. If the record date is Tuesday, go back Monday and then...*Friday* for the ex-dividend date.

In the real world, it looks like this:

```
Equity Office declares first quarter common dividend

Mar 16, 2005— Equity Office Properties Trust (EOP), a publicly
held office building owner and manager, has announced today that
its Board has declared a first quarter cash dividend in the amount
of $.50 per common share. The dividend will be paid on Friday 15
April 2005, to common shareholders of record at the close of
business on Thursday 31 March 2005.
```

So, March 16 is the Declaration Date. The Payable Date is April 15. The Record Date is Thursday, March 31. The article doesn't mention the Ex-Date (because that's not established by the company), but we can figure that it must be...right, Tuesday, March 29. If you bought the stock on Tuesday, your trade wouldn't settle until Friday, April 1, which means the seller's name would be on the list of shareholders at the close of business on Thursday, March 31. When stock is purchased on the ex-date, the seller is entitled to the dividend, not the buyer.

Companies can pay dividends in the form of cash, stock, shares of a subsidiary, and even the product they make.

> ➢ Rights and Warrants

Another right common stockholders enjoy is the right to maintain their proportionate ownership in the corporation, known as a **pre-emptive right**. The corporation can sell more shares to the public, but it must give the existing shareholders the right to buy their proportion of the new shares before others get to buy theirs. If they didn't do that, current shareholders would have their equity "diluted" or diminished. If you own 5% of a company now, it must give you the right to maintain your 5% ownership, so for every share owned, investors receive what's known as a **subscription right**. It works like a coupon that lets the current shareholders purchase the new stock below the market price over the course of a few weeks. If a stock is trading at $20, maybe the existing shareholders can take one right plus $18 to buy a new share. Those rights act as coupons that give the current shareholders two dollars off the market price. So, the investors can use the subscription rights, sell them, or let them expire in a drawer somewhere, like most coupons.

A **warrant** is a long-term security that allows the holder to purchase a company's stock at a predetermined price. If you hold a warrant that lets you buy XYZ for $30 per share, then you can buy a certain number of shares at that price whenever you feel it makes sense to do so, like when XYZ is trading for a lot more than $30. When issued, the price stated on the warrant is above the current market price of the stock. It usually takes a long time for a stock's price to go above the price stated on the warrant —if it ever makes it, that is. But, they're good for a long time, typically somewhere between 2 and 10 years.

Warrants are often included with a bond offering as an enticement to investors. Corporations pay interest to borrow money through bonds. If they attach warrants to the deal, they can offer investors a lower interest payment in exchange for the potential upside on the common stock. Sometimes warrants are referred to as "sweeteners" for this reason. If you watch *The Shark Tank*, perhaps you can picture an entrepreneur asking to borrow money from Mr. Wonderful and then asking for a lower interest rate in exchange for giving him the right to buy up to 49% of the company for a fixed $2 million over the next several years. That would be exactly how it works when companies include warrants with a bond offering. The word "attach" is metaphorical, by the way—there is no glue being applied to any certificates here. If the investor wants to hold the bond and sell the warrant, or vice versa, no problem.

> ADR

"**ADR**" stands for **American Depository Receipt**, and like many of the acronyms you'll need to know for the exam, this one means exactly what it says. It's a <u>receipt</u> issued to somebody in <u>America</u> against shares of foreign stock held on <u>deposit</u> in a bank. If you want to buy stock in Toyota, for example, you'll buy the Toyota ADR, which trades on the NYSE under the symbol "TM." This way, you don't have to buy a stock trading at 1,176.568 yen, and you don't have to wake up in the middle of the night to trade your stock while the exchange is open in Japan.

The exam might say that ADRs make it convenient for Americans to buy stock in foreign corporations such as Toyota, Nokia, etc. They are just shares of stock that might receive dividends, but they have a special risk the exam might talk about, called foreign currency or **currency exchange risk**. See, when Toyota declares a dividend, they declare it in the yen. That is then converted to dollars. Therefore, if, say 1,000 yen are being converted to American dollars for you, would you want the American dollar to be strong or weak versus the yen?

If the dollar were strong, those 1,000 yen wouldn't work out to many dollars. If the dollar were weak, those 1,000 yen would convert to *more* dollars, so the owner of an ADR would be better off with a weak dollar, in case the exam feels like playing hardball.

ADR holders have the ability to exchange their ADRs for the actual foreign share certificates, should the exam ask such a question. The voting rights on the stock is typically retained by the bank creating the ADR, but not always.

> Preferred Stock

Preferred stock is a little peculiar. It's a fixed-income security, but it's also an equity security. See, usually when you hear "fixed income," you think about debt securities, which we'll look at in a few pages. But, preferred stock, which also pays a fixed income, is an equity security.

So, wait, is preferred stock equity, or is it fixed-income?

Yes, it is. The exam might point out that "equity" securities are held by "owners," while most "fixed-income investments" are held by "creditors." Well, preferred stock is, as I said, a little different. It pays a fixed-income stream, but it's an equity position. See, there are two basic types of ownership in a company—common stock and preferred stock. Common stock might pay dividends or not, but its value can rise infinitely with the profits of the company. Preferred stock, on the other hand, simply pays a fixed-income stream and does not rise in market value if and when the company's profits increase.

As an owner of the company, the question is whether you're more interested in a stated rate of income paid out to you on a regular schedule or an unlimited potential gain. If you want the income stream to be predictable, buy the preferred stock. If you are patient over dividends or only care about capital appreciation, buy the common stock instead.

Why do we call it "preferred" stock, by the way? Because preferred stock owners get preferred treatment over common stock owners if the company must be liquidated to pay their creditors/lenders, and they always get their dividend before the company even thinks about paying common stockholders. Common stock simply gives the investor an ownership stake in the company—not a stated rate of return. If you buy 1,000 shares of MSFT, you don't get a piece of paper telling you you'll earn, say, 3% every year in dividends or interest. You just get a piece of paper showing that you own shares of a public corporation.

Preferred stock, unlike common stock, does pay a stated rate of return, which just means that the dividend is printed right on the stock certificate and on the trade confirmations and account statements you get from your broker-dealer. The stock is named according to its rate of return: 4% preferred stock, for example, or 5.5% preferred stock. The par value for a preferred stock can be any amount the issuer wants, but let's use $100 as the par value for preferred stock because it works well for a test question. The stated dividend to the investor is a percentage of that par value. Six percent preferred stock would pay 6% of $100, or $6 per share per year. What if the company's profits increased? Six percent preferred stock would still pay $6 per share per year.

We hope.

See, dividends still must be declared by the Board of Directors. Preferred stockholders aren't lenders. They're owners, who like to receive dependable dividends. But, if the board doesn't declare a dividend, do you know how much an owner of a 6% straight preferred stock would receive?

Nothing. However, if the investor owned cumulative preferred stock, he wouldn't necessarily get the dividend now, but the company has to make up the missed dividend in future years before it could pay dividends to any common stockholders. If the company missed the six dollars per share this year and wanted to pay the full six dollars per share next year, cumulative preferred stockholders must get their $12 before the company could pay a dividend to the owners of its common stock.

By the way, this 6% works more like a maximum than a minimum. If an investor wants the chance to earn more than the stated 6%, he'd have to buy participating preferred stock. Now, if the company raises the dividend for common stock, they raise the dividend on this participating preferred stock, too. A correct answer on participating preferred stock might be something like "a type of preferred stock whose dividend rate is fixed as to the minimum, but not as to the maximum."

Again, increased profits mean nothing to a preferred stockholder. That is the concern for the owner of common stock. Rather, the two main concerns for a preferred stock investor are interest rates and credit quality. If you receive a fixed income stream, the market will re-price your investment whenever interest rates in general move around. Your interest rate risk is that when interest rates rise, the market price of your fixed-income security will drop. If interest rates rise, the market price of preferred stock drops. The par value never changes, but the amount someone would pay for your preferred stock will drop if interest rates rise. On the other hand, when interest rates drop, the market price of your preferred stock will rise. That, however, is not a risk. That is known in the financial services industry as "a good thing." Credit quality means that the issuer must be able to make steady profits and manage those profits wisely if they're going to be able to pay the promised dividend. So, most preferred stockholders look for companies with financial strength before buying their preferred stock. It's not about growth of profits with preferred stock. It's about the company's ability to pay the promised dividend.

There is one exception. As I said, common stock represents the opportunity to make an unknown amount of money should the corporation become the next Microsoft, Coca-Cola, Apple Computer, etc. Preferred stock, on the other hand, is a fixed-income security, which means the income it pays is fixed. So, you might feel smart getting a likely 6% return every year on your 6% preferred stock, but what if the company pulls a Google on you? The common stock goes from $85 to $750 a share. What would that do for you, as a preferred stockholder?

Probably annoy the heck out of you, since you wouldn't enjoy any of that upside. If you want the chance to ride the upside on common stock, you buy a type of preferred stock known as convertible preferred stock. This type lets an investor exchange one share of preferred stock for a certain number of common shares whenever the investor wants to make the switch. If the convertible preferred stock is convertible into 10 shares of common stock, the convertible preferred stock is usually worth at least whatever 10 shares of common stock are worth. If so, they trade at parity, which means "equal." Just multiply the price of the common stock by the number of shares the investor could convert the preferred into. That gives you the preferred stock's parity price.

So, if the convertible preferred stock were convertible into 10 shares of common stock and the common stock went up to $15 a share, how much would the convertible preferred be worth at parity?

10 X $15 or $150.

That's known technically as a good thing. So, other types of preferred stock are income investments, while convertible preferred stock is growth-and-income. While other types of preferred stock are interest-rate sensitive, convertible preferred stock is not as dependent on interest rates, since its value has that other factor—the market price of the company's common stock.

Finally, while the par value of preferred stock and bonds is meaningful, to an investor the par value of common stock is meaningless. It's just an arbitrary value (1 penny, 1 dollar, no par value) that the lawyers assign in the articles of incorporation.

The market price of a company's preferred stock has nothing to do with the price of its common stock. Only the unusual convertible preferred stock has a market price tied in any way to the price of the issuer's common stock.

	COMMON	PREFERRED
Ownership stake	X	X
More likely to receive dividends		X
Priority in bankruptcy		X
Growth potential	X	
Voting rights	X	
Stated rate of return		X

> Yield, Total Return

Measuring the return on equity securities comes down to two concerns: growth and income. The exam might call growth **capital appreciation** and refer to the income as "dividends" because everything must have at least two or three names in this industry. But, whatever we call it, this stuff is simple. If you buy a stock at $10, and a year later it's worth $12, that's capital appreciation or "growth" of 20%. If the stock pays $2 in dividend income after you paid $10, that's a **yield** of 20%. Notice how capital appreciation refers to the stock price rising, while yield just refers to the income you receive compared to what you paid for the stock. So, what if you wanted to factor in the growth in share price plus the dividend? Now, you're talking about **total return**. So, this stock that went up by $2 and distributed $2 in dividends showed a total return of 40%. Put down $10, receive $2 in dividends and $2 in growth for a "total return" of $4. Compared to the $10, you got back a 40% total return, right?

Dividends are paid quarterly or four times a year. So, if the test question says it's a 25-cent quarterly dividend, you may need to annualize it (multiply by 4) to get a $1 annual dividend first.

Annual Dividend divided by the Market Price = YIELD

I would generally expect the exam to test this concept like this:

   If the dividend paid on XYZ common stock remains stable while the market price falls, current dividend yield will

A. Increase

B. Decrease

C. Remain stable

D. Be relatively unaffected

If you were getting $1 on an investment of $10, your yield is 10%. If you get a dollar for paying just $5, that's a much higher yield of 20%. So, the yield would increase as the market price drops, right? The answer is Choice A. As always, if the question says that price goes one way, tell it that yield goes the other way. This is known as an **inverse relationship**, like the relationship between your velocity and the time it takes to get where you're going. When one goes up, the other goes down, and vice versa.

INVESTMENT COMPANY PRODUCTS

Think of a mutual fund as a big investment portfolio that can serve up as many shares as investors care to buy. Investors send in money to buy shares of the big portfolio. The fund uses the money to buy securities. When an investor sends in, say, $10,000, the portfolio gets bigger, but it also gets cut up into more slices—however many she is buying with her $10,000. The shares of the fund don't change value when investors buy or sell them. Rather, the shares become more valuable when the securities in the portfolio pay income, go up in market value, or both. And, nobody is guaranteeing that shares of the mutual fund portfolio will become more valuable. Even though the portfolio is diversified and run by a professional investment adviser, it is not uncommon to see mutual funds lose value very quickly.

Now, couldn't an investor bypass the mutual fund and just buy stocks and bonds directly in whatever companies or governments he chooses? Sure, but most people refuse to change the oil in their car— why would they suddenly become do-it-yourselfers with six- and seven-figure retirement nest eggs? Takes a lot of work to decide which stocks or bonds to purchase. If you only have $400 to invest, you can't take a meaningful position in any company's stock, and even if you tried, you'd end up owning just one company's stock. Virtually no investor would put all his money in just one two stocks but would, rather diversify. The diversification of a mutual fund is considerably greater than what an individual investor could achieve investing directly in stocks and bonds. Also, the portfolio is run by professionals who know when it's time to rebalance the portfolio as sure as the crew at JiffyLube knows when it's time to rotate the tires and replace the filters.

There are many advantages to mutual fund investing versus picking stocks and bonds individually:

- Investment decisions made by a professional portfolio manager
- Ease of diversification
- Ability to liquidate a portion of the investment without losing diversification
- Simplified tax information (Form 1099-DIVs make tax prep easier)
- Simplified record keeping (rather than getting 50 annual reports from 50 companies, you get two reports per year from one mutual fund)
- Ease of purchase and redemption of securities
- Automatic reinvestments of capital gains and income distributions at NAV
- Safekeeping of portfolio securities

The first point is probably the main reason people buy mutual funds—no way are they willing to try this stuff at home. They have no knowledge of stocks, bonds, taxation, etc., and they have even less interest in learning. Let a professional portfolio manager—often an entire *team* of portfolio managers—decide what to buy and when to buy and sell it. As we mentioned, it's tough to have your own diversified portfolio in individual stocks and bonds because a few hundred or thousand dollars will only buy a few shares of stock or a few bonds issued by just a few companies. Any one company could go bust, and most investors don't have the emotional capacity to withstand a $10,000 investment that drops to zero when the company declares bankruptcy.

On the other hand, a mutual fund would usually hold stock in, say, 300 or more companies, and their bond portfolios are also diversified. Therefore, even with the smallest amount of money accepted by the fund, the investor is immediately diversified. The exam calls this the "undivided interest concept." That means $50 owns a piece of all the ingredients in the portfolio, just as a large investor's $1 million does. Yes, the small investor owns a much smaller piece, but he is also just as diversified as the large investor is. They both own their percentage of everything inside the portfolio. They both have an undivided interest in all securities owned by the fund.

Notice that another bullet point said, "Ability to liquidate a portion of the investment without losing diversification." See, if you own 100 shares of IBM, MSFT, and GE, what are you going to do when you need $5,000 to cover an emergency? If you sell a few shares of each, you'll pay three separate commissions. If you sell 100 shares of any one stock, your diversification is seriously reduced. With a mutual fund, you redeem a certain number of shares and remain just as diversified as you were before the sale. And, you can usually redeem/sell your shares without getting hit up for any fees.

What exactly do we mean by "diversification"? As the FINRA exam outline indicates, mutual funds can diversify their holdings by:

- Industries
- Types of investment instruments
- Variety of securities issuers
- Geographic areas

If it's a stock fund, it is basically a growth fund, a value fund, an income fund, or some combination thereof. No matter what the objective, the fund will usually purchase stocks from issuers across many different industries. In a mutual fund prospectus you'll often find a pie chart that shows what percentage of assets is tied up in a specific industry. Maybe it's 3% in telecommunications, 10% retail, 1.7% healthcare, etc. That way if it's a lousy year for telecommunications or retail, the fund won't get crushed the way a small investor who owns securities in just one telecommunications company and one or two retailers.

A bond fund can be diversified among investment instruments. That means they buy some debentures, some secured bonds, some convertible bonds, some zero coupons, some mortgage-backed securities, and even a few money market instruments to be on the safe side. Even if the fund did not spread their investments across many different industries (telecomm, pharmaceutical, retail, etc.) and chose instead to focus on just a few industries, they would still purchase securities from a variety of issuers. So, if they like retail, they can still buy stock in a variety of companies—Walmart, Target, Sears, Nordstrom, Home Depot, etc. And, since any geographic area could be hit by an economic slump, a tsunami, or both, most funds will spread their holdings among different geographic areas. I mean, the Pacific Rim countries sure look promising, but I don't want all my holdings in companies from Japan, Taiwan, and Singapore.

Let's go to the most important document on mutual funds, the Investment Company Act of 1940, which defines a **diversified company** like so:

> "Diversified company" means a management company which meets the following requirements: At least 75 per centum of the value of its total assets is represented by cash and cash items (including receivables), Government securities, securities of other investment companies, and other securities for the purposes of this calculation limited in respect of any one issuer to an amount not greater in value than 5 per centum of the value of the total assets of such management company and to not more than 10 per centum of the outstanding voting securities of such issuer.

So, how does the "Act of 1940" then define a "**non-diversified company**"?

> "Non-diversified company" means any management company other than a diversified company.

Hmm. That just means that if the fund wants to promote itself as being "diversified," it must meet the definition—on 75% of the portfolio, no more than 5% of its assets are in any one company, and they don't own more than 10% of any company's outstanding shares. What happens if the mutual fund allocates exactly 5% of its assets to XYZ common stock, and then XYZ rises so much that the investment now represents more than 5% of assets? Does the fund must sell off some shares? No. They just don't buy any more XYZ at this point. If the fund doesn't feel like meeting the definition under the 75-5-10 test it will simply must refer to itself as a "non-diversified fund." Also, if the Board of Directors wanted to change the fund from being diversified to non-diversified, or vice versa, that would require a shareholder vote.

I like to own a percentage of various companies of my own choosing. I'm also willing to do a little homework on the companies I invest in. Unfortunately, I end up getting proxy (voting) materials and annual reports from, perhaps, 20 different companies. And, keeping track of all the dividends I've received from the various sources is annoying. With a mutual fund, I'd get one 1099-DIV that would keep track of all the dividends and capital gains distributions, and I'd also get just one semi-annual report and one annual report from the fund.

But, I'd have to give up maybe 1.5% a year in operating expenses, and over 20–40 years that adds up to a lot more than the meager commissions I pay to purchase and occasionally sell shares of stock. Just something to think about, something that might help you understand mutual funds, and their differences from individual stocks, a little better. It's not a slam against mutual funds. For most retail investors, mutual funds are going to provide the best investment vehicle. And for many retirement plans mutual funds are the only investment vehicle available.

➢ Types of Mutual Funds

>   Equity Funds

The primary focus of **equity funds** is to invest in equity securities. But, not all approaches to equity investing are the same. **Growth funds** invest in companies that appear likely to grow their profits faster than competitors and/or the overall stock market. These stocks usually cost a lot compared to the profits that they might or might not have at this point. In other words, the market price compared to the earnings is high.

A share of stock is a slice of the company's profits, also called earnings. The question is, how many times the earnings per share are investors willing to pay for the stock? If the investor is willing to pay high price-to-earnings ratios," he is a growth investor. Dividend income, if any, would be secondary to the goal of finding growth opportunities. In other words, if your investor is seeking income, she doesn't want growth funds.

What if the investor prefers to buy stocks trading at low price-to-earnings ratios? He is looking for value, so the industry calls him a value investor. **Value funds** seek companies trading for less than the portfolio management team determines they are worth. Volkswagen is struggling even more than most auto manufacturers as I write this. But, if a value fund thinks the stock is worth more than the market realizes, they'll snap it up now at a low price-to-earnings multiple and wait for the turnaround.

The exam might say that value funds buy stocks in established companies that are currently out of favor. Since the share price is depressed while the dividend keeps getting paid, value stocks tend to have high dividend yields. Therefore, they are considered more conservative than growth stocks.

What if the investor just can't make up his mind between a growth fund and a value fund? Luckily, there are funds that blend both styles of investing, and the industry calls these **blend funds**. They would be a little more aggressive than "value funds" and a little less volatile than "growth funds." The test might also bring up "core" or "blend/core" funds. If the question uses the phrase "middle of the road approach," it is talking about a blend/core fund. These funds are not purely growth or purely value. They may also blend blue-chip stock with more speculative small cap investments. The idea is to allow investors to get a diversified investment that can also maximize their growth potential.

If your investor's objective is to receive income from equities, you might recommend an **equity income fund**. These funds buy equity securities that provide dependable income. While a growth fund would not look for dividend income, dividend income is the main reason that an equity income fund would purchase a specific stock. We would probably see oil companies, utility companies, and drug companies in the typical equity income fund portfolio. Receiving dividends tends to reduce the volatility of an investment, so equity income funds are lower risk than equity growth funds. Also, companies that pay dividends are paying them out of actual profits, which means the stock is not completely speculative; it has a value that can be determined.

What if we can't decide between a mutual fund family's growth funds and its income funds? Chances are they'll be happy to sell us a **growth and income fund**. A growth and income fund buys stocks in companies expected to grow their profits and in companies that pay dependable, respectable dividends. Or, maybe the same company offers both a steady dividend and the prospect of future growth. Either way, since they've added the income component, growth & income funds would have lower volatility than growth funds. So, from highest to lowest volatility, we would find growth, then growth & income, and then equity income funds. I have a catalog from one of the largest mutual fund families in the world which puts them in exactly that order, and even uses the color red for the highest volatility—growth—as in, "Warning! This stuff can burn!"

Both **international** and **global funds** appeal to investors who want to participate in markets not confined to the U.S. The difference between the two is that an international fund invests in companies located anywhere but the U.S. A global fund would invest in companies located and doing business anywhere in the world, including the U.S. When we move away from the U.S., we take on more political/social risk as well as currency exchange risk.

> Bond Funds

Stock is not for everyone. Even if an investor wants to own some equity funds, chances are you'll still put a percentage of her account in bond funds. A rule-of-thumb is that whatever her age is, that's the percentage the investor should put into fixed-income.

Which type of fixed-income (bond) funds should the investor purchase? If the investor is not in a high tax bracket or is investing in an IRA, 401(k), etc., we'll recommend taxable **bond funds**. The investor's time horizon will determine whether she should purchase short-term, intermediate-term, or long-term bond funds. Her risk tolerance will tell us if she needs the absolute safety of U.S. **Treasury funds** or is willing and able to take on the extra risk involved with high-yield **corporate bond funds**. If the investor is in a taxable account and wants to earn interest exempt from federal income tax, we might put her into a **tax-exempt bond fund**, which purchases municipal bonds. If the investor is in a high-tax state such as Maryland, Virginia, or California, we can sell her the "Tax-Exempt Fund of Maryland," Virginia, or California. Now, the dividends she receives will generally be exempt from both federal and state income taxes.

But, we're not done just because we put her into a tax-exempt bond fund. How much of a yield does she want and how hard is she willing to chase it? If she's willing to roll the dice, we can put her into a high-yield **tax-exempt fund** and pray that not too many of the cities or water and sewer districts default. If she's more conservative, we buy funds that focus on issuers with higher credit ratings from S&P, Moody's, and Fitch.

> Money Market Mutual Funds

We've seen that an investor's need for liquidity tells us how much to park in **money market mutual funds**. There are both taxable and tax-exempt money market mutual funds. The **tax-exempt money market funds** buy short-term obligations of states, counties, cities, school districts, etc. They pay low rates of interest, but since it's tax-free, rich folks still come out ahead. But, you would only sell a "tax-exempt" fund to an investor in one of the top marginal tax brackets.

The whole point of the money market mutual fund is its **stable value.** The money investors put here can be turned right back into the same amount of money without worrying, unlike the money in a bond fund or, especially, a stock fund. Investors earn low returns but can often write checks against these accounts, which are treated like a sale of so-many shares times $1 each.

When an investor says that he is currently "25% in cash," he probably means that 1/4th of his account is currently in a **money market mutual fund.** Another use for these funds is as a vehicle in which to sweep a brokerage customer's cash after a deposit, dividend, interest payment, or sale occurs. Money market mutual funds are a holding place for cash that is not ready to be either invested long-term or spent by the customer.

As the SEC explains, "Money market funds pay dividends that reflect prevailing short-term interest rates, are redeemable on demand, and, unlike other investment companies, seek to maintain a stable NAV, typically $1.00. This combination of principal stability, liquidity and payment of short-term yields has made money market funds popular cash management vehicles for both retail and institutional investors."

Some of these funds keep at least 99.5% of their portfolio in Treasury securities and are called government money market funds. The funds that hold municipal securities are tax-exempt money market funds. Those holding corporate debt securities are known as prime money market funds. These three types can be for retail or institutional investors.

Because of the financial crisis of 2008 the SEC wants to prevent future runs on money market funds during extraordinary situations. The problem is that if funds artificially maintain an NAV of $1 when their portfolio may suddenly not be worth that amount, there is a first-mover advantage for investors to hurry up and pull out. To prevent this the SEC now requires institutional prime and tax-exempt money market mutual funds to value their NAV at the actual market value of the securities--called floating the NAV. This way, there is a natural disincentive to run for the exits and end up receiving only, say 97 cents on the dollar.

Also, except for government money market funds, both retail and institutional prime and tax-exempt funds can now impose both liquidity fees of up to 2% to discourage redemptions and even a temporary halt to redemptions if the situation is dire. If the board of directors for the fund decides the **redemption gate** is in the best interest of the shareholders, they can impose it for up to 10 business days. No more than one 10-day gate or halt could be imposed, however, in any 90-day period.

As with all funds, investors agree to pay operating expenses in exchange for the benefits provided by the investment product. Money market funds do not charge sales charges per se, but typically impose a 12b-1 fee of .25% as well as management fees and transfer agent fees, etc.

So, while money market mutual funds are still a safe and liquid investment, their liquidity is not as automatic and across the board as it once was, especially outside of government money market funds.

> Specialized Funds

Specialty/specialized funds focus their approach to investing. Some funds specialize in an industry, some in geographic regions, some in writing covered calls, etc. Investors can buy the Latin America, the Europe, or the Pacific Rim fund. They would then hope that those regions don't go into a major economic slump or suffer a natural disaster. See, when the fund concentrates heavily in an industry or geographic region, it generally takes on more volatility.

Most equity funds hold stocks in many different industries. On the other hand, there are **sector funds** that do exactly as their name implies—focus on industry sectors. If we buy a "growth fund," so far we have no idea which industries the so-called "growth companies" compete in. On the other hand, if we buy the Communications Fund, the Financial Services Fund, or the Healthcare Fund, we know which industry space the companies operate in. Concentrating in just one sector is the definition of aggressive investing. Investment results are unpredictable year by year. So, make sure the investor has a long anticipated holding period and high risk tolerance before recommending sector funds in a test question.

There are **asset allocation** funds for conservative investors. Rather than maintaining one's own mix of, say, 20% large cap value, 20% small cap growth, 40% high-yield bond, and 20% short-term Treasuries and constantly having to rebalance, investors can invest in an asset allocation fund that matches their goals. A similar type of fund is called a **balanced fund.** Here, the portfolio is always balanced between stocks and bonds and generally diversified among various types of each. There is not a set percentage for us to know here. Rather, the fund's prospectus would explain the parameters established by the board of directors.

A popular way to invest these days is through **age-based portfolios** or **lifecycle funds.** These funds shift the allocation from mostly-equity to mostly-fixed-income gradually as the investor gets closer and closer to his goal of retirement. Another name for these investments is **target funds.** If she plans to retire in or around 2050, for example, the individual would invest in the Target 2050 fund offered by a mutual fund family. The investments would be diversified, and that mix would become more conservative as we get closer and closer to the year 2050.

529 Savings Plans typically offer an age-based portfolio that is much more aggressive for kids 1-6 years old than those who are now 18 and in need of the funds. For example, the allocation for the youngsters might be 90% equity/10% fixed-income, while those 18 years old would be in a portfolio closer to 70% fixed-income/20% money market/10% equity.

Both international and **global funds** appeal to investors who want to participate in markets not

confined to the U.S. The difference between the two is that an **international fund** invests in companies located anywhere but the U.S., while a global fund would invest in companies located and doing business anywhere in the world, including the U.S. When investors move away from the U.S., they take on more political risk as well as currency exchange risk. For developed markets like Japan and Singapore, the political risk would be lower than in emerging markets such as Brazil and China. Both types of markets, however, would present currency exchange risk to U.S. investors.

Precious metals funds allow investors to speculate on the price of gold, silver, and copper, etc. by purchasing a portfolio usually of mining companies who extract these metals. Since a mine's costs are fixed, it only makes sense to open them for production when the price of what you're mining goes high enough to make it worth your while. Therefore, these funds typically hold stock in mining companies as opposed to holding precious metals themselves.

What if the investor does not believe that portfolio managers are likely to beat an index such as the S&P 500 with their active management over the long-term? He can buy an **index fund** that tracks an index as opposed to a fund trying to trade individual stocks. An index is an artificially grouped basket of stocks. Why are there 30 stocks in the Dow Jones Industrial Average, and why are the 30 stocks that are in there in there?

Because the company who put the index together says so. Same for the S&P 500. S&P decided that these 500 stocks make up an index, so there you have it. Investors buy index funds because there are no sales charges and low expenses. Since there's virtually no trading going on, the **management fees** should be—and typically are— low. So, for a no-brainer, low-cost option, investors can put their money into an index and expect to do about as well as that index.

Well-known indexes include the Dow Jones Industrial Average. The "Dow" is price-weighted, which means the stock price itself determines how much weighting the stock receives within the index. If a stock trades at $100, for example, its weighting is much higher than a stock trading at $11 per-share. The S&P 500, like most indexes, is market-cap-weighted. The share price of MSFT doesn't matter, but the fact that all their outstanding shares are worth, say, $200 billion means MSFT could be weighted 20 times more heavily than other stocks within the index. Because the S&P 500 contains such a large percentage of the major stocks trading on the secondary market, its movement is considered to represent the movement of the overall stock market. We mentioned this when looking at beta, which measures how much one stock moves compared to the overall market, as measured by the S&P 500.

Note that neither the Dow nor the S&P 500 cares whether the stock trades on the NYSE or NASDAQ. It's the size of the company and the market cap that matter here. And, all 30 stocks within the Dow Jones Industrial Average would also be included with the 500 stocks in the S&P 500.

The most famous "Dow" is the **Dow Jones Industrial Average** (DJIA). But, there is also the Dow Jones Transportation Average and the Dow Jones Utility Average. Together, these three make up the Dow Composite, which provides what the publishers of the indices call a "blue-chip microcosm of the U.S. stock market."

As much as I hate to confuse you, the company that owns Standard & Poor's now owns the Dow Jones indices, too, so if you "google" it, you will find that the Dow Jones averages are now part of the "S&P Dow Jones Indices."

Another well-known market-cap-weighted index is the **NASDAQ 100.** This index represents the 100 largest non-financial company stocks, all trading on NASDAQ. Stocks such as Facebook, Google, Microsoft, and Amazon are found here.

A well-known small cap index is the **Russell 2,000.** There are also bond indices for bond investors who want to pay low management fees and engage in passive investing.

Open-end index funds are for long-term investors. If an investor wants to do as well as one of the indices above, this is where he goes. But, because it is an open-end fund, the shares must be redeemed, with everyone who redeems that day receiving the same NAV next calculated by the fund. In a few pages we'll see that Exchange-Traded Funds (ETFs) are another low-cost way to match the performance of an index, only these shares are traded throughout the day just as shares of MSFT or IBM are traded throughout the day. For a small investment of money, the open-end index funds are more cost-effective because the ETFs charge commissions. An investment of $100 into an ETF would be a bad move, even if the commission were just $9. That is like a self-imposed 9% front-end load!

But, for investments of several thousands of dollars, the ETF is at least as cost-effective as its open-end cousin.

The other night I helped a friend review the investments in her 401(k) plan, and I was able to quickly point out that her "35 and up" fund was a fund made up of several other funds, all from the same company, with the allocation based on her anticipated retirement date. Since this fund was comprised of other funds, your industry went ahead and named the product a **fund of funds.** Funds of funds are usually associated with higher fees as opposed to picking just one or two of the funds within the group.

➢ Comparisons of Mutual Funds

Once we decide which types of funds an investor should purchase, how do we go about comparing one fund to another? The mutual fund prospectus would be a darned good place to go. In this document, we find the fund's investment objectives and style. Do they focus on companies with outstanding stock valued at $5 billion and above? $1 billion and below? Do they use fundamental analysis, poring over income statements and balance sheets, possibly meeting with senior management of the companies whose stock they hold? Or, do they rely more on technical analysis—charts, patterns, trends, etc.? Is this a small cap, mid-cap, or large cap fund, and how is the fund defining "small, mid-, and large cap," anyway?

There are also investment policies disclosed in the prospectus and the statement of additional information. Maybe the fund is telling you that it may invest up to 10% of its assets in securities of issuers outside the United States and Canada and not included in the S&P 500. Or, that they allow themselves to invest 10% of their assets in lower-quality debt securities rated below BB/Ba by S&P and Moody's, or even in debt securities no one has ever rated. If that stuff all sounds too risky for the investor, well, that's why we're disclosing it here in the prospectus.

The prospectus provides information on the party managing the portfolio. We call that party the investment adviser or the portfolio manager. Often, it's a team approach, so we can see the names of the individual portfolio counselors and how much experience they have doing this sort of thing. The prospectus I happen to be looking at now has a team of eight advisers, and their experience in the industry ranges from 18 to 40 years.

One of the most misunderstood aspects of mutual fund investing involves **fees and expenses**. You'll often hear people say, "No, there are no expenses on any of my mutual funds—they're all no-load." As we'll see in more detail later, whether the fund is "no load" or not, all funds charge operating expenses. You might not get a bill for your share of the expenses, but the fund takes out enough money from the portfolio to cover their expenses, whether this happens to be a "no load" fund or one that charges either front- or back-end sales charges. **Sales charges** are one thing; **expenses** are another. Not all funds have sales charges, but all funds have expenses. Even the lowest of the low-cost ETFs charge management fees and other operating expenses.

In the prospectus, the investor can see how much of her check is going toward the sales charge, and how much of the dollars she then invests will be eaten up by ongoing operating expenses. The section that details the fees and expenses of the fund has been entitled "Fees and expenses of the fund" in the prospectus sitting on my desk. If two growth funds have similar 10-year track records but one has expenses of 1.5% while the other charges just .90%, this could be the tiebreaker the investor is looking for. **Expense ratios**, in other words, are important factors when determining your investment into a fund. An index fund would have low management fees (or should), since there is no active trading going on. A fund with a high turnover rate is actively trading the portfolio and would, therefore, typically charge higher management fees. Basically, if a fund is charging high operating expenses, there must be a good explanation for those charges; otherwise, look for another fund. If the fund has a stellar track record of actively trading its portfolio and/or provides all kinds of services then maybe it's worth it to investors. If not, keep looking.

So, what are these sales charges all about? Well, if you and your friends wanted to launch a new mutual fund, how would you go about doing that? Forget the nightmare of SEC registration, I mean just from a business standpoint—how would you go about launching this mutual fund? You would need investors, right? Okay, how do you find investors? You have to advertise the fund and give people a number to call or a website to visit for more information. You'd have to print colorful prospectuses and mail them out whenever somebody requests one. And, most of these customers are going through a sales representative, and sales representatives like you do not generally work for free. So, those distribution costs are going to have to be covered somehow.

One way to cover them is with a sales charge. If the net asset value (NAV) of our aggressive growth fund is $9.50, we might charge people $10.00 for a stock worth $9.50 and call the difference of 50 cents a sales charge. What's more, we will get away with it. Yes, mutual fund investing is somewhat unique in this way. It's a little bit like going into a high-end retail store and hearing the sales clerk say, "That will be $274 for the sandals, plus $12.50 to cover the cost of the ad we had to put out to bring you into the store."

What? They're charging the customer an additional fee to cover the expense of bringing the customer into the mutual fund? Absolutely. If the mutual fund is sponsored/underwritten/distributed by an outside member firm, there could be a sales charge on purchases or redemptions of the fund. This sales charge covers the **distribution expenses** of printing, selling, mailing, and advertising the fund, and leaves a profit for the underwriter/sponsor/distributor of the fund. How much of a sales charge will the investor pay?

Depends on the fund. 5.5% is not uncommon for small investments. The maximum allowed sales charge is 8.5%, but anything over 5.75% is generally considered rude. So, if a mutual fund charges a maximum sales charge of 5.5%, that means that when the investor cuts her check, 5.5% of it goes to the distributors. Only the other 94.5% goes into the mutual fund for investment purposes.

Please keep two categories entirely separate in your mind: shareholder fees vs. expenses, as explained in the following table. Both sales charges and redemption fees can be avoided or reduced, as we'll see. And, many funds do not have sales charges or redemption fees. But all funds have expenses.

SHAREHOLDER FEES	EXPENSES
Sales charge (one-time charge, added to purchase price of mutual fund share)	Deducted from fund's assets on ongoing basis; examples include:

SHAREHOLDER FEES	EXPENSES
Added to investor's check when he buys	Management fee
Redemption fee (designed to discourage investors from redeeming shares soon after they buy them)	12b-1 fee
Subtracted from investor's proceeds when he sells	Custodial fee
	Transfer agent fee
	Consulting and legal work
	Board of director salaries

So, that stuff has to do with how much the fund costs to buy and hold. How well does the fund perform for investors? The prospectus will show you total return, usually as a bar chart and a table of numbers. Since I'm looking at a growth fund prospectus, the red bars are often long and pointing in both upward and downward directions. Over the past 10 years, the fund has gone up as high as 45% and down as much as 22% over a calendar year. As we said, investing in growth stocks requires a high risk tolerance, a long time horizon, and a healthy supply of antacid. There was a 3-year period here where the fund averaged returns of negative 9%. Sure hope you didn't need any of this money during that little blip.

What is "total return"? The point of buying a mutual fund share is that it might go up. We call that "capital appreciation." The mutual fund usually pays dividends from all those stocks and bonds in the portfolio. And, at the end of the year, if they took more profits than losses while trading their stocks and bonds, they distribute a capital gains check to shareholders.

Total return takes all three of those things and compares it to where the fund started. If the fund started out with a **net asset value** or **NAV** of $10 and finished the year at $11 per share, that's $1 of "capital appreciation." If the fund also paid a dividend of 50 cents per share and a $1 capital gains distribution, we would add that $1.50 to the capital appreciation of $1 for a total of $2.50 of good stuff. Comparing that $2.50 to where we started—$10—gives us a total return of 25%. How likely is it that a fund could have a total return of 25%?

The prospectus I happen to be looking at did 26%, 31%, and 45% during 1997, 1998, and 1999. So, naturally, it had a similar return the next three years, right? No, after that, it was anybody's guess: 7% in 2000, negative 12% in 2001, *negative* 22% in 2002. Which means the following year was probably even worse, right? No. In 2003 the fund had a total return of nearly 33% in a positive direction. Now we see why the prospectus says that "past results are not predictive of future results." Yeah. I guess not.

As you can see from the completely unpredictable returns on a growth fund, mutual funds, especially equity funds, are not short-term investments. Investors need a long time horizon, as this prospectus indicates on the first page. Nobody knows what will happen this year or next. We can show you the returns over 1, 5, and 10 years and let you be the judge. If we've only been in existence four years, we'll show you the figures for one year and "life of fund" or "since inception." But no one can tell you which funds will go up this year, let alone which funds will go up the most. If they could do that, why wouldn't they just buy the funds that will go up the most each year and quit their day job?

Taxation always plays a part on an investor's returns, so the prospectus also shows results after taxes have been figured in. Of course, this is a little tricky, as we see from the caveat in the prospectus on my desk:

> Your actual after-tax returns depend on your individual tax situation and likely will differ from the results shown below. In addition, after-tax returns may not be relevant if you hold your fund shares through a tax-deferred arrangement, such as a 401(k) plan, IRA, or 529 Savings Plan.

> ## A-, B-, and C-Shares

A mutual fund that adds sales charges can get the sales charge from investors either when they buy or when they sell. **A-shares** charge a front-end load when the investor acquires them. *A = acquire.* **B-shares** charge a back-end load when the investor sells them. *B = back end.* For a B-share, the investor pays the NAV when she buys the shares, but she will leave a percentage behind when she sells. The percentage usually starts to decline in the second year, and after several years (6 to 8), the back-end load goes away completely—effectively, the B-shares are converted to A-shares at that point, to keep things nice and simple. B-shares are associated with **contingent deferred sales charges**. Break down those words. The sales charge is deferred until the investor sells, and the amount of the load is contingent upon when the investor sells. For a test question on the proceeds of a B-share redemption, take the NAV and deduct the appropriate percentage from the investor's proceeds. If the NAV is $10, the investor receives the $10, minus the percentage the fund keeps on the back end. So, if she sells 100 shares and there is a 2% back-end sales charge, she gets $1,000 minus $20, or $980 out the door.

So, since the back-end or deferred sales charge eventually goes away, provided the investor isn't going to sell her shares for, say, seven years, she should purchase B-shares, right? Wouldn't it be great if things were *ever* that simple? See, we've been acting as if distribution expenses are covered only by sales charges, either on the front-end (A-shares) or back-end (B-shares). Turns out, distribution expenses are covered only by the sales charge, unless the fund has a **12b-1 fee**.

What?

Yes, a "12b-1" fee also covers distribution costs. 12b-1 fees, like sales charges, go to salespersons. No doubt you've heard about so-called "**no-load funds**." Well, you may not have gotten the whole story. A no-load fund can still charge a 12b-1 fee, provided it doesn't exceed .25% of the fund's assets. Every quarter, when they take money out to cover expenses, these "no-load funds" can also take an amount not to exceed 25 basis points. Money market mutual funds are "no load," but that also means they can charge 12b-1 fees up to .25%.

So, again, should the investor buy the A-share or the B-share? The choice involves this 12b-1 fee. The A-shares for our aggressive growth fund might be as high as 5.5%, but the 12b-1 fee will often be

.25% going forward, while the B-shares will pay an ongoing 12b-1 fee of, say, 1.00%. That complicates things, doesn't it? While the person who bought the B-shares is waiting for that contingent deferred sales charge schedule to hit zero, he's paying an extra .75% every year in expenses. .75% times seven years is an extra 5.25%. But still, the A-shares start out with a maximum of 5.5% upfront sales charge, so the B-shares are still better. Right?

This 12b-1 fee is a percentage. As the investor's account assets are growing over time, that .75% is also taking more money from him, even if it's a flat percentage.

And, as we'll soon see, 5.5% would probably be the maximum sales charge on the A-shares. If the investor puts in more money, she can maybe knock down the sales charge to 3% or even 2%, which is why long-term investors with a decent amount of money should almost always buy the A-shares.

Just to make the decision harder, there are also **C-shares**, which usually don't charge an upfront load but do carry a high 12b-1 fee. The level 12b-1 fee is where we got the "level load" nickname, by the way. Some C-shares also charge a contingent deferred sales charge if the investor sells in less than 1 year or 1½ years.

So, which type of share should an investor buy? Although I think this concept is a little too subjective, I'd recommend the following answers.

- Long-term investor with $50,000+ to invest – A-shares
- Intermediate or Long-term investor with small amount to invest – B-shares
- Short-term investor with < $500,000 to invest – C-shares

The difference in expenses between A-shares on one hand, and B- and C-shares on the other involves the 12b-1 fee. The fund also charges a management fee to cover the cost of the portfolio manager. That would be the same for every share class and must be a separate line item. A mutual fund can't bury their management fees under the 12b-1 fees or sales charges. Sales charges and 12b-1 fees cover distribution costs. The management fee covers portfolio management—the fund must keep the two separate.

The next item in the expenses table of the prospectus is "other expenses." When we add the management fee, the 12b-1 fee and the "other expenses" fee, we have the expense ratio for the fund. For the A-shares, maybe the expense ratio is .70%. But, the expense ratio for the B- and C-shares could be 1.45%, due to that extra .75% 12b-1 fee. Please don't assume that the difference would always be .75%, though. I'm just using that as a typical, credible number.

If the investor purchases a B-share, she pays the NAV or net asset value. Only when she sells would the fund take a sales charge from her. If the investor purchases the A-shares, she pays more than the NAV. That extra that she pays is the sales charge, as we said. When we add the sales charge to the NAV, we arrive at the public offering price (POP).

POP - NAV = Sales Charge

If the POP is $10 and the NAV is $9.45, the sales charge is the difference of $.55 (55 cents). If you're asked to calculate the sales charge as a percentage, use this formula:

If we took $10 minus $9.45, we'd get a sales charge of 55 cents. Divide that 55 cents by the POP of $10, and you see that the sales charge percentage is 5.5%. The sales charge is expressed as a percentage of the POP, not the NAV.

How and when is this net asset value (NAV) figured? Mutual funds use **forward pricing**. That means that if you take my check for $10,000 at 11 a.m., you won't know how many shares I'll end up buying yet. The fund will re-figure the NAV when trading closes that day, and then put my $10,000 into the fund at the NAV they come up with then.

Same thing for a seller. A seller "redeems" her shares to the fund. When she turns in a redemption order at 1 p.m. she won't know the exact dollar amount of her check because the NAV won't be determined until after the markets close at 4 p.m. Eastern. The "net asset value" or NAV is nothing more than the value of one slice of the portfolio. The assets of the portfolio would be the value of the securities plus any cash they've generated minus any liabilities.

Where did the liabilities come from? The fund might borrow money from time to time to handle redemptions. If the fund has $10,000,000 in assets and $550,000 in liabilities, the net assets of the fund would be $9,450,000. If there are 1 million shares, the NAV per share is $9.45. Sellers will receive $9.45 per share when they redeem their A-shares today, but they'll pay a POP higher than that if they're buying. Buyers of the B-shares will pay $9.45, but those redeeming/selling their shares will receive $9.45 per share minus whatever percentage they leave behind to the contingent deferred sales charge.

To figure the POP (public offering price) that an investor pays, use the following formula:

NAV / (100% – sales charge) = POP

So, if the NAV is calculated at $9.45 today, an investor paying a 3% sales charge would pay a public offering price of $9.74. To calculate that, divide $9.45 by .97. If the investor were paying just a 1% sales charge, the POP would be $9.55. To calculate that, divide $9.45 by .99.

➤ Reducing the Sales Charge

Although A-shares do charge the front-end sales charge, you can also reduce that sales charge by employing various methods laid out in the prospectus.

> Breakpoints

Perhaps you've noticed that in general the more you want to buy of something, the better the deal. Doesn't a small box of Lucky Charms™ at the convenience store cost a lot more per ounce than a shrink-wrapped pack of 10 boxes from Sam's Club? Same with mutual funds. If you want to invest $1,000, you're going to pay a higher sales charge than if you want to invest, say, $100,000. For mutual funds, investors are rewarded with **breakpoints**. Let's say that the L & H Fund had the following sales charge schedule:

INVESTMENT	SALES CHARGE
< $25,000	5.5%
$25,000 – $49,999	5.0%
$50,000 – $99,999	4.0%
$100,000 – $199,999	3.0%

That means that an investor who buys $100,000 worth of the fund will pay a much lower sales charge than an investor who invests $20,000. In other words, less of her money (as a percentage) will be deducted from her check when she invests. A breakpoint means that at this point the fund will give you this break. A lower sales charge means that an investor's money ends up buying more shares. For mutual funds, we don't pick the number of shares we want; we send in a certain amount of money and see how many shares our money buys us. With a lower sales charge, our money will buy us more shares. Keep in mind that fractional shares are common. For example, $1,000 would buy 12.5 shares if the POP were $80.

> Letter of Intent

So, what if we didn't have the $100,000 needed to qualify for that breakpoint? We could write a **letter of intent** explaining to the mutual fund our intention to invest $100,000 in the fund over the next 13 months. Now, as we send in our money, say, $5,000 at a time, the fund applies the lower 3% sales charge, as if we'd already invested the full amount. The lower sales charge means we end up buying more shares, right? So, guess what the fund does? It holds those extra shares in a safe place, just in case we fail to invest that $100,000 we intended to. If we don't live up to our letter of intention, no big deal. We just don't get those extra shares. In other words, the higher sales charge applies to the money invested.

Also, that letter of intent could be backdated up to 90 calendar days to cover a previous purchase. If an investor bought $3,000 of the L & H fund on March 10, he might decide in early June that he should write a letter of intent to invest $50,000 over 13 months. He could backdate the letter to March 10 to include the previous investment and would then have 13 months from that date to invest the remaining $47,000.

Breakpoints are available to individuals, husbands & wives, parents & minor child in a custodial account, corporations, partnerships, etc. So, if the mom puts in $30,000 and puts in $20,000 for her minor child's UGMA account, that's a $50,000 investment in terms of achieving a breakpoint. The child cannot be an adult; he must be a minor. Corporations and other businesses qualify for breakpoints. About the only folks who don't qualify for breakpoints are investment clubs.

Another important consideration for breakpoints is that a sales rep can never encourage an investor to invest a lower amount of money to keep him from obtaining a lower sales charge offered at the next breakpoint. That's called breakpoint selling and is a violation of FINRA rules. Likewise, if a rep fails to point out to an investor that a few more dollars invested would qualify for a breakpoint, that's just as bad as actively encouraging him to stay below the next breakpoint. Sales representatives and their broker-dealers typically receive part of the sales charge. It would be to their advantage to get the highest sales charge possible. Unfortunately, they are required to keep their clients' interests in mind, too.

Yes, unfortunately, they take all the fun out of this business.

> ### Rights of Accumulation
If an investor's fund shares appreciate up to a breakpoint, the investor will receive a lower sales charge on additional purchases. In other words, when an investor is trying to reach a breakpoint, new money and account accumulation are counted the same way. So, if an investor's shares have appreciated to, say, $42,000 and the investor wanted to invest another $9,000, the entire purchase would qualify for the breakpoint that starts at $50,000. In other words, the $42,000 of value plus an additional $9,000 would take the investor past the $50,000 needed to qualify for the 4% sales charge.

This is known as rights of accumulation.

Please note that this has nothing to do with a letter of intent. If the investor writes a letter of intent to invest $100,000, he must invest $100,000 of new dollars into the fund to get the breakpoint he is intending to get. Rights of accumulation means that an investor could save money on future purchases, based on the value of the account.

> ### Combination Privilege
Most funds are part of a family of funds—Fidelity, Vanguard, American Funds, etc. Many of these fund families will let investors combine a purchase of their Income Fund with, say, their Index or Growth Fund to figure a breakpoint. They call this a **combination privilege**. So, if the individual invests $20,000 in the Income Fund and $30,000 in the Growth Fund, that's considered a $50,000 investment in the family of funds, and that's the number they'd use to figure the breakpoint.

> ### Conversion/Exchange Privilege
The fund might also offer a **conversion/exchange privilege**. This privilege allows investors to sell shares of, say, the L & H Growth Fund, to buy shares of the L & H Income Fund at the NAV, rather than the higher POP. If we didn't do that, the investor might get mad enough to leave our family, since there would be no immediate benefit to his staying with us.

Buying the new shares at the NAV is nice for the investor, but the IRS still considers the sale a taxable event. So, if you get a test question on the tax treatment, tell the exam that all gains or losses are recognized on the date of the sale.

➢ ### Buying and Selling Mutual Fund Shares
A no-load fund is purchased at the NAV, but every quarter 12b-1 fees are deducted from the fund's assets to cover the cost of distribution. If the fund has a "load," you can pay it upfront by buying an A-share and then save money on expenses going forward. You can also knock down your front-end sales charge by purchasing in quantity either all at once or through a Letter of Intent (LOI). If you buy the B-shares, you avoid the front-end sales charge, but you have two other concerns to keep in mind: 1) you'll leave a percentage on the table if you sell for the first several years and 2) the fund will take

a much higher 12b-1 fee on your behalf every quarter, driving up your expenses. If you were only going to hold a fund for, say, two or three years, the C-shares would probably make sense. You would pay no front-end or back-end sales charge, and even though the 12b-1 fee of 1% is a bit annoying, it's only being charged for two or three years.

> Purchasing Shares

Investors typically invest in mutual funds through a financial sales representative. However, an investor could also set up an account with the fund company and buy shares directly from them. Usually, the fund company will strongly encourage the investor to go through a registered representative, though, who is licensed to discuss investments with customers. If an investor goes directly through the fund, the people on the phone are just taking whatever order he wants to place. Would the investor save money by bypassing the registered representative? No. The distributor of the fund would keep all the sales charge, rather than sharing it with the registered rep's broker-dealer and the registered representative.

And, most people do not wake up thinking, "You know, I think I need to buy some shares of a well-diversified growth & income mutual fund today." A registered representative will be the one getting the ball rolling 99% of the time.

Once they've set up an account through the registered representative, customer can purchase additional shares in any of the following ways:

- Contacting their registered representative
- Mailing in their payment to the fund's customer service department (transfer agent)
- Telephoning the fund company
- Purchasing online
- Wiring the money from a bank account

Many people choose to set up an automatic investment program whereby, say, $300 per month is drawn from their bank account and sent to the fund company. This puts them on a disciplined schedule of investing and makes sure they don't purchase all their shares at just one price. The automatic plan uses "dollar cost averaging," which will be explored later.

When the investor opens her account, the fund needs to know if she wants to receive dividends and capital gains in the form of a check, or in the form of more shares. If she decides to automatically reinvest, there will be no tax advantages, but there is a big advantage to her in that she gets to reinvest at the net asset value, avoiding sales charges. Her money will grow faster this way, since every dollar she reinvests goes back into the fund and not a dime to the distributor. If she's in a retirement plan, she will automatically reinvest, since there are penalties for early withdrawals from retirement plans.

Mutual funds have minimum initial investments that are usually lower for IRA accounts than taxable accounts. Some funds will let investors in the door for as little as $25 or $50. Others are upscale clubs who won't talk to us for less than $3,000. The minimum initial investment is found in the prospectus, along with all the other vital information.

Open-end mutual fund shares are not traded with other investors. Rather, when an investor wants to sell shares of the L&H Aggressive Growth Fund, she sells them back to the L&H Aggressive Growth Fund. This is called a **redemption**. When we **redeem** shares, we receive the NAV per share if it's an A-share, and the NAV minus the back-end sales charge if it's a B-share.

Shareholders can redeem in any of the following methods:

- By contacting the registered representative
- By writing to the fund company
- By telephoning or faxing the fund company
- By going through the fund company's website

The fund company reserves the right to require what's known as a "signature guarantee" on any redemptions. A signature guarantee is an official stamp that officers of a bank can put on the required paperwork. When I inherited shares from a family member a few years back, I had to go to my bank for a signature guarantee to transfer ownership from the individual to the individual's estate, of which I was the executor. A "signature guarantee" is a common requirement when stock is being transferred or sold. They are usually obtained from a bank officer, or a member of a stock exchange.

The prospectus on my desk tells me that the fund reserves the right to require the pain-in-the-neck signature guarantee on any redemptions. The fund will require a signature guarantee if the redemption is:

- Over $75,000
- Made payable to someone other than the registered shareholder(s); or
- Sent to an address other than the address of record, or an address of record that has been changed within the last 10 days

Also, note that some mutual fund shares are issued (or were) as paper certificates. If that's the case, the investor must send in the certificates after signing them and obtaining the signature guarantee.

Mutual funds are not in love with redemptions. In fact, many charge a redemption fee during the first year or so to encourage investors to sit tight. If they sell too soon, investors might leave 1% of their investment behind. Note that this is not a back-end sales charge going to the distributors. This is just a penalty that compensates the fund for the hassle of having to pay out redemptions.

But, whether mutual funds enjoy redeeming shares or not, the fact is they must redeem shares promptly. Promptly means within 7 days at the latest, and that requirement could only be suspended if an emergency shut down the exchanges and there was no way to value the fund's portfolio. So, be skeptical of any answer that's trying to convince you that the fund can "halt redemptions." Not usually.

We looked at how a dividend is declared and paid for common stock trading on the secondary market. For an open-end fund, it's even simpler. The Record Date comes first, followed by the Ex-Dividend Date, and then, finally, the Payable Date. These occur on three successive days.

Many investors choose to invest into the fund systematically through an automatic deduction from their bank account. This way they invest rather than procrastinating, and they also use "dollar cost averaging," which avoids buying all the shares at high prices. When they go to redeem their shares, it would stink to sell them all at low prices, too.

Therefore, some investors set up **systematic withdrawal plans**. To set up a systematic withdrawal plan, the investor must have a minimum account value, often $5,000 or so. Payments are made first from dividends and then capital gains. If the dividends and capital gains don't cover the amount the investor wants to withdraw, the fund then starts redeeming shares. It's also a good idea to stop putting money into the fund once the investor begins the withdrawal plan.

There are several payout or withdrawal options.

......Fixed-Dollar Period Payments (Fixed-Dollar Plan)

As the name implies, if the investor wants to receive a fixed-dollar payment periodically, we can offer her the "fixed-dollar periodic payment" option. If she wants $300 per month, the fund will send her $300 a month. How long will her investment last? Until it's all gone. She's not fixing the period—she's fixing the monthly payment, which will keep coming until the money has been exhausted through regular withdrawals.

......Fixed-Percentage Periodic Payments (Fixed-Percentage Plan)

The investor might prefer to receive 2% of her account value each month, or maybe 5% each quarter. How much will the investor receive with each withdrawal? Who knows? Whatever 2% or 5% of the current account value happens to be. How long will the funds last? That is also a variable. What is fixed here is the percentage of the account value to be withdrawn regularly.

......Fixed-Shares Periodic Payments (Fixed-Share Plan)

The investor can also have the fund redeem/liquidate, say, 10 shares per month and send a check. How large will that check be? Whatever 10 shares are worth that month.

......Fixed Time

Finally, if the investor wants her account liquidated/withdrawn over, say, three years, she'll give the fund an exact date, and they'll figure out how much to redeem each month (or other period) to exhaust the account by that date.

➢   Structure and Operation of the Mutual Fund Company

So far, we've been looking at mutual funds in terms of what they are, who buys which ones, and how investors go about buying and selling them. Now, let's look at a mutual fund as a company—who performs which functions at, say, Fidelity, American Funds, and Vanguard, etc.?

>   Board of Directors

A mutual fund has a **Board of Directors** that oversees operations of the fund or family of funds. The board's responsibilities include:

- establish investment policy

- select and oversee the investment adviser, transfer agent, custodian
- establish dividends and capital gains policy
- review and approve 12b-1 plans

Just like at a public company such as McDonald's or Starbucks, the Board of Directors does not do the business of investing. Rather, it oversees operations of the company. The shareholders of the fund elect and re-elect the board members. Shareholders also vote their shares to approve the investment adviser's contract and 12b-1 fees.

> Investment Adviser

The Board of Directors oversees operations and establishes policies. The party investing the portfolio is called the **investment adviser**. The investment adviser to the fund manages the fund's investments according to the stated objectives and policies handed down by the Board. Shareholders and the Board of Directors vote to hire and retain investment advisers, who are paid a percentage of the fund's net assets. That's why they try so hard. The more valuable the fund, the more they get paid. Their fee is typically the largest expense to a mutual fund. Investment advisers must advise the fund in keeping with federal securities and tax law. They must also base their investment decisions on careful research of economic and financial trends rather than on hot stock tips from their bartender. The investment adviser is also called the portfolio manager.

> Custodian

The **custodian** is a bank that has legal responsibility for all the cash and securities owned by the mutual fund. What an amazing responsibility it must be to keep track of all the purchases and sales of maybe 1,000 different portfolio stocks or bonds, all the dividends and interest received, all the stock splits or mergers with other companies! Of course, somebody's got to do it, and that somebody is called the "custodian."

The custodian receives the dividends and interest payments made by the stocks and bonds in the fund portfolio. The custodian is also responsible for the payable and receivable functions involved when the investment adviser buys and sells securities for the portfolio. That means they release the funds to cover purchases by the investment adviser and receive those securities that were purchased. And, they receive funds after the adviser sells securities and deliver those securities to the buy side. Think of the custodian as the record keeper for the mutual fund portfolio. The next entity keeps records of shareholders and often acts as a customer service provider to the shareholders.

> Transfer Agent

The **transfer agent** is the party that issues new shares to buyers and cancels the shares that sellers redeem. Most of these "shares" are electronic files, but it still takes a lot of work to "issue" and "redeem" them. While the custodian receives dividends and interest payments from the portfolio securities, it is the transfer agent that distributes income dividends to the investors. The transfer agent provides shareholder services for the fund and often sends out those semi-annual and annual reports that investors must receive. As we just saw, investors can purchase and redeem shares directly with the transfer agent, although most will probably go through their registered representative.

Some funds are sponsored by **underwriters**, who bear the costs of distributing the fund up front and then get compensated by the sales charge that they either earn themselves or split with the broker-dealers who make the sales. Underwriters (a.k.a. "wholesalers," "distributors," or "sponsors") also prepare sales literature for the fund, since they're the ones who will be selling the shares, either directly to the public or through a network of broker-dealers. If a fund acts as its own distributor, it usually covers the distribution costs through a 12b-1 fee, as we mentioned. The fund can call itself "no load" provided the 12b-1 fee does not exceed .25% of net assets.

These are the methods of distribution for mutual fund shares:

- Fund/to underwriter/to dealer/to investor
- Fund/to underwriter/to investor
- Fund/to investor

> Shareholder Voting

Mutual fund shareholders vote on:

- Changes in investment policies and objectives
- Approval of investment adviser contract
- Approval of changes in fees
- Approval of and discontinuation of 12b-1 fees
- Election of board members
- Ratification of independent auditors

A mutual fund that distributes its own shares directly to the public does so under SEC Rule 12b-1 and covers distribution costs with this ongoing, asset-based "12b-1" sales fee. To approve and renew (at least annually) a 12b-1 fee, there must be a majority vote of outstanding shares and the Board of Directors, including a majority of the non-interested board members. But, to discontinue the 12b-1 fee, it requires only a majority of the outstanding shares and a majority of the non-interested board members.

Also, know that investment companies may not do any of the following without getting a majority vote of outstanding shares:

- Change from an open-end to a closed-end fund and vice versa
- Change from a diversified to non-diversified fund and vice versa
- Borrow money, lend money, purchase real estate or commodities contrary to their registration statement
- Cease functioning as an investment company

> Closed-End Funds

The third type of investment company defined by the Investment Company Act of 1940 is the **management company**. Within this category, we find both **open-end funds** and **closed-end funds**. So far, we've been talking about the open-end funds. Let's say a few words on the closed-end variety at this point. The main difference between the two is that open-end fund companies continually issue and redeem shares. When you find an investor for the L&H Aggressive Growth Fund, the fund will issue brand-new shares to the investor, which is why you had to sell them with a prospectus. Open-end funds don't do an IPO and then force shareholders to trade the fixed number of shares back and forth. Rather, they issue new shares every time somebody wants to buy them, and they let the shareholders sell back the shares whenever they need or want to.

On the other hand, closed-end funds issue shares that work the way shares of Starbucks of Microsoft work. Closed-end funds do an IPO, at which point there is a fixed number of shares. What if you want to sell your closed-end fund? You trade it the same way you trade any other share of stock. How much will you receive? Whatever a buyer is willing to pay. These shares can trade at a discount to their NAV, or at a premium. It just depends on the supply and demand for these shares.

So, if the test question says that the NAV is $9.45 with the POP at $9.00, something's up, right? Investors can't buy an open-end fund at a discount. As we saw, the cheapest we can buy it is at the NAV. B-shares are sold at the NAV, and so are no-load funds. But, no way can an investor buy open-end shares at a discount. So, if the fund shares are selling below NAV, they must be closed-end fund shares.

That does not mean that closed-end funds always trade at a discount. If investors want the shares, they might pay a premium. I'm not saying that closed-end funds always trade at a discount to their NAV. I'm saying that only the closed-end fund could do that.

And, since closed-end shares trade the same way that GE or MSFT shares trade, investors can both purchase them on margin and sell them short. To "sell short" involves borrowing shares from a broker-dealer and selling them, with the obligation to buy them back and replace them later. If the price falls, the investor buys low after already selling high. If the price goes rises, the investor suffers a loss.

Another difference between open and closed-end funds is that an investor would purchase, say, 100 shares of the closed-end fund and pay whatever that costs. For an open-end fund, we just cut a check for, say, $1,000, and see how many shares we end up with. In almost all cases, we get "full and fractional shares" with an open-end fund, which is just a way of saying that $100 would turn into 12.5 shares if the POP were $8.00. That little "point-5" of a share is the "fractional share." For a closed-end fund, we would either buy 12 shares or 13 shares, not 12.5.

Open-end funds only issue common stock to investors. That's right—even if it's a bond fund, the investor isn't buying bonds in the mutual fund company. The investor is buying a percentage of the bond portfolio. How do investors evidence ownership? Common stock.

Another way to say it is that the open-end fund does not issue "senior securities." A closed-end fund, on the other hand, can use leverage by issuing bonds to investors. They can also issue preferred stock and even common stock with greater or lesser voting rights. So, open-end funds do not use a lot of leverage and do not issue "senior securities." Just the opposite is true for closed-end funds.

The investment objectives between an open-end and a closed-end fund could be the same—there are closed-end corporate bond funds, tax-exempt bond funds, aggressive growth funds, etc. Nuveen Investments is a major issuer of closed-end municipal bond funds (www.nuveen.com offers a primer on open-end and closed-end funds). Why would we want those versus the open-end variety? Well, what happens to yield when the price of the bond drops—it goes up, right? So, if we can buy somebody's closed-end bond fund at a discount, we just pumped up your yield a little bit. What about when we want to sell your shares? Well, let's hope they're trading at a premium by then. If not, welcome to the NFL.

OPEN-END	CLOSED-END
Continuous offering of unlimited # of shares and shareholders	Fixed offering of shares
Issues only one class of stock	Can issue different classes of common stock, preferred stock, and bonds
Shares are purchased and redeemed with issuer/primary market only	Shares are not redeemable; must be traded on secondary market
Ex-Date established by Board of Directors	Ex-Date established by exchanges

> Face Amount Certificate Companies, Unit Investment Trusts

Okay, so that's a compare/contrast between open-end and closed-end investment companies. They both represent the type of investment company called the "management company." These two types of "management companies" make up the lion's share of questions on investment companies, but we can't forget the other two types: face amount certificate company and unit investment trust. When purchasing a face amount certificate, the investor either pays installments or a lump sum into the program, and later receives the higher face amount on the certificate on a future date. The exam might ask if these carry sales charges and/or management fees. The answer to both questions is yes. Sales charges cover the cost of marketing and selling the shares; management fees cover the cost of managing the investments to pay out more than they took in.

Then, there is the unit investment trust or UIT. These pooled investments are not actively managed portfolios, so they don't charge a management fee. If it's a portfolio of bonds, they just let the bonds mature. So, like any trust, it just kind of sits there holding title to assets, and receiving income from those assets. Investors buy units of this investment trust, which is why they are called unit investment trusts. The units are redeemable, meaning they can be cashed in for their current value.

> ETFs

Perhaps you have heard of "ETFs" or seen advertisements for the well-known varieties called "Spiders," "Diamonds" and "Cubes." An **ETF** is an **exchange-traded fund**. Why did they name it that? Because it is a fund that trades on an exchange and this is not an industry brimming with creative types. An ETF is organized as a Unit Investment Trust (UIT) and it trades among investors throughout the day, unlike a mutual fund, which shareholders redeem for the same NAV next calculated by the fund.

An ETF is typically an index fund. That means that if an investor wants to do as well as an index, she can track that index with an exchange traded fund (ETF). To track the S&P 500, she can buy the

"Spider," which is so named because it is an "SPDR" or "Standard & Poor's Depository Receipt." Of course, she could already have been doing that with an S&P 500 open-end index fund. But, that is a boring old open-end fund, and how does an investor buy or sell those shares? Directly from the open-end fund. No matter what time of day, if we put in a redemption order, we all receive the same NAV at the next calculated price—forward pricing. So, if the S&P 500 drops 80 points in the morning and rises 150 points by mid-afternoon, there is no way for us to buy low and then sell high with an open-end fund.

But with the ETF version investors can buy and sell their shares as often as they want to. They can try to buy when the index drops and sell when it rises. Unlike the open-end versions, these ETFs can be bought on margin and can be sold short for those who enjoy high-risk investment strategies. The test might say that ETFs facilitate "intra-day trading," which means that we can buy and sell these things as many times as we want throughout the day.

So, are ETFs cheaper than the open-end index fund versions?

Depends how you do it. If you were only going to invest $500, the open-end fund would probably be cheaper. You wouldn't pay a sales charge and the expenses are only about .18% (18 basis points) at the time of this writing. The ETF has an expense ratio of only .11% (11 basis points). But, since the ETF version (Spider) is a stock, you would pay a commission to buy it, just as you would pay to buy shares of GE, Walmart, etc. So, if you invested $500 into the ETF and paid a $10 commission, that commission would work out to be 2% (200 basis points), which is much higher, and that's before we factor in the expenses. On the other hand, if you're investing a larger amount, such as $100,000, the same $10 commission is now 1 basis point (.0001) versus the 18 basis points (.0018) for the open-end index fund's operating expenses. So, I think it's safe to say that for a small amount of money—as usual—the open-end mutual fund is a great option. For larger amounts of money, though, the ETF might be cheaper, assuming the investor is paying low commissions.

As with the open-end index funds, ETFs offer **diversification**. For a rather small amount of money, an investor can own a little piece of, say, 500 different stocks with the SPDR, or 30 different stocks for a Dow-based ETF. It is also easy to implement asset allocation strategies with ETFs. An investor can find ETFs that track all kinds of different indexes (small cap, value, growth, blue chip, long-term bonds, etc.). If an investor wanted to be 80% long-term bonds and 20% small cap stock, that goal could be achieved with just two low-cost ETFs. This point is not necessarily a comparison to the open-end index funds, which would offer the same advantage. Rather, it is a comparison to purchasing individual bonds or small cap stocks. To spread the risk among many bonds and small cap stocks, an investor must spend large sums of money. With an ETF (as with the open-end index funds) diversification can be achieved immediately with a much smaller investment.

ETFs:

- Trade like shares of stock, intra-day
- Investors pay a commission rather than a sales charge
- Shares can be bought on margin, sold short
- ETFs have low expense ratios
- ETFs are convenient for investors seeking diversification/asset allocation

- ETFs are very low-cost when purchased in larger quantities
- Indexes include small cap, mid-cap, large cap, growth, value, S&P 500, Dow Jones, NASDAQ, even fixed income
- Series 6 holders can't sell ETFs (or closed-end funds) trading on secondary market

OPTIONS

Those sweeteners called warrants that we discussed gave an investor the right to buy stock at a set price. They were sold to the investor by the issuing corporation.

Options, on the other hand, are contracts between two parties not related to the issuing corporation that let the owner buy 100 shares of stock for a set price or sell 100 shares of stock for a set price. The options that give investors the right to buy stock at the strike price are called **calls**. The options that give investors the right to sell stock at the strike price are called **puts**. So, if you hold a MSFT Mar 30 call, you have the right to buy 100 shares of Microsoft common stock for $30, no matter how high the stock goes. What if it gets stuck at $30, or falls to $20? You bought the wrong call. Maybe you're so ticked about being burned on the calls that, next month, you decide to buy the right to sell Microsoft for $25, figuring it's going to drop to, like $7, and wouldn't it be fun to sell it to somebody for $25, after buying it for $7? Well, that's what you think when you pay your premium of, say, $250, only the stock doesn't fall that far. It only falls to $26, so, once again, your option expires worthless. I guess I could have come up with an example of somebody making money by purchasing options, but I chose to be realistic instead.

In any case, if you think a stock price is about to rise, you are bullish on the stock. Bulls buy calls. If you think a stock price is about to drop, you are bearish on the stock. Bears buy puts. What if you want to sell an option? That just means you're willing to give somebody the right to buy stock from (call) or the right to sell stock to (put) you because you want that $200, $300, whatever the premium is, and you figure they'll lose the bet and never be able to force you to do anything beyond laugh your way to the bank. What if they win the bet?

That could be painful. If you gave somebody the right to buy Google at $150 a share, and they paid you $800 for that call option, you probably felt smart taking their bet. See, you'd get $800 per contract, and maybe you sold 100 contracts for $80,000 in premiums. Which would have been great except that Google went up to, say, $350, and the call buyer has the right to buy stock at the strike price. You now are required go buy 10,000 shares of Google for $3.5 million and then turn around and sell them for just $1.5 million.

So, if you sold somebody a call, you figured they were wrong. They're a bull—you're a bear. If you sold somebody a put, you figured they were wrong. They're a bear—you're a bull.

Bulls are in a position to buy stock. If they bought a call, they have the right to buy stock at the strike price. If they sold a put, they are obligated to buy stock at the strike price.

Bears are in a position to sell stock. If they bought a put, they have the right to sell stock at the strike price. If they sold a call, they have the obligation to sell stock at the strike price.

SUITABLE INVESTMENT RECOMMENDATIONS

Let's now look at some typical investors here and try to figure out what you should recommend to them and—just as important—what you should not recommend.

```
Investor: Heather Sams

Age: 42

Occupation: real estate agent

Profile: Heather earned $50,000 last year as a full-commission
real estate agent. She made 2/3 of her income in May, June, and
July, closing on just one property from August through December.
Heather has two children, ages 3 and 5. She is a single parent.
Her monthly mortgage payment is $1,100. She has a $100,000 term
life policy. Your firm's risk tolerance survey determines that she
falls within the "moderate risk tolerance" category.

Objective: save for retirement (in 20+ years) and the college
education of her two children.
```

What should you recommend to a client such as Heather Sams? Luckily, she does have life insurance, and there is no credit card debt, so Heather can afford to invest some money, even if it's a small amount. What are her specific needs? She wants to grow her investment dollars over the next 13 years for the eldest child, 15 years for the youngest child, and at least 20 years for herself. Those are long time horizons. However, she also has serious liquidity needs right now—she's going months without a paycheck during the seasonal slump in home sales. So, we can't just focus on capital appreciation over the long term We also must put a percentage of her capital into safe money market mutual funds. During the lean times when she's unable to sell a house, she can write checks against the money market shares to meet monthly expenses. How much should we invest there? We should probably just take her monthly expenses and figure out how much she'd need to invest to generate that much income for at least four or five months each year. If it turns out to be 75% or more allocated to the money market, I would not be surprised.

Okay, so we've got her doing better than a bank savings account or CD. Surely we can do more than that for her. Heather's time horizon for retirement is 20 years. There haven't been many 20-year periods where the S&P 500 was anything less than decent. She doesn't have a lot of money to waste on sales charges and operating expenses, so why don't we put half of her remaining 25% into an S&P 500 index fund? Or, if the index fund doesn't strike her fancy, I don't have a problem with just about any lower-risk equity fund for a small percentage of her investment capital. Maybe it's a growth & income fund, an equity income fund, a large cap value fund, or a "conservative growth fund." Maybe it has the words "blue chip" in it and a portfolio that is, truly, "blue chip," meaning dependable. If she had a higher risk tolerance, I would recommend small cap or aggressive growth funds, but the investor must be able to tolerate wide price fluctuations financially *and* psychologically. I can't impose my own views about risk on my clients. After all, it's their money. I get a commission either way.

That leaves us with about 12.5% of Heather's investment capital for education. When you hear the word "education," you might automatically think "529 plan." Those are effective for people with a lot of money to invest, people interested in making gifts that take things right up to the limit (currently $14,000 per year). That sounds like a pair of wealthy grandparents, not a single mom with two kids working a hit-or-miss full commission sales job. A Coverdell Savings Account will allow $2,000 per child per year to grow on a tax-deferred basis. I don't think Heather will end up maxing out either child's account this year, so we could certainly go with a Coverdell account and invest the money conservatively.

There are alternate solutions, too. Her high expenses relative to income tell me that reducing her current tax burden would be a major benefit. How can we reduce her tax burden? Instead of simply investing in mutual funds in a taxable account, we might persuade her to set up a Traditional IRA. That way when she files her 1040 in April, maybe she'll get a refund from Uncle Sam. A few hundred or even a thousand dollars would go a long way toward helping her keep her head above water. If her income increases steadily over the next few years, we can get her set up with a SIMPLE IRA, which allows for much higher annual contributions and, therefore, bigger tax benefits.

How will the Coverdell accounts help her current tax situation? They won't. But, she does need to save for her children's education, and why not get the benefit of tax deferral and tax-free withdrawals. Think about that—maybe she'll contribute $20,000 for each child over the next 13–15 years. If those investments are worth $40,000 when the kids go to college, there is no tax due on the $20,000 of growth. The money doesn't have to be tapped between here and there, so why not lock it up in a tax-deferred account meeting a long-term goal? In the Coverdell, she can invest as conservatively as she wants.

Or, forget the Coverdell. I-bonds might be the ticket. An I-bond is a savings bond issued by the U.S. Treasury, which means it's safe and exempt from state and local income taxes. An I-bond pays a guaranteed rate that is fixed over the life of the bond, but also pays out more interest income when inflation rises. So, there's no default risk and no real purchasing power risk, either. There are also tax advantages. First, the interest isn't paid out; it's added to the value of the bond. You can, therefore, defer the taxes until you cash in/redeem the bond. And, if you use the proceeds for qualified education costs in the same calendar year that you redeem the bonds, the interest is tax-*free*. Heather would not even have to declare that the I-bonds will be used for educational purposes when she buys them. Provided she uses the proceeds in the same year she redeems the bonds—and meets the other requirements of the Education Savings Bond Program—the interest is tax-free.

Am I saying that a "mid-cap growth fund" or 10-year Treasury notes have been ruled out? Not at all. Both could easily fit into or replace our recommendation. The point is, she needs liquidity for sure. She also needs some capital appreciation without taking on extreme risk. And, she must take care of her children's education. Therefore, there are some things that we can rule out. Municipal bonds have no place in Heather's portfolio—she is not in a high tax bracket. Of course, we're not even going to talk about options (puts and calls), as speculation is clearly not for Heather. I don't see how we could justify a recommendation for emerging market or sector funds, not when the test question is pointing out a "moderate risk tolerance."

So, as you can see, it's tough to know for sure what the right answer is for suitability questions. Your best bet is to think through things analytically and try to eliminate recommendations until you get to something that seems to work best for the investor given the facts provided.

Let's try another one.

Investor: Linda McManus

Age: 69

Occupation: school teacher, semi-retired

Profile: Linda taught third graders for 45 years before finally retiring. Only, she didn't completely retire. As soon as she added her name to the district's substitute teaching list, she has been teaching at least twice a week since her so-called "retirement." Education is, not surprisingly, a major theme of Linda's life. Although her grandchildren have yet to show that they share her love of learning, the thought that they would not attend at least four years of college has never entered Linda's mind. Even though her children earn modest livings and are both saddled with too much credit card debt and too much of what she calls "champagne tastes on beer salaries," Linda decided long ago that her grandchildren would not miss out on college due to their parents' financial blunders. Linda's teacher's pension is decent, paying 65% of what she made during her last year as a full-time teacher. The house was paid off long ago, although the property taxes have risen beyond the comfort level. Her husband died five years ago and left an insurance policy of $110,000, most of which is now sitting in bank CDs. Linda would like to invest for her three grandchildren's educations, ages 8, 11, and 12 currently. She would like to cover her property taxes without using so much of her monthly pension check. And, she would like to protect her purchasing power against the threat of inflation. Your firm's survey determines that Linda has a low-to-moderate risk tolerance.

Objective: current income, capital appreciation.

What should you recommend to an investor like Linda McManus? Her grandchildren are not 3 and 5 years old, so the time horizon for a 12-year-old is considerably shorter than that of a 3-year-old in terms of investing for educational needs. The portfolio will have a higher allocation to fixed-income and a lower allocation to equity/stock than it would for younger children's education funds. If we do go mostly fixed-income for the educational needs, the maturities must fit the time horizon. An income investor wants her bonds to mature within her time horizon. If she has a 10-year time horizon, a 30-year bond would force her to sell before maturity at who knows what price. If rates have risen, she could get taken to the cleaners. So, if Linda's granddaughter is six years away from her freshman year, we need debt securities that mature in six years or sooner. Maybe an intermediate-term, investment-grade corporate bond fund would work best. Yes, Treasury notes are safer, but investment-grade corporate bonds are not exactly high-risk, either, and they pay a higher return. She might also purchase I-bonds and use the proceeds for the grandkids' education without paying taxes on the interest that gets paid out upon redemption.

A 529 Savings Plan might be a good idea, too. She has about six figures sitting in bank CDs. When the next one matures, maybe she could put it into a 529 Savings Plan for her oldest grandchild, and do the same for the younger grandchildren when the next two CDs mature. Linda can put up to the current gift tax exclusion per year without triggering gift taxes. And, when the grandkids use the money for education, there will be no taxes due at the federal level. What about the state level? That's the tricky part of 529 Plans. You would typically start by looking at the plan offered by Linda's state, since she may get to deduct her contributions from state taxes.

If Linda preferred to just buy tuition credits at today's prices, she could do that, too. But it's important that we know the grandkids are going to be okay with attending college in a specific state. If Linda buys tuition credits from the State of Virginia, the grandkids will need to attend a state college in Virginia; otherwise, things could get ugly. So, if we aren't sure in which state the kids will be willing to attend college, the I-bonds might be looking real tempting. Those are Treasuries and, therefore, not taxed as ordinary income at the state level.

However we take care of the grandkids' education, we're still going to devote part of Linda's money for Linda. She has property taxes due twice a year, so we need a safe, dependable debt security that pays interest semi-annually. Sounds like United States Treasury Bonds to me. Or, maybe we don't want to lock into a fixed interest rate for such a long time period and choose to buy 5-year T-Notes, instead. As they mature, we can buy new T-Notes at, perhaps, a higher (or lower) interest rate. Either way, Linda's principal is as safe as it gets, and we can use the semi-annual interest payments to cover part or all her semi-annual property tax bills.

Since she wants to protect her purchasing power, we'll put a percentage of her capital into the stock market, but we'll be about as conservative as a stock investor can be. Blue chip stocks are issued by dependable, mature companies. Linda can reinvest the dividends into a blue chip or conservative growth fund for now. As time goes by, she can always choose to start cashing the dividend checks instead to keep the lights on or maybe update her kitchen. And, if she redeems a few shares of the funds once in a while to replace an old furnace or washing machine, well, that's why we invest. Eventually, somebody has to spend the money. Otherwise, what's the point?

How much should we allocate to each? I would probably start with her property tax bill. Let's say she qualifies for a senior citizen exemption and pays $1,500 a year in property taxes. How much would she be required to invest to generate $1,500 a year on a U.S. Treasury security? Treasury bonds are yielding a little more than 5% as I write this, so how much principal must be invested to generate $1,500 per year? $30,000. Of course, before she pays her property tax, she gets taxed on the interest by the federal government. So, we should probably invest enough to leave her with $1,500 *after-tax*. If she's in the 25% bracket, she'll need to invest $40,000. And, since her property taxes will rise over time, she should consider investing a little more than that just to be on the safe side.

The amount she invests for her grandchildren's education will depend largely on her monthly expenses versus her pension check and the modest amount she earns as a substitute teacher. She currently receives a pension check of $2,000 and grosses between $800 and $1,100 per month as a substitute teacher. So, with $2,800 in employment income and about $300 in CD interest, let's say she has $3,100 per month to cover the following expenses:

$200	heating and cooling
$100	prescriptions, healthcare
$350	groceries
$100	clothing
$250	automobile, insurance, etc.
$150	miscellaneous

Looks like she has about $2,000 a month to invest, or $24,000 per year.

That means she can easily max out a 529 Plan for her oldest granddaughter this year and still have $10,000 to invest for herself. Or, she can max out 529 Savings Plans for her two oldest grandchildren if she chooses to be more self-sacrificial. Or, she can use the maturing bank CDs to fund the 529 plans and invest the rest for herself. Whatever you recommend here, chances are the numbers will end up getting tweaked before the signature goes on the dotted line. It's just important that you begin with an appropriate recommendation and a good understanding of the issues.

Again, I see no reason to talk about municipal securities and even less reason to talk about puts and calls, emerging market funds, sector funds, funds of hedge funds, or any other speculative, high-risk, aggressive investment strategy. I would also be leery of a registered representative recommending a deferred annuity. A deferred variable annuity will promise that Linda receives an income stream for the rest of her life, but we don't know how much that income will be from month to month. There is also going to be a surrender period of about eight years during which she'd get penalized for taking out money. A 69-year-old could easily end up with a medical emergency, a busted water heater, a leaky roof, etc., and so we would assume that her need for liquidity is too high to be tying up a bunch of money into a deferred annuity. Annuities also charge "mortality and expense risk charges," "administrative fees," "management fees," etc., that might make them worthwhile for a long-term investor. But, the older the investor, the more skeptical I'd be about recommendations for variable annuities, especially on a regulatory exam, especially when both FINRA and NASAA have written explicitly of their own skepticism of senior citizens being pitched variable annuities.

What if Linda still wanted some tax deferral? Given her age, a Traditional IRA doesn't work, given that she'll be required to start taking distributions on April 1 following her 70½th birthday, which is just around the corner. I mean, if she already has one started, she can make a few more contributions up to the current maximum, but that's about it. However, a Roth IRA would work just fine. Since that money comes out after-tax, the IRS will let her make continued contributions to a Roth. She has ordinary income from the substitute teaching, so, she can always buy her stocks or equity mutual funds within a tax-deferred Roth IRA, putting in up to the current maximum contribution. Her grandkids aren't going to college for at least five years, so Linda can make tax-free withdrawals and send part or all it to her grandkids once they get set up at college.

As always, there are many ways to take care of an investor's objectives. The registered representative just needs to know as much as possible about the investor's financial situation, needs, objectives, and risk tolerance.

```
Investor: Bryan Biesterfield

Age: 37

Occupation: sales manager

Profile: Bryan was never much of a student, but within one year of
finishing college, he hit the ground running as a software sales
rep. He made $110,000 his first full year in the business,
followed by $250,000 and, finally, peaked at $320,000 during 2001,
after which he has had to learn how to squeak by on just $120,000
a year, give or take. Mostly, Bryan's income is tied to the
overrides he makes on a team of five sales representatives. Maybe
it's the 15 years of marriage, the two children, or the 55-minute
commute, but something has started to douse the fire that used to
rage in his belly. Now, as he approaches middle age, Bryan is
focused more on the end game strategy—will he have enough money
to retire and how long will it take to get there? Are his wife and
kids protected should he get clipped in Philadelphia traffic on
the way to and from the office? If he got pushed out of his
current cushy management position, how long would it take to land
a comparable job?

Objectives: capital appreciation consistent with a conservative
strategy, capital preservation.
```

Given his high-risk career, generous salary, and relatively young age, you'd probably be leaning toward an aggressive growth/speculative strategy. But everything he's telling me is pointing toward a much more conservative strategy. His bright-lights-big-city days are far behind him at this point. Of course, a wife and two kids in the suburbs will do that, even to a former hell-raising bachelor from the big city. So, the first thing you would probably discuss is his need for insurance. If he's been earning six figures for many years, his family has become accustomed to buying what they want when they want it, within certain limits. I mean, no, you can't have a new Porsche this week, Sweetie, but as far as the cashmere sweater goes, well, we can probably swing it. If Bryan's wife and daughters had to someday choose between designer blue jeans and a Walmart private label brand, well, let's not even consider a fate so cruel. Let's make sure he has enough life insurance to cover their lifestyles for several years. Sounds like about a $1 million death benefit to me. Now, you might think that's a little excessive, given the fact that the mortgage balance is surely quite low given Bryan's high salary.

Au contraire. Like many high earners, this family is leveraged. They have taken so many home equity lines of credit and done so many re-financings that their mortgage balance still sits at an astonishing $485,000. So, the $1 million life policy will only leave slightly over $500,000 after paying off the house, slightly less after funeral expenses. It may take a few years for Bryan's wife to go back to school, finish her degree, and get a job that pays anything like what Bryan earned, so let's leave a nice cushion there.

Assuming Bryan has sufficient insurance coverage, we could then move on to other objectives. Notice how he wants to make sure he can retire young enough to enjoy his retirement, which is sort of a thin line to walk. On the one hand, he'll need sufficient capital appreciation to get where he wants to go. On the other hand, he can't risk losing it all on speculation. Reminds me of when I'm running late for an appointment. On the one hand, I have to go fast enough to get there on time. On the other hand, if I get caught speeding, I'll be pulled over and end up not even making the appointment.

So, we need a conservative mutual fund—perhaps a growth & income fund or a balanced fund. That way, part of his investments will seek the capital appreciation/growth required to put together a nest egg big enough to retire on, and another part will seek a dependable income stream that can be reinvested for now and spent later if needed. This could make for a tricky test question, though. Exactly how I would choose "balanced fund" over "growth & income fund" or even a "value fund" I'm not sure. They could all provide growth and dependable income, so I'm hoping the other choices can be easily ruled out because they're too risky, or they don't offer enough growth potential.

So, Bryan has played defense by purchasing enough life insurance to pay off the mortgage and give his wife and kids some breathing room should tragedy strike. We're considering an equity strategy that offers growth at a reasonable risk and seeks income to smooth out an otherwise bumpy ride. What about his concern that he could lose his job and need a cushion to carry him to the next position? That's a need for liquidity. A sales manager will get fired if he doesn't make his numbers, and getting fired from one position doesn't exactly help land the next one, especially as he gets older and grayer. If he loses his job, would he have enough of a reserve to tap for at least a year, maybe two? Maybe go back to school, retrain for a new career, etc.? That all costs money, and with no employment income, who's going to cover that stuff, let alone all the cashmere sweaters his wife and daughter might require at a moment's notice?

I think he should try to build up a money market or Treasury portfolio with a principal of around $100,000. I don't think he has the cash flow to cut a check all at once, so I'd figure out how much of each monthly paycheck can go toward this safety net, with the excess going into a conservative equity mutual fund, maybe a balanced fund to add some exposure to the bond market, as well.

```
Investor: Michelle Mathers

Age: 33

Profile: Michelle is a divorced woman with no kids earning $62,000
a year in middle management for a large printing company in
Sandusky, Ohio. After a messy divorce, Michelle is basically
starting over financially. Since her ex-husband is a semi-
professional musician earning $10,000 in a good year, Michelle is
required to pay $350 per month in alimony to her former husband.

Michelle lives in a modest two-bedroom townhouse with a monthly
mortgage payment of $900. She drives a five-year-old Toyota
```

Corolla and does not spend excessively on clothes. Although she likes to go out, she generally keeps the activities low-cost: coffee, window shopping, lounging at a local bookstore, maybe a museum.

Michelle's former employer in Columbus is still holding her $30,000 401(k) plan, which Michelle would like to roll over to her current company's plan. Unfortunately, her current employer is a little on the frugal side—they offer no matching contributions. Therefore, the only benefit to participating in the non-matching 401(k) would be the higher contribution limits versus a Traditional or Roth IRA. She also invested a modest sum into a deferred variable annuity a few years back. The annuity contract is currently worth $15,000, and Michelle is less than pleased with the slow growth in value and high fees.

Your firm determines that Michelle's risk tolerance is moderate.

Objective: capital preservation, primarily for retirement and possibly the purchase of income/investment property.

Well, we obviously can't help Michelle with the whole alimony-to-a-former husband thing. But, we can help her move the 401(k) money into our more trustworthy, competent hands. Unless the test question calls it a "Roth 401(k)" we assume this account has been funded with pre-tax dollars. Therefore, it can be rolled into her own Traditional IRA without any tax implications. Not only will there be no tax hassles when we move the $30,000 from her 401(k) to a Traditional IRA, but also the money won't even be counted towards her current year contribution limit.

So, we'll help her fill out the paperwork for a "direct rollover," whereby the 401(k) custodian—which happens to be Fidelity—cuts a check directly to the IRA custodian, which happens to be us. Michelle can also contribute to the IRA this year, which will reduce her taxable income for the year and grow tax-deferred until retirement. Since Michelle does not have an IRA set up, we will help her set up a "Rollover IRA." This is not an investment in and of itself. An IRA is a protective shell that we wrap around the mutual funds we plan to sell her to provide for current tax deductions on the contributions and tax-deferred growth. Since she has a moderate risk tolerance and is looking to build a nest egg for retirement and possibly the purchase of investment property, I'm leaning toward a mid-cap growth fund for most of her account, possibly a more conservative fund for the remainder—large cap value, equity income, even a balanced fund.

What about the annuity? Is she stuck with what she purchased? Not necessarily. The IRS allows us to do a tax-free "1035 contract exchange." This means that we can take her current annuity and turn it into one of our superior offerings. However, nothing is simple in this business, not even the simple stuff. The 1035 exchange allows Michelle to move the value of her annuity to another annuity contract without paying ordinary income or a 10% penalty tax. However, it has nothing to do with the agreement between Michelle and the insurance/annuity company. See, the insurance company wants Michelle to leave her money alone for the first eight years. To help encourage her to play along, they charge her 7% of the contract value if she surrenders during the first year. In the second year, the surrender charge drops to 6%. In the third year it drops again, all the way down to 6%. Michelle is only in the third year of her contract, which means she would lose 6% of whatever the contract is worth, or about $900.

While we can help with the tax-free contract exchange and would certainly enjoy spending the commissions earned on the sale of the annuity, we must keep FINRA's suitability rules in mind. Is it suitable to do something that costs Michelle 6% of her contract value? Are we convinced that our own product will provide for superior performance at lower expenses?

Time to consult with your principal/supervisor. He or she will help you figure out if it is, in fact, a suitable transaction and, if so, what type of documentation will be needed to cover the firm's backside.

What about Michelle's need for supplemental income? Frankly, I don't see it. She earns $62,000 and has a $900 monthly mortgage payment. She doesn't buy $700 business suits or $500 handbags. She doesn't own a boat or collect wine. She's already been promoted to middle management, and she's confident that she'll continue to climb the ladder, either at this or another company. The $350 alimony payment to the husband is annoying but not devastating financially.

I think we should help her with the 401(k) direct rollover (the check is cut to our custodian, not in Michelle's name) to a rollover IRA. We should proceed with the 1035 annuity exchange carefully, under the guidance of our compliance principal. And, we should recommend equity funds that are neither too stodgy nor too aggressive.

Finally, it might be fun and educational to consider your own age, occupation, profile, objectives, and risk tolerance to come up with some investment recommendations for yourself. Or for your mom, sister, brother-in-law, bowling buddy, what have you. The more "real world" we can make this process, the more comfortable you'll be at the testing center. Reading several mutual fund prospectuses would be a great way to familiarize yourself with the different options out there, the pros and cons of different funds, etc.

THE PRIMARY MARKETPLACE: ISSUING SECURITIES

Facebook made headlines several years ago with their **initial public offering** or "**IPO**," in which they sold stock to investors at $38 per share and those investors then watched the stock climb to $100 or more per share! The difference between the initial $38 price and the eventual market price of, say, $104, is the difference between the primary and secondary markets. Securities are issued to investors on the **primary market**. Securities are traded among investors on the **secondary market**.

To perform an initial public offering on the primary market a privately-owned company sells a percentage of ownership to public investors in exchange for an infusion of cash that can be used to expand the business. In an initial public offering of stock the company takes the money investors pay for the stock and buys factories, manufacturing equipment, and computers, etc. In exchange for their investment into the business the investors end up owning a percentage of the company's profits, nothing more, and nothing less.

Now, nothing makes the securities regulators more nervous than to hear that a company wants to raise money from investors. Let's face it, many business owners would say just about anything investors wanted to hear to get their hands on a few million dollars. That's why the state and federal securities regulators like to slow down the issuers in much the same way they're slowing you down right now. Just tying you up with a little paperwork, giving you a chance to rethink your whole decision, making sure it's something you want to do. Because, if you go through with it, you will subject yourself to full disclosure to the public going forward.

The SEC requires the issuer to file a detailed **registration statement** because they want to see exactly what the issuer will be telling their potential investors in the prospectus. They want the issuer to provide the whole story on the company: history, competitors, products and services, risks of investing in the company, financials, Board of Directors, and officers, etc. And, like a fussy English composition instructor, they want it written in clear, readable language. Only if investors clearly understand the risks and rewards of an investment do they have a fair chance of determining a good investment opportunity from something better left alone. If investors consistently get burned on the primary market, soon investors will stop showing up to provide companies with capital, which means companies would have one heck of a time expanding, hiring more workers, and pushing along the local and national economies.

So, the federal government is interested in what goes on in the securities markets, which is why Congress passed the **Securities Act of 1933**. The Securities Act of 1933 requires issuers of securities to register the securities offering and provide full disclosure to investors before taking their money. The SEC will make the issuer write and rewrite the registration statement, just like a composition instructor might make you do four rewrites of a research paper before finally agreeing to let you graduate. If this section is awkward and this paragraph is unclear, rewrite it. The SEC calls their equivalent of red pen marks "letters of deficiency" and sometimes, **deficiency letters**.

Now, an issuer would know their own business and industry sector well, but they probably know little about issuing securities. So, they hire underwriters, also called "investment bankers." An underwriter or investment banker is a broker-dealer who helps issuers raise money by issuing securities to investors. All the big-name Wall Street firms such as Morgan Stanley, Goldman Sachs, and Merrill Lynch have major underwriting or investment banking departments.

Once these underwriters help the issuer file registration papers under the Securities Act of 1933 the offering goes into a **cooling off period**, which will last a minimum of 20 days. This process can drag on and on if the SEC is finding problems with the registration statement, but no matter how long it takes, the issuer and underwriters can only do certain things during this "cooling off" period. Number one, they can't sell anything. They can't even advertise the offer of securities. About all they can do is take **indications of interest** from investors, but those aren't sales, just names on a list of people expressing some interest in a securities offering. And those who indicate their interest must receive a **preliminary prospectus** or "red herring." This disclosure document contains almost everything that the final prospectus will contain except for the **effective date** and the final **public offering price** or "POP." A registered representative may not send a research report along with the red herring and cannot highlight it or alter it in any way.

The issuer and the underwriters perform due diligence during the cooling off period, which just means they make sure they provided the SEC and the public with accurate and full disclosure. It's up to them to do this—the SEC is only reviewing the information for clarity. It had better be accurate.

Even though the SEC makes issuers jump through all kinds of hoops, they don't approve or disapprove of the security. They don't guarantee the accuracy or adequacy of the information provided by the issuer and its underwriters. In other words, if this whole thing goes belly up because of inaccurate disclosure, the liability still rests squarely on the shoulders of the issuers and underwriters, not on the SEC. And there must be a disclaimer saying basically that on the prospectus. In fact, look at the cover of any mutual fund prospectus. The one I'm looking at now says it this way:

> The Securities and Exchange Commission has not approved or disapproved of these securities. Further, it has not determined that this prospectus is accurate or complete. Any representation to the contrary is a criminal offense.

Some securities offerings are exempt from registration requirements based on the security or the way it is to be offered and sold. The Securities Act of 1933 is a piece of federal legislation, so it's not surprising that the folks who passed it gave themselves an exemption from the rule. That's right, government securities are exempt from this act. They don't have to be registered.

Neither do municipal securities, e.g., a State of California General Obligation bond or a School District 207-U capital improvement bond. Charitable organization securities, such as church bonds, are exempt from the act. So are bank securities, which are already regulated by bank regulators. Debt securities that mature in 270 days or less—commercial paper, banker's acceptances—are also exempt from this arduous registration process.

So, **exempt securities** don't have to be registered under the Securities Act of 1933 because they get a special excuse from that requirement. Then, there are also transactions that qualify for an exemption to registration requirements, called **exempt transactions**. If an entity issues their securities through a certain type of transaction, they can avoid the typical registration requirements. For example, if the issuer and underwriters sell the securities through a **private placement**, the SEC won't even make them register the securities offering.

Why would an issuer choose to go that route? A company like Five Guys Holdings, Inc. might want to raise $10 million by offering stock to sophisticated investors like those on the Shark Tank panel, without having to file a public registration statement that their competitors and the whole world can see. In fact, Five Guys did exactly that, and you can find their notice of the exempt offering here: http://www.sec.gov/Archives/edgar/data/1467164/000146716409000001/xslFormDX01/primary_doc.xml.

This issuer provided full disclosure of all material facts, but only to the few investors involved in the offering. Five Guys had to notify the SEC that the exempt transaction took place, but they didn't have to provide much information about themselves or the offering. For example, rather than including an income statement, they simply indicated that their annual revenues are somewhere between $25 million and $100 million. And, that seems like something McDonald's and their other competitors would have already known, anyway.

So, they got the best of both worlds: they raised their money, and they didn't have to file detailed registration statements with the SEC that anyone can see the way McDonald's, Microsoft, Apple, and all other public companies must.

PRIVATE PLACEMENTS

The federal government requires most securities to be registered primarily to protect the typical unsophisticated investor. If the investors are all sophisticated, the regulators can ease up a bit. While the Securities Act of 1933 would require a company doing a public offering of stock to provide a standard registration statement and prospectus, the Act also offers companies the ability to do a much easier private placement. A private placement is sold to sophisticated, well-funded investors, and because these investors are so sophisticated the offering does not even have to be registered. That's right, if you purchase a private placement, that offer has not been registered. Of course, if no one has ever called to interest you in one of these private placements, don't feel bad. You'd have to find yourself on the following list before expecting a phone call:

Accredited Investors:

- Bank, savings & loan, other similar institution
- Broker-dealer
- Insurance company
- Registered investment company, business development company, small business investment company
- Employee benefit plans with > $5,000,000 in assets (includes government, ERISA, and 501c3 plans)
- Any trust with assets > $5,000,000
- Any director, executive officer, or general partner of the issuer of the securities being offered or sold
- Any natural person whose individual net worth, or joint net worth with that person's spouse, at the time of his purchase exceeds $1,000,000 (not including primary residence)
- Any natural person who had an individual income in excess of $200,000 in each of the two most recent years or joint income with that person's spouse in excess of $300,000 in each of those years and has a reasonable expectation of reaching the same income level in the current year
- Any entity in which all the equity owners are accredited investors

If you didn't see yourself on that list, you could still get in on one of these private placements, as they allow the issuer to sell to no more than 35 non-accredited investors. The issuer/underwriters must be reasonably sure that you and the other non-accredited investors are sophisticated enough to get in on a private placement.

Since the shares are unregistered, a legend must be printed on the certificates reminding the investor that the transfer/sale of the shares is restricted. Therefore, since everything needs at least three names in this industry, private placement securities are also referred to as "legend stock" or "restricted stock." They must be held fully paid for a specified period of time before the investor sells them—that is the "restriction" that gives them their name.

> Purchaser Representatives

Since a private placement may be sold to 35 unsophisticated, non-accredited investors, the regulators decided to provide some protection to those folks. So, a non-accredited investor who lacks sufficient knowledge of financial matters must have a **purchaser representative** to help evaluate the risks/suitability of the investment. The purchaser representative is simply someone who can help act as a mentor to the investor, explaining the merits and potential risks of the investment. The purchaser representative cannot be some guy who steps out of an office at the issuer's headquarters volunteering his time to the buyer. The purchaser representative cannot be affiliated with the issuer unless they also happen to be a relative of the buyer. So, if the guy stepping out of the office happens to be the buyer's father-in-law, that's a different story.

There used to be a general prohibition against soliciting *any* investor for a private placement, but the rules have been relaxed so that solicitation is allowed *if all investors are accredited.* That would make an issuer think long and hard on whether they want to include any of the non-accredited purchasers in the offering.

Variable life insurance is sometimes sold through a private placement to sophisticated, wealthy investors who want more sophisticated investment options than those offered from conventional variable products.

UNDERWRITING COMMITMENTS

Different issuers receive different levels of commitment from their underwriters. Under a **best efforts** commitment, the underwriters act as agents. In other words, no money at risk. They try to sell, and whatever they can't sell goes back to the issuer.

Underwriters have money/capital at risk only when they give **firm commitments**. Now, they're agreeing to buy the securities outright, then turn around and sell them to the public. The difference between the value at which they buy from the issuer and sell to the public is known as the **spread**. The managing underwriter takes a manager's fee, the underwriters split up the underwriting fee, and whoever makes the sale gets the selling concession. Maybe the POP or "public offering price" is $10.00 and the issuer receives $9.20 per share. That would be a total spread of 80 cents per share. So, if the underwriters can sell 1 billion shares, they can keep $800 million.

If you get a question about a **standby offering**, tell the exam that this is a firm commitment underwriting for a rights offering. A rights offering is done in connection with an additional offer of stock. With a standby underwriter in place, the issuer is assured of distributing all the shares of the additional offer.

FREERIDING & WITHHOLDING

If the underwriters have set the POP of a stock at $10, what happens if it becomes clear that the stock will likely trade the way Facebook did soon after the IPO? Wouldn't it be tempting to hold all the shares for their own account and sell them later for a big profit? It might be tempting, but it's not allowed by FINRA, who calls the violation "freeriding and withholding." These public offerings must be bona fide (good and true) distributions. That means if your firm is an underwriter or a selling group member, it must make a good faith effort to sell all the shares it is allotted to investors, no matter how tempting it might be to keep most of them for its own account and take a "free ride" by "withholding" the securities from hungry buyers. In other words, investment bankers cannot pretend to be offering stock to the public and then sort of change their minds and keep the good ones for themselves.

THE NEW ISSUE RULE

Not so long ago it seemed that the only IPOs that were readily available to investors were the lousy ones. The good ones seemed to get snatched up by people in the industry. These days, there are many investors who are not allowed to buy initial equity offerings. An investor who may not purchase a new issue of common stock is called a restricted person. **Restricted persons** include:

- Member firms and their owners
- Broker-dealer personnel (not restricted to registered persons)
- Finders and fiduciaries (finders, accountants, consultants, attorneys, etc.)
- Portfolio managers for institutions (banks, S&Ls, insurance companies, etc.) buying for their own account

Of course, it would be fun to help your immediate family members profit from a wildly successful IPO. Unfortunately, FINRA prohibits the offering of new issues to immediate family members, defined as:

- parents
- mother-in-law or father-in-law
- spouse, brother or sister
- brother-in-law or sister-in-law
- son-in-law or daughter-in-law
- children
- any other individual to whom the person provides material support

Notice that the above list did not mention all family members. Specifically, aunts, uncles, grandparents, and cousins are not considered to be restricted. And, the immediate family members above are only restricted if they give or receive "material support," which FINRA defines as:

> *"Material support" means directly or indirectly providing more than 25% of a person's income in the prior calendar year. Members of the immediate family living in the same household are deemed to be providing each other with material support.*

Or, they would be restricted only if the family member working for a broker-dealer works for a firm that is selling the new issue (not a ban for employees of all broker-dealers), or if the employee has the ability to control the allocation of the new issue to investors. The new issue rule also requires that before selling a new issue to any account, a member firm must obtain a representation that the account is eligible to purchase new issues in compliance with this rule. The firm can obtain these "affirmative statements" either in paper form or electronic, but must not rely on oral statements from customers. And, these affirmative statements must be re-verified every 12 months, with copies maintained at least three years. Note that an investment club could buy a new issue, but not if a registered rep is part of the club.

Finally, the new issue rule only covers initial public offerings (IPOs) of common stock. The following are not subject to this rule:

- Secondary offerings
- Debt security offerings
- Preferred stock
- Investment company offerings
- Exempt securities
- REITs
- DPPs

ISSUING SECURITIES TIMELINE		
QUIET PERIOD	COOLING OFF PERIOD	EFFECTIVE DATE
• Prepare documents • No discussions with investors	• File registration statement • No sales or $ collected • Deficiency letters SEC • Blue sky the issue • Indications of interest • Preliminary prospectus • Due diligence meeting	• Sales confirmed • Final prospectus delivered

THE SECONDARY MARKETPLACE: TRADING SECURITIES

The primary market refers to an issuer raising money by selling brand new securities to investors and using investors' capital to expand the business. In the secondary market, on the other hand, investors trade those securities back and forth. Shares of Google were sold to investors on the primary market for $85 per share. After giving the underwriters the spread, Google kept the proceeds and reinvested the money into the business. After that, investors became so enthusiastic over Google's common stock that the price rose to more than $800 a share on the secondary market. Why? Same reason the price of anything rises—supply and demand. High demand and a tight supply will lead to high prices on corn, natural gas, and common stock.

It may also help to keep in mind that you will be selling annuities, variable life insurance, and mutual funds with your Series 6, and those products do not trade on a secondary market. An investor purchases those packaged products from the issuer and sells them back to the issuer when it's time to cash in. We don't sell our shares of the open-end ABC Aggressive Growth Fund to other investors. We redeem the shares, which means we sell them back to the issuer for what they're currently worth.

But, you're not that far removed from trading securities, because the mutual funds that you sell are buying and selling stocks and bonds for the portfolio. They purchase shares of initial public offerings on the primary market, and they also trade the portfolio securities with other investors on the secondary market. And that is why you must know the basics here for your exam.

Within the secondary market, there are different marketplaces that people use to trade securities. Let's start with the "first" or "exchange market," which the exam will likely call an **auction market**. The New York Stock Exchange (NYSE) IS the main part of the **first market**. There are also regional exchanges in Chicago, Boston, Philadelphia, and San Francisco that are based on the NYSE. Since there are both buyers and sellers, the exam could call this a "double auction" market. Either way, associate the word "auction" with "exchanges" or "the first market." Even though most trading is done electronically, each day the trading session starts and ends with a live auction at the NYSE. The exchange also reverts to the auction or "open outcry" system during periods of order imbalances between buys and sells or extreme market volatility.

The OTC or over-the-counter market is not a physical marketplace, but it's definitely a market. It is also known as the **second market**, and the exam will refer to it as a **negotiated market**. Market makers put out a **bid** and **ask** price, and stand ready to take either side of the trade, for at least one round lot. For stocks a round lot is 100 shares. So if a dealer or market maker says their quote is 20.00–20.11, they stand ready to buy 100 shares at $20.00 or sell 100 shares at $20.11. The difference between where they buy and where they sell is called the "spread," just like the difference between what a car dealer will pay for your trade-in, and what he'll sell it for to a buyer later on.

People trade these "OTC" stocks by computer rather than gathering at a big building on Wall Street. The big names such as ORCL, MSFT, or CSCO trade on an electronic system you have no doubt heard of called "NASDAQ." That stands for the National Association of Securities Dealers Automated Quotation system, by the way. Maybe you bought some of those wild and crazy Internet stocks a few years ago and watched them get kicked off NASDAQ when the share price became embarrassingly low. When that happens, they end up in a purgatory known as the "OTC Bulletin Board," where, no matter how hard investors pray, the stocks never seem to make it back to that electronic paradise known as NASDAQ.

The exam may refer to "Non-NASDAQ OTC" stocks, which is what we're talking about. Also, the "pink sheets." The problem with OTC stocks that don't trade on NASDAQ is the problem of "liquidity." There isn't as much buying interest on these stocks, so when you go to sell, you take a big haircut. If your stock trades on NASDAQ, there is more activity and, therefore, usually you get a better price when you buy or sell. In other words, NASDAQ offers better liquidity, while the Bulletin Board, Pink Sheets, or any "illiquid market" would leave you with serious "liquidity risk." Similarly, a car dealer would probably give you a better trade-in price for your Camry™ and sell it for a smaller markup later on compared to the deal he'd give you and the ultimate buyer of some car no one wants.

Anyway, the exam may also bring up the third and fourth markets. If a broker-dealer purchases a large block of stock that normally trades on the NYSE/exchange markets off the floor through a market maker, we have ourselves a negotiated or "over-the-counter" transaction of an exchange-listed stock. Sort of a hybrid between the two markets I just described where a broker-dealer buys a block of

GE or IBM not on the New York Stock Exchange, but over-the-counter through a dealer. Let's just call this the third market and keep moving.

The fourth market is where big institutional investors—pension funds, insurance companies, mutual funds, etc.—trade directly through electronic communications networks (ECNs). Sort of like an eBay for institutional investors. A famous ECN is called INSTINET. INSTItutional investors trade directly over INSTINET. They don't, in other words, call up a registered representative and ask for some hot recommendations. They know what they want to buy and sell, so they just buy and sell electronically without anybody's help, thank you very much.

SECONDARY MARKET

1st Market

• NYSE, auction market

2nd Market

• Negotiated market

• Functions through "market makers"

• NASDAQ

• OTC BB, Pink Sheets

3rd Market

• OTC transaction of an NYSE-listed security

4th Market

• Direct institutional trading, e.g., "INSTINET"

ECONOMIC FACTORS

The US economy is a large and mighty machine. Whether you picture the furious activity going on in America's large cities—New York, Los Angeles, Chicago, and Houston, etc.—or whether you picture all the small towns with mom and pop businesses eking out a living—somebody measures the value of all that activity and calls it our Gross Domestic Product (**GDP**).

GDP measures the total output of the American economy. It's the total value of all goods and services, measured as the price paid by the consumer for, say, all the gallons of milk or haircuts purchased over a 3-month period. If GDP is increasing, the economy is growing. If GDP is declining, so is the economy. The American economy rides a continuous roller coaster known as the business cycle. The phases of the **business cycle** are: expansion, peak, contraction, trough, recovery. All this means is that the economy goes up (expands), hits a peak, declines, hits bottom (trough), and then comes back up again (recovery). Because this progression is typically volatile, some refer to it as the "boom and bust" cycle.

Rising prices (known as inflation) are factored into this GDP calculation to arrive at "real GDP." In other words, we don't want to kid ourselves that rising prices is the same thing as rising economic output. We use the CPI (consumer price index) to factor in the effects of inflation, which we'll discuss shortly. Note that the word "real" generally means to subtract the rate of inflation from something. If you got a test question that said Orville Olmeyer has an investment that grows 6% while the CPI rises 3%, Orville's "real rate of return" is 3%—the amount above inflation.

The period of contraction/decline can be referred to as either a **recession** or a **depression**. A recession is associated with an economic slowdown, unemployment, dropping consumer confidence, and other negative indicators that lasts for at least a few months. A more prolonged and severe version of a recession is known as a depression.

INFLATION, DEFLATION

If the economy expands too fast, prices can go higher and higher until they're out of control. That's called **inflation**. Inflation is measured by the CPI, or "consumer price index." The CPI surveys the prices consumers are paying for the basic things consumers buy (movie tickets, milk, blue jeans, gasoline) and tracks the increases in those prices. They give more weighting to the stuff people buy more of, and sometimes they exclude certain items that are volatile (food and energy) because how many people buy food or gasoline in any given month? When we exclude food and energy, we're measuring "core inflation," which will not be on the exam, unless it is. The exam might say that inflation occurs when the demand for goods and services is growing faster than the supply of these items. Or, it could say something like, "too many dollars chasing too few goods." I like to think of inflation in terms of what would happen if they ran out of beer during the third inning at Wrigley Field and suddenly everyone realized they have nothing to do but watch a baseball game. Luckily, some enterprising young fella stands up and says he'd be happy to sell a cold six-pack he somehow managed to smuggle past security. How high would the price of cold beer rise on a hot August afternoon with 40,000 thirsty fans vying for six cold, sweaty cans of beer?

That's inflation. Sometimes economists worry about the opposite scenario, **deflation**. A beach ball can be inflated or deflated, and so can the economy. If you over-inflate a beach ball it will pop; if you under-inflate it, it's just as useless. Same for the economy. While inflation can make things too expensive for consumers to buy, deflation can make things ever cheaper. "Cheaper goods" sounds good until you consider that profit margins at businesses will be ever shrinking, as they pay last month's prices for raw materials and then struggle to sell them at next month's cheaper prices. Assuming they can sell anything to anyone—would you rush out to buy something today if you knew it would be cheaper tomorrow? Wouldn't you be tempted to put off your purchases indefinitely, waiting for the price of DVD players, clothing, and automobiles to drop in your favor?

That's an economic slowdown, right? Everybody sitting around waiting to see who'll be the first one to open his or her wallet. Which is why deflation—while rare—is just as detrimental to the economy as inflation. And that's why the **Federal Reserve Board** is forever manipulating interest rates trying find the right economic temperature—not too hot, not too cold. Like Goldilocks, they hope to find the economic porridge just right. Which is another way of saying that demand for stuff and the supply of that stuff are in the right balance. If we have strong demand and tight supply, prices will rise. If demand for stuff is weak and the supply of that stuff is high, prices will fall.

To review, if the economy grows too fast, we can end up with inflation. And, as we'll soon see, the Federal Reserve Board (or **FOMC**) will raise interest rates to let some air out of the over-expanding economy. If the economy starts to sputter and stall, we can end up with deflation. And, as we'll soon see, the Fed will pump some air back into the economy by lowering interest rates. A likely approach for an exam question would be to combine economics with bond prices and yields. As we saw earlier, during an inflationary period, bond prices usually drop. During a deflationary period, bond prices rise. And, yes, that means that their yields do the opposite in both cases.

FISCAL AND MONETARY POLICY

Fiscal policy is what the President and Congress do: tax and spend. To stimulate the economy, just cut taxes and increase government spending. Lower taxes leave more money for Americans to spend and invest, fueling the economy. If the government is spending more on interstate highway construction, a lot more folks are going to be hired for construction crews. Or maybe the federal government orders 10 million computers from Hewlett-Packard. HP would suddenly buy more equipment and raw materials and hire more workers, which is how to push the economy forward.

On the other hand, if we need to cool things down, the federal government increases taxes and cuts spending. Higher taxes leave less money for Americans to spend and invest, and decreased spending puts less government money into projects that would otherwise be hiring subcontractors, laborers, etc. The economists who view things this way are known as **Keynesian** economists.

Monetarists—the Federal Reserve Board—feel that controlling the money supply (**monetary policy**) is the key to managing the economy. What is the money supply?

It's the supply of money. Money, like any commodity, has a cost. The cost of money equals its "interest rate." If there's too much demand and too little supply, the cost of money (interest rate) goes up. That slows down the economy and fights inflation. If there's too little demand and too much supply, the cost of money (interest rate) goes down. That helps to stimulate the economy and pump some air back into a deflated economy.

Wait, money has a cost? I thought I paid the cost of things *with* money. Sure, but if I want to start a business, I need money. How much do I have to pay to borrow this money? That's the interest rate—the cost of borrowing money.

So, how can the money supply be influenced? Through monetary policy, enacted by the Federal Reserve Board. Because of that embarrassing little fiasco known as the 1930s, the Fed likes to make sure that banks don't lend out and invest every last dollar they have on deposit. So, the Fed requires that banks keep a certain percentage of their customer deposits in reserve. This is called, surprisingly enough, the reserve requirement. If the Fed raises the reserve requirement, banks have less money to lend out to folks trying to buy homes and start businesses. So, if the economy is overheating, the Fed could raise the reserve requirement to cool things down, and if the economy is sluggish, they could lower the requirement to make more money available to fuel the economy. The most often used tool is open market operations. The Fed can either buy or sell Treasury and agency securities. If they want to cool things down, they can raise rates by selling Treasuries. If they want to fuel a sluggish economy, they can buy Treasuries, thereby pushing rates down to help consumers buy big-ticket items.

Again, interest rates can be thought of as the price of a commodity known as money. Whenever a commodity—corn, sugar, concert tickets—is scarce, its price rises. Whenever something is widely available, its price drops. When money is tight, its cost (interest rate) rises. When money is widely available, its cost (interest rate) falls. So, if the Fed wants to drop rates, they make money more available by buying T-Bills. If they want to raise rates, they make money scarce by selling T-Bills.

Then there's the tool that gets talked about the most in the news, the **discount rate**. When people talk about the Fed raising interest rates by 25 basis points, they're talking about the discount rate. The discount rate is the rate the Fed charges banks that borrow directly from the Fed, while banks lend each other money at the **fed funds rate**. Either way, if banks must pay more to borrow, you can imagine that they will in turn charge their customers more to borrow from them. So, if the Fed wants to raise interest rates, they just raise the discount rate and let the banking system take it from there. The Fed doesn't directly set the **prime rate** or the fed funds rate. They do have influence over the rates through the discount rate, but they don't set the other rates. And, of course, they never, ever have anything to do with taxes.

So, think of the Fed as the driver of the economy. If the economy starts going too fast, they tap the brakes (raise interest rates) by raising the reserve requirement, raising the discount rate, and selling T-Bills. If the economy starts to stall out, the Fed gives it gas by lowering the reserve requirement, lowering the discount rate, and buying T-Bills.

INTEREST RATES

Interest rates represent the cost of borrowed capital. If you wanted to borrow $100,000 to expand your business as opposed to taking on owners, you would pay some money on top of the money you borrow. How much you pay for that borrowed "capital" is what we call interest rates. When there's a lot of money to be loaned out, lenders will drop their rates to get you to borrow. When money is tight, however, borrowers compete with each other to get a share of the limited capital and pay higher and higher rates.

The exam may ask you to work with the following interest rates:

- Discount rate: the rate banks pay when borrowing from the Federal Reserve Board
- Fed funds rate: the rate banks charge each other for overnight loans in excess of $1 million. Considered the most volatile rate, subject to daily change
- Call money rate or "broker call loan rate": the rate broker-dealers pay when borrowing on behalf of their margin customers
- Prime rate: the rate that the most creditworthy corporate customers pay when borrowing

Whether we use fiscal or monetary policy, our efforts will influence interest rates. And interest rates can make it either easier or harder for companies to do business and for consumers to consume.

VALUE OF U.S. DOLLAR VS. OTHER CURRENCIES

If you do business with foreign companies, you might have to pay for the stuff you buy in their currency, or you might receive their currency when you sell them the stuff you make. If so you are now subject to currency exchange risk. If you import hard drives from Japan and pay for them in yen, your risk is that the American dollar will weaken, which is the same thing as saying the yen will strengthen. How does that work? Well, you have signed on the dotted line to pay 1 million yen in 90 days. You will convert dollars to yen, in other words, so if the dollar is suddenly weak, you will lay more dollars on the table. If you export to Japan and receive 1 million yen in 90 days, what happens if the dollar has strengthened/yen has weakened? The 1 million yen you receive won't be worth much.

A weak dollar helps our exports because our goods suddenly look cheap to the other country. A strong dollar hurts our exports, because our goods suddenly look expensive to the other country. Of course, if you've ever vacationed in Mexico when the dollar was strong vs. the peso, you know that that makes for a much better vacation. If the dollar were weak, everything would suddenly seem expensive.

What causes one currency to strengthen or weaken when measured against another? If interest rates were rising in this country, that fact would attract foreign investment into American fixed-income securities, which tends to strengthen the dollar. If interest rates were falling, there would be less incentive for foreign investors to park their money in Treasuries, for example, and, therefore, we would expect the dollar to weaken.

FINRA RULES

In this chapter we have looked at the features of various investment vehicles and looked at their risk and reward characteristics. We looked at suitability requirements when making investment recommendations to customers, and will soon discuss the tax consequences of buying, holding, and selling securities. While Chapter 4 is focused on rules and regulations, the exam outline also places several regulatory concerns within the context of the other sections. So, let's see what concerns FINRA has when recommending securities and dealing with customers.

FINRA RULE: STANDARDS OF COMMERCIAL HONOR AND PRINCIPLES OF TRADE

The FINRA Conduct Rules could all be boiled down to this:

> *A member, in the conduct of his business, shall observe high standards of commercial honor and just and equitable principles of trade.*

Putting your investor's money in your own bank account would be inconsistent with this rule, wouldn't it? So would buying stock in your customer's account without first discussing the idea with the customer. If a broker-dealer is pushing a specific mutual fund just because the fund has agreed to trade through the broker-dealer and generate fat commissions, this would also be "conduct inconsistent with just and equitable principles of trade."

FINRA RULE: CUSTOMERS' SECURITIES OR FUNDS

This rule is telling member firms to watch what they do with the funds and securities they hold on behalf of customers. Since some of the customers might not pay close attention to their account statements, it might be tempting to, like, borrow a few grand here and there, provided you put it back, right? Maybe even add a little bit of interest since you're such an honest broker, right?

Tempting, sure. And real stupid. The firm cannot lend out customer securities to themselves or others who might want to sell them short, unless the customer has authorized that in writing. Also, the firm must segregate (separate) customer securities that have been fully paid from the firm's own securities.

I'm sure it's tempting to tell a skeptical customer, "Even if you lose money on this stock transaction—don't worry. We'll guarantee you and give you your money back." I have recently seen many real-world examples of registered reps dropping the ball on customer accounts and then trying to appease the angry investor with a personal check.

Don't do that. Firms may not offer guarantees against loss, nor would they want to. You make a suitable recommendation and help your customer manage risk, but when he buys a stock, anything can happen.

The word "sharing" is a red-flag word. If a registered representative wants to share in the account of a customer, they will need the customer's written authorization and the firm's written authorization, and they must share only in proportion to their investment in the account. The exception to the proportional sharing requirement is if the customer happens to be a member of the rep's immediate family (parents, mother-in-law or father-in-law, husband or wife, children, or any relative to whose support the member or person associated with a member otherwise contributes directly or indirectly).

Let's not be confused over the use of the word "guaranteed." We looked at several types of U.S. Treasury securities, all which are guaranteed as to timely interest and principal payments. There are even corporate bonds and stocks that are guaranteed as to interest, principal, or dividends by a third-party. Notice that we're talking about what an issuer of securities has promised to do. On the other hand, agents and broker-dealers don't guarantee customers against a loss. To do so is a violation and does not represent high standards of commercial honor, even if it seems like it when you offer to personally guarantee a nervous customer against any further losses in her account.

Securities involve various risks, and an agent's job is not to shield investors from these risks. Rather, an agent's job is to help them plan for and manage these risks. I have seen many agents up on the FINRA website after they mess up a customer's account, then offer to meet him or her for lunch and slip a big check under the table. The customer generally cashes that check before turning the agent into the appropriate supervisor. Agents are adults, and adults must face up to bad news. Trying to make it all go away with "personal guarantees" is a recipe for disaster, one FINRA will not let you or your firm cook up, no matter how honest or forthright it might feel to offer to make the pain go away. This is not the insurance industry—individuals can and do lose money investing in securities.

Note that we're only talking about investment losses. On the other hand, when a broker-dealer or agent mess up, the firm will routinely refund the customer for an over-charge, or even go back and fill a security purchase or sale order at a price the customer was due but did not receive because of a mistake. Still, an agent would never try to enact some sort of refund like this without a supervisor/principal getting on board. Right?

Again, if you put a customer into a mutual fund that goes down—that happens, and there is nothing you can do about it except discuss strategies with the customer going forward. If you started to process a purchase or redemption order on a Monday and then for some reason never followed through, your firm would likely go back to that date and execute a purchase or redemption order based on the price the customer should have paid or received, making up the difference from their own account. These are completely different situations.

FINRA RULE: BORROWING FROM OR LENDING TO CUSTOMERS

A registered representative may never borrow money from or lend money to a customer without following this FINRA rule:

> *No person associated with a member in any registered capacity may borrow money from or lend money to any customer unless the member has written procedures allowing the borrowing and lending of money between such registered persons and customers of the member and the lending or borrowing arrangement meets one of the following conditions.*

Here are the conditions that would allow a registered rep to borrow from/lend to a client:

- the customer is a member of such person's immediate family
- the customer is a financial institution regularly engaged in the business of providing credit, financing, or loans, or other entity or person that regularly arranges or extends credit in the ordinary course of business
- the lending arrangement is based on a personal relationship with the customer, such that the loan would not have been solicited, offered, or given had the customer and the associated person not maintained a relationship outside of the broker/customer relationship
- the lending arrangement is based on a business relationship outside of the broker-customer relationship
- the customer and the registered person are both registered persons of the same member firm

How does FINRA define "immediate family"? Broadly:

> *parents, grandparents, mother-in-law or father-in-law, husband or wife, brother or sister, brother-in-law or sister-in-law, son-in-law or daughter-in-law, children, grandchildren, cousin, aunt or uncle, or niece or nephew, and shall also include any other person whom the registered person supports, directly or indirectly, to a material extent.*

Also, note that the member firm would always have to pre-approve the borrowing/lending arrangement, except when they wouldn't. If it's an arrangement with a lending institution or an immediate family member, the firm can write their policy in a way that does not require notification. But the arrangement between a fellow registered rep or somebody with whom you have a business relationship—that must be pre-approved.

Just to keep everything nice and simple.

But, the bottom line is this—the borrowing and lending policies are established by your firm. If you get a test question implying that a registered representative can borrow money from a client because the client is a family member or a lending institution, read carefully. The firm can allow this activity or not allow it. Whatever the written policy is, that's how things work at that broker-dealer.

FINRA RULE: VARIABLE CONTRACTS

This rule tells member firms that when they accept payment from a customer for a **variable contract**, the price at which the money is invested is the price next computed when the payment is accepted by the insurance company. The member firm must transmit the application and payment promptly to the insurance company. No member who is a principal underwriter may sell variable contracts through another broker-dealer unless the broker-dealer is a member, and there is a sales agreement in effect between the parties. The agreement must also provide that the sales commission be returned to the insurance company if the purchaser terminates the contract within seven business days. Sorry, that rule doesn't favor you very much, but it is what it is. Also, member firms can only sell variable annuities if the annuity/insurance company promptly pays out when clients surrender their contracts.

Associated persons may not accept compensation from anyone other than the member firm. The only exception here is if there is an arrangement between you and the other party that your member firm agrees to, and your firm deals with a bunch of other requirements. Associated persons (you) may not accept securities from somebody else in exchange for selling variable contracts. The only non-cash compensation that can be offered or accepted would be:

- gifts that do not exceed an annual amount per person fixed periodically by the Association, and that are not preconditioned on achievement of a sales target. The gift limit is still $100, by the way.
- an occasional meal, a ticket to a sporting event or the theater, or comparable entertainment that is neither so frequent nor so extensive as to raise any question of propriety and is not preconditioned on achievement of a sales target
- payment or reimbursement by offerors in connection with meetings held by an offeror or by a member for the purpose of training or education of associated persons of a member

For that last bullet, the associated person must get the firm's permission to attend and that his attendance and reimbursement of expenses cannot be preconditioned on meeting a sales target. Only he—not a guest—can have expenses reimbursed. The location of the meeting must be appropriate, too, meaning if the offeror's office is in Minneapolis, it looks suspicious when the meeting is held in Montego Bay.

And—as always—the recordkeeping requirements are tougher than we'd like. As the rule states, the "member firm shall maintain records of all compensation received by the member or its associated persons from offerors. The records shall include the names of the offerors, the names of the associated persons, the amount of cash, the nature and, if known, the value of non-cash compensation received."

A firm can give their registered representatives non-cash compensation for selling variable contracts, but they can't compensate them more for selling one variable contract than for another. This rule states that the non-cash compensation arrangement requires that the credit received for each variable contract security is equally weighted.

FINRA RULE: INVESTMENT COMPANY SECURITIES

Mutual funds and variable annuities are both investment companies covered under the Investment Company Act of 1940. Since they are so similar, it's not surprising that this FINRA rule on investment company securities is similar to the one we just looked at on variable contracts. Like the previous rule, this one tells member firms who act as underwriters/distributors of investment companies that they must have a written sales agreement between themselves and other dealers. If the other dealer is not a FINRA member, they must pay the full public offering price, which would make it real tough for them to make a profit. As before, member firms must transmit payment from customers to the mutual fund companies promptly.

➤ Excessive Charges

This rule also tells member firms not to offer or sell shares of investment companies if the sales charges are excessive. What makes the sales charges excessive? 8.5% of the public offering price is the maximum sales charge. Also, note that if the fund does not offer breakpoints and rights of accumulation that satisfy FINRA, the fund cannot charge 8.5%. Of course, it would be a violation to describe a mutual fund as being "no load" or as having "no sales charge" if the investment company has a front-end (A shares) or deferred (B shares) sales charge, or if their 12b-1 fees exceed .25 of 1%.

➤ Withhold Orders

Although I would have thought this truth were self-evident, this FINRA rule states that, "No member shall withhold placing customers' orders for any investment company security so as to profit himself as a result of such withholding." Another part of this rule says that member firms can only purchase investment company shares either for their own account or to fill existing customer orders—they can't just pick up a batch of shares and then see if anybody wants them, in other words.

➤ Anti-Reciprocal Rule

This next thing seems highly testable to me. Broker-dealers cannot decide to sell investment company shares based on how much trading business the investment company does or would consider doing through the firm. The "pay to play" method is a big no-no, in other words. Be broad in your understanding of this rule—if it looks at all as if a member firm is tying the promotion of certain funds to the amount of trading commissions they receive when the fund places trades through them, it's not passing the smell test. This would also apply to a member firm offering to compensate their branch managers and reps more for selling the shares of those investment companies who execute transactions through the firm, generating fat commissions.

So, I just told you that a broker-dealer (member firm) cannot sell mutual fund shares if the mutual fund trades through the broker-dealer, generating commissions for the member firm, right?

No. What I'm saying is that the firm can't tie the promotion/sale of the mutual fund to the level of trading the fund does or intends to do through the firm. Similarly, firms compensate their branch managers and representatives for selling mutual fund shares; they simply can't compensate them more for selling the shares of the funds willing to "pay to play."

Interestingly, as I look at FINRA's website this morning, I see that the regulators just fined a firm over $12 million for placing mutual funds on a "preferred list" in exchange for those funds doing lots of lucrative trading business through the firm. The news release calls it a "shelf-space program," which is a great name for it. See, in the supermarket, all the products you see are there because the company paid a fee for "shelf space." Well, that's okay for cookies and crackers, but not for mutual funds.

This all boils down to the fact that a broker-dealer should recommend a mutual fund because it's the best investment for a customer, not because the broker-dealer will make money from the mutual fund when it executes its trades through the firm.

If a transaction involves the purchase of shares of an investment company that imposes a deferred sales charge when the investor redeems the shares someday, the written confirmation must also include the following legend: "On selling your shares, you may pay a sales charge. For the charge and other fees, see the prospectus." The legend must appear on the front of a confirmation and in at least 8-point type.

I am not making that up. 8-point type.

If a customer buys mutual fund shares but then redeems them within seven *business* days, any compensation earned by the broker-dealer and the registered rep must be returned to the underwriter. This puts a damper on registered representatives getting all their fraternity brothers to buy mutual fund shares and then dump them so that their buddy can earn sales charges, apparently.

Finally, everything I told you about the FINRA rule concerning receipt of payment from other sources, including non-cash compensation, holds true here, too. So, assuming you haven't fallen asleep or died of boredom yet, you might want to do a quick review of that section.

FINRA RULE: BREAKPOINT SALES

Open-end mutual funds with front-end loads typically offer **breakpoints,** as we saw earlier. Preventing a customer from receiving a breakpoint, or failing to inform her of the breakpoints—even though they are printed in the prospectus—is a violation called **breakpoint selling**. An exception to this concern is when a broker-dealer offers a diversification/asset allocation program that spreads the customer's investments among many funds. Provided the firm discloses to the customers that this program may prevent them from receiving breakpoints and keeps records of this, there is no breakpoint selling occurring.

FINRA RULE: INFLUENCING OR REWARDING EMPLOYEES OF OTHERS

In many ways, financial services sales efforts must be tamed down considerably from what might fly in other industries. For example, if I were still in the carpet cleaning business, no one would have a problem with my offering large cash payments to sorority sisters who can get my company a contract with various sorority houses. Or, if I knew someone who worked at a rival janitorial services company, there would be no law against paying him or her to flip some of the smaller accounts my way.

So, if you come from a sales career in a different industry, you might need to tone down the approach. FINRA doesn't want you or your firm rewarding or influencing other firms or their members with large cash payments or gifts worth over a certain amount. That annual limit on gifts has been at $100 for quite some time, and, of course, not much influence can be purchased with things worth $100 or less, which is exactly how the regulators want it. If your firm sponsors a mutual fund, they may not offer a $500 cash prize to the broker-dealer or agent who sells the most shares, for example. If you start a small underwriting firm, you may not buy your way into the next syndicate by sending the decision makers at Goldman Sachs Cuban cigars worth thousands of dollars.

FINRA is prohibiting payments for influence; they are not prohibiting legitimate compensation for work performed in connection to a legitimate written contract between the member and the person receiving payment. If your firm agrees to let you work for another firm on weekends structuring small bond offering, and there is a written agreement in place, that would be an exception. Provided the other member is paying you to do legitimate work and not trying to influence you or your firm, they are not violating this rule. Also, note that a gift of $100 includes cash and items that could easily be resold for. So, you can't give a big player at another firm $400 cash-money or $400 worth of imported wine. You could take him out for an occasional business meal or take him out to the ballgame. How about slipping him season tickets to your company's skybox? No—slip them to me, instead. I'm not associated with any FINRA-member firm, and neither will you be if you don't appreciate all these rules we're going over.

FINRA RULE: USE OF INFORMATION OBTAINED IN FIDUCIARY CAPACITY

Broker-dealers and their various affiliated companies provide services we might not think of right off. If a member firm acts as the "paying agent" for the issuer of a bond, they have access to information on all the bondholders to whom they pay interest and, eventually, principal. Therefore, FINRA prohibits that member firm from using the information in any way without the consent of the issuer. As the rule states:

> *A member who in the capacity of paying agent, transfer agent, trustee, or in any other similar capacity, has received information as to the ownership of securities, shall under no circumstances make use of such information for the purpose of soliciting purchases, sales or exchanges except at the request and on behalf of the issuer.*

NASD RULE: DEALING WITH NON-MEMBERS

FINRA still uses NASD rules—many have been retired, but many are still effective. This one, which is obviously still in effect, states, "No member shall deal with any non-member broker or dealer except at the same prices, for the same commissions or fees, and on the same terms and conditions as are by such member accorded to the general public." What they're saying is that member firms can't treat broker-dealers who don't belong to FINRA or another registered securities association any differently from how they treat any other public customer. Section 15A of the Securities Exchange Act of 1934 calls for registration of securities associations, such as FINRA, NYSE, MSRB, etc. So, if the broker or dealer is not registered under that Act, the member firm can't share commissions with them, or participate in a syndicate with them, or trade securities with them at special prices not available to any member of the public.

The rule would allow a FINRA member firm to do business on more favorable terms with a member of a different securities association—provided it's registered under Section 15A of the Securities Exchange Act of 1934.

NASD RULE: CONTINUING COMMISSIONS

Provided there is an agreement in place, a retired representative can receive continuing commissions from his former firm on business placed when he was in the industry. There can be no payment for any new business, of course, since the retired rep is no longer registered. Member firms can also have a contract to pay a widow or other beneficiary for the former rep's business pursuant to an agreement.

INSIDER TRADING

Let's say you got an invitation for dinner from an old college friend, who is now an attorney working on mergers and acquisitions. Over a few cocktails he quietly explains that Pfizer is going to announce the acquisition of a small biotech company trading on the OTC Bulletin Board for just 75 cents a share. When the announcement comes out, the stock should hit $4 almost immediately. And, he happens to know that Pfizer is willing to pay as much as $11 a share to acquire the smaller firm.

At this point, it would be tempting to buy as much of the stock trading for 75 cents as you possibly can. Unfortunately, it would also be unethical, illegal, and extremely painful if you got caught. See, like the other federal securities Acts, the Securities Exchange Act of 1934 is frequently amended and updated, just like the Series 6 exam.

In 1988 Congress passed the **Insider Trading and Securities Fraud Enforcement Act**, which amended the Securities Exchange Act of 1934. The Act of '34 had already prohibited insider trading, but the legislation in 1988 raised the penalties a bit. Even if the person doesn't end up in prison, the SEC can sue him in civil court and extract the following penalties:

- For the individual who passed out the inside information or was dumb enough to use it, the court can impose a civil penalty of three times the profit gained or loss avoided as a result of such unlawful purchase, sale, or communication.
- If that person happened to be "controlled" by somebody else (a boss, the broker-dealer who hired the agent, for example) that "controlling person" could receive a civil penalty of the *greater* of $1,000,000, or three times the amount of the profit gained or loss avoided as a result of the controlled person's violation.

A person caught trading on inside information can also be held liable to "contemporaneous traders." That means that if you profit big time from your little put-call play, I might sue you and show how your actions caused me to lose money. How much would you be required to pay me for "pain and suffering"?

You wouldn't. The maximum under this statute is the profit you made or the loss you avoided by trading on inside information.

Broker-dealers often come into possession of material inside information involving impending mergers, bankruptcies, etc. Therefore, they must maintain a **Chinese wall** around investment banking personnel to prevent the sharing of insider information among them, registered representatives and other employees.

INVESTMENT COMPANY ACT OF 1940

Back in 1940 the United States Congress formed a committee and several subcommittees who after many hours of extensive effort and expense concluded that a <u>company</u> whose primary activity is <u>investing</u> shall henceforth be referred to as an "investment company."

The legislation lays it out with the following passage:

```
1. When used in this title, "investment company" means any issuer
which—

A. is or holds itself out as being engaged primarily, or proposes
to engage primarily, in the business of investing, reinvesting, or
trading in securities
```

So, if the company is primarily engaged in making investments in securities, that company is an **investment company**. The definition also states that if more than 40% of the company's total assets are tied up in securities investments, that's an investment company.

The most well-known type of investment company is commonly called a "mutual fund." Under the Investment Company Act of 1940, the mutual fund represents the third type of investment company, formally called **management companies**. A management company is either an open-end or a closed-end fund. An open-end fund issues securities that investors sell back to the fund when they want to cash in. How much will the investor receive? Whatever the securities happen to be worth at the time.

The **closed-end fund** sells their securities in an IPO, but if investors want their money later, they must trade the closed-end fund shares with other investors on the secondary market. How much will they receive? Whatever a buyer is willing to pay. As the Investment Company Act of 1940 says, "*Open-end company* means a management company which is offering for sale or has outstanding any redeemable security of which it is the issuer." So, what is a "closed-end company"?

"*Closed-end company* means any management company other than an open-end company."

So, open-end companies allow investors to redeem the shares to the company for the net asset value. Closed-end companies might have the same investment objective as an open-end fund (growth, income, etc.), but when shareholders want to sell, they trade these shares exactly as they trade shares of IBM, GE, or Walmart. Investors buy at the Asked price and sell at the Bid price. Sometimes the bid price is much lower than we would like, unlike the open-end shares that simply pay out the NAV.

Open-end shares don't trade. Instead, investors sell them back to the issuer, which is called "redeeming" the shares.

Let's look at the other two types of investment companies, and—please—keep this organizational chart clear in your mind. There are three types of investment companies. One type is called the "management company," and there are either open-end or closed-end management companies.

Another type is called the **face amount certificate company**. Here, the investor either pays installments or a lump sum into the investment program, and receives the higher face amount on the certificate on a future date. The exam might ask if these carry sales charges and/or management fees. The answer to both questions is yes. Sales charges cover the cost of marketing and selling the shares; management fees cover the cost of managing the investments to pay out more than they took in.

Then, there is the **Unit Investment Trust** or UIT. These are not actively managed/traded portfolios, so they don't charge a management fee. If it's a portfolio of bonds, they just let the bonds mature. So, like any trust, it just kind of sits there holding title to assets and receiving income. Investors buy units of this investment trust, which is why they are called unit investment trusts. The units are redeemable, meaning they can be sold for their current value.

The main point of this Act is that if the company fits the definition of an "investment company," it must register your securities with the Securities and Exchange Commission.

REGISTRATION OF INVESTMENT COMPANIES

Investment companies submit a registration statement to the SEC. The registration statement has two parts. Part 1 is what all prospects must receive before purchasing a mutual fund, the prospectus. Part 2 contains more detailed information that must be made available but is not automatically provided. Part 2 is called the **statement of additional information**, or SAI.

Of course, the fact that a mutual fund or other investment company has been registered does not imply approval or endorsement by the SEC or any other regulator. The front cover of a mutual fund prospectus will make that clear.

RESTRICTIONS

Unless the fund meets some stringent financial and disclosure requirements, it is prohibited by the SEC from engaging in the following activities:

- Selling securities short (unlimited loss potential)
- Purchasing securities on margin (high-risk)
- Selling uncovered options (covered calls okay)
- Participating in joint investment or trading accounts
- Acting as a distributor of its own securities (use an underwriter, or a 12b-1 plan)
- Borrowing or lending money

If the fund wants to do any of the above, it must disclose the activities and explain the extent to which it plans to engage in them in the registration statement/prospectus. An open-end fund can borrow money from a bank but must maintain a 3-to-1 **asset-to-debt** coverage. And, the fund may not lend money to one of its officers or directors, no matter what it says in its registration statement. Finally, open-end funds do not issue "senior securities" giving those investors higher claims. Open-end funds issue only common stock. It's the closed-end funds that can issue senior securities, provided they follow the rules under the Investment Company Act of 1940.

We looked at the various players at a mutual fund: distributor, investment adviser, Board of Directors, transfer agent, and custodian. The Investment Company Act of 1940 stipulates that investment companies (e.g., The American Balanced Fund) cannot act as the distributor of their own shares unless they do so under SEC Rule 12b-1, which is why we've already discussed such 12b-1 fees, as an operating expense deducted against fund assets. As SEC Rule 12b-1 states

> A registered, open-end management investment company may act as a distributor of securities of which it is the issuer: *Provided,* That any payments made by such company in connection with such distribution are made pursuant to a written plan describing all material aspects of the proposed financing of distribution and that all agreements with any person relating to implementation of the plan are in writing." Also, the plan is only implemented when a majority of the outstanding shares, a majority of the Board of Directors, and a majority of the non-interested/independent board members approves it. The plan can also be terminated with a majority vote of the shareholders or a majority vote of the non-interested/independent board members. The plan must be approved annually by a majority of the shareholders, a majority of the Board of Directors overall *and* within the Board of Directors, a majority of the non-interested/independent members of the board.

12b-1 fees cannot exceed .25% of the fund's average net assets if the fund wants to call itself "no load" and act as its own distributor. On the other hand, since I used the example of the American Balanced Fund, you would see quickly from their summary prospectus that the fund is distributed by American Funds Distributors and is not a "no load" fund. Basically, any fund family with B- and C-shares is not a "no load" fund family and has its shares marketed and sold by a separate-but-related distributor/underwriter.

Paying 12b-1 fees to broker-dealers and agents pursuant to a written agreement is fine, but a registered investment company cannot reward member firms for selling their shares by giving them portfolio securities or by giving them commissions when they agree to execute buy and sell orders through the broker-dealer. If the ABC Funds Distributors worked it out so that their related investment adviser executed the most transactions for the fund portfolios through the broker-dealers selling the most shares of the funds to their retail investors, this would be a violation. Without this rule, investors would end up being pitched mutual funds for reasons that have nothing to do with suitability. Each broker-dealer would end up using various mutual fund products as nothing but a way to generate trading commissions and profits from the mutual fund companies, at the expense of investors.

Open-end funds and their underwriter can only offer to exchange shares of one fund for shares of another based on the relative Net Asset Values (NAV) of the funds, unless they have first filed the offer with the SEC and gotten their approval of the terms. This rule does not cover the case where the majority of the shares of an open-end fund have voted to reorganize the fund into something different. We're talking about the case where the ABC Fund Family offers to exchange shares of their Growth Fund for shares of their new Growth and Income Fund. If they do that, the exchange must be based on the relative net asset values of the fund shares unless they have first presented the offer to the SEC and received its okay. This rule also applies among the types of investment companies, too, so if you get a question about a fund company offering to exchange shares of an open-end fund for units of a unit investment trust, or vice versa, same deal.

Open-end and closed-end funds, as well as unit investment trusts, frequently pay dividend distributions to their share or unit holders. When doing so, they must either pay the dividend only from their net income, or—if it is being paid from some other source—a written statement must accompany the payment of the dividend or special distribution. Why? Dividend distributions tend to be steady and predictable; if an investor gets a one-time payment of $5 per-share, we don't want her to start making plans to keep on receiving it, right? Dividend distributions are not paid from portfolio trading profits (capital gains), so when capital gains or other distributions are made to shareholders, the fund must go out of its way to clarify that this is not a regular dividend distribution. Also, investment companies do not distribute capital gains to shareholders more than once every 12 months under the Investment Company Act of 1940.

The pricing of investment company shares is subject to regulation. First, when an investor redeems shares of an open-end fund, the price he receives is based on the next calculated price, not yesterday's NAV. Mutual funds price their shares once a day Monday through Friday provided the exchanges are open and there are requests from investors to turn their shares back into cash—**redemption orders.** The fund does not must allow member firms to buy shares for their customers and then immediately redeem them; in fact, if that happens within a certain time frame, any sales charges earned will be forfeited. Member firms cannot purchase shares of open-end funds below the net asset value. Instead, they make part of the extra fee added to the NAV called a **sales charge.** As we saw, the sales charges are laid out in the breakpoint schedule shown in the summary or statutory prospectus for the fund. If the fund ever changes this sales charge schedule, it must provide full disclosure to prospective and existing shareholders, revise its prospectus and Statement of Additional Information (SAI), and must apply the new sales charge schedule uniformly to all investors who invest the certain stated amounts in the new breakpoint schedule.

Open-end funds and Unit Investment Trusts are both registered investment companies that issue redeemable securities. Under the Investment Company Act of 1940, they may only suspend the investor's ability to redeem or turn shares back into cash under limited circumstances and, otherwise, complete a redemption order within 7 days. As the Investment Company Act of 1940 states:

> No registered investment company shall suspend the right of redemption, or postpone the date of payment or satisfaction upon redemption of any redeemable security in accordance with its terms
>
> for more than seven days after the tender of such security to the company or its agent designated for that purpose for redemption, except—

(1) for any period (A) during which the New York Stock Exchange is closed other than customary week-end and holiday closings or (B) during which trading on the New York Stock Exchange is restricted;

(2) for any period during which an emergency exists as a result of which (A) disposal by the company of securities owned by it is not reasonably practicable or (B) it is not reasonably practicable for such company fairly to determine the value of its net assets; or

(3) for such other periods as the Commission may by order permit for the protection of security holders of the company.

So, in general mutual funds and UITs must redeem their investors' securities within 7 days. But, since investment company products are used as the investment vehicle for variable annuities, a rule had to be written to exempt them in the case where an annuitant is receiving payments under a "life contingency" payout option, e.g. a "life with period certain" settlement option.

The ways in which closed-end funds distribute and/or repurchase their shares is also regulated under the Investment Company Act of 1940. The same way that public companies such as ORCL or SBUX might decide to repurchase their shares on the secondary market, a closed-end fund could buy its shares back on the secondary market. If so, they must inform the existing shareholders at least six months ahead of time, and they must do so in a way that satisfies SEC requirements. For example, if their shares are listed on the NYSE, and they purchase them from investors through that medium, everything looks fine. But, if they quietly buy 1,000,000 of their shares from a hedge fund or secretive trader from Bora Bora, that wouldn't work. Closed-end funds also cannot issue their securities at special prices to member firms except in connection to an offering/underwriting of securities. In other words, when the fund is capitalizing or doing an additional offer of shares, then member firms can make customary underwriting fees. But, when the closed-end fund shares are trading on the secondary market, a broker-dealer does not get to buy shares from the fund at a deep discount. Rather, trades in closed-end funds yield either commissions (broker) or markups/markdowns (dealer) to member firms executing the transactions for or with their customers, as do trades in any other common stock issues. Also, closed-end funds may not issue their shares in exchange for services rendered or for property. Why not? If you were an existing shareholder, you would only want to see new owners come in if they contributed *money* to the fund, right? The fact that they did tax planning for the principals at the fund company wouldn't help you much but would, rather, dilute your equity or devalue your ownership stake in the fund.

The names of funds and the words connected to them could end up being misleading, and we know how much the SEC hates it when investors are misled. Therefore, the Investment Company Act of 1940 stipulates:

It shall be unlawful for any person, issuing or selling any security of which a registered investment

company is the issuer, to represent or imply in any manner whatsoever that such security or company—

(A) has been guaranteed, sponsored, recommended, or approved by the United States, or any agency, instrumentality or officer of the United States;

(B) has been insured by the Federal Deposit Insurance Corporation; or

(C) is guaranteed by or is otherwise an obligation of any bank or insured depository institution.

So, whether it's the investment company itself or anyone selling the shares, the fund is not guaranteed by the United States Treasury even if every single security in the portfolio is a U.S. Treasury security. The U.S. Treasury issues their bills, notes, and bonds to whomever; they do not guarantee mutual fund companies who might decide to buy such securities as part of their business model. Similarly, the money market mutual fund is basically a worry-free investment, but it is still not a bank product and, therefore, not backed up by the FDIC or any bank. Making statements or implications that the securities you sell are safer than they are in fact is exactly the sort of thing that FINRA finds "inconsistent with high standards of commercial honor." It's a deceptive sales practice that has gotten many an agent removed from the industry.

Finally, the Investment Company Act of 1940 lays out its own penalties for larceny or embezzlement of fund assets, just in case the police or FBI weren't already all over the case. The "Act" states, "Whoever steals, unlawfully abstracts, unlawfully and willfully converts to his own use or to the use of another, or embezzles any of the moneys, funds, securities, credits, property, or assets of any registered investment company shall be deemed guilty of a crime, and upon conviction thereof shall be subject to the penalties provided in section 49. A judgment of conviction or acquittal on the merits under the laws of any State shall be a bar to any prosecution under this section for the same act or acts." That means that if somebody working for the investment adviser to the ABC Growth Fund accidentally "converts" $500,000 for her own benefit, she could be prosecuted under the Investment Company Act of 1940 in federal court if the local District Attorney's office didn't feel like making an example of her. But, if the DA does file charges, then the Investment Company Act of 1940 is not used to take another swing at her.

What are the "penalties provided in Section 49"? A $10,000 fine and/or up to five years in federal prison. But, if the defendant sustains the burden of proving he had no actual knowledge of the rule, regulation, or order, then he won't be convicted under the Act.

TAX CONSIDERATIONS

Most of us pay income taxes at several different rates due to the graduated, progressive income tax system in the United States. At the time of this writing, there are seven tax brackets. For most taxpayers, the first $9,275 of income is taxed at 10%. The next dollars earned up to $37,650 are taxed at 15%. The next dollars up to $91,150 are taxed at 25%, and so on.

Notice that we don't pay 25% on all our income just because we reach that bracket. Rather, we pay 25% on the dollars we make above a certain amount. If the highest rate of tax applied is 25%, then

25% is the taxpayer's **marginal tax rate**. An exam question might define an investor's marginal rate as "the rate of tax paid on the last dollar of income earned."

Beyond the different tax brackets there are also different methods of filing income taxes, and these methods affect the rate of taxes paid. For example, a single filer is pushed into the 15% tax bracket and then the 25% bracket at a certain dollar amount, while a married couple filing jointly would get to make twice those amounts before being pushed into the 15% and then the 25% bracket.

On the other hand, if they choose "married-filing-separately," the dollar amounts are different. Turns out a married couple choosing to file separately can each earn as much as single filers, until we get to those middle tax brackets and, suddenly, they get pushed into the 28% and 33% brackets sooner than if they'd stayed unattached. The reasoning for this is that married couples share expenses and should, therefore, be pushed into higher marginal brackets at lower dollar amounts. Those who disagree with the notion refer to it as the "marriage penalty."

There is another method of filing called "head of household." If the test question says that your client is now raising two children orphaned when her sister was killed in a car crash, that individual should file as "head of household" versus "single filer." For a "head-of-household" filer, the dollar amounts of income allowed before being pushed into the next tax bracket are much higher compared to a single filer. For example, using this method the individual would not reach the 15% bracket until her adjusted gross income rose above $13,250, compared to just $9,275 for the other methods ($18,550 for married filing jointly).

For a more detailed look: https://www.irs.com/articles/projected-us-tax-rates-2016.

Whatever the marginal tax bracket, what we're talking about is **ordinary income**. Ordinary income includes wages, salaries, bonuses, commissions, some dividends, and bond interest. We'll talk later about investments held within retirement accounts, but for now, let's talk about the regular, old taxable brokerage account.

PORTFOLIO INCOME

Bonds pay interest, and many stocks pay dividends. This income is a major part of a portfolio's total return. Unfortunately, it is also taxable.

> Dividends

Let's say you buy 1,000 shares of GE for $30 per-share. Every three months you receive a quarterly dividend of 25 cents per-share, or $250. Believe it or not, it's only taxed at a maximum rate of 15% in most cases nowadays. Before the big change to the tax code, those dividends were taxed at ordinary income rates. Many investors paying a 39% tax on dividends a few years ago are now paying no more than 15%. Imagine that. You're a wealthy individual receiving $200,000 in dividend income each year. You used to pay about $78,000 in taxes on that money; now you pay only $30,000.

But, it's also not correct to make a blanket statement such as, "Dividends are taxed at 15%." The dividends that get taxed at 15% are called **qualified dividends**. These include dividends from GE, MSFT, or most any C-corporation. But there are **ordinary dividends**, which we'll get to in a second.

First, however, why are dividends now taxed at just 15%? This relates to our look at the income statement. Remember the phrase "net income after tax"? That reminds us that corporations such as GE and MSFT pay dividends after they've paid tax on their profit. Unlike bond interest, dividends are not deducted from a company's income to reduce their tax burden. Since GE or MSFT already paid tax on the profits before paying some of them to shareholders in the form of a dividend, why should shareholders get fully taxed on that money?

Turns out they shouldn't, and they don't. We pointed out that C-corporations subject the owners to the double taxation of income, but at least, the taxation on dividends is reduced for most investors. If your marginal tax rate is 25%, 33%, or 35%, you pay only 15% on qualified dividends. But, check this out—if your tax bracket is lower than 25%, the tax you pay on qualified dividends is zero percent.

Zero. But, again, not all dividends are qualified and taxed at the kinder, gentler rates. The dividends that don't qualify for this tax treatment include ordinary dividends, which are taxed at ordinary income rates. REITs pay out 90% of their earnings pre-tax to shareholders to act as a conduit to the investors. But, since the REIT receives a tax break on the dividend, the unit holders do not. REIT investors pay ordinary dividends taxed at ordinary income rates.

For investors who reach the 39.6% marginal bracket, qualified dividends and long-term capital gains are now taxed at 20%.

Finally, I am giving you the "real-world" tax rates on dividends. The exam will likely avoid the issue entirely and say something like, "If the tax on dividends is 20%, what is Joe's after-tax return?" The exam generally wants to see if the test taker can work with a concept rather than seeing if he has memorized endless tables of data.

> Bond Interest

Interest paid on corporate and government bonds is taxable at ordinary income rates. This explains why wealthier investors often try to hold their corporate bonds in tax-advantaged accounts, which we'll discuss in a few pages. Corporate bond interest is taxable at the federal, state, and local government levels, while US government bond interest is taxable at the federal level exclusively.

Corporate bond interest is taxable in states that have an income tax, and even a few cities tax the corporate bond interest that their residents earn. GNMA, FNMA, and FHLMC are taxable at the federal, state, and local levels, also, just like corporate bonds.

> Taxation of municipal securities

The interest on general obligation bonds is tax-exempt at the federal level, but your state could tax the interest if you buy a bond from an out-of-state issuer. If you live in Georgia and buy a bond issued by the State of Alabama, Georgia can tax that interest. Plus, if you live in Atlanta, Georgia, and Atlanta has a tax on bond interest, your city could tax you as well.

How could you avoid being taxed by Georgia and the city of Atlanta? Buy a bond issued by Atlanta, Georgia. The state will give you a break, and so will Atlanta.

Finally, if you live in Atlanta and buy a bond issued by Valdosta, Georgia, the federal government will give you the tax break, and so will the State of Georgia, since both Valdosta and Atlanta are in that state. But, what about Atlanta—did you help them out? No, so they can tax you. How do you get Atlanta off your back? Buy one of their municipal securities. You help us finance our schools, we'll help you reduce your tax burden.

SITUATION	FEDERAL	STATE	LOCAL
Resident of Topeka, KS, buys a Toledo, OH, municipal bond	EXEMPT	TAXABLE	TAXABLE
Resident of Topeka, KS, buys a Wichita, KS, municipal bond	EXEMPT	EXEMPT	TAXABLE
Resident of Topeka, KS, buys a Topeka, KS, municipal bond	EXEMPT	EXEMPT	EXEMPT

Not all municipal securities pay tax-free interest. The ones used for public purpose/essential services do, but if the tax code says that the bond is a "private activity" bond, the interest is subject to **alternative minimum tax** (**AMT**). Most municipal bond investors are subject to AMT, which would force them to add some of the interest received on a private activity bond back into their taxable income. For that reason, **private activity bonds** usually offer higher yields (before tax). An example of a private activity bond is a bond issued to finance a parking garage that will be operated by a private company, or bonds issued to build a sports stadium. If the exam says your customer wants a municipal bond but is concerned about AMT, put her into a general obligation bond, such as a school bond. Or look for the concept of "essential, public purpose."

And, some municipal bonds are taxable. For example, if a public university has already issued a certain amount of GO debt that is outstanding, additional bond issues could be taxable, requiring the issuer to offer much higher yields to investors. Or, if the bond issue is a refunding issue used to call bonds, there is no exemption for the interest paid to investors in that case, either.

So far, we have been discussing the income that securities provide to investors through interest and dividend payments.

➢ Capital Gains

On the other hand, think of a **capital gain** as the profit you take when you sell a security for more than you bought it.

Back to our GE example. You bought 1,000 shares @$30 each. Let's say you sell 100 shares for $40 to take a vacation. If you held GE for more than 1 year, you'd realize a long-term gain of $1,000, since $10 times 100 shares = $1,000 in capital gains. Go ahead and take your vacation, and at the end of the year, you'll owe Uncle Sam 15% of that $1,000, or $150. Your state may tax the gain as well. And, if you're in the top tax bracket of 39.6%, you pay 20% to the U.S. Treasury.

If you had sold that stock within a year, the gain would be taxed at your ordinary income rate since it's a short-term capital gain. If your ordinary income rate is 25%, you owe the IRS $250. If it's 35%, you only kept $650 of that capital gain when the dust settles.

A capital gain is the difference between your **proceeds** (what you sell it for) and your **cost basis** (what you paid for it). Think of your "cost basis" as all the money that has gone into an investment after being taxed. When you buy GE for $30 a share, you don't deduct that from taxable income, so $30 a share is your cost basis. You also pay a commission in most cases, so you add that to your cost basis. When you bought 1,000 shares of GE @$30, you paid a $50 commission. So, while we used round numbers above to introduce the concept, your cost basis is really $3,050 divided by 1,000 shares, or $30.05 per-share.

If an investor purchases shares of the same stock at different times and for different prices, there are different methods of determining the cost basis when he sells the stock someday. For example, if he bought 100 shares for $50, 100 shares for $60, and 100 shares for $75 over the past several years, which 100 did he just sell? The IRS assumes the method used is **first in first out (FIFO)**. That means, he just sold the shares with the $50 cost basis, leading to a much larger taxable capital gain vs. using the shares purchased for $75.

Could he use the $75 cost basis? Yes, but he and the broker-dealer would have to identify the shares with the **CUSIP number** when the sell order is placed. That method is called **share identification**.

The method many investors use is **average cost**, in which they total all the money spent on the shares and divide that by the current number of shares. This method is available only when a broker-dealer or other custodian holds the shares on the investor's behalf.

> Proceeds

Broker-dealers charge commissions when customers buy and when they sell securities. So, when you buy shares of GE, you add the commission to the cost basis, and when you sell those shares of GE, you subtract the commission from your proceeds. If you sell 100 shares of GE @40 and pay a $50 commission, your proceeds would be $3,950, or $39.50 per-share. On your tax returns for the year in which you sell the stock, you would report that your proceeds were $3,950, while your cost basis on those 100 shares was $3,005. The capital gain on that sale is $945.

> Holding Period

If you sell a security held for one year or less, that is a short-term gain or loss. If it's a gain, it is taxed at your marginal rate. If you hold a security for more than one year, that is considered a long-term gain or loss. If it's a gain, it is taxed at the same 15% currently used for qualified dividends for most investors (0% for low-bracket, 20% for top-bracket investors).

One advantage of a buy-and-hold investment strategy is that any gains will likely be taxed at the lower long-term capital gains rates. This helps portfolio performance.

How do you count your **holding period**? In Publication 564 the IRS explains:

> To find out how long you have held your shares, begin counting on the day after the trade date on which you bought the shares. (Do not count the trade date itself.) The trade date on which you dispose of the shares is counted as part of your holding period. If you bought shares on May 6 of last year (trade date), and sold them on May 6 of this year (trade date), your holding period would not be

more than 1 year. If you sold them on May 7ᵗʰ of this year, your holding period would be more than 1 year (12 months plus 1 day).

As with qualified dividends, if the investor's marginal tax rate hits 25-35%, he pays no more than 15% tax on long-term capital gains, and if his marginal rate is lower than that, he could end up paying zero percent on capital gains. Zero percent.

> ## Capital Losses

You don't pay the tax on the day you sell the stock. Rather, you figure it into your income taxes when you file for the year. But you'll want to keep track of the gain, because the IRS will want to know, and because when you sit down with your accountant at the end of the year, you might decide to sell some other stocks at a loss to balance out that gain. You took a $945 gain on GE. If you sell another stock at a $1,000 **capital loss**, you'd end up at zero capital gains for the year.

Congratulations, you made no money this year. And, therefore, you have no capital gains taxes to pay. You could sell even more stock at a loss. If you lost, say, $10,000 for the year, you could use $3,000 of your total or net loss to offset (reduce) your adjusted gross income for the year. So, if your AGI was going to be $53,000, now it's only $50,000. That reduces your tax bill.

But you really did lose money. See the relationship? If you're paying no tax, it's because you're making no money. If you're paying taxes, it's because you're making money. Personally, I prefer the latter, but that's not the point, and many would argue that it's better to reduce your tax burden than to have the misfortune of making money in the stock market.

Some will even purposely take a net loss for the year and continue to carry the excess that's over the $3,000 limit forward. I know a few investors who have enough capital losses to last the rest of their lives, $3,000 at a time. They took about $100,000 in capital losses in 2002, and it's going to take quite some time to use that up at three grand a year.

Lucky devils.

> ## Wash Sale Rules

So, the "benefit" of selling securities at a loss is that you can offset your ordinary income by up to $3,000 per year. But, to use that loss, stay out of that stock for at least 30 days. If you sell MSFT at a loss, don't buy any Microsoft stock for 30 days. And, you could not have purchased any 30 days *before* you made the sale, either.

Also, don't get clever and buy warrants, convertible bonds, convertible preferred stock or call options that convert to Microsoft common stock. Just take your capital loss and stay out of Microsoft for 30 days both before and after the sale.

What if you promise not to buy any Microsoft common stock over the next 30 days but can't stop yourself? Then, you can't use the loss now to offset ordinary income on your taxes because of wash sale rules. Never fear, though, because if you took a $7-per-share loss on Microsoft, you would add $7 per-share to your cost basis on the new purchase. If you were to repurchase MSFT @$40, your cost basis would be $47. In other words, you would eventually get the benefit of that loss you took, but not now. And, if you recall our discussion of the time value of money, now is always a better time to get those dollars rather than at some point in the future.

When you sell a bond at a loss, there is a similar rule. Either wait 30 days to buy a replacement, or, if you want to sell a GE bond at a loss and buy another GE bond, you'll need to substantially alter some features of the bond: interest rate, maturity, call feature, or some combination. Or, just buy a bond from a different issuer. The test might call this process a **bond swap**.

When an investor makes regular and frequent investments into a mutual fund, he would typically end up executing wash sales whenever selling shares for a loss. Why? Chances are he either bought or is about to buy more of the same shares with his automatic investments.

➢ Unrealized Capital Gains

An **unrealized capital gain** is just an increase in value, a "paper gain," as some say. There is no tax to pay just because your asset has become more valuable. As with your house, you owe no capital gains tax on your securities just because they have gone up in value. Only if the investor sells the security or the house and realizes a profit would there be a capital gains tax to pay.

➢ Capital Gain or Loss on a primary residence

Selling a house for a capital gain is usually more pleasant than doing the same with shares of stock. If a homeowner owns and lives in a primary residence any two of the previous five years leading up to the sale of the property, any capital gain taken when he sells his house is tax-free up to $250,000 for individuals and up to $500,000 for married couples. He must meet the "ownership and use tests" to claim up to those maximum amounts. But, even if he doesn't meet the two-year ownership and use tests, he may qualify for a reduced maximum amount if suffering a financial or health-related hardship.

If two people jointly own a house, each could claim up to $250,000 on his or her separate return. A married couple claiming up to $500,000 as a tax-free capital gain is required to file jointly for the year they take advantage of this maneuver. For more information look up IRS Publication 523.

What about a capital loss on a primary residence? What if you put on a $100,000 addition to your house but end up selling for less than your cost basis? That is always painful. If you wanted to take a capital loss on your primary residence, you would first need to convert it to a rental property. If you rent it out, you can take depreciation on the property as we did under our look at partnerships. And, now, if you end up selling for less than your cost basis, you do get to claim a capital loss to offset taxable capital gains for the year.

Then again, if you have no capital gains for the year, that loss doesn't help much.

MUTUAL FUND TAXATION

The owner of the securities inside a mutual fund is the investment company itself. The fund sells pieces of this portfolio to investors in the form of common stock.

➤ Income Dividends

So, like any common stockholder, a mutual fund holder will probably receive dividends. A stock mutual fund earns dividends from the stocks that they own. A bond fund receives regular interest payments on their fixed-income portfolio. A balanced fund earns both dividends and interest from the securities held in the portfolio. The funds pay expenses with that money and if there's a profit left over, they distribute it to the shareholders. The shareholders receive convenient **1099-DIV** statements that help keep track of this income, which will be taxable at some rate.

If it's a stock fund, the investor is taxed at ordinary or qualified dividend rates, depending on the composition of the fund.

If it's a bond fund, income checks will be taxed just like bond interest, because that's where the income is derived. If it's a government bond fund, the interest is only taxable at the federal level. If it's a corporate bond fund, the interest is taxable at all levels. And if it's a municipal bond fund, the interest is tax-exempt at the federal level, but the investor's state government often taxes the interest received on out-of-state municipal bonds. For that reason, there are many state-specific municipal bond mutual funds for residents of high-tax states such as California, Virginia, and Maryland.

➤ Capital Gains in Mutual Funds

There are two ways that capital gains come into play for mutual funds. If the investment adviser realizes more gains than losses, the fund realizes a net gain for the year. They can either distribute this to the shareholders or not. Either way, investors are taxed on their proportional share of this capital gain. That's the trouble with investing in funds that buy low and sell high. It's called a capital gain, and the **capital gains distribution** is taxed at the investor's long-term capital gains rate.

> Distributions to Shareholders

A fund almost always makes sure that when it takes a capital gain, it's a long-term capital gain, since, as we saw, the difference to a high-tax-bracket investor could be significant. Assume it's a long-term gain on the exam. Could it be a short-term gain?

Sure, but that is the exception rather than the rule.

We've been saying that the interest on U.S. Treasury securities is exempt from state and local taxation, and it is. Notice we've said nothing about capital gains until now. Yes, capital gains (not interest payments) on U.S. Treasuries are taxable at the federal, state, and local levels.

And, on the tax-free front, even though the dividend checks received from tax-exempt municipal bond funds are usually tax-exempt at the federal level, any capital gains distributions are treated as capital gains.

> Shareholder Sales

The second capital gains issue with mutual funds is within the investor's control, just as it is on a share of GE or MSFT. If she sells her mutual fund shares within a year, any gain is a short-term gain, taxed at her ordinary income rate. If she holds them for more than one year, it's a long-term gain, taxed at a maximum of 15% for most investors.

If a mutual fund buys a stock at $10, and the stock now trades at $15, there is no tax to pay. Unrealized gains make the NAV of the fund go up, but that doesn't affect the investor unless or until A) the fund realizes a gain on the shares by selling for a profit, or B) the investor does by redeeming his shares at a higher value.

➢ Cost Basis on Reinvestments

Many investors choose not to take the income and capital gains distributions as checks. Rather, they apply that money towards more shares of the fund, which they buy without a sales load (at the NAV). Since the distributions are taxed either way, the investor adds to her cost basis by the amount of the distribution.

Let's say she bought the ACE Equity Income Fund at $10 per-share. Last year, she received $1 in dividends and $1 in capital gains distributions per-share. If she reinvests the $2 per-share, she pays tax on that amount, and her cost basis rises by that amount, too.

TAXATION OF ANNUITIES

➢ Accumulation Period

During the accumulation phase of a deferred variable annuity, the investment grows tax-deferred. So, all the dividends and capital gains distributions from the subaccounts are reinvested into more units, just like most people reinvest distributions back into a mutual fund. If the individual dies, the death benefit is paid to the beneficiary. The death benefit is included in the annuitant's **estate** for estate tax purposes, and the beneficiary pays tax on anything above the cost basis. If the husband bought the annuity for $50,000, and it's now worth $60,000, she'll receive $60,000 and pay ordinary income rates on the $10,000 of earnings.

Sometimes people cash in their contract earlier than expected. If they're under 59½ and don't have a qualifying exemption, they will not only pay ordinary income tax on the earnings, but also a 10% penalty tax, too. So, if it's a $60,000 annuity, and a 49-year-old surrenders the contract that he bought for $50,000, he'd pay his ordinary income rate on the $10,000 of earnings and a 10% penalty of $1,000. You didn't think the IRS would, like, penalize him 10% and then take his ordinary income rate on what's left, did you? It's his ordinary income rate plus 10% of the excess over his cost basis.

Notice how only the excess over cost basis is taxed and/or penalized on a non-qualified annuity. The cost basis was taxed before it went into the account.

So, if he's not 59½ yet, the IRS is giving him all kinds of reasons not to surrender the contract. And, we already mentioned that the insurance company will keep a percentage on the back end if he surrenders during the early years of the contract. So, he can have his money if he wants to, but if he takes it out too soon, there will be penalties and taxes to deal with.

> 72(t) and Substantially Equal Periodic Payments

We've mentioned that the magic age for taking distributions is 59½ because, otherwise, the individual is hit with early withdrawal penalties. Annuities are by nature retirement plans and are subject to the 10% penalty for early withdrawals made without a qualifying exemption. One exemption available is to utilize IRS rule "**72(t)**." A reference to "72t" relates to an individual taking a series of substantially equal periodic payments (SEPP). The IRS won't penalize the early withdrawal if the individual sets up a schedule whereby he or she withdraws the money by any of several IRS-approved methods.

Once he starts the SEPP program, he must stay on it. The IRS requires him to continue the SEPP program for five years or until he is 59½, whichever comes last. So, if the individual is 45, she'll have to keep taking periodic payments until she's 59½. If the individual is 56 when she starts, she'll have to continue for 5 years. Either that, or cut the IRS a check for the penalties she was trying to avoid.

> Loans

Some insurance companies allow contract owners to take a loan against the value of the annuity during the accumulation period. Usually, the interest charge is handled by reducing the number of accumulation units owned. If the owner pays back the loan in full, the number of units goes up again. Unlike a loan against a life insurance policy, however, a loan from an annuity is treated as a distribution. In other words, it is not tax-free.

> 1035 Exchanges

Both annuities and insurance policies allow the contract owner to exchange their contract for another without paying taxes. That's fine, just don't forget the surrender period. If someone has a 6% surrender fee in effect, and an agent pushes them to do a 1035 exchange, the IRS won't have a problem with it, but FINRA almost certainly will.

Also, this isn't the same thing as a life insurance contract. With a life insurance policy, people often cash in part of their **cash value**. If they're only taking out what they put in—or less—the IRS treats it as part of their cost basis. In an annuity, however, if someone does a **random withdrawal** for, say, $10,000, the IRS considers that to be part of the taxable earnings first.

Most annuities are non-qualified, which means they are purchased with non-tax-deductible dollars. When you cut the check for, say, $50,000 for the annuity, you get no tax deduction from the IRS that year against adjusted gross income. In other words, that $50,000 was taxed that year, so the tax collectors won't tax that money again when you take it out someday. That $50,000 will be your cost basis. You will only pay taxes on the amount of earnings above that and only when you finally take out the money.

On the other hand, a "tax-qualified variable annuity" or "individual retirement annuity" is funded with pre-tax or tax-deductible contributions with the same maximums used for Traditional IRA accounts. Like the Traditional IRA—and unlike the non-qualified variable annuity—withdrawals from the IRA annuity account must begin at age 70½.

The IRS refers to these plans as "individual retirement annuities," and they are basically just IRAs funded with an investment into a variable annuity. Why do that? Probably for the death benefit during the accumulation phase that guarantees your beneficiaries will receive at least the amount you contributed. Or, some people like the idea of an annuity payout that lasts for as long as they live, perhaps longer.

So, most questions focus on non-qualified variable annuities funded with after-tax dollars. But, don't be shocked if you get a question about variable annuities funded with tax-deductible dollars.

> Annuity Period

When the annuitant begins receiving monthly checks, part of each check is considered taxable ordinary income, and part of it is considered part of the cost basis. Once the annuitant has received all the cost basis back, each additional annuity payment will be fully taxable.

Also, if the beneficiary is receiving annuity payments through a "life with period certain" or a "joint with last survivor" settlement option, she will pay ordinary income tax on part of each monthly check, too—as always, on the "excess over cost basis."

TAXATION OF LIFE INSURANCE

When we pay life insurance premiums, we don't take a deduction against income, so they are made after-tax. They usually grow tax-deferred, however, which is nice. When the insured dies, the beneficiary receives the death benefit free and clear of federal income taxes. But the death benefit is added to the insured's estate to determine estate taxes. It's that simple when the beneficiary has the lump-sum settlement option, anyway. If we're talking about those periodic settlement options that generate interest, some of those payments could be taxed as interest income.

Rather than take a loan, the policyholder can also do a "partial surrender," whereby the policyholder takes out some of the cash value—not enough to make the policy lapse, of course. Depending on how much has been paid in premiums, taxes may be due on the amount withdrawn. Unlike for variable annuities, the IRS uses FIFO here, assuming the first thing coming out is the cost basis, not the earnings. Only the part taken out above the premiums paid would be taxed.

If a loan is taken out, there are no immediate tax consequences.

TRANSFERRED SECURITIES

A securities issuer's transfer agent keeps track of the transfers of ownership among shareholders. Usually a transfer of ownership is the result of a sale, but there are other ways to transfer ownership of stock. Stock can be inherited, received as a gift, or received as a charitable donation.

> Inherited Securities

What if your grandmother bought stock at $10 a share several decades ago and passed it to you through her will when she—you know? What is your cost basis? Whatever the stock was worth on the day your grandmother—you know. If it's worth $30 on the date of death, then that's your cost basis, $30. For an inherited stock the recipient steps up the cost basis to the fair market value on the date of death. If the recipient sells the stock for $30 when the stepped-up basis is $30, there are no capital gains taxes.

Also, if the recipient sells this stock for more than $30, the capital gain is treated as long-term no matter how long he holds it. Most estates close out within a few months. If they liquidate the securities for more than the cost basis, there is a capital gain, but it's treated as long-term, even if it all happened in a few months.

The heirs who inherit appreciated securities can either value them as of the date of death or six months after. Estates often close out within six months and would, therefore, find it easier to value the stocks and bonds as of the date they sell it to cut checks to all the beneficiaries named in the will and trigger no capital gains taxes.

If they want to value the securities as of six months after the date of death, they must value all assets as of that date. That means the estate may be required to pay a real estate appraiser to value the house as of the same date the securities are valued. When the house is sold, the buyer might not be willing to pay the appraised value, or even if the house is sold for the appraised value, there are generally seller's expenses. In either case, the estate could end up showing a loss on the sale of the deceased's primary residence, or on the securities for that matter.

➤ Gifted Securities

What if Grandma decided to give you the stock while she's alive? In that case, you would take her original cost basis of $10. If the stock is worth $40 when you sell it, your gain is $30 a share. Not like when you inherited the shares. Then, your gain would have only been $10.

You would take over Grandma's holding period, and not necessarily have to hold it for 12 months plus one day to get the long-term capital gains treatment. If she has already held the stock for years, your holding period is also long-term.

➤ Tax-deductible Charitable Donations

What if Grandma decided to donate the stock to a charity instead of giving it to her grandkids? If she does that, she deducts the fair market value of the stock on the date of the donation. If it's worth $30,000 when she donates it, she can deduct $30,000 when figuring her taxes--up to a maximum of 40% of her adjusted gross income for the year.

What should an investor do if he has a stock that has appreciated significantly and one that has gone down in value? A good tax move might be for him to donate the appreciated stock to a charity and sell the loser for a capital loss. This way he will avoid a capital gain on the appreciated stock while also getting the tax deduction. And, he can use the capital loss on the other position to offset other gains or even some of his ordinary income. From there, he can donate the cash to a charity, or, of course, find other uses for it.

AMT

If an investor is in a certain income bracket, he is subject to an "Alternative Minimum Tax," or "AMT." That means that even though people say that municipal bonds pay tax-free interest, he will report *some* municipal bond interest on his AMT form as a "tax preference item." Generally, municipal bonds that are considered "private purpose" by the tax code subject investors to reporting income on their AMT forms. That's why many tax-exempt mutual funds also buy bonds that are not subject to AMT taxes.

The following is from IRS Publication 556 – Alternative Minimum Tax.

> The tax laws give preferential treatment to certain kinds of income and allow special deductions and credits for certain kinds of expenses. The alternative

minimum tax attempts to ensure that anyone who benefits from these tax advantages pays at least a minimum amount of tax. The alternative minimum tax is a separately figured tax that eliminates many deductions and credits, thus increasing tax liability for an individual who would otherwise pay less tax. The tentative minimum tax rates on ordinary income are percentages set by law. For capital gains, the capital gains rates for the regular tax are used. You may have to pay the alternative minimum tax if your taxable income for regular tax purposes plus any adjustments and preference items that apply to you are more than the exemption amount.

A test question might also bring up the fact that the owner of a limited partnership interest will be required to consult the instructions to his K-1 and may have to add certain tax preference items such as "accelerated depreciation" to his AMT form. The test question might say that "straight-line depreciation" would not be a tax preference item.

PROGRESSIVE AND REGRESSIVE

Progressive taxes include income, estate, and gift taxes. The bigger the income, estate, or gift, the higher the percentage rate the IRS charges.

Estates that are large get taxed, too. So, when Bill Gates passes away, his heirs will receive a ton of money, but the IRS will take some first in the form of estate taxes. The bigger the estate, the higher the rate of taxation. Progressive.

A **regressive** tax, on the other hand, is a flat tax. A list of regressive taxes would include sales, gas, payroll, and excise taxes. Everyone pays the same rate there. When you check out your items at Walmart, the cashier doesn't ask you your marginal tax bracket before giving you your total, right? No, it's a flat tax. Just like gas taxes are applied equally to gallons of gas whether they're pumped into a clunker or a Cadillac.

Lower-income Americans put a higher percent of their incomes into buying gasoline than high-income Americans do. If the secretary and the CEO both drive to work, they consume a similar amount of gasoline and pay a similar amount of gas taxes. If the amount of tax is, say, $800, that represents a much higher percentage of the secretary's income than it does the CEO's.

Unlike with income taxes, as the income levels drop, a flat tax represents a larger percentage of income. So, while the secretary's income might be taxed at no more than 15%, the gas and sales taxes she pays represent a much higher percent of her income than they do for the CEO in this example.

CORPORATE TAXES

Corporate profits are taxed at corporate tax rates. On the income statement bond interest is deducted pre-tax, while profits are taxed before dividends are paid to shareholders. Corporate profits (net income after tax) are taxed at that corporation's tax rate.

On the other hand, some companies use the IRS's Subchapter M to set themselves up as a "conduit" to investors. REITs do this. Many mutual funds do it, too. If a mutual fund has $1,000,000 in net income, for example, they often send at least 90% of it (900K) to shareholders as a dividend or "income" distribution. That way, the mutual fund company only pays tax on the remaining $100,000.

The shareholders pay tax on the money the fund sends them. The company must send at least 90% of its net income to qualify for this tax treatment, and they can send more if they want.

When a corporation invests in the stocks of other companies, they receive dividends like any other investor. Unlike ordinary investors, though, the corporation receiving these dividends from shares of other companies' stock gets to exclude the first 70% from tax. That means they only get taxed on 30% of what they receive. And, if they're really an owner of the other company because they own 20% or more of it, they can exclude 80% of the income from tax. Berkshire Hathaway purchases smaller companies outright. They typically receive preferred dividends from those acquired companies, and if the smaller entity is being taxed on the net income, why should the parent company be fully taxed, too?

On the other hand, if a corporation holds the bonds of another corporation, they do not get to deduct any of the interest. That's because the company who paid the interest already deducted it from their taxable income. Municipal bond interest is tax-exempt to a corporate owner just as it is to any other owner.

RETIREMENT PLANS

In a taxable account the principal is reduced each year when the investor is taxed on interest, dividends, and capital gains. In a tax-deferred account the principal is not taxed unless and until the individual finally takes distributions. The account balance grows faster when it is growing on a tax-deferred basis.

Tax-deferral is an advantage offered by deferred annuities and through retirement accounts. Whether one's contribution is tax-deductible, the fact that the interest, dividends, and capital gains will not be taxed each year is an advantage to the investor. That's why so many individuals participate in at least one retirement plan. Some retirement plans are started by the individual, and some are offered through an employer.

Let's start with the plans an individual can open, provided he has **earned income.** Earned income includes salary, bonuses, tips, alimony, and any income derived from actively participating in a business. It does not include passive income such as rental income from an apartment building or portfolio income such as bond interest, dividends, or capital gains.

Retirement plans are for working people who need to save up for retirement. If someone's sole source of income is rent checks or dividends, he probably doesn't need to save for retirement. And, if he does, he'll just have to do it outside a retirement account.

INDIVIDUAL PLANS

An **IRA** is an **Individual Retirement Account**, or an Individual Retirement Arrangement.

➢ Traditional

To contribute to a **Traditional IRA** the individual must be younger than 70 ½ and have earned income for the year. If the individual's income consists solely of dividends and bond interest, he can't make an IRA contribution for that year.

Contributions to an IRA are tax-deductible. If he contributes $5,000 to his IRA this year, that $5,000 no longer counts as taxable income. If he was going to pay tax on $52,000, now it's only $47,000 of taxable income for the year.

If he does have earned income for the year, an individual can contribute 100% of that earned income up to the current maximum. So, if she earns $1,800, then $1,800 is her maximum IRA contribution for that year. People 50 years and older can add a **catch-up contribution**. That amount is currently an extra $1,000.

At the time of writing, the maximum contribution to a Traditional IRA is $5,500, $6,500 for those 50 or older.

> Penalties

Over-funding an IRA results in a 6% penalty on the amount above the maximum contribution for the year and any earnings associated with it. If the individual realizes she has over-funded her IRA for the year, she can remove the excess by the tax filing deadline the following year, or re-characterize the excess as part of the following year's contributions. If it's March 17, 2017 when she realizes she has over-funded her IRA by $1,000 for 2016, she can remove the $1,000 to avoid a penalty or fill out a form to re-characterize it as part of her 2017 contributions. If she does nothing, she pays a 6% penalty.

While we can always pull the money out of a Traditional IRA, if we take it out before age 59½, we'll pay a 10% penalty on top of the ordinary income tax that we always pay on withdrawals from IRAs. However, the following are qualifying exemptions to the 10% penalty. Although the withdrawal is taxable, the 10% penalty is waived for withdrawals made pursuant to:

- Death
- Permanent disability
- First home purchase for residential purposes

- A series of substantially equal periodic payments under IRS Rule 72-t
- Medical expenses
- Higher education expenses

A withdrawal pursuant to death means that the IRA owner has died and someone else is receiving the account balance as a named beneficiary. The beneficiary will be taxed but will not be penalized because the account owner died before age 59 1/2.

So, an individual can't have the money until he's 59½ without paying a penalty unless he uses one of the exemptions above. That's on the front end.

On the back end, he also is required to start taking it out by the time he's 70½. If not, the IRS will impose a 50% insufficient distribution penalty. We're talking about RMDs here, or **required minimum distributions**. When someone turns 70½, he has until April 1st of the following year to take out at least the required minimum distribution. If not, the IRS will levy a 50% penalty.

That's 50% of what he should have taken out at this point, not half the account value.

The absolute latest date that an individual can take his first withdrawal from a Traditional IRA without penalty is April 1st following the year he turns 70 1/2 . However, if he does that, he must take *two* distributions that year, which can push him into a higher tax bracket and make more of his social security benefits taxable. So, it's easier to take the first distribution in the year the individual turns 70½.

Unlike the Roth IRA, no contributions can be made into the Traditional IRA after age 70½.

➢ Roth

The **Roth IRA** is funded with non-deductible contributions. However, the money comes out tax-free in retirement if the individual is 59½ years old and has had the account at least 5 years.

In retirement, then, the withdrawals you take from a Traditional IRA are taxable income. If you withdraw $30,000, you might only keep $22,000 after-tax. A withdrawal of $30,000 from your Roth IRA, on the other hand, leaves you with $30,000 to spend.

Unlike the Traditional, for the Roth IRA there is no requirement to take a distribution by age 70½. Since the IRS isn't going to tax that money, they couldn't care less when or even if it is withdrawn. In fact, individuals can keep contributing if they have earned income. So, a 72-year-old can refrain from taking Roth IRA withdrawals and can keep making contributions into the account if she has earned income. Neither option is available, on the other hand, for her Traditional IRA.

If the individual or married couple have adjusted gross incomes above a certain amount, they cannot contribute to their Roth IRAs. Period. So, get those Roth IRA accounts started while you're young and before you strike it rich. The money you contribute in your 20s and 30s can compound for decades, even if the IRS cuts off new contributions by age 40 based on your income.

If an individual has both a Traditional and a Roth IRA, the contribution limit is the total allocated among the two accounts. As I said, that is currently either $5,500 or $6,500 depending on age.

Also, the Roth IRA allows the individual to remove her cost basis, or the amount she has contributed, after five years without penalty. So, if he has contributed $25,000 into a Roth IRA and seven years later the account is worth $40,000, he could take the $25,000 out without a penalty and keep the remainder of $15,000 in the account. He could not put that $25,000 back in, however, and would not earn the tax-deferred and tax-free returns going forward.

But, as always, it's his money.

➢ Converting a Traditional to a Roth IRA

Some individuals start out with a Traditional IRA and then decide to convert it to a Roth IRA. This requires the individual to pay tax on the entire amount going into the new Roth IRA, since Roth IRAs are funded with after-tax dollars. Even if the individual makes too much money to contribute to his Roth IRA, he can convert a Traditional IRA to a Roth IRA.

➢ Investment Restrictions

I'm not sure why they do it, but some people like to use their Traditional IRA to invest in collectible items such as artwork, Persian rugs, antiques, coins, gems, stamps, etc. Funds withdrawn from the IRA to buy such items are considered distributed, which means the individual would pay ordinary income rates, plus a 10% penalty if he is not yet 59½.

US-minted gold or silver bullion coins are allowed, as they have intrinsic value. Collectible coins, on the other hand, are not suitable. Municipal bonds typically make poor investments for a Traditional IRA. Municipal bonds pay tax-exempt interest, which is why their coupon payments are so low. All money coming out of the Traditional IRA is taxed, so the municipal bond's tax-advantage is destroyed and all the individual is left with is a lower coupon payment.

➢ Rollovers and Transfers

To move an IRA from one custodian to another, the best bet is to do a **direct transfer**. Just have the custodian cut a check to the new custodian. The IRA owner can do as many of these direct transfers as he wants. If, however, he does a **rollover**, things get tricky. First, he can only do one per year, and, second, it must be completed within 60 days to avoid tax ramifications.

In a rollover, the custodian cuts a check in the individual's name. The account owner cashes it and then sends the money to the new custodian, but any shortfall is subject to taxes and a 10% penalty. If the individual withdrew $50,000 but could only come up with $10,000 sixty days later, that $40,000 difference is taxed as ordinary income, plus a penalty tax of $4,000.

EMPLOYER-BASED PLANS

Plans offered through an employer either define the benefit to be received when the employee retires or the contributions made into the account. Usually, it is only the contributions that are defined.

➢ Defined Contribution Plans

A **defined contribution plan** only defines the contributions the employer and/or the employee can make into the plan. The employer is not defining or promising any benefit at retirement. We'll talk about **defined benefit pension plans** in a bit, but let's focus first on the more familiar defined contribution plans.

At many companies new employees receive paperwork to fill out concerning the **401(k) plan** sponsored by the employer as an employee benefit. The employees choose a few mutual funds, and tell the HR department to deduct X amount from their paychecks to go into the 401(k) account. This way, part of their salary goes straight into a retirement fund and is not taxable currently, just like the money that goes into a Traditional IRA. Pretty attractive, especially if the employer matches what the employees elect to defer from each paycheck.

The amount of the employee's contribution is known as an **elective deferral.** Employers generally match all or part of an employee's elective deferral up to a certain percentage of compensation, as stipulated in their plan literature. But, they are not required to make **matching contributions**. Why might someone choose to participate in a 401(k) even if the company was not matching contributions? Maybe he likes the higher maximum contribution limit vs. the IRA or Roth IRA.

The advantage to a business owner setting up a 401(k) plan is that a vesting schedule can be laid out over several years, meaning that the employer's contributions don't belong to the employee until he is fully vested. However, 401(k) plans come with complicated **top-heavy** rules, which means the plan cannot provide benefits to just the key, highly compensated employees. A plan in which 60% of the benefits go to key employees is a plan that shows signs of being "top-heavy," and will be required to adjust things or deal with tax problems.

For-profit companies offer 401(k) plans to their employees. Non-profit organizations such as schools and hospitals offer **403(b) plans** to their employees. As with a 401(k) plan, the employee indicates how much of her paycheck should go into the 403(b) account, which simultaneously gives her a tax break now and helps her save up for retirement later. As with a 401(k) plan, the contributions go in pre-tax but come out fully taxable when the participant starts taking distributions.

While a 401(k) plan might offer participants the ability to purchase stocks and bonds a la carte, a 403(b) plan only offers annuities and mutual funds as investment vehicles. The 403(b) plans can also be referred to as **Tax-Sheltered Annuities** or **TSAs**.

Some states and cities have begun to shift the burden of funding retirement benefits to their employees. These so-called **457 plans** are for state and local government employees, e.g., police and fire workers. Contributions are tax-deductible, and the plans use the same maximum contribution limits used by 401(k) and 403(b) plans.

Profit sharing plans are also defined contribution plans, but the contributions are never required. If the company does contribute, it must be made for all eligible employees based on a predetermined formula. For example, maybe all workers receive up to 10% of their salaries when the company has a banner year. The profit-sharing plan uses much higher maximum annual contributions than the 401(k), 403(b) or Section 457 plans. Of course, that would only matter if you happened to work for a profitable and generous employer.

A **money purchase plan** is not flexible the way a profit sharing plan is. The money purchase plan requires the employer to make a mandatory contribution to each employee's account, based on his/her salary, whether the company feels like it or not. The exam might say something like "in a money purchase plan, contributions are mandatory on the part of the employer and discretionary on the part of the employee."

Keogh plans are for individuals with self-employment income or for those working for a sole proprietorship with a Keogh plan in place. They're not for S-corps, C-corps, LLCs, etc.—only sole proprietors. If the individual in the test question has side income or is self-employed, he or she can have a Keogh. They can contribute a certain percentage of their self-employment income into the Keogh.

How much? A lot. As with the SEP-IRA, the business owner can put 20% of her compensation into a Keogh, and she can put in 25% of her employees' compensation. Some readers find it shocking that there may be employees at a "sole" proprietorship. But, trust me, there can be. A "sole proprietorship" is just a business with one owner, a guy doing business as himself. The number of employees he has? Anybody's guess. Also, to avoid confusion, remember we said that Keogh plans are for sole proprietorships only; we did not say that sole proprietorships can only have a Keogh plan. A SEP-IRA or SIMPLE IRA would also be available to a sole proprietor, for example.

A small business can establish a **SEP-IRA**, which stands for "Simplified Employee Pension" IRA. This allows the business owner to make pre-tax contributions for herself and any eligible employees. Twenty-five percent of wages can be contributed to an employee's SEP, up to the current maximum. SEP contributions are not mandatory on the part of the business owner. It's just that if the business makes any contributions, they must be made to all eligible employees as stipulated in the plan agreement.

Notice how the business makes the contributions, not the employees. So, if you're self-employed, you can contribute to your own SEP-IRA, but if you're an employee at a company with a SEP-IRA, it's the company who will make the contributions on your behalf. To establish a SEP, the employer uses a model agreement put out by the IRS (download it from www.irs.gov) that they and the employees sign. It does not have to be filed with the IRS, which does not issue an opinion or approval.

Keep in mind that even though a large contribution can be made to a SEP-IRA, that amount must represent 25% of wages. In other words, we often focus on the maximum amounts that can be contributed, but to make contributions at all the small business owner must be making a profit, and when contributing for employees, the contributions are 25% of wages. That means that the only way to put a lot of money into a SEP-IRA is to earn a lot of money—since 25% of a $33,000 salary is not going to make for a large contribution.

In that case, maybe the small business owner decides to set up a **SIMPLE Plan** instead. A SIMPLE plan can be either an IRA or a 401(k). The SIMPLE plan is for businesses with no more than 100 employees and with no other retirement plan offered. In a SIMPLE plan, business owners choose to either match the employee's contributions up to 3% of compensation, or to contribute 2% of the employee's compensation if he does not make an elective deferral from his paycheck.

Unlike with a 401(k) plan, employees are immediately vested in a SEP-IRA or SIMPLE plan.

Many companies reward key employees by offering them **employee stock options.** These options do not trade among investors but are essentially free call options that allow employees to buy the company's stock at a set strike/exercise price. To keep the employee around a while, the company usually awards the options to buy the stock on a vesting schedule by which the employee gradually receives options. An **ESOP** or **employee stock ownership plan** is what it sounds like. Through these plans the company allows all workers to purchase company stock at a discount and through a payroll deduction. The stock and the dividends/cap gains generated on it grow tax-deferred, like a 401(k) plan.

> ➤ Defined Benefit Plans

Defined benefit pension plans are the opposite of defined contribution plans. In a defined contribution plan the employer puts in some money and then wishes employees the best of luck with retirement. For a defined benefit plan, the employer bears all the risk and, therefore, must earn sufficient returns on their investments to pay a defined benefit to retirees and their survivors.

Maybe that defined benefit is 70% of average salary figured over the employee's last three years of service, paid out each year in retirement, plus maybe a benefit to a spouse or children if he dies within a certain time.

A defined benefit pension plan is established as a trust and does not pay tax on the income it generates. In fact, the company gets to deduct the contributions it makes into the pension fund from taxable income. Therefore, these plans do not typically invest in municipal securities, since they are already tax-advantaged accounts.

Because corporations typically try to fund these plans only as much as required, defined benefit plans require an actuary to certify that funding levels are sufficient to cover future pension fund obligations.

Education savings plans offer tax deferral to help someone achieve a long-term goal, much as do retirement plans. Another similarity is that, as with retirement planning, age is a key factor. The portfolio used for a one-year-old child will be more aggressive than the one used for a 16-year-old. As always, the closer you get to your target date, the more you shift your money into bonds and away from stocks.

➢ 529 Plans

529 Plans allow investors to plan for future education expenses. In a **529 Savings Plan** the account is invested in various mutual fund-type accounts for future educational needs, with the withdrawals coming out tax-free if used for qualified education expenses. In a **529 Prepaid Tuition Plan** someone simply purchases tuition credits today to be used in the future, when college could be a lot more expensive.

> 529 Savings Plan

Usually it would be a family member socking money away for a child's education, but the beneficiary does not have to be a child, or even a blood relative of the donor. In fact, you can set up a 529 plan for yourself, in case you're still in the mood for more schooling after studying for this exam. The person who opens the account is the custodian; the beneficiary is the person who will use the money for education. For 529 savings plans, the owner controls the assets at all times.

Contributions are made after-tax (non-deductible), and the withdrawals used for qualified education expenses are tax-free at the federal level. That means the contributions are not deducted from taxable income when figuring federal taxes owed, although most states offer a deduction for state income taxes. For example, an Illinois resident could contribute $10,000 into the State's 529 Savings Plan and deduct that amount when figuring his state income taxes. To receive the benefit of the account—tax-free withdrawals—the withdrawals must be qualified withdrawals that cover tuition, room & board, books, etc. Qualified education expenses do include computer technology, which as the IRS explains, "includes the cost of the purchase of any computer technology, related equipment and/or related services such as Internet access. The technology, equipment or services qualify if they are used by the beneficiary of the plan and the beneficiary's family during any of the years the beneficiary is enrolled at an eligible educational institution."

If the beneficiary decides he doesn't need the money, the account can name a second beneficiary without tax problems, provided the second beneficiary is related to the first. And there's one area that can easily lead to confusion. When setting up a 529 plan it makes no difference whether the account owner is related to the beneficiary—I mean, the kid might just be the world's luckiest paperboy. It's just that if you start a 529 Savings Plan for your paperboy and then discover that the kid has no intention of going to college or even technical school, then if you want to avoid tax implications, you can only change the beneficiary to a blood relative of the paperboy (or back to yourself). If you want to change beneficiaries to someone not related to the paperboy, you'll deal with the 10% penalty and ordinary income tax. Just to keep things nice and simple.

Don't forget that when Grandma, for example, is putting money into a 529 savings plan on behalf of her granddaughter, she is making a gift. Gifts over a certain amount are taxable to the one making the gift. With a 529 savings plan, Grandma can contribute up to the gift tax exclusion without incurring gift taxes, and can even do a lump-sum contribution for the first five years without incurring gift tax hassles. In other words, if the annual gift tax exclusion is $14,000, she can put in $70,000 for the next five years. Or, she and her spouse can contribute a combined $140,000. Note that if somebody uses the five-year-up-front method, they can't make any more gifts to the beneficiary for the next five years without dealing with gift taxes.

Each state sets the maximum amount that may be contributed on behalf of a beneficiary, which the IRS defines as, "the amount necessary to provide for the qualified education expenses of the beneficiary."

The owner of the plan maintains control over the assets, deciding when withdrawals will be made. The money can be withdrawn to cover higher education expenses, such as tuition, books, and room and board. As with the CESA we are about to discuss, the assets in a 529 Plan are counted more favorably for purposes of financial aid than assets held in the beneficiary's UTMA/UGMA account.

Also, bear in mind that it doesn't have to be "college," necessarily that the account is funding—just any school higher than high school, basically. So if the exam asks if you can use the assets to go to heating & air-conditioning school, tell it that provided the school is an accredited post-secondary institution eligible to participate in a student aid program, the answer is yes.

>   Prepaid Tuition

If you're sure that Junior won't mind going to college in-state, you might want to lock him in as a future Boilermaker, Hoosier, or Sycamore through a **prepaid tuition** plan whereby you pay for his tuition credits now for any public school in the fine state of Indiana. I didn't say you were locking him into being *accepted* at IU or Purdue, but he would get to go to a state school with a certain number of credits already paid for.

And, if he ends up wanting to attend college in another state, the parents would have checked to see if their state's plan is transferrable to another state system. Similarly, if Junior gets a scholarship and doesn't need all the credits that were purchased, these plans provide refunds plus a modest rate of interest. Note that these credits cover tuition and fees only. And, the exam could refer to them as "defined benefit plans," because, well, they are. You pay for the tuition credits now. You hope the state can afford to provide the benefit of education when your kid needs it.

The two basic types of 529 Plans, then, are the ones that let the custodian invest the money and withdraw all the earnings tax-free, and the ones that let people purchase tuition credits now to be used in the future. In other words, one is a defined contribution plan, the other a defined benefit plan.

> Coverdell Education Savings Account

A **Coverdell Education Savings Account** (CESA) also allows for after-tax contributions (non-deductible), but the current maximum is only a few thousand dollars per year per child. While the 529 Plan is for higher education only, the Coverdell plan can be used for elementary, secondary, and higher education expenses. The distributions will be tax-free at the federal level if used according to the plan guidelines.

As with the 529 savings plan, the Coverdell ESA account can be used for education expenses, including tuition, books, and room and board. However, the contributions to a CESA must stop on the beneficiary's 18th birthday and must be used or distributed to him by age 30 subject to a 10% penalty and ordinary income taxes due on the earnings in the account. In some cases, CESA accounts can be transferred to another beneficiary who is a family member; however, some agreements say only the beneficiary can make that call. In the 529 Savings Plan the account owner is the custodian, while in a CESA the custodian is the financial institution holding the account—as with an IRA. The parent who set up the CESA would only be the "responsible individual," rather than the custodian. If your child never goes to college, you cannot refund the money to yourself, as you can in the 529 Savings Plan. From a CESA all payments must go to the beneficiary. Also, there are income limits on the donors of a CESA, similar to the limits placed on people trying to fund their Roth IRAs. In general, CESAs are clearly not for high-income investors.

Compared to money in an UTMA/UGMA account, assets in a 529 or Coverdell account do not count against the minor's chance of receiving financial aid to the same extent.

A 529 Savings Plan would typically allow contributions of a few hundred thousand dollars total into the account. For the CESA, however, the maximum is stated as the maximum that can be put into the account per-child, per-year. That number is currently just $2,000 per year.

So, should the investor use a 529 plan or a CESA? Generally, it would come down to the amount of money he wants to contribute. If he is going to contribute only a few thousand dollars, he might use the CESA. But, if he wants to put large amounts of money away and/or maintain flexibility and control over the assets, he'll use the 529 Savings Plan. Either way, he will enjoy tax-free withdrawals at the federal level, assuming he does everything according to plan.

HEALTH SAVINGS ACCOUNTS

As nice as it is to take money out of a Roth IRA tax-free, there was no tax deduction back when that money went in. With the Health Savings Account (HSA), on the other hand, contributions are deductible and withdrawals used to pay medical expenses are tax-free.

The account receives favorable tax treatment and is tied to an insurance policy called a high deductible health plan (HDHP). To be eligible for one of these accounts the individual can be covered under no other plan and must be below the eligibility age for Medicare. HSAs are owned by the individual, even though these plans are frequently offered through an employer. If an employee changes jobs, his HSA is portable—it's his account. There is no pressure to spend any amount of money from one's health savings account each year. Even if there is money in the account, the individual is not required to use the account to pay for medical expenses. Many people choose instead to pay expenses out-of-pocket and let the account balance continue to grow tax-deferred until they need it in their golden years.

NOW WHAT?

Securities agents are not tax professionals, so they can't give tax planning advice or tackle big problems related to estate planning. But, they have to talk about the tax implications of investing, accurately, and without harming the investor. Therefore, a possible question could be:

One of your customers has received a distribution from the ABCD All-American Tax-Exempt Bond Fund you recommended to her 37 months ago. If this is a distribution of net long-term capital gains, you would accurately inform the customer that
   A. The distribution is exempt from federal but not state taxation
   B. The distribution is exempt from state but not federal taxation
   C. The distribution is exempt from both federal and state taxation
   D. The distribution is subject to both federal and state taxation
EXPLANATION: with the name "tax-exempt" right in the name of the fund, it sure is tempting to assume that all distributions from the fund are tax-exempt. Of course, nothing is ever that simple. First, even if this were a regular distribution from the interest payments received by the fund, it would be subject to state taxation. Right there, we can eliminate Choice B and Choice C. Again, if this were an income/dividend distribution coming from the bond interest received by the fund, then the answer would be A. However, this is a capital gains distribution, and, therefore, it is subject to taxation at both the federal and state levels. Eliminate Choice A, leaving us with
ANSWER: D

If the agent in the situation above gets in a hurry one day, he might accidentally tell this client to spend the distribution on a new Cadillac, thinking it is all tax-exempt. Later, when the customer finds out it was subject to her long-term capital gains rate of maybe 15 or even 20%, well, that's the kind of problem you and the regulators would rather avoid.

Registered representatives sell a lot of mutual funds. A test question might ask something like this:

A mutual fund investor receives a dividend distribution of $500 and a long-term capital gains distribution of $250. What is true if the investor reinvests both distributions into more shares of the fund?
  A. She defers taxation until the new shares of the fund are ultimately sold
  B. The full amount of the reinvestment is added to her cost basis
  C. The amount of any taxes due is added to her cost basis
  D. The dividend is added to the cost basis, while the capital gains distribution is subtracted

EXPLANATION: even though Choice A is tempting, remember that mutual funds offer no tax deferral. Tax-deferral is provided by various tax-advantaged accounts, which we will look at in the next chapter. Eliminate Choice A. Choice B kind of seems logical at first maybe— let's put in on the side. Choice C looks even more logical—again, put it on the side. Choice D makes no sense at all, so we can eliminate that one. Okay, so we know it's either B or C. Do we add the full amount of the reinvestment or just the amount of the taxes paid on the reinvestment? What is "cost basis"? Cost basis can be thought of as all the money that has gone into an investment and been taxed. What you pay for a stock or bond is your cost basis. What you pay for a mutual fund is your cost basis. And then, since your dividends and capital gains are taxable whether you reinvest or spend the check, you add the full amount of the distribution to your ever-rising cost basis any time you reinvest. Eliminate Choice C, leaving us with
ANSWER: B

Questions relating to investment company products and the Investment Company Act of 1940 are expected to be plentiful on the Series 6 Exam. Like this one:

An investment company whose shares trade independently of Net Asset Value is known as which of the following?
  A. An open-end fund
  B. A Unit Investment Trust
  C. A Real Estate Investment Trust
  D. A closed-end fund

EXPLANATION: when you read a question like this, it's natural to assume that all four choices are, in fact, investment companies. However, that is not, in fact, the case. A REIT is not an investment company at all, so you can eliminate Choice C. So, our big-picture perspective first narrows it down to the three choices that are, at least, investment companies. Do open-end funds trade independent of NAV? Big picture again—open-end funds don't trade, period! The idea of securities trading on a secondary market is so familiar that some candidates will accept that open-end funds trade just like shares of common stock do. , no. Open-end funds are redeemed to the issuer as opposed to being traded among investors. Eliminate Answer A. Do Unit Investment Trusts trade? No, they are redeemable. Eliminate Choice B, and you are left with
ANSWER: D

An exam question could point out the similarities and differences between open- and closed-end funds using all kinds of different language. The question above said that a closed-end fund "trades independent of Net Asset Value." Another way to say it is that a closed-end fund "makes no provision for future offerings of shares." Or, that a closed-end fund is "associated with a fixed number of shares." Or even that a closed-end fund "is a management company under the Investment Company Act of 1940 whose shares are non-redeemable and whose portfolio is either diversified or non-diversified."

This almost limitless variety explains why I don't write, say, 15 practice questions here. I don't want you to think those questions somehow cover what you be required to know or should be used to measure what you know.

Time to take the Chapter 2 Review Quiz, watch the two associated lessons in the Training Videos, and move onto the next chapter in the book.

CHAPTER 3:
Obtains, Verifies, and Confirms Customer Purchase and Sale Instructions

Once you are registered you will open customer accounts, get to know your customers' investment profiles, and make suitable recommendations of mutual funds, variable annuities, and/or variable life insurance policies to your customers based on their goals and financial situations.

EXECUTING ORDERS

REGULATION T

With your Series 6 designation you will execute purchase and sale orders for open-end funds, variable annuities, and variable life insurance. However, your exam will likely ask questions about terms and processes that are only used by Series 7 licensees. For example, if you had your Series 7 designation, you could help a customer buy 1,000 shares of MSFT today and earn a commission for your trouble. If so, you would enter the transaction on the **trade date,** but the **settlement date** would not occur for three more business days.

Transactions in stock, corporate bonds, and municipal bonds settle **regular way** on "T + 3," which means whatever the **Trade** date is, count forward three business days to the settlement date. The settlement date is when both sides of the transaction complete their obligations to make payment and deliver the securities. If the trade date is Tuesday, the settlement date is Friday. If the trade date is Wednesday, the settlement date is Monday. Unless there is a holiday; weekends and holidays don't count.

If a customer enters an order to buy 500 shares of ABC on Tuesday, the broker-dealer would generally expect payment by the settlement date of Friday. Under the Federal Reserve Board's **Regulation T**, payment must be made within 2 business days of regular way settlement. If not, the firm must impose a **frozen account** status on the customer. When an account is frozen, no purchase orders can be executed unless the customer already has the cash in the account. No more credit for 90 days. Besides being a slow payer, another way for a customer to have his account frozen is to engage in **freeriding.** An example of this violation of Regulation T occurs if a customer buys 1,000 shares of MSFT on Monday for $30 a share, only instead of sending in $30,000, he sells the shares for $31 on Wednesday, using the proceeds to cover the purchase side of the transaction.

That is freeriding and will lead to an account freeze.

Broker-dealers don't have to extend credit to their customers at all. The one that I use, in fact, would reject any purchase order that involves more funds than I have in the account. If they wanted to let me slide, they would do so according to the requirements of Regulation or "Reg" T. Regulation T requires broker-dealers to get prompt payment from customers or request a formal extension. If the firm gets an extension and the customer still doesn't pay, that's the firm's problem. They must settle regular way with the other side of the transaction, so if they must buy or sell securities at prices that cause a loss, yes, they can take that from the customer's account—or not. Either way, they must settle with the broker-dealer on the buy or sell side of the transaction and work things out with their customer.

If a firm has a big customer—maybe the quarterback for the city's NFL franchise—what if he buys $80,000 worth of ABC common stock, but then goes out of town before he gets a chance to make payment? Could his agent or the firm lend him the $80,000?

No. I know of a former agent who was caught lending customers money to buy his investment products, allowing him to make commissions-plus-interest, and hit his sales targets. That worked well, for about four months. Not sure which industry he went into after his employer found out about his creative business practices, but it had nothing to do with securities, that's for sure.

ORDER TICKETS

Rules under the Securities Exchange Act of 1934 require that brokerage orders be evidenced by a written **memorandum** or **order ticket.** As the rules state, the firm must make and keep "a memorandum of each brokerage order, and of any other instruction, given or received for the purchase or sale of securities, whether executed or unexecuted." The "unexecuted order" might seem strange, but when trading individual shares of stock it is common for investors to place an order to buy or sell shares at a certain price; if that price never materializes, the orders are unexecuted. The firm would still need records of these orders—limit and stop orders, for example.

What must be contained on such a "memorandum" or "order ticket"? Here we go:

```
The memorandum shall show the terms and conditions of the order or
instructions and of any modification or cancellation thereof; the
account for which entered; the time the order was received; the
time of entry; the price at which executed; the identity of each
associated person, if any, responsible for the account; the
identity of any other person who entered or accepted the order on
behalf of the customer or, if a customer entered the order on an
electronic system, a notation of that entry; and, to the extent
feasible, the time of execution or cancellation.
```

If a test question asks what is *not* on the order ticket, a possible correct answer could be "the agent's commission" or "the rating of the bond." Or, of course, anything not in the list I just quoted. It's a hard test—you knew that, right?

Excellent.

The rule goes on to point out that:

```
an order entered pursuant to the exercise of discretionary
authority by the member, broker or dealer, or associated person
thereof, shall be so designated.
```

Broker-dealers must keep a memorandum for each order executed for their own account. Also, note that order tickets/memoranda are for "trades" of securities. If securities are purchased on a subscription basis from the issuer of the securities, the firm can just keep a copy of the subscription agreement. An investor purchasing a limited partnership interest in a natural gas project, for example, would be signing a subscription agreement and attaching payment to the issuer of the securities. Not that you can sell limited partnership interests with a Series 6 license, but, again, the exam goes much wider and deeper than that.

So, whether they are selling shares of common stock or shares of mutual funds, the regulators require firms to obtain and maintain certain information for each order. They also require that members confirm transactions with their customers.

TRADE CONFIRMATIONS

An order ticket or order memorandum is an internal document of the broker-dealer. Once the order has been executed, a **trade confirmation** is sent to the customer to confirm the trade. FINRA and SEC rules require the confirmation to be delivered no later than settlement of the transaction. For corporate and municipal bonds and for common stock, settlement is T + 3. For U.S. Treasury securities, however, trades settle regular-way on the next business day (T + 1). In either case, trade confirmations must be delivered to customers, who are encouraged to review them for accuracy and keep them for their records. Trade confirmations must include the following information:

- Date and time of the transaction (or furnish the time upon request)
- Identity of the securities purchased or sold
- Price of the securities purchased or sold
- Number of shares/units
- Whether member acted as an agent or principal—if principal, indicate if acting as a market maker in the security
- If acting as agent: name of the person from whom security was purchased or to whom it was sold (or furnish upon request), and the amount of any remuneration received

FINRA now requires additional information to be provided for fixed-income transactions in certain cases. For non-municipal fixed-income securities--which includes corporate and agency debt for purposes of the rule--in which the member firm acts in a principal capacity with a non-institutional customer the member must disclose the member's mark-up or mark-down from the prevailing market price for the security on the customer confirmation.

BEST EXECUTION

FINRA rules require broker-dealers and their agents to use "reasonable diligence to ascertain the best market for the subject security" and get the transaction done on terms "as favorable as possible under prevailing market conditions." The fairness of transactions with customers is a major regulator concern. To determine the fairness that a brokerage customer received, the following factors are taken into consideration:

- The character of the market for the security (price, volatility, liquidity, etc.)
- The size and type of transaction

- The number of markets checked
- Accessibility of the quotation
- The terms and conditions of the order as communicated to the member and associated persons

Some stocks trade infrequently and only on the Non-NASDAQ Over-the-Counter Market. The liquidity and volatility of these stocks could easily justify a price not as good as the customer had hoped. On the other hand, a stock as liquid as MSFT should not involve large markups or markdowns to the customer.

FINRA rules also prohibit the violation known as **interpositioning**. This violation entails involving a third party in a transaction that is not necessary and in a way that hurts the customer. As FINRA rules state:

> *In any transaction for or with a customer or a customer of another broker-dealer, no member or person associated with a member shall interject a third party between the member and the best market for the subject security in a manner inconsistent with this rule.*

The rule also says that when a firm must use a third party to get the transaction done—as they often do for municipal bonds—the burden of showing the necessity of the third party and the benefit to the customer would be on the member.

ACCOUNT STATEMENTS

Member firms must send to their customers at least quarterly **account statements** that show the current values for cash and securities, and any activity that took place since the last statement in terms of purchases and sales or deposits and withdrawals of securities. My own account statements tend to be 5 or 6 pages long and would be much longer if I held more stock positions or did any amount of trading. As the NASD rule stipulates:

```
Each general securities member shall, with a frequency of not less
than once every calendar quarter, send a statement of account
("account statement") containing a description of any securities
positions, money balances, or account activity to each customer
whose account had a security position, money balance, or account
activity during the period since the last such statement was sent
to the customer.
```

The account statement also must contain a statement to the customer "that advises the customer to report promptly any inaccuracy or discrepancy in that person's account to his or her brokerage firm."

COMPENSATION TO REGISTERED REPRESENTATIVES

The Securities Exchange Act of 1934 requires broker-dealers to keep detailed records regarding the compensation paid to their registered representatives. As one of the rules under this Act stipulates, member firms must make and keep a record:

as to each associated person listing each purchase and sale of a
security attributable, for compensation purposes, to that
associated person. The record shall include the amount of
compensation if monetary and a description of the compensation if
non-monetary. In lieu of making this record, a member, broker or
dealer may elect to produce the required information promptly upon
request of a representative of a securities regulatory authority.

The firm also needs a record:

of all agreements pertaining to the relationship between each
associated person and the member, broker or dealer including a
summary of each associated person's compensation arrangement or
plan with the member, broker or dealer, including commission and
concession schedules and, to the extent that compensation is based
on factors other than remuneration per trade, the method by which
the compensation is determined.

Also, as a registered representative you may not share your commissions with anyone who is not a
registered agent and who does not work for your firm or an affiliated firm. And, in any case, your
supervisor must approve of the sharing of commissions or payment of referral fees. So, if you get a
test question about a big customer who wants the agent to "rebate a third of his commissions" to him
to help offset the large purchase price, this is not an acceptable business practice.

NASD RULE: SUPERVISION

A member firm must monitor its **registered principals**, who must monitor their **registered
representatives**. Both registered representatives and their principals are "associated persons of a
member firm." This rule is clear all by itself:

Each member shall establish and maintain a system to supervise the
activities of each registered representative, registered
principal, and other associated person that is reasonably designed
to achieve compliance with applicable securities laws and
regulations, and with applicable NASD/FINRA Rules.

Written Procedures

Each member shall establish, maintain, and enforce written
procedures to supervise the types of business in which it engages
and to supervise the activities of registered representatives,
registered principals, and other associated persons that are
reasonably designed to achieve compliance with applicable
securities laws and regulations, and with the applicable Rules of
FINRA/NASD.

A copy of a member's written supervisory procedures shall be kept
and maintained in each OSJ and at each location where supervisory
activities are conducted on behalf of the member. Each member
shall amend its written supervisory procedures as appropriate

within a reasonable time after changes occur in applicable securities laws and regulations, including the Rules of this Association, and as changes occur in its supervisory system, and each member shall be responsible for communicating amendments through its organization.

When a member firm violates the conduct rules, they usually get penalized for violating the rule and for not having adequate supervisory systems in place that should have prevented what happened from happening.

The exam outline also mentions the definitions of **OSJ** and **branch office**:

(g) Definitions

(1) "Office of Supervisory Jurisdiction" means any office of a member at which any one or more of the following functions take place:

(A) order execution and/or market making;

(B) structuring of public offerings or private placements;

(C) maintaining custody of customers' funds and/or securities;

(D) final acceptance (approval) of new accounts on behalf of the member;

(E) review and endorsement of customer orders, pursuant to paragraph (d) above;

(F) final approval of communications for use by persons associated with the member, pursuant to Rule 2210(b)(1); or

(G) responsibility for supervising the activities of persons associated with the member at one or more other branch offices of the member.

(2)(A) "Branch Office" means any location identified by any means to the public or customers as a location at which the member conducts an investment banking or securities business, excluding:

(i) any location identified in a telephone directory line listing or on a business card or letterhead, which listing, card, or letterhead also sets forth the address and telephone number of the branch office or OSJ of the firm from which the person(s) conducting business at the non-branch locations are directly supervised;

(ii) any location referred to in a member advertisement, as this term is defined in Rule 2210, by its local telephone number and/or local post office box provided that such reference may not contain the address of the non-branch location and, further, that such reference

FINRA CODE OF PROCEDURE

FINRA investigates violations of the conduct rules through **Code of Procedure** (COP). All requests for information must be met within 25 days. Members and associated persons are required to cooperate with the investigation, producing documents or testimony as required. If they don't file a response or cooperate with the process, a disciplinary order will be issued without them—a **default decision**. And if it's decided that they broke a rule, the firm, agent, or principal could be censured, fined, suspended, expelled, or barred.

They would get to appeal, assuming they can afford the legal fees. If they chose a contested hearing, the appeals first go to the **National Adjudicatory Council** (NAC), then to the SEC, and even into the federal courts.

But it would be easier if they didn't get in trouble in the first place.

Under **Acceptance, Waiver, and Consent**, or "AWC," the respondent chooses not to dispute the allegations. In that case the Department of Enforcement has the respondent sign a letter accepting a finding of violation, consenting to the sanctions imposed, and waiving the right to a hearing or to an appeal. If the respondent agrees, the letter is sent to the NAC for review. If accepted, it becomes final. If not, the next step is a formal hearing.

If the activity is considered a "minor rule violation," the maximum fine would be a relatively low amount, and the process would involve having the respondent sign a minor rule violation letter. When the respondent signs the letter, the settlement is final, and the NAC can tack on a limited fine and/or a letter of censure.

Other times, the respondent makes an **offer of settlement,** in which he proposes what FINRA ought to do about his activities.

In many cases a settlement can't be reached and there is a hearing. If so, the decision will be listed as **contested** when FINRA announces it on their website along with all the other recent disciplinary actions. Whether the punishment is arrived at through Acceptance, Waiver and Consent (AWC), an offer of settlement, or through a contested hearing, any of the following penalties can be assessed:

- Censure
- Fine (any amount)
- Suspension (temporary)
- Expulsion (the firm is done)
- Barred (associated person is done)

As I mentioned, if either side is unhappy with the decision of the hearing panel, an appeal can be filed to the NAC within 25 days. From there, the case can be appealed to the SEC (Securities and Exchange Commission) and even the federal civil court system from there.

FINRA RULE: PROVISION OF INFORMATION AND TESTIMONY AND INSPECTION AND COPYING OF BOOKS

When FINRA wants to review records or take testimony, we have two options: cooperate, or find a new career. As FINRA Rule 8210 makes clear:

> *For the purpose of an investigation, complaint, examination, or proceeding authorized by the FINRA/NASD By-Laws or the Rules of the Association, an Adjudicator or Association staff shall have the right to:*
>
> *(1) require a member, person associated with a member, or person subject to the Association's jurisdiction to provide information orally, in writing, or electronically and to testify at a location specified by Association staff, under oath or affirmation administered by a court reporter or a notary public if requested, with respect to any matter involved in the investigation, complaint, examination, or proceeding; and*
>
> *(2) inspect and copy the books, records, and accounts of such member or person with respect to any matter involved in the investigation, complaint, examination, or proceeding.*
>
> *(c) Requirement to Comply*
>
> *No member or person shall fail to provide information or testimony or to permit an inspection and copying of books, records, or accounts pursuant to this Rule.*

But, since they do have a heart, FINRA/NASD also stipulates that:

> *Inspection and Copying*

FINRA CODE OF ARBITRATION PROCEDURE

As in major league baseball, disputes in the brokerage industry are settled in **arbitration**. Member firms can't sue each other in civil court if an underwriting turns sour and one member of the syndicate is convinced they are owed $1 million from the managing underwriter, who promised more shares than they delivered. That sort of dispute must be submitted to arbitration.

CUSTOMER CODE

The Code of Arbitration Procedure is separated into a code for customer disputes and a code for industry disputes. Let's look at the customer code first. As we saw earlier, firms get their customers to sign pre-dispute arbitration agreements, but they must be clear what arbitration means to the customer in the document they're getting the customer to sign. The rule stipulates that the warning must look like this:

```
This agreement contains a pre-dispute arbitration clause. By
signing an arbitration agreement the parties agree as follows:

(A) All parties to this agreement are giving up the right to sue
each other in court, including the right to a trial by jury,
except as provided by the rules of the arbitration forum in which
a claim is filed.

(B) Arbitration awards are generally final and binding; a party's
ability to have a court reverse or modify an arbitration award is
very limited.

(C) The ability of the parties to obtain documents, witness
statements and other discovery is generally more limited in
arbitration than in court proceedings.

(D) The arbitrators do not have to explain the reason(s) for their
award.

(E) The panel of arbitrators will typically include a minority of
arbitrators who were or are affiliated with the securities
industry.
```

(F) The rules of some arbitration forums may impose time limits for bringing a claim in arbitration. In some cases, a claim that is ineligible for arbitration may be brought in court.

(G) The rules of the arbitration forum in which the claim is filed, and any amendments thereto, shall be incorporated into this agreement.

Only by getting the customer to sign this agreement would your firm know that when somebody loses a bunch of money investing through you and your firm, he will not be able to drag them through civil court, with appeal after appeal. Arbitration is faster and cheaper for all involved. Claims under arbitration can be filed up to six years after the event, which is why written customer complaints are maintained on file for six years by broker-dealers. What if a customer loses money investing through a firm that goes bankrupt, or has its license canceled, suspended, or revoked? Then the customer would be free to sue them in civil court.

When a claim goes before an arbitration panel, some of the arbitrators come from the industry, and some don't. The ones that don't come from the industry are called "public arbitrators." The ones that do come from the industry are called "non-public arbitrators." To simplify the rule, let's define the two types of arbitrators like this:

Non-Public Arbitrator	Public Arbitrator
<ul><li>is associated with a broker-dealer</li><li>was associated with a broker-dealer within the past 5 years</li><li>is a member of a commodities exchange or associated with a commodities firm</li><li>is retired from a broker-dealer or commodities exchange/member firm</li><li>is an attorney, accountant, or other professional who has devoted 20% or more of their professional work in the last two years to broker-dealers, commodities firms</li><li>is an employee of a bank or other financial institution and either executes transactions in securities or supervises those who do for compliance</li></ul>	<ul><li>person who doesn't fit the bullet points above</li><li>person who is not an investment adviser</li><li>person is not the spouse or immediate family of anyone in the above list</li><li>person is not an employee of any entity in the securities industry</li><li>person is not a director or officer of any entity in the securities industry, or his/her spouse or immediate family member</li></ul>

HEARINGS

The arbitration panel consists of various numbers and types of arbitrators, depending on the severity of the dispute. For a claim of $50,000 or less, FINRA will appoint one public arbitrator. If the claim is more than $50,000, the panel consists of one arbitrator unless both parties agree to three. If three arbitrators are on the panel, two will be public and one non-public (from the industry). For claims over $100,000 or for claims of unspecified damages, or for claims seeking non-monetary awards, the default setting is three arbitrators unless both parties agree to only one. Note that even if there is only one arbitrator, FINRA still refers to him as a "panel."

Claims of $50,000 or less	Claims > $50,000 up to $100,000	Claims > $100,000, or Unspecified/Non-$
• 1 arbitrator, simplified arbitration • Public arbitrator, unless agreed in writing otherwise	• 1 arbitrator unless parties agree to 3 • Public arbitrator if panel of 1, unless agreed in writing otherwise • 2 of 3 public arbitrators if panel of 3	• 3 arbitrators unless parties agree to 1 • 2 of 3 public arbitrators if panel of 3 •

Even though we're not in court here, smart respondents appear with attorneys who guide them through this potentially expensive process. Arbitration can lead to a big payout to an aggrieved customer, which is something an agent would then disclose in his U4 information, which is then open to anyone using FINRA's broker-check system at www.finra.org. If you think about it, many of FINRA's rules would likely either confuse a customer or seem like something outside his concern, while, on the other hand, seeing that a registered representative has had to pay out large amounts to dissatisfied customers would likely hit home for most potential and/or former customers.

Failure to appear is a bad idea, since the panel can decide to hold the hearing without the respondent provided proper notice was provided. The same thing happens for disciplinary hearings—if the respondent won't cooperate, the panel usually just reaches a default decision. And, for not cooperating, the panel usually makes sure the respondent is permanently removed from the industry.

SIMPLIFIED ARBITRATION

If the dispute is between a public customer and either an associated person or a member firm and involves no more than $50,000, the customer submits a statement of claim in writing to the Director of Arbitration. In the statement of claim, the customer details the dispute, the relevant facts, the remedies sought, and whether she's so worked up she's demanding a hearing. See, if the customer doesn't request a hearing in writing, and the arbitrator doesn't call one, these things are usually just decided by the public arbitrator knowledgeable in the securities industry and appointed by the Director. The Director serves the other side a copy of the claim, and the other side (the "respondent") sends its written response to the Director and the customer within 45 days, including documentation to support his side of the story if he wants. The arbitrator examines the facts of the case and makes his decision promptly.

If the amount of monetary damages rises above $50,000 during the process, the claim would no longer be eligible for simplified arbitration.

AWARDS

Arbitration is supposed to be as fast and painless as possible, so the arbitrator(s) "shall endeavor to render an award within 30 business days from the date the record is closed." The **award** is a document summarizing the dispute, the damages sought and damages awarded, and the names and signatures of the arbitrators. Surely, since it's FINRA arbitration it's a private matter, right? Not. As the FINRA manual states, "All awards and their contents shall be made publicly available." That's why the firms might want to settle—settlements are private affairs. How long does the respondent have to pay an award? 30 days. What if the other side doesn't pay right away? As the FINRA Manual says:

> An award shall bear interest from the date of the award: (1) if not paid within thirty (30) days of receipt, (2) if the award is the subject of a motion to vacate which is denied, or (3) as specified by the arbitrator(s) in the award. Interest shall be assessed at the legal rate, if any, then prevailing in the state where the award was rendered, or at a rate set by the arbitrator(s).

If the respondent simply won't pay, they will end up being disciplined by FINRA under Code of Procedure, and you can go after them like any other creditor, reporting the debt to the big credit reporting agencies.

FINRA rules require agents and broker-dealers to report within 30 days whenever the firm or an associated person has been found to have violated securities laws, rules, or regulations, has been named in a written customer complaint, or has been the subject of arbitration, litigation, or a settlement involving more than $15,000. As a registered representative, your Form U4 information is made public through FINRA's BrokerCheck system. Obviously, no registered representative wants disciplinary problems or arbitration awards paid out to angry customers being disclosed through the FINRA website. Unfortunately, any such situations will go into that system. If an agent fails to update his U4 information promptly, we will see that he has now been barred by FINRA for that and, most likely, for failing to cooperate with the disciplinary process that proceeds from these unfortunate oversights.

Some of the disclosures agents must make could happen outside the industry. For example, if an agent were charged with felony possession of a controlled substance with intent to distribute, he might be tempted to conceal that fact from his employer and FINRA. Unfortunately, when his employer and FINRA do, in fact, find out, there will be even more disclosures going into the CRD system, allowing the public to find the special report on this individual who used to be registered with a FINRA member broker-dealer.

The only way to get a customer dispute **expunged** from the Central Registration Depository (CRD) system is through the courts. As FINRA rules state, members or associated persons who want to get a customer dispute expunged "must obtain an order from a court of competent jurisdiction directing such expungement or confirming an arbitration award containing expungement relief." If a member or associated person goes to court seeking an expungement, they must name FINRA as one of the parties and serve FINRA with all appropriate documents—unless FINRA formally waives that requirement.

And, if we are talking about a criminal conviction being expunged, this is tricky. Although the courts could expunge the conviction, Form U4 still asks if the individual has ever been charged with any felony or any misdemeanor relevant to the securities industry. Therefore, even though the individual could say "No" to the question of whether he's ever been convicted of such a crime, he would still have to answer "Yes" to the question of whether he was ever charged with such a crime.

As you can see, criminal and regulatory problems, as well as customer disputes, lead to nothing good. The firm and/or the agent either properly disclose everything and live with the consequences, or they try to conceal the information and usually end up with a set of even worse consequences that usually involve a permanent vacation from the securities industry. As many parents would agree, making a mistake is seldom as bad as trying to conceal it from the powers that be.

INDUSTRY CODE

FINRA's Code of Arbitration Procedure for Industry Disputes requires industry members to settle disputes through arbitration.

> *(a) Generally*
>
> *Except as otherwise provided in the Code, a dispute must be arbitrated under the Code if the dispute arises out of the business activities of a member or an associated person and is between or among:*
>
> *• Members*
>
> *• Members and Associated Persons*
>
> *• Associated Persons.*
>
> *(b) Insurance Activities*
>
> *Disputes arising out of the insurance business activities of a member that is also an insurance company are not required to be arbitrated under the Code.*

So, if you should ever leave a firm under a cloud of bitterness, where you feel you are owed money, you would not be able to sue. You would submit your claim to arbitration. If you fail to convince the arbitration panel that your firm owes you, you won't be getting anything out of your firm. But, if you do convince the panel that your firm owes you, say, $50,000, they must honor that award. Failure to honor an arbitration award, or to produce documents or attend a hearing are all examples of "conduct inconsistent with just and equitable principles of trade," which is the ultimate sin as far as FINRA is concerned. If the parties use mediation and reach a settlement, failure to honor the terms of that settlement would also be considered conduct inconsistent with just and equitable principles of trade. It is also considered a violation of just and equitable principles of trade for a broker-dealer to require agents to waive their right to settle disputes in arbitration. As FINRA states:

> *Action by members requiring associated persons to waive the arbitration of disputes contrary to the provisions of the Code of Arbitration Procedure shall constitute conduct that is inconsistent with just and equitable principles of trade and a violation of Rule 2110.*

The number of arbitrators based on the dollar amounts we looked at are the same for industry disputes as they are for customer disputes. However, the composition of the panel is different, depending on whether an associated person and a member are in dispute or if the dispute is between two members. If the dispute is between an associated person and a member firm, the composition of the panel is the same as it is for customer disputes. If it's just one arbitrator, it will be a public arbitrator (unless both sides agree in writing otherwise), and if the panel uses three arbitrators, two of them will be public arbitrators. On the other hand, if the dispute is between members, a panel of one arbitrator will consist of one non-public arbitrator (unless both sides agree in writing otherwise), and a panel of three all will be non-public arbitrators. As mentioned, the dollar amounts we saw for the customer code are the same, and simplified arbitration is available for amounts of no more than $50,000.

MEDIATION

Sometimes both parties agree to try and avoid arbitration by using the **mediation** process. Here, a mediator listens to both sides and delivers a non-binding settlement. But, if a settlement cannot be reached, the matter goes to arbitration. The mediator cannot sit on that arbitration panel.

NOW WHAT?

The Series 6 Exam is expected to ask several questions about the documentation involved with processing customer orders. Like this one:

Three of the following pieces of information would be on both an order ticket and a trade confirmation. Which one would ONLY be recorded on the trade confirmation?
 A. Account number
 B. Commission
 C. Account executive identifier
 D. Number of shares, units

EXPLANATION: agents and member firms are not allowed to enter transactions and then decide in which accounts to place them. The account number must be indicated for each trade about to be placed. Also, a customer could have several accounts with the firm—identifying the account associated with this trade is important, so eliminate Choice A. Choice B does not necessarily look like something to be on the trade ticket, so let's put that one to the side. The registered representative (account executive) must be identified on the order ticket and on the trade confirmation. Eliminate Choice C. I don't

see how an order could be placed without specifying the number of shares to be bought or sold. And, it wouldn't be much of a trade confirmation if it lacked such basic information. Eliminate Choice D, leaving us with
ANSWER: B

FINRA recently updated a rule on the holding of customer mailings—e.g., account statements, trade confirmations, proxies, and annual reports. Therefore, a question like this seems likely:

One of your elderly customers, who does not use electronic communications, calls this morning and asks you to please hold back the delivery of any account-related mailings while she is in South Africa for 61 days. Which of the following is accurate of this customer request?
   A. The customer must make the request in writing, and your firm must both send disclosure of alternative methods of monitoring the account and receive confirmation the customer received this disclosure
   B. Because she is traveling overseas for less than 3 months, you may fulfill this request with prompt principal approval
   C. Because she is traveling for more than two consecutive months, your firm will need her to supplement the request in writing
   D. With the passage of Dodd-Frank, member firms are no longer permitted to hold back the delivery of any account-related customer mailings

EXPLANATION: the former rule was rigid—the firm could hold back customer mailings for two months if traveling domestically and three months if traveling abroad. Now, the time frame is not the main concern. The main concern, as always, is that the firm first has this request in writing. Choice B implies this oral request can simply be approved by a principal, so eliminate Choice B. Choice C says you only need it in writing in this specific case. That is wrong, so eliminate Choice C. Choice D seems official-like with the reference to Dodd Frank, but, clearly the passage in this chapter would have read quite differently if this were the case. Eliminate Choice D, leaving us with
ANSWER: A

Investors need to know about the handful of registered representatives who harm investors and end up paying out big arbitration awards. Therefore, you could see a question like this:

A registered representative fails to follow through on instructions to sell a customer's mutual fund holdings after which the account drops by a total of $25,000. The customer plans to file an arbitration claim that names the member firm specifically and not the registered representative. Therefore, which of the following statements is accurate?
   A. If the amount of the award is $15,000 or more, the member must update the agent's U4/U5 information with a disclosure report concerning the incident
   B. Because the registered representative is not named, the member need not update the agent's U4/U5 information regardless of any award
   C. Because the amount of money was only $25,000, the customer may not file an arbitration claim based solely on this incident

D. Because the amount of money was only $25,000, the member need not update the agent's U4/U5 information

EXPLANATION: at first all four answer choices look okay. $25,000 was an amount you read about. Unfortunately, you have to now remember what that had to do with. Was the customer precluded from filing a claim, or was a claim of this size simply handled by simplified arbitration? That's it, right? The $25,000 figure had to do with simplified arbitration versus the bigger amounts that involve three or five arbitrators? If you're sure that's right, you can eliminate both Choices C and D. What if you're not sure? Put them to the side. Never eliminate an answer choice unless you *know* why you're eliminating it. What about the first two choices? Again, they both make sense—if the agent wasn't named, maybe the firm takes the hit? That is how things *used* to work. Trouble was, customers eventually understood that if they wanted to get paid, they should name the firm, who would then conceal from the public that the agent is a bad boy. Nowadays, members must disclose any arbitration award related to an agent's activities if the amount is at least $15,000, even if the claim fails to name the agent specifically. We can now eliminate Choice B. Then, we can go back and eliminate Choice C and D, leaving us with

ANSWER: A

It's time to take the Chapter 3 Review Quiz. Then, please watch the associated lesson in the Training Videos, and move onto the next chapter in the textbook.

CHAPTER 4:
Regulatory Fundamentals and Business Development

At this point we have looked at what a registered representative does for a living in chronological order: opens a customer account, determines and makes suitable recommendations to the customer, and handles purchase and sale orders for the customer. Now, we must look more closely at the federal securities Acts and also at FINRA. FINRA still uses some NASD rules, while many former NASD rules have either been incorporated or retired. Don't worry about whether a rule is an NASD or FINRA rule. Rather, learn the rule and understand its importance to customers and the regulators.

Let's start with the federal securities Acts, again, in chronological order.

SECURITIES ACT OF 1933

The exam outline lists some specific definitions from this "Truth in Securities Act," including:

- **Issuer**: every person who issues or proposes to issue any security.
- The term **"sale"** or **"sell"** shall include every contract of sale or disposition of a security or interest in a security, for value.
- The term **"offer to sell,"** **"offer for sale,"** or **"offer"** shall include every attempt or offer to dispose of, or solicitation of an offer to buy, a security or interest in a security, for value.
- **Underwriter**: any person who has purchased from an issuer with a view to, or offers or sells for an issuer in connection with, the distribution of any security, or participates or has a direct or indirect participation in any such undertaking, or participates or has a participation in the direct or indirect underwriting of any such undertaking.

Let's take them one at a time. First, an issuer is considered an issuer as soon as they propose to issue a security. In other words, once any person declares their intentions by filing a registration statement or putting together an offering circular, they are an issuer and are subject to all the rules that issuers must follow. They can't take money from investors, for example, until the securities have been declared effective for sale. And, they had better not deceive anyone in any way with the offer or sale of these securities. An issue of securities could be something as legitimate as an IPO for a well-known company like Starbucks or just some promissory note issued by an individual with no intention of repaying the investor. Both Starbucks and the individual issuing worthless paper are issuers as soon as they propose to issue any security.

The definition of *offer* includes every attempt to sell a security or any attempt to solicit an offer to buy a security. A securities offering must be registered before it is offered to investors. When the securities are offered to investors, anyone connected to the offer is subject to anti-fraud regulations. If investors are misled due to inaccurate or incomplete disclosure of all material facts, the issuer can end up in trouble with the securities regulators as well as the attorneys for the investors who were harmed.

Whenever a contract of sale for a security is entered, or whenever a security is disposed of for value, a *sale* has occurred. The anti-fraud regulations under federal and state securities law prohibit deceptive or manipulative behavior through either the offer or sale of a security or an interest in a security.

The definition of *underwriter* includes any individual or firm who has agreed to purchase securities from an issuer to offer or sell them to investors as part of a securities distribution. Many broker-dealers have underwriting departments that derive a large percentage of the firm's profits, while other broker-dealers simply execute trades for their customers on the secondary market, and still others sell mutual funds and variable annuities almost exclusively. While it is easy to remember that firms including Goldman Sachs and JP Morgan are underwriters, the Securities Act of 1933 also makes it clear that investors who buy unregistered securities from the issuer and then quickly resell them on the secondary market would be acting as underwriters, too. That's why there are rules involved whenever an issuer does a **private placement**, which we'll look at below. Since those securities are unregistered, the SEC has many concerns about investors buying and then quickly releasing them into the secondary market, acting just like an underwriter.

To offer securities to investors on the primary market, most issuers are required to file a **registration statement** with the Securities and Exchange Commission under the Securities Act of 1933. The registration statement discloses what the business is, what properties it owns, its financial documents, the important risks associated with the security being offered, and information on the officers and directors of the company.

Not all securities are subject to this registration requirement, however. The following securities are considered **exempt securities** not required to register under the Act:

- Security issued or guaranteed by the United States
- Security issued or guaranteed by any territory or state of the United States
- Note, draft, bill of exchange, or banker's acceptance which arises out of a current transaction with a maximum maturity of 9 months
- Security issued by a person organized exclusively for religious, educational, benevolent, fraternal, charitable, or reformatory purposes and not for profit
- Security issued by a savings and loan, building and loan, cooperative bank, etc.
- Insurance and annuity contracts (not variable contracts!)

Municipal bonds, commercial paper, and common stock in a savings & loan are examples of securities offered and sold to investors without registration statements being filed with the SEC. That saves the issuers time and money, but it doesn't imply the SEC has approved these securities or determined they are safer, better, or anything like that. In fact, while a Treasury bond might be safe, some religious or bank securities could turn out to be the shakiest things any fixed-income investor ever bought. The offering documents prepared for investors of church bonds would not be filed with the regulators, but the documents still must be clear that no regulator has "passed upon" (rendered a judgment on) the merits of the securities being offered or the issuer itself. Any statement or implication to the contrary is fraudulent, and since securities are offered both through the mail and electronically, mail and wire fraud charges can be filed against operators trying to take money from people through deception. So, an exempt security is still a security, and an offer of exempt securities will still include offering documents to investors. If any material facts are misstated or omitted from those documents, the issuers can be sued by investors and the SEC, and—in some cases—prosecuted for criminal offenses. Registration is a line of defense in the SEC's fight to protect investors, but the fact that a security escapes registration in no way implies that it escapes the anti-fraud regulations. If it is a security, it is subject to anti-fraud statutes. If it is an exempt security, it is not subject to registration requirements.

U.S. Treasury Notes and State of Oregon municipal bonds are exempt securities. As we saw elsewhere, there are also **exempt transactions**. That means that if the issuer sells the securities in a certain way, they can either avoid registration altogether, avoid registration with the SEC, or perhaps just do a scaled-down disclosure document like an offering memorandum or an offering circular as opposed to the standard registration statement or S1.

Under **Reg A**, an issuer can sell up to $5,000,000 worth of securities in a year without having to jump through all the usual hoops. Rather than filing a standard registration statement, the issuer files an offering circular, a much more scaled-down document.

The SEC is in charge of interstate commerce, meaning commerce among many states. Therefore, if the issuer wants to sell only to residents of one state, the SEC doesn't get involved—there is already a state securities regulator who can deal with this one. So, if the issuer agrees to sell the stock to residents of only one state, they will qualify for a **Rule 147** exemption. The issuer's main business must be located in the state, and 80% of its assets located there. Also, the buyers can't sell the security to a non-resident for nine months. The issuer registers with the state, rather than the SEC, since it's all taking place in that one state. This is also called an **intrastate offering**, which means it all takes place within one state.

The SEC is out to protect the average investor from fast talking stock operators pushing worthless investments. But, the SEC doesn't provide as much protection to big, sophisticated investors such as mutual funds, pension funds, or high-net-worth individuals. If anybody tries to scam these multimillion-dollar investors, they'll be in just as much trouble as if they scammed an average investor, but the SEC doesn't put up as much protection for the big, institutional investors, who can usually watch out for themselves to a large extent.

Therefore, if the issuer wants to avoid the registration process under the Act of 1933, they can limit the sale to these institutional, sophisticated investors. These investors are often referred to as **accredited investors**. They include institutions and the officers and Board of Directors of the issuer. Also, if an individual or married couple meets the net worth or the income requirements, he or she is accredited. So, an issuer can place their securities under a **Reg D** transaction with as many of these folks as they want. This "private placement" is not being offered to the general public, so the SEC eases up a bit.

If there will be any solicitation of investors, the regulators allow the issuer and underwriters to sell to no more than 35 non-accredited purchasers. Either way, if the investor is an individual, he must hold the stock for a certain time before selling it. Or, he must hold it for "investment purposes" as opposed to buying it and immediately flipping it. After the holding period, a non-affiliated investor must comply with volume limits on any sales of the stock for only a specified time, while an affiliated investor (10% owner, officer, or director of the issuer) must comply with volume limits all the time.

An affiliate of the issuer always files Form 144 with the SEC, announcing that he intends to sell a certain amount of the issuer's stock over the next 90 days. We don't want the large shareholders to sell too much stock at once, which usually drives the price down for everyone else who might want to sell. The volume to be sold over the 90-day period is limited to 1% of the shares outstanding or the average weekly trading volume over the four most recent weeks, whichever is larger.

The securities offered and sold through a private placement don't have to be registered, but FINRA still requires member firms to file a copy of the private placement memorandum (PPM) with their Firm Gateway. The PPM must be filed no later than 15 calendar days after the first sale is made. Or, if no PPM is going to be used with the offering, that fact must be reported to FINRA.

Rule 144 covers both restricted stock and control stock. There is nothing different about control stock. It's just that the stock is owned by officers and directors of the issuer, or large shareholders. the people who hold the stock that are different. If the shareholder is the CEO of a corporation, or the CFO, or the owner of a major chunk (10%) of the stock, he is required to notify the SEC when selling his shares. This is done by filing a Form 144, the same form that covers resales of **restricted stock**.

Stock sold through a private placement is unregistered and therefore restricted. Restricted means its transfer or sale is restricted—investors must hold it for a specified time before selling it. If the transaction is not larger than 5,000 shares and $50,000, the sale can be made without reporting. Basically, a transaction that small does not make the regulators nervous as it won't impact the price of the stock due to the low volume of shares traded.

And, those people can never sell the company's stock short. They can't profit from their company's poor stock performance, in other words. And, if they make a profit on their company's stock held less than 6 months, they'll wish they hadn't. This is called a short-swing profit, and it must be turned back over to the company with the gain still being taxed by the IRS.

FINRA is concerned that agents and their firms sometimes help clients sell unregistered restricted securities, which violates federal securities law. In other words, if the customer does not conform to all the stipulations we just went over, but wants to simply take his unregistered restricted shares and sell them, firms must be sure they don't help him skirt securities law in this manner. FINRA alerts its member broker-dealer firms that some customers are companies trying to sell their shares illegally. If the customer deposits certificates representing a large block of thinly traded or low-priced securities, that's a red flag. If the share certificates refer to a company or customer name that has been changed or that does not match the name on the account, that's another red flag. If a customer with limited or no other assets under management at the firm receives an electronic transfer or journal transactions of large amounts of low-priced, unlisted securities, that's another red flag. Broker-dealer firms must do a reasonable inquiry to make sure that they are not helping people get around securities law. The SEC has said that "a dealer who offers to sell, or is asked to sell a substantial amount of securities must take whatever steps are necessary to be sure that this is a transaction not involving an issuer, person in a control relationship with an issuer, or an underwriter." For this purpose, it is not enough for him to accept "self-serving statements of his sellers and their counsel (attorneys) without reasonably exploring the possibility of contrary facts."

Rule 144a allows the restricted securities we just discussed to be re-sold to institutional investors including banks, insurance companies, broker-dealers, investment advisers, pension plans, and investment companies without meeting the usual registration requirements under the Securities Act of 1933. So, if an investor acquires restricted securities through a private placement, he/they can re-sell them to qualified institutional buyers such as those mentioned without messing up the exemption the issuer is claiming from the registration requirements. As usual, the regulators want to prevent the shares from being distributed in a general public offering without registration requirements being met. When the buyers are all sophisticated institutions, the regulators can ease up.

This SEC rule also states that the seller must be reasonably certain that the buyers are qualified institutional buyers, which generally means that the institution invests on a discretionary basis at least $100 million, or is a registered broker-dealer, an investment company, a bank, or a federal covered investment adviser. To check that the buyers are qualified institutional buyers, the SEC says that the seller can rely on the buyer's most recent publicly available financial statements, or a certification from the CFO or other officer of the institution.

CIVIL LIABILITY

Registration and disclosure help to protect investors, but whether an offer of securities had to be registered or not, the persons connected to the offering have civil liability to the investors if material facts are omitted or misstated. Think of that for a second—if you are a registered representative, maybe you help five customers purchase $1 million worth of an offering in a high-risk start-up company. What does "civil liability" mean in that sense? In terms of money, the Securities Act of 1933 is on the same page with state law, where you would be liable to the person you harmed for "the consideration paid for such security with interest thereon, less the amount of any income received thereon."

And, in a civil action, the burden would shift to the plaintiff. As the Securities Act of 1933 states, if the defendant is connected with the offer of a security, and the purchaser relied on statements and did not know they were bogus, he would be liable if he couldn't prove he didn't know any better and couldn't have. The phrase in the Securities Act of 1933 is "and who shall not sustain the burden of proof that he did not know, and in the exercise of reasonable care could not have known, of such untruth or omission."

An agent with a Series 7 license might offer a few wealthy investors looking for tax shelter a limited partnership investment in several oil wells in Wyoming. Turns out, the offering documents for the investment made some statements that were not accurate. They claimed that two of the wells were in production when, in fact, they were not, and they overstated the production of the five wells that were currently producing.

Can the agent sustain the burden of proving he didn't know the statements were bogus and could not have known even after exercising reasonable care? Depends. If there were red flags in the offering document, the firm—who is charged with reviewing the document to determine suitability of any recommendations—should have done some digging. However, if they rely on a seemingly reputable geological report, then they probably couldn't be expected to know or assume otherwise. But neither the agent nor the firm can shrug these things off as if the buyer has the burden of doing more digging on his own. No, the agent and his broker-dealer have suitability obligations to each customer. FINRA has a system of arbitration to handle agents and broker-dealers. But the officers and directors of a public company have civil liability to stock and bondholders who rely on the information contained in registration statements/prospectuses.

SECURITIES EXCHANGE ACT OF 1934

An offer of stock that was not registered would violate the Securities Act of 1933 and would also violate the anti-fraud sections of the Securities Exchange Act of 1934 if important information were left out or misstated to investors.

ANTI-FRAUD PROVISIONS

Why? Because the **Securities Exchange Act of 1934** has anti-fraud provisions that apply to any person and any security. As the Securities Exchange Act of 1934 makes clear:

> It shall be unlawful for any <u>person</u>:
>
> • To employ any device, scheme, or artifice to defraud,
>
> • To make any untrue statement of a material fact or to omit to state a material fact necessary to make the statements made, in the light of the circumstances under which they were made, not misleading, or
>
> • To engage in any act, practice, or course of business which operates or would operate as a fraud or deceit upon any person, in connection with the purchase or sale of <u>any security</u>

The security could be offered on the primary market or the secondary market. Either way, full and fair disclosure is what it is all about.

➤ What Is a Security?

So, what is a "security"? The Securities Exchange Act of 1934 defines it this way:

```
The term "security" means any note, stock, treasury stock,
security future, bond, debenture, certificate of interest or
participation in any profit-sharing agreement or in any oil, gas,
or other mineral royalty or lease, any collateral-trust
certificate, pre-organization certificate or subscription,
transferable share, investment contract, voting-trust certificate,
certificate of deposit for a security, any put, call, straddle,
option, or privilege on any security, certificate of deposit, or
group or index of securities (including any interest therein or
based on the value thereof), or any put, call, straddle, option,
```

or privilege entered into on a national securities exchange relating to foreign currency, or in general, any instrument commonly known as a "security"; or any certificate of interest or participation in, temporary or interim certificate for, receipt for, or warrant or right to subscribe to or purchase, any of the foregoing; but shall not include currency or any note, draft, bill of exchange, or banker's acceptance which has a maturity at the time of issuance of not exceeding nine months, exclusive of days of grace, or any renewal thereof the maturity of which is likewise limited.

Among that long list we find the investment contract, which was defined through the Supreme Court's Howey Decision as:

- An investment of money
  - in a common enterprise
  - with an expectation of profits
  - derived through the efforts of others

For example, if an Iowa farmer needed to raise $500,000 to expand his soybean and hog farming operation, maybe he prints up 10 certificates. Each one costs the investor $50,000 and gives the investor a 3% ownership stake in the farm's profits. That's an investment of money in a common enterprise whereby each investor hopes to benefit solely through the efforts of others—the farmer. The investors aren't getting up at 5 a.m. on a cold, February morning in Iowa to feed the livestock, right? They're neither farm hands nor managers, and what they just bought was an "investment contract," which is one example of a "security" as listed in the Securities Exchange Act of 1934. So, if the farmer gives the investors offering documents with inflated profits or exaggerated crop yields, he has probably committed securities fraud. Fraud can carry criminal penalties and civil liabilities to the investors.

On the other hand, if the investment of money is not a security, it is not subject to anti-fraud statutes under securities law. The following investments are not securities:

- Fixed annuities
- Whole life, term life
- Commodities futures contracts

But, if those aren't securities, who is going to regulate them to make sure investors don't get burned? Luckily, we already have insurance regulators for the insurance products and commodities regulators for the commodities futures. The securities regulators only want to regulate securities.

So, why is a fixed annuity not a security when a variable annuity is? A fixed annuity is an insurance contract guaranteed by an insurance company's general account. Money is not at risk when an investor buys a fixed annuity. The insurance company guarantees a rate of return and must live up to the guarantee. But, once they start tying contract values to the stock and bond markets, anything can happen. This is no longer an insurance contract. Rather, it is an investment of money into various mutual-fund-like subaccounts, so it must be registered and regulated as a security.

The most important concept in securities regulations is that if the investment of money fits the definition of a security, and this security is offered or sold through any deceptive or manipulative device, that constitutes securities fraud.

SECTION 17 – RECORDS AND REPORTS

This section of the Securities Exchange Act of 1934 dictates that broker-dealers must file a balance sheet and income statement certified by a registered public accounting firm and any other documents the SEC rules say are needed to determine if the firm is in sound financial condition. Broker-dealers also must send a certified balance sheet to their customers and any other document the SEC decides ought to be sent, as well.

DEFINITIONS UNDER THE SECURITIES EXCHANGE ACT OF 1934

A broker-dealer is a firm that can either help a customer buy and sell securities, or they can take the other side of the transaction with the customer. If they act as a "broker" that means they charge a commission for finding a buyer or seller for the security. They take no risk here, as they hold no inventory. On the other hand, they could take the other side of the transaction with the customer, acting as a dealer. That means they can sell some of their stock for a profit or buy some at a markdown.

When they send a trade confirmation, they indicate whether they acted as a broker/agent, or as a dealer/principal. The definition of **broker** is "any person engaged in the business of effecting transactions in securities for the account of others." The definition of **dealer** is "any person engaged in the business of effecting transactions in securities for its own account." As you might imagine, the definition of "broker-dealer" is "any person engaged in the business of effecting transactions in securities for the account of others or its own account." Some firms are only brokers, carrying no inventory. Most large firms act in various capacities. In fact, there are types of broker-dealers, literally, from A through Z on the form used to register a broker-dealer, **Form BD**.

SECURITIES AND EXCHANGE COMMISSION

The Securities Exchange Act of 1934 established the **SEC** as the ultimate securities regulator. This organization is not just an SRO (**self-regulatory organization**) such as FINRA. The SEC is a federal government entity with whom a mere SRO such as FINRA or CBOE must register.

> ➤ Registration of Securities Associations

Section 15A of the Securities Exchange Act of 1934 requires national securities associations to register with the SEC. That means that exchanges and associations such as the NYSE, NASDAQ, FINRA, CBOE, etc., must register. When the SROs want to change a rule, it must be signed off on by the SEC as well. These SROs may not allow members to join the association unless the members are registered. And, they don't necessarily let everybody who wants in, in. Section 15A talks about **statutory disqualification**, which means that, by statute, FINRA, etc., can deny membership to a firm if it lacks financial strength or has engaged in "acts or practices inconsistent with just and equitable principles of trade." As you may have noticed, FINRA and other SROs can deny membership if a firm or associate fails to meet "standards of training, experience, and competence as are prescribed by the rules of the association." A possible test question would have you say that any felony or securities-related misdemeanor in the past 10 years will likely lead to a statutory disqualification.

Please note that a "securities-related misdemeanor" would include anything involving money or deception: forgery, bribery, perjury, shoplifting, embezzlement, counterfeiting, extortion, fraud, etc. Misdemeanor DUI, for example, would not be a "securities-related" or "investment related" offense.

An important amendment to the Securities Exchange Act of 1934 was the **Maloney Act.** This Act of Congress provided for the registration of national securities associations, such as—at the time—NASD. Turns out, the NASD is the only national securities association that ever registered with the SEC under the Maloney Act.

Let's see how the Securities Exchange Act of 1934 explains the SEC that it empowers:

> The rules of the association are designed to prevent fraudulent and manipulative acts and practices, to promote just and equitable principles of trade, to foster cooperation and coordination with persons engaged in regulating, clearing, settling, processing information with respect to, and facilitating transactions in securities, to remove impediments to and perfect the mechanism of a free and open market and a national market system, and, in general, to protect investors and the public interest;

➢ Fingerprinting

Rule 17f-2 of the Securities Exchange Act of 1934 requires officers and certain employees of member firms to submit fingerprints. As the Act says:

> ...every member of a national securities exchange, broker, dealer, registered transfer agent and registered clearing agency shall require that each of its partners, directors, officers and employees be fingerprinted and shall submit, or cause to be submitted, the fingerprints of such persons to the Attorney General of the United States or its designee for identification and appropriate processing.

But, of course, not everyone must submit fingerprints. Persons who fit the following descriptions are exempt from the fingerprinting rule:

- Is not engaged in the sale of securities;
- Does not regularly have access to the keeping, handling or processing of:
    - securities,
    - monies, or
    - the original books and records relating to the securities or the monies; and
- Does not have direct supervisory responsibility over persons engaged in the activities referred to in paragraphs (a)(1)(i)(A) and (B) of this section.

Also, the following exempts those firms who fit this description:

> Is engaged exclusively in the sale of shares of registered open-end management investment companies, variable contracts, or interests in limited partnerships, unit investment trusts or real

```
estate    investment    trusts;    provided,    that    those    securities
ordinarily are not evidenced by certificates.
```

SECURITIES ACT OF 1933 AND INVESTMENT COMPANIES

A public company such as Starbucks or Microsoft registers their offerings on a standard registration form called an **S-1**. Investment companies use registration **Form N-1A** to accomplish two things at once: register the fund under the Investment Company Act of 1940 and register the shares under the Securities Act of 1933. Form N-1A has two parts. Part A of the registration statement becomes the prospectus that will be used to sell the fund shares to investors. The SEC declares that the prospectus should "disclose fundamental characteristics and investment risks of the Fund, using concise, straightforward, and easy-to-understand language." Part B of the form provides a statement of additional information, which is why they named it the "statement of additional information" or SAI for short. The SEC explains that the SAI should "provide additional information about the Fund that the SEC concludes is not necessary to be in the prospectus, but that some investors may find useful."

In general, the prospectus should:

- emphasize the fund's overall investment approach and strategy
- elicit information for an average or typical investor who may not be sophisticated in legal or financial matters
- help investors evaluate risks of an investment and decide whether to invest in a fund by providing a balanced disclosure of positive and negative factors

Specifically, the following information is required:

- Objectives and goals, risk, performance
- Fee table
- Management of fund
- Purchase and sale of fund shares
- Tax information
- Financial intermediary compensation
- Objectives, strategies, related risks, overview of portfolio holdings
- Management, organization
- Financial highlights

The summary prospectus is all that is legally required to sell a mutual fund to an investor, but to get the investor's interest supplemental sales materials are often used as well. When they are used, these materials must point out how important it is for an investor to read the full or statutory prospectus plus the Statement of Additional Information before investing money in the fund. If you listen closely to a radio advertisement for a mutual fund, you will hear this caveat at the end being read quickly, as if the studio has suddenly caught fire.

What's the big deal about reading a prospectus? A prospectus is a disclosure document completely void of advertising slogans. Its only aim is to inform a prospective investor of all relevant facts he might need to know before investing in the fund. If we let investors simply watch a 30-second TV ad and then send their money into the investment company—without even requesting a prospectus—that would negate the Securities Act of 1933's requirement that investors receive full disclosure.

The prospectus is what it is. A registered representative may not highlight it or make a written summary of it for a customer. If an agent highlighted sections of the prospectus, some customers would conclude they were supposed to ignore the rest of the document. And, if a registered representative wrote his own summary of a prospectus, imagine all the material facts he could end up leaving out, and all the statements he might end up making that have never been reviewed by FINRA or the SEC.

So, an agent should walk a customer through the prospectus, but not alter, highlight, or rewrite the prospectus, ever. Of course, the customer can mark up and highlight a prospectus all she wants. The point is, we don't want a registered representative to do that and hand her a disclosure document she might assume is only to be skimmed.

In the prospectus, an investor can quickly see what the fund is trying to achieve and what the important risks are. He can see the performance record for 1, 5, and 10 years, depending on how long the fund has been around. Right up front, the sales charges and expenses are laid out so investors can compare funds and fund families. While the mutual fund's portfolio is described in the prospectus, an investor often comes away with only a vague sense of what the individual securities are—9% financials, 8.2% consumer discretionary, 11.1% healthcare, etc. As the SEC notes, some investors might find it useful to see the statement of additional information, especially when it comes to looking at what's in the mutual fund portfolio.

The Statement of Additional Information includes a list of each security held in the portfolio and a recent value of the fund's total position in that stock, bond, etc. The prospectus would tell us what percentage of assets are devoted currently to financial companies, and might tell us that Wells Fargo is one of their ten largest holdings. But it wouldn't tell us how many shares of Wells Fargo are owned and what their total market value is. On the other hand, if the fund owns 41,235,800 shares of Wells Fargo (WFC) recently valued at $1.27 billion, the SAI lists that information along with each other position and its value. Any debt securities the fund holds are also listed, including both the par value and the current market value.

So, while the prospectus might state that the balanced fund devotes 29% of assets to fixed-income investments, the SAI, on the other hand, would tell us every debt security held by the fund—the issuer, the nominal yield, the par value, and the current market value. If the fund holds $10 million par value (currently trading at $10.12 million) of 4.5% ABC subordinated debentures maturing in 2019, the SAI will tell us so.

The SAI also includes financial statements for the fund portfolio. An investor can, therefore, see what all the assets are worth—minus any liabilities—on the balance sheet. The assets are the securities values and any cash the fund is holding, while the liabilities are usually minimal and include borrowings used to pay out investors who want to sell/redeem their shares. On the income statement investors can see how much income the portfolio securities generated through dividends and interest payments, minus all the expenses of the fund for all the parties involved with running it: investment adviser, distributor, transfer agent, custodian, etc.

The SEC requires the following information in the SAI:

- Fund History
- Fund Policies, e.g., borrowing, issuing, underwriting securities, etc.
- Detailed information on officers and directors
- Detailed information on all advisers and related entities
- Brokerage allocation
- Audited financial statements (income, balance)
- Portfolio securities in detail

The two documents come together again on the back cover of the prospectus, which must disclose how to obtain an SAI by calling a toll-free number, visiting the company's website, or mailing in a request. I tend to just go to the mutual fund company's website and download the SAI in a few seconds. The one I'm looking at now for the American Balanced Fund is 193 pages long, and it shows exactly what is in the fund's portfolio and exactly how much money it generated for investors and for all the entities running the fund. For example, for the most recent year, the American Balanced Fund portfolio generated about $1.8 billion in dividends and interest and then took about $537 million of that to cover operating expenses before sharing the net income—about $1.3 billion—with investors. That, I got from the income statement. The balance sheet tells me that the securities and cash, minus all liabilities, left the fund with just under $85 billion in net assets.

If you visit an investment company's website, you will find the prospectus and SAI for each mutual fund. You will also find links to the **semiannual report** and the **annual report** to shareholders. Note that while public companies report quarterly to shareholders, mutual funds report only twice per year, with the annual report audited by an independent accountant. As with public companies, only the annual report for a mutual fund must be audited, not that the other reports can be bogus or sloppy. It's just that a certified public accountant must certify that the numbers presented in the annual report have been verified.

The **summary prospectus** is the most scaled-down document used to offer and sell an open-end fund. The document must be clearly identified as a summary prospectus and on the cover page or toward the beginning of the document the following statement must be made:

```
Before you invest, you may want to review the Fund's prospectus,
which contains more information about the Fund and its risks. You
can find the Fund's prospectus and other information about the
Fund online at [_____]. You can also get this information at no
cost by calling [_____] or by sending an e-mail request to [_____].
```

To assist investors in getting the full or **statutory prospectus**, the summary prospectus must have a toll-free phone number, an email address, and a website address for obtaining the more complete document. The website address must take the user directly to the document, too, should the test get that detailed. Since this is a summary of the statutory prospectus, the information that is contained in both documents must be the same—in other words, the summary prospectus contains less information than the statutory prospectus—not a different set of facts.

GENERIC ADVERTISING

Generic advertising is defined as any type of notice that does not specifically refer by name to the securities of a specific investment company or to the investment company itself. Generic advertising would include communications that:

- relate to securities of investment companies generally or to the nature of investment companies, or to services offered in connection with the ownership of such securities
- mention or explain different types of funds, for example—growth, value, blend, bond, no-load, variable annuities, etc.
- invite the reader to inquire further

Generic advertising must contain the name and address of a registered broker or dealer or other person sponsoring the communication. Generic advertising is not considered an offer for sale and, therefore, falls under different rules from, say, a prospectus or advertisement for a specific mutual fund.

SALES LITERATURE MUST NOT BE MISLEADING

The Securities Act of 1933 stipulates that **sales literature** for investment company shares must not be misleading, either by making untrue statements of material fact or omitting material facts that must be included to avoid misleading investors. For example, if the aggressive growth technology fund wants to brag about a 20% total return, they must compare that to the appropriate technology index. If a technology fund is up 20% when the NASDAQ Composite is up 35%, the investor needs the whole story, right? And, of course, whenever past returns are mentioned, the sales literature must also point out that this does not imply that future results will be similar. Also, inappropriate comparisons among funds are prohibited. For example, if an aggressive growth fund tries to compare a 5% return to the 2% return on a money market fund, this would be misleading. The literature should compare the aggressive growth fund to other aggressive growth funds and an appropriate index—not to bank CDs, T-Bills, money market funds, or even growth & income funds.

Benefits of investing in securities and, specifically, the securities of the fund being promoted can be listed. This is, after all, sales literature. It's just that whenever a benefit is mentioned, a statement of risk can't be far behind. The prospectus I'm looking at tells the reader:

```
Your investment in the fund is not a bank deposit and is not
insured or guaranteed by the FDIC or any other government agency.
```

In case that didn't make the point, the next statement is:

```
You may lose money by investing in the fund. The likelihood of
loss is greater if you invest for a shorter period of time.
```

ADVERTISING

The Securities Act of 1933 authorizes the SEC to consider the purpose of each offering when writing requirements for the prospectus. As Section 10 of the Act states: The Commission shall have the authority to classify prospectuses according to the nature and circumstances of their use or the nature of the security, issue, issuer…and to prescribe as to each class the form and contents which it may find appropriate and consistent with the public interest and the protection of investors.

When an investment company advertises its products in a magazine, or on TV and radio, they are omitting many material facts contained in the prospectus. Therefore, such an advertisement for a mutual fund may be referred to as an **omitting prospectus.**

An advertisement must include a statement that advises an investor to consider the investment objectives, risks, and charges and expenses of the investment company carefully before investing. The ad also must explain that the prospectus contains this and other information about the investment company, and it must identify a source from which an investor may obtain a prospectus.

An advertisement containing performance data must include a legend disclosing the following:

- the performance data quoted represent past performance
- past performance does not guarantee future results
- the investment return and principal value of an investment will fluctuate so that an investor's shares, when redeemed, may be worth more or less than their original cost
- current performance may be lower or higher than the performance data quoted

The legend must also identify a toll-free telephone number or a website where an investor may obtain performance data current to the most recent month-end. If a sales load or any other nonrecurring fee is charged by the fund, the advertisement must disclose the maximum sales charge, and it must be clear whether the performance figures cited are including the deduction of sales loads. If they aren't including that, there must be a statement pointing out that returns would be reduced if we factored in the sales loads.

An advertisement for a money market fund that presents itself as maintaining a "stable value" must include the following statement:

> An investment in the Fund is not insured or guaranteed by the Federal Deposit Insurance Corporation or any other government agency. Although the Fund seeks to preserve the value of your investment at $1.00 per share, it is possible to lose money by investing in the Fund.

Of course, a loss on a money market fund investment could happen, but almost certainly won't happen. Most investors alive today have only heard of such craziness one time in their lives, no matter how old they might be. So, think of a money market mutual fund investment as a "safe-money investment" that isn't guaranteed by a bank, an insurance company, or the United States Treasury. It's backed up by the prudence of the portfolio managers buying the highest quality short-term debt securities they can buy that will also generate some sort of yield for the investors. If the exam asks you to compare the safety of a money market mutual fund and, say, a U.S. Treasury Note, or a $125,000 bank CD, the T-Note and the CD are in an entirely different world of safety—investors are not going to experience a default on these unless the United States Government basically just gives up and rolls over like a beached whale.

A money market mutual fund, on the other hand, could end up being run by a group of guys who turn out to be, contrary to popular belief, maybe only the second or third smartest guys in the room—if the portfolio managers buy commercial paper in companies that then go bankrupt, the fund may not be able to keep the share price at $1. Once that news got out, investor redemptions would probably skyrocket, and the panic could force the fund to liquidate all kinds of holdings at fire-sale prices, further worsening the problem.

So, as an investor, please don't worry about such an outcome, but, as a registered representative, please make sure your customer understands what could happen and why some safe-money investments are much safer than others. An investment guaranteed by the United States Treasury is always the safest thing out there, and that includes any FDIC-insured bank deposit. Insurance companies and mutual fund companies also offer products that provide a more stable principal and an extremely low chance of loss-of-principal.

DEFINITIONS UNDER INVESTMENT ADVISERS ACT OF 1940

A "broker-dealer" makes money through transactions in securities. So, of course, the investment in question must be a "security" as defined by law, not a fixed annuity, whole life insurance policy, etc. But if any person is effecting transactions for the accounts of others in securities, they fit the definition of a broker-dealer. These transactions can take place on the primary market, as with IPOs, or on the secondary market, when an investor decides to buy or sell securities trading back and forth among investors.

An **investment adviser**, on the other hand, does not make money because someone is buying or selling securities. Rather, an investment adviser is compensated for providing investment advice related to securities. If I draw up a detailed financial plan for a client and charge $3,000, I just got compensated for investment advice.

The **Investment Advisers Act of 1940** defines an investment adviser as:

> ...any person who, for compensation, engages in the business of advising others, either directly or through publications or writings, as to the value of securities or as to the advisability of investing in, purchasing, or selling securities, or who, for compensation and as part of a regular business, issues or promulgates analyses or reports concerning securities.

If the person is compensated for advising others on securities, they are acting as an investment adviser. What if the person is advising them on fixed annuities? Those aren't securities, so they wouldn't be an investment adviser. If they did something stupid, they would be disciplined under insurance laws.

An investment adviser often does more than simply tell someone what he or she ought to do. Many investment advisers are portfolio managers who trade their clients' accounts in exchange for a percentage of the account value. So, the number of transactions has no bearing on their compensation. Rather, their motivation is to make the account value rise. Which, as it turns out, is usually what their clients want, too. Even when an investment adviser places a buy or sell order for their client's account, that trade is executed at a broker-dealer.

Some clients bypass the investment adviser and simply ask their registered rep what to do before making their own decision—if they buy or sell, the registered rep makes a commission. Some clients like using a portfolio manager to decide what to do, knowing the investment adviser only gets paid more money if the client's account value rises.

INVESTMENT ADVISER REPRESENTATIVES

When investment advisers hire people to sell the services of the firm or manage customer accounts, those people must be registered, too. These individuals represent the investment adviser, so the industry decided to call them **investment adviser representatives**. The investment adviser registers either with the SEC or certain states. When they do so, they use Form ADV and indicate whether they're registering with the federal regulators or the state regulators. They submit **Form U4** applications to the states in which their investment adviser representatives must be registered, too. The exam might say that employees of an investment advisory firm would be considered representatives if they:

- manage accounts
- sell the services of the firm
- determine recommendations for clients
- make recommendations to clients
- supervise those who do any of the above

So, the receptionist or IT guy would not have to pass the Series 65 exam and get licensed. The regulators call the individuals who don't have to register "ministerial personnel."

FINRA (AND NASD) RULES

COMMUNICATIONS WITH THE PUBLIC

As we've seen, communications with the public must be approved or at least monitored by a principal, with copies of certain materials kept in a separate file at the firm. Communications going out to retail investors not only must be pre-approved and filed internally by the firm, but a copy of the material must also be filed with FINRA. Since these communications are regulated so tightly, it's important that each firm have sufficient written supervisory procedures governing the whole process. One of the more frequent violations that firms get nailed for is inadequate written supervisory procedures (WSPs).

Let's look at the important definitions involved here. First, a "communication" is defined as correspondence, retail communications and institutional communications:

- Correspondence: any written (including electronic) communication that is distributed or made available to 25 or fewer retail investors within any 30 calendar-day period.
- Institutional Communications: any communication that is distributed or made available only to institutional investors. NOTE: **Institutional investors** (as opposed to retail investors) include: a bank, savings and loan association, insurance company, registered investment

company, registered investment adviser, any other entity (whether a natural person, corporation, partnership, trust, or otherwise) with total assets of at least $50 million, a governmental entity or subdivision thereof, a 403(b) or Section 457 plan that has at least 100 participants, a qualified plan that has at least 100 participants, a FINRA member or registered associated person of such a member, and a person acting solely on behalf of any such institutional investor.

- Retail Communications: any written (including electronic) communication that is distributed or made available to more than 25 retail investors within any 30 calendar-day period

So, correspondence is any written communication going to 25 or fewer retail investors. Whether these investors are prospects or existing customers makes no difference. FINRA is now only focused on the number 25 (or fewer). Correspondence is not required to be pre-approved by a principal or filed with FINRA, so that number 25 is important. For example, if your test question says that a registered representative provides a handout at a live seminar for 22 investors, that material is merely correspondence. But if it is handed out to, say, 32 investors, it is now a "retail communication."

Who cares? Well, retail communications must be pre-approved and filed internally by a principal, with a copy also filed with FINRA. Failure to file these communications will lead to disciplinary action. Even though FINRA has changed the names of their categories, the following are still examples of written communications that could either be considered correspondence or retail communications, depending on whether they're delivered to 25 or fewer (correspondence) or more than 25 retail investors (retail communications):

- Form letter
- Computer slide show
- Brochure
- Market letter making investment recommendations
- Independently prepared reprint

For that last item, the "independently prepared reprint," if a registered representative sends a copy of a favorable magazine or newspaper article to 20 retail investors, that is still correspondence, but if it goes to more than 25 retail investors, it is considered a retail communication.

Clearly, the written communications going to institutional investors are not regulated as tightly as those going to folks who often don't know much about investing. Communications to banks, pension funds, etc., cannot be misleading, of course, but the audience is not so unsophisticated that everything must be pre-approved and/or filed with FINRA.

No matter how we define the communications with the public, it all comes down to this idea:

> *All member communications with the public shall be based on principles of fair dealing and good faith, must be fair and balanced, and must provide a sound basis for evaluating the facts in regard to any specific security or type of security, industry, or service. No member may omit any material fact or qualification if the omission,*

The communications put out by a member firm are a big deal, which is why most of them must be approved internally by a compliance principal and many require that a copy also be filed with FINRA. Retail communications must be approved by a principal before they are used. This would include, for example, a form letter to prospects, a display ad in a local business directory, handouts from an investment seminar, or even an independently prepared reprint of a magazine article sent to more than 25 retail investors. Basically, what FINRA used to call "sales literature" or "advertising" would be examples of what they now call "retail communications." We used to split hairs between whether the communication was broadcast out to a general audience (advertising) or delivered to a controlled audience (sales literature). Either way, the stuff had to be pre-approved and filed internally and with FINRA. It still does, but it's now considered "retail communications," and you'll notice it's based on the sophistication level of the audience rather than the delivery method of the message.

The reason the test might sweat you on the difference between "correspondence" and "institutional communications" on one hand and "retail communications" on the other is that correspondence and institutional communications must be monitored, while retail communications must be approved by a principal internally before they are used, and filed with FINRA within 10 days of first use. Also, note, though, that if materials have already been filed with FINRA, they do not need to be filed again provided they are not being altered by the firm using them. In other words, the sponsor for a mutual fund files virtually all communications connected to it; from there, member firms selling the fund just need to be sure they use the material as it was filed. There is a big difference between a registered representative using a piece of supplemental sales literature on a mutual fund that was filed with FINRA long ago and that same registered representative creating his own PowerPoint slide show on the benefits of mutual fund investing. Right?

Retail communications must prominently disclose the member firm's name and if any other entity is named, the communication must reflect the relationship between the member firm and that entity and make clear which products and services are offered by the member firm itself. Retail communications include advertising, which is why all TV and radio ads name the broker-dealer. The exception to that rule is a "blind recruitment ad" looking for employees—in these the firm can leave its name off the ad and ask candidates to submit their information to a nondescript mailing address. This makes sense, as a well-known firm might not want 10,000 aggressive sales professionals clogging up all lines of communication once they know who is hiring. A new member broker-dealer is required to file its retail communications before they are used. Established companies file most communications with FINRA within 10 days of first use—meaning no later than 10 days *after* the stuff already went out. But, certain materials must be pre-filed with FINRA even if the member broker-dealer is established. If the communication, for example, includes investment company rankings that are either not generally published or are created by the investment company itself or an underwriter/affiliate, the material must be filed before it's used.

When a member firm files copies of retail communications with FINRA, they provide the following information:

- Date of first use
- Name, Title, CRD # of principal approving it
- Date approval given

Not surprisingly, institutional communications are not regulated as tightly as retail communications are. As FINRA explains in a notice to member firms, the rules on communications "permit a firm to distribute an institutional communication without having a registered principal approve the communication prior to distribution, provided that the firm establishes and implements certain written procedures for the supervision and review of such communications." So, an institutional communication is treated similarly to correspondence—monitor it, have a procedure in place to supervise it, but prior principal approval is not required.

A retail communication, on the other hand, is subject to internal principal pre-approval, with a copy usually also filed with FINRA. Correspondence, as opposed to retail communications, comes down to the number 25. So, a seminar handout provided to 25 or fewer retail investors within a 30 calendar-day period would be considered correspondence under the new definition. Under the old definition, it would have been considered "sales literature." Either way, the materials must conform to the rules on communications of a member firm.

TYPE OF COMMUNICATION	MONITORED?	PRIOR APPROVAL?	FILED WITH FINRA?
Correspondence	Yes	No	No
Retail Communications	Yes	Yes	Usually
Institutional Communications	Yes	Not usually	No

COMMUNICATIONS REGARDING VARIABLE CONTRACTS

Communications regarding variable contracts are subject to the same FINRA standards for communications generally, plus a few that are specific to these products. First, a customer must understand clearly that she's being offered a variable annuity or variable life insurance (VLI) no matter what the name of the product might be. And in neither case is she being offered a mutual fund, even if there are similarities. Liquidity is not available on many variable contracts, so if a customer is sold a variable annuity or variable life policy believing it makes a good short-term investment that can be liquidated for a good price, that's a problem. Contingent deferred sales charges and tax ramifications must be made clear to the customer, since cashing in a variable annuity can subject the investor to a 10% penalty plus surrender charges.

There are "guarantees" offered in variable contracts, such as the minimum guaranteed death benefit on a VLI policy, or the death benefit offered on a variable annuity. But, these guarantees are subject to the insurance company's ability to pay claims. Make that clear to the customer. Even though variable life insurance ties cash value and death benefit values to the investment markets, it must be marketed foremost as a life insurance product. If the regulators feel that an agent is selling VLI primarily as a way to invest in the stock and bond market or achieve tax deferral, he could have problems. To that end, we don't compare VLI to mutual funds, stocks or bonds; compare it to other types of insurance, including term, whole life, or variable universal life (VUL).

Unlike when an agent sells a mutual fund, when selling insurance, illustrations are routinely used. Chances are, the agent will show illustrations of a whole life insurance policy compared to a VLI and perhaps a VUL policy. The illustrations are not guarantees, and the insurance company must be careful how they present this information. They can show a hypothetical illustration as high as a "gross rate" of 12%, provided they also show how things would work out with a "gross rate" of 0%. Whatever the maximum rate used is, it must be reasonable given recent market conditions and the available investment options. Since mortality and expense charges reduce returns, illustrations must be figured using the maximum charges. Current charges may also be included.

SPECIFIC TYPES OF COMMUNICATIONS

Retail communications for investment company securities that contain a ranking or performance comparison used to require members to file a copy of the ranking or comparison used when filing the retail communication with FINRA. The rule was created back when FINRA staff did not have ready access to such rankings or comparisons. Now that such information is readily available online, members simply must maintain back-up materials supporting what was cited in their retail communications.

FINRA also used to require any retail communication involving bond mutual fund volatility to be filed 10 days prior to first use. Also, any such communication had to be preceded or accompanied by a prospectus when delivered to an investor. Now, FINRA allows these retail communications to be filed within (after) 10 days of first use and has eliminated the prospectus-delivery requirement for these communications.

Members offering or providing investment analysis tools allowing customers to make their own investment decisions used to be required to provide access to the tools to FINRA staff. Now, members simply must provide such access upon FINRA's request. Members also no longer file report templates and the retail communications themselves with FINRA.

PAYMENTS INVOLVING PUBLICATIONS THAT INFLUENCE THE MARKET PRICE OF A SECURITY

Advertising in a magazine is fine, provided the member firm follows all the SEC and FINRA requirements. What is not fine is for a member firm to get a magazine or website to write favorable reviews of the member's family of mutual funds in exchange for cash or anything of value. The Securities Act of 1933 requires that any communication put out to influence the market price of a security must include disclosure that the person putting it out is receiving compensation. Research reports put out by broker-dealers are covered under different rules. A research report is used to increase business for the broker-dealer as opposed to prop up the price of the stock that is being researched and possibly rated highly by the firm.

OUTSIDE BUSINESS ACTIVITIES OF AN ASSOCIATED PERSON

Many students seem shocked when I tell them that they'll be required to notify their employing broker-dealer before doing any type of work outside the firm. As this rule stipulates:

No person associated with a member in any registered capacity shall be employed by, or accept compensation from, any other person as a result of any business activity, other than a passive investment, outside the scope of his relationship with his employer firm, unless he has provided prompt written notice to the member. Such notice shall be in the form required by the member.

Notice that a "passive investment" does not count here. So, if you get a question about a registered representative who owns a vacation property that he rents out each summer, this is not covered under this rule. That is a passive investment.

PRIVATE SECURITIES TRANSACTIONS OF AN ASSOCIATED PERSON

Some people studying for this exam seem to imagine that they'll be maintaining their independence and autonomy even after associating with a member firm. They can't believe they must tell the firm about the bar and grill they're planning to open with their brother-in-law Billy next spring. They're appalled that TD Ameritrade or the Charles Schwab Company would have the audacity to inform their employer that they just opened an investment account with them. They also don't see why they can't join up with a member firm but continue to offer whatever type of investment opportunity comes up to their clients through whatever other firm wants to do the deal.

Well, FINRA wants all activities of a registered representative to be supervised, so if the registered representative is sitting in his office offering investors a chance to invest in his sister's new diner down the street without telling his firm, there is no way the firm could monitor his activities to protect investors. That could even be the answer to a Series 6 question asking why **selling away** is a violation—because it gives the principal/firm no opportunity to supervise the activities. A registered representative cannot offer securities to investors that his firm knows nothing about. As this rule makes clear:

No person associated with a member shall participate in any manner in a private securities transaction except in accordance with the requirements of this Rule.

(b) Written Notice

Prior to participating in any private securities transaction, an associated person shall provide written notice to the member with which he is associated describing in detail the proposed transaction and the person's proposed role therein and stating whether he has received or may receive selling compensation in connection with the transaction.

Once the registered representative has provided written notice to the employer, the member firm can either approve or disapprove of the plan. If they approve the activities, the transaction must be recorded on the books and records of the member firm, and the member must supervise the registered representative's participation in the transaction as if the transaction were executed on behalf of the member. If there is no compensation to be received, the firm mudt acknowledge receipt of the agent's intentions and indicate whether the activity is to be allowed. What if the firm says they disapprove of the activity?

Doing so anyway is a violation known as selling away or selling away from the firm.

NASD RULE: PERSONS SERVING IN THE ARMED FORCES OF THE UNITED STATES

What happens when a registered representative volunteers or is called into active military duty? If he or she is away from the firm more than two years, does the license expire? Does he have to take continuing education courses in some cave in Afghanistan? Does she lose all the commissions she could have made on her "book of business"?

Not surprisingly, FINRA and the SEC are extremely accommodating when a registered representative or principal is called away from the firm to serve Uncle Sam. Here are the basic facts:

- license is placed on "inactive status"
- continuing education requirements waived
- dues, assessments waived
- two-year expiration period does not apply—exam might refer to this as "tolling"
- can earn commissions, usually by splitting them with another rep who will service the book of business
- the "inactive" representative cannot perform any of the duties of a registered rep while on inactive status

You could see a question about a "sole proprietor" called into active military duty. If so, tell the test that the same bullet points above would apply.

TELEMARKETING

So, you'd like to spend your day smiling and dialing, huh?

Careful. As you may have noticed, there has been a major backlash against telemarketing in general, and FINRA has codified how the smile-and-dial process must be approached. Let's bring up a few quick facts:

- Don't call the residence of any person before 8 a.m. or after 9 p.m. in the prospect's local time zone, unless that person has given express written/signed permission, is an established customer of your firm, or is a broker-dealer
- Check your firm's specific do-not-call list. If the prospect is on that list, should you go ahead and dial them anyway? Only if you're planning an early retirement
- Check the Federal Trade Commission's national do-not-call list and do not call anyone on that list
- A member or person associated with a member making a call for telemarketing purposes must provide the called party with the name of the individual caller, the name of the member, an address or telephone number at which the member may be contacted, and that the purpose of the call is to solicit the purchase of securities or related service. The telephone number provided may not be a 900 number or any other number for which charges exceed local or long distance transmission charges
- The provisions set forth in this rule are applicable to members telemarketing or making telephone solicitations calls to wireless telephone numbers

- If a member uses another entity to perform telemarketing services on its behalf, the member remains responsible for ensuring compliance with all provisions contained in this rule

Prior to engaging in telemarketing activities, the firm must:

- Create a written policy for maintaining a do-not-call list
- Train personnel who will be smiling and dialing
- If anyone requests to be put on your firm-specific do-not-call list, put them on the list
- Identify all callers—who you are, who you work for, the fact that you are trying to interest them in securities

> ➢ Tape-Recording Rule

This do-not-call stuff is a major pain. For some firms, the pain is even greater. If certain sales representatives have an employment history that includes working at a "disciplined firm," the firm is going to must start tape-recording all telephone conversations between the member's registered persons and both existing and potential customers. The firm will be required to establish procedures for reviewing the tape recordings and must maintain the recordings for three years. At the end of each calendar quarter, such firms must report to FINRA on their supervision of the telemarketing activities. The reporting is due within 30 days of the end of each quarter.

What is a disciplined firm? Basically, any firm that has been disciplined by the SEC, any SRO, or the Commodity Futures Trading Commission. So, if a certain number of registered reps used to work at disciplined firms, break out the tape recorder and start taping. You can probably find a list of firms currently subject to this rule at www.finra.org.

SELLING DIVIDENDS

As a mutual fund prospectus explains, there is no reason to hurry up and buy the fund simply because it's about to pay a dividend to investors. The share price will drop by the amount of the dividend, and the investor will be taxed. So, if you push your customer to hurry up and buy the fund or the common stock to receive the next dividend, that's a violation called **selling dividends**. That is a great name for it, as it implies the registered representative is trying to sell an upcoming dividend as opposed to a long-term investment in a dividend-paying portfolio of stocks. As the prospectus on my desk informs investors:

> On the ex-dividend date for a distribution, a fund's share price is reduced by the amount of the distribution. If you buy shares just before the ex-dividend date, in effect, you "buy the dividend." You will pay the full price for the shares and then receive a portion of that price back as a taxable distribution.

So, selling an equity income fund to an investor seeking dividend income is probably a good idea. Trying to hustle that investor into hurrying up to collect a dividend from that mutual fund—bad idea. The portfolio will receive all kinds of dividends from all kinds of diverse issuers and industry groups going forward, which will help your investor achieve his goal. Playing games with the temporary share-price fluctuation most mutual fund investors would never notice—that's the deceit that FINRA and the SEC frown upon.

USE OF MANIPULATIVE, DECEPTIVE OR OTHER FRAUDULENT DEVICES

As mentioned, the Securities Exchange Act of 1934 prohibits the use of deception in connection with the offer, sale, or purchase of any security. When you sit for the Series 63 exam, you'll see that state securities law is not just on the same page but sounds like an echo of the federal act. FINRA is also on the same page, which is why they decided to make it a violation of FINRA rules to mislead investors. As this rule states:

> No member shall effect any transaction in, or induce the purchase or sale of, any security by means of any manipulative, deceptive or other fraudulent device or contrivance.

For example, if you needed $3 million to execute a business plan based on a communications device that is not quite ready for production, you could present a prototype to large investors with a phony report touting its many benefits and maybe a production engineer's assertion that the product can be made this quickly for this amount of money. You could do all this, that is, if you were reasonably sure the investors won't mind losing their money while you drive around in a new Cadillac CTS. I never seem to forget about an agent who took $50,000 from a 75-year-old widow, told her he was investing it in a specific mutual fund, but put the money into his own day-trading account, where whatever he didn't lose on bad tech-stock picks was eventually spent on personal items at the local mall.

That's manipulative, deceptive, or fraudulent. That's a career-ender.

TRANSACTIONS, ACCOUNTS AND ASSOCIATED PERSONS

On a new account form, the agent asks if the customer is associated with a member firm. If the broker-dealer knows the customer is associated with a member firm, or if an associate of a member firm has discretion over the account, the firm must:

- notify the employer member in writing, prior to the execution of a transaction for such account, of the executing member's intention to open or maintain such an account;
- upon written request by the employer member, transmit duplicate copies of confirmations, statements, or other information with respect to such account; and
- notify the person associated with the employer member of the executing member's intention to provide the notice and information required

Broker-dealers must go a little farther than just notifying the other firm that an employee is going to start executing transactions through the firm. All member firms have a duty to determine that any transaction entered for an employee of another member will not adversely affect the other member. The rule on adverse interest requires the executing member to use reasonable diligence to determine that a transaction will not adversely affect the employer member firm. Notice how FINRA puts the burden on the executing member firm to determine that the transaction will not harm the other member as opposed to forcing the other side to prove they've been harmed. These regulators—they think of everything.

You will soon be an associate of a member firm, so when you want to open an investment account with another firm, the rules state:

A person associated with a member, prior to opening an account or placing an initial order for the purchase or sale of securities with another member, shall notify both the employer member and the executing member, in writing, of his or her association with the other member; provided, however, that if the account was established prior to the association of the person with the employer member, the associated person shall notify both members in writing promptly after becoming so associated

Not only must you inform your employing broker-dealer about other brokerage accounts, but also FINRA requires employees to notify their employer in writing prior to any transactions in an account with an investment adviser, bank, or other financial institution. Upon written request from the employing member firm, the employee must request in writing and assure that the investment adviser, bank, or other financial institution provides the employer member with duplicate copies of confirmations, statements, etc.

FINRA RULES, PROCEDURES

The most important FINRA rule states that "A member, in the conduct of his business, shall observe high standards of commercial honor and just and equitable principles of trade." So, if the conduct is inconsistent with high standards of commercial honor and isn't fair to customers, FINRA has a problem with that. What can they do about it? As we'll see, they can fine violators, and they can end their careers.

REGISTRATION

As we mentioned, if a firm tries to register with FINRA, or if they try to hire an agent or principal, they could get shot down by what's called a statutory disqualification. If the person trying to get registered has already been disciplined by a securities regulator, his chances aren't good. If they've been convicted of any felony or any securities related misdemeanor in the past 10 years, same thing. The FINRA Manual explains that if the misdemeanor "involves the purchase or sale of any security, the taking of a false oath, the making of a false report, bribery, perjury, burglary, any substantially equivalent activity however denominated by the laws of the relevant foreign government, or conspiracy to commit any such offense," the agent, principal, or firm could lose his license or be prevented from getting registered.

FINRA makes it clear that filing bogus or misleading information would be a bad idea:

> *Filing of Misleading Information as to Membership or Registration*
>
> *The filing with the Association of information with respect to membership or registration as a Registered Representative which is incomplete or inaccurate so as to be misleading, or which could in any way tend to mislead, or the failure to correct such filing after notice thereof, may be deemed to be conduct inconsistent with just and equitable principles of trade and when discovered may be sufficient cause for appropriate disciplinary action.*

Individuals who try to conceal felonies or investment-related misdemeanors are filing misleading information and will be removed from the business when they are found out.

> ### Failure to Register Personnel
>
> *The failure of any member to register an employee, who should be so registered, as a Registered Representative may be deemed to be conduct inconsistent with just and equitable principles of trade and when discovered may be sufficient cause for appropriate disciplinary action.*

Secretaries and receptionists working for member firms don't have to be registered, but any employee who is selling mutual funds, annuities or other securities must be.

Here's how FINRA puts it:

> ### All Representatives Must Be Registered
>
> *All persons engaged or to be engaged in the investment banking or securities business of a member who are to function as representatives shall be registered as such with FINRA/NASD in the category of registration appropriate to the function to be performed as specified in Rule 1032. Before their registration can become effective, they shall pass a Qualification Examination for Representatives appropriate to the category of registration as specified by the Board of Governors.*

FINRA defines a representative like this:

> ### Definition of Representative
>
> *Persons associated with a member, including assistant officers other than principals, who are engaged in the investment banking or securities business for the member including the functions of supervision, solicitation or conduct of business in securities or who are engaged in the training of persons associated with a member for any of these functions are designated as representatives.*

There are different categories of "registered representative," too. A General Securities Representative has a Series 7 and can sell individual stocks, bonds, municipal securities, options…generally just about anything. A person with a Series 6 is called a Limited Representative—Investment Company and Variable Contracts Products. This allows the individual to sell only mutual funds and variable contracts, plus something that seldom gets mentioned: a Series 6 holder can also be part of an underwriting for a closed-end fund. Just the underwriting, though, which is done through a prospectus.

Once they start trading in the secondary market between investors, they're just shares of stock, and a Series 6 holder can't sell individual shares of stock. Everything they sell must come with a prospectus.

FINRA does not allow inactive representatives to park their license at a broker-dealer:

> *A member shall not maintain a representative registration with FINRA/NASD for any person (1) who is no longer active in the member's investment banking or securities business, (2) who is no longer functioning as a representative, or (3) where the sole purpose is to avoid the examination requirement prescribed in paragraph (c).*

So, if the agent is out for two years or more, he must take this exam again, so (3) is saying that the firm had better not pretend he is associated just so he can skip the Series 6 requirement.

A broker-dealer also could not sponsor someone for the Series 6 exam just so the person could sit for the test. As the rules say:

> *A member shall not make application for the registration of any person as representative where there is no intent to employ such person in the member's investment banking or securities business.*

FINRA also now requires registrations to be made electronically, and member firms must identify a principal or corporate officer responsible for supervising the registration process.

EXAM CONFIDENTIALITY

How serious is FINRA about protecting the surprise element in their exams? Let's see:

> *FINRA/NASD considers all its Qualification Examinations to be highly confidential. The removal from an examination center, reproduction, disclosure, receipt from or passing to any person, or use for study purposes of any portion of such Qualification Examination, whether of a present or past series, or any other use which would compromise the effectiveness of the Examinations and the use in any manner and at any time of the questions or answers to the Examinations are prohibited and are deemed to be a violation of Rule 2110.*

Individuals have been caught cheating on their exams, which is a violation of this FINRA rule:

FORM U4, FORM U5, AND CRD

When a broker-dealer hires a securities agent, the **U4** form must be completed. When an agent in training fills out the U4, he must be sure that what he's filling out is the truth, the whole truth, and nothing but the truth. The agent also must manually sign the U4, as FINRA rules state:

Every initial and transfer electronic Form U4 filing and any amendments to the disclosure information on Form U4 shall be based on a manually signed Form U4 provided to the member or applicant for membership by the person on whose behalf the Form U4 is being filed. As part of the member's recordkeeping requirements, it shall retain the person's manually signed Form U4 or amendments to the disclosure information on Form U4 in accordance with SEA Rule 17a-4(e)(1) and make them available promptly upon regulatory request. An applicant for membership also shall retain in accordance with SEA Rule 17a-4(e)(1) every manually signed Form U4 it receives during the application process and make them available promptly upon regulatory request.

As you can see, Form U4 is important. Form U4 is filed by the broker-dealer on behalf of the agent, but the agent must complete and sign (manual signature) several sections involving information such as:

- Name, address, any aliases
- 5-year residency history
- 10-year employment history
- Information on any charges of any felony or any "securities-related misdemeanor" such as fraud, forgery, theft, counterfeiting, extortion, embezzlement, etc.

After a member firm submits U4 information on an individual, they must also promptly submit fingerprint information. If the fingerprint information is not provided to FINRA within 30 days of application, the registration will be deemed inactive.

An exam question might add a couple of incorrect choices, so remember that on Form U4, the applicant does not disclose his marital status or level of education.

When an agent leaves one broker-dealer to work at another firm, the broker-dealer fills out a U5 within 30 days of the agent's termination date. Then, the agent can do the whole U4 process all over again with the new firm. In other words, an agent's registration is not transferred from one firm to the next. U5 out. U4 in. The hiring broker-dealer is required to get a copy of the agent's U5 filed with

FINRA's **Central Registration Depository** or **CRD**, or they could require the agent to provide a copy, in which case he must do so within two business days of the request. Member firms must keep their U5 records for three years, two years in an easily accessible place. The U5 information is just as important to the regulators as is the U4 information. Why? Because if an agent has a history of getting fired for bad deeds, the public needs to know that. In fact, it might be the biggest benefit provided by the BrokerCheck system.

Speaking of BrokerCheck, FINRA only releases information considered relevant to the investing public. While you do provide your residential history on Form U4, FINRA does not provide that to the public. Nor do they provide your physical description.

The CRD is a place that maintains information on all persons registered with FINRA, including information on customer complaints and disciplinary history. If you know somebody you don't like at the firm, it might be fun to see if you can find any dirt on him at FINRA's broker check at www.finra.org. It's public information; you would not be spying. Member firms need principals who supervise the registered representatives, review correspondence and other communications going out to investors, approve every account, initial order tickets, handle written customer complaints, and make sure there's a written supervisory manual for the office to use to stay in compliance with regulations. In other words, somebody at the firm is ultimately responsible for the business of the firm—that person is the principal.

FINRA puts it like this:

All Principals Must Be Registered

All persons engaged or to be engaged in the investment banking or securities business of a member who are to function as principals shall be registered as such with FINRA/NASD in the category of registration appropriate to the function to be performed as specified in Rule 1022. Before their registration can become effective, they shall pass a Qualification Examination for Principals appropriate to the category of registration as specified by the Board of Governors.

Here is how FINRA defines a "principal":

Definition of Principal

Persons associated with a member who are actively engaged in the management of the member's investment banking or securities business, including supervision, solicitation, conduct of business or the training of persons associated with a member for any of these functions are designated as principals.

Also, note that, in general, each member must have at least two principals taking care of the stuff that principals are supposed to take care of.

CONTINUING EDUCATION

Registered representatives must complete continuing education requirements including the **regulatory element** and the **firm element**. The regulatory element requires registered representatives to participate in a training exercise that must be completed within 120 days after a person's second registration anniversary, and every three years thereafter. If the rep does not complete the regulatory element, his registration can become inactive, meaning he can't do any business. If the registration remains inactive for two years, it is terminated. A test question might ask what would happen if a registered rep left his firm, and then re-associated with another firm, say, 15 months later—when would he be required to complete the regulatory element? If so, tell the test that the regulatory element would be based on his initial registration date with the previous firm, not the new date of hire.

The firm element is completed annually. Member firms design a written training program that is interactive and covers the following topics:

- Regulatory requirements that apply to business performed
- Suitability and ethical sales practices
- Overall investment features and related risk factors

ANNUAL CERTIFICATION OF COMPLIANCE

FINRA member firms don't just write a supervisory manual once and let it ride for years. Rather, each year, they must certify that they have sufficiently reviewed their own firm for all important areas of compliance. As the FINRA rule states, "Each member shall have its chief executive officer(s) (or equivalent officer(s)) certify annually that the member has in place processes to establish, maintain, review, test and modify written compliance policies and written supervisory procedures reasonably designed to achieve compliance with applicable FINRA rules, MSRB rules and federal securities laws and regulations, and that the chief executive officer(s) has conducted one or more meetings with the chief compliance officer(s) in the preceding 12 months to discuss such processes."

FEES TO FINRA

FINRA determines how much member firms must pay in fees based on the number of registered representatives employed by the firm, and the number of branch offices the firm has.

USE OF THE FINRA NAME

Members cannot use the FINRA name in any way that might falsely imply that FINRA has endorsed them. For example, printing up business cards with the phrase "a FINRA-approved brokerage firm" would be a violation. The firm should simply state "member of FINRA" in a way that places no undue emphasis on that simple statement of fact. You will have business cards printed, and on these cards, you may not print your name and contact info in a small font with "FINRA Registered Representative" in a big font. Doing so might imply that you belong to some rare group of registered representatives who belong to FINRA, or that, perhaps FINRA is giving you credentials like "CFP" or "CPA."

FEDERAL RESERVE BOARD'S REGULATION T, REG U

The Federal Reserve Board was granted the authority to regulate the extension of credit by broker-dealers under the Securities Exchange Act of 1934. Broker-dealers extend credit to customers by letting them buy securities on credit. The collateral backing the loan is the current market value of the securities the customer bought on credit.

No, seriously. If you want to buy $100,000 of stock today, you do not need to have $100,000 to do it. Get yourself set up with a margin account, and your broker-dealer will spot you half. You put down $50,000, they put down $50,000. Bet you didn't realize broker-dealers were so generous!

Oh, that's right—they charge interest on the loan, just like the credit card company does when we take a cash advance. In fact, a margin account is a lot like a credit card, only you usually get a better interest rate because there is some collateral here. So, **Regulation (Reg) T** regulates the extension of credit from a broker-dealer, and the percentage of the stock's value that the firm can lend the customer has been 50% for quite some time.

In a cash account, customers must make full payment for securities purchases no more than two business days after regular way settlement. So, when we purchase stock in a cash account, regular way settlement is T + 3. Regulation T says that we can make payment within two full business days of that. And, if we are a deadbeat, the firm can request an extension from FINRA or another self-regulatory organization, who will usually grant it. But, if the firm bends over backwards and the customer still lets them down, or if they're just tired of bending over backwards for him, they can put a 90-day freeze on the account. That just means that for the next 90 days, they won't take any buy orders from the customer unless the cash is already in the account.

Regulation U regulates the extension of credit by a bank to a broker-dealer. In a margin account, securities are pledged as collateral to a bank, who is providing the loan to the broker-dealer, who is going to mark it up a few points. Reg U dictates how much credit a bank can extend in this situation.

SIPC

We mentioned that broker-dealers must indicate if they are not members of **SIPC** on trade confirmations. That's because being a member of SIPC protects a customer's assets against a broker-dealer going bankrupt. The broker-dealer holding the customer's cash and securities could end up going under. If the creditors seize those assets, the customer is still protected by SIPC, which is the Securities Investor Protection Corporation. If an investor buys $100,000 of stock that quickly becomes worthless, that has nothing to do with SIPC. SIPC only protects customer assets from broker-dealer failure. Rather than having to fight to get their cash and securities back for years in court, SIPC will distribute money to the firm's customers.

Basic coverage is $500,000 per account, of which no more than $250,000 can be un-invested cash. So, if the question says that the customer's securities are worth $220,000 and there is $280,000 of cash in the account, she is not covered up to the full $500,000. Rather, SIPC covers the $220,000 of securities and the maximum $250,000 of cash, for a total of $470,000. What about the other $30,000? For that amount the investor becomes a general creditor.

Since SIPC does not cover against fraud or bad investments, it is important that registered representatives never tell a customer that SIPC and FDIC are basically the same thing. FDIC insures bank deposits, which don't fluctuate in value to begin with. SIPC protects brokerage customers against missing assets due to broker-dealer failure.

NOW WHAT?

As we saw, there are many activities that registered representatives must not engage in. Therefore, you could see a question like this:

Which of the following statements is accurate concerning a registered representative who wants to work a few hours a week outside his employing FINRA-member firm for compensation?

   A. Provided the compensation does not exceed $100 weekly, the registered representative may perform the work without notification to the member
   B. The registered representative must provide prior written notice to the member firm
   C. The member firm must first grant permission for this activity
   D. Provided the work is performed within the financial services industry, the registered representative may perform the work without notification to the member

EXPLANATION: the dollar amount of $100 is designed to distract you with the rule on gifts to associated persons of other member firms. There is no dollar amount associated with the rule on outside employment, so eliminate Choice A. Candidates too often grow frustrated with choices as close to each other as B and C. Instead, put them both to the side and look at Choice D. Does this make sense? Or, would FINRA worry even more that the work is done in financial services? Eliminate Choice D. Now, unfortunately, both B and C look equally tempting. Series 7 questions are not only about your ability to use reasoning skills. At this point, you must know the rule. What you don't have to do is assume that since this is a regulatory exam, your job is to pick the most stringent answer. The rule states that the registered representative simply must provide written notification. Even though the member can reject or restrict his activities, the rule does not require "written permission" from the member. Eliminate Choice C, leaving us with

ANSWER: B

Misusing the word "guaranteed" can do major harm to an investor. The Series 6 will, therefore, want to see if you know the important concepts surrounding guarantees in the securities industry, like this:

What is true of the word "guaranteed" as it relates to the securities industry?
   A. The word may not be used in connection with any security subject to investment risk
   B. Broker-dealers—but not their agents—may guarantee certain customers against investment losses on securities recommended by any agent of the firm
   C. Only U.S. Treasury—but never corporate—bonds may be described using this word
   D. Agents and broker-dealers may not guarantee any person against an investment loss

EXPLANATION: the word "guaranteed" can be used if used responsibly, so eliminate Choice A. Choice B seems logical—maybe these big firms can do it but not their agents? Choice

D says that neither one can offer guarantees. Let's put them to the side, then, and see about Choice C. This one almost seems tempting, except that we know a corporate bond or preferred stock could be "guaranteed" by a third party promising to pay dividends, interest, or principal if the issuer is unable to. So, eliminate Choice C. Now, the question is whether a broker-dealer can guarantee customers against a loss, or maybe neither firms nor agents can offer guarantees. Broker-dealers are not insurance companies. They have far riskier business models and far different net capital requirements. Neither they nor their agents can offer to guarantee any customer against investment loss or promise a specific result. Eliminate Choice B, leaving us with

ANSWER: D

As you can probably guess, time to take the Chapter 4 Review Quiz. Next up, watch the lesson in the training videos, and then move onto the 100-question practice exams.

Sample Questions

For those who don't have our complete Pass the 6(TM) Success Program we will now provide 30 sample questions that should look similar to many questions encountered at the exam center.

1. Which of the following may a 72-year-old not do regarding a Roth IRA account?
A. Change the beneficiary
B, Elect to take no distributions
C. Continue to make contributions from earned income
D. Make deductible contributions from earned income

2. If an investor purchases a bond for more than par value, yield to maturity will be
A. Equal to current yield
B. Equal to nominal yield
C. Lower than current yield
D. Higher than nominal yield

3. Which of the following is not an operating expense in an open-end mutual fund?
A. Sales charges
B. Management fees
C. 12b-1 (asset-based distribution) fees
D. Board of director compensation

4. AIR is 3.5%. Two months ago, the separate account grew at an annualized rate of 4.5%, and an annuitant received a check for $1,000 as a result. The following month, the separate account grew at an annualized rate of just 4%; therefore, the annuitant would have received a check for
A. ½% less than $1,000
B. More than $1,000
C. $1,000
D. Less than $1,000

5. If an investor invests the required minimum and then chooses to have $300 deducted from her checking account every month and used toward purchasing more mutual fund shares, the main advantage of this method would be
A. Tax deferral
B. Dollar cost averaging
C. Avoiding front-end sales charges
D. Avoiding wash sales

6. When a registered representative uses the term 'guaranteed by the full faith and credit'---
what is he referring to?
A. A revenue bond
B. An investment-grade corporate bond
C. The interest on a US Treasury bond
D. The interest and principal on a US Treasury bond

7. A broker-dealer delivers a trade confirmation to a customer. The trade confirmation
indicates that the firm acted in a "principal" capacity. Therefore, the firm acted as a
A. Fiduciary
B. Broker
C. Dealer
D. 3rd party

8. Which of the following customer requests would be considered a discretionary order
requiring written authorization from the client?
A. Purchase shares of MSFT today
B. Sell 100 shares of MSFT today
C. Purchase 300 shares of MSFT this afternoon
D. Sell 300 of my 500 shares of MSFT today

9. A customer's account is frozen for 90 days under Regulation T. Which of the following
statements is correct?
A. The customer may make sales but not purchases
B. The customer may make purchase transactions if the full purchase price is in the account
before the order is executed
C. The customer may not make any transactions under any circumstances
D. The customer may make purchases but not sales

10. An investor whose portfolio is 85% devoted to intermediate-term investment-grade
bonds likely views which of the following as least important?
A. Income
B. Capital appreciation
C. Yield
D. Capital preservation

11. A client deposits $6,000 cash at 10 AM. If the client deposits $5,000 cash at 4:00 PM, your firm would file
A. a Reg T extension request
B. no report at this time
C. a currency transaction report (CTR)
D. a suspicious activity report (SAR)

12. What must a firm do if it discovers that one of its clients is on the OFAC list of suspected terrorists?
A. notify federal law enforcement authorities immediately
B. Notify the SEC
C. Notify FINRA
D. all choices listed

13. The Bank Secrecy Act requires broker-dealers to obtain detailed information on wire transfers in excess of
A. $5,000
B. $15,000
C. $10,000
D. $3,000

14. In order for a registered representative to borrow money from a customer,
A. The customer must be a bank
B. The customer must be an immediate family member
C. The firm must approve the policy orally
D. The firm's written supervisory procedures (WSP) must allow this practice

15. Open- and Closed-end funds share all of the following characteristics except
A. issued on the primary market
B. may invest in debt securities
C. trade on the secondary market
D. not required to maintain diversified portfolios

16. Variable annuities and mutual funds have all of the following in common except
A. the individual retains investment risk
B. income and capital gains grow on a tax-deferred basis
C. portfolios are managed by an investment adviser
D. they are registered as investment companies

17. Your customer would like to purchase an insurance policy that offers a flexible premium. You would recommend
A. variable life insurance
B. term life insurance
C. whole life insurance
D. universal life insurance

18. If an employee transfers a 401(k) to a rollover IRA upon leaving a job,
A. The employee must pay tax on the excess above cost basis
B. There will be no penalties or taxation to pay at this time
C. The employee must be 59 ½ to avoid penalties
D. The employee may only perform one transfer per year

19. The maximum gift that a donor may make to a UTMA account for tax year 2017 is
A. $12,000
B. $13,000
C. $14,000
D. None of these choices

20. A 1035 contract exchange may not take place in which of the following ways?
A. one annuity to another offered by a different company
B. one annuity to a life insurance policy issued by the same company
C. one insurance policy to another issued by a different company
D. one insurance policy to another issued by the same company

21. The net investment income from an open-end investment company equals the
A. Dividends and interest paid on securities in the fund's portfolio less operating expenses
B. Dividends and capital gains on sales of portfolio securities
C. Net capital gains on sales of portfolio securities only
D. Profits from the investment company's operations

22. Which of the following retirement plans comes with the least flexible contributions on behalf of the employer?
A. Profit sharing plan
B. Defined benefit pension plan
C. SIMPLE plan
D. Money purchase plan

23. Sue Ellen originally invested $10,000 into the Argood Value Fund. She has since reinvested dividend distributions of $1,000 and capital gains distributions of $500. If Sue Ellen currently holds 1,000 shares of the Argood Value Fund, her cost basis per-share is

A. $10.00

B. $11.00

C. $11.50

D. $10.50

24. Which of the following statements is/are accurate of insurance policies?

A. death benefits are not taxable to the beneficiary, but are includable in the insured's estate for purposes of estate taxes

B. loans against the policy are charged interest, and both the principal and interest reduce the contract values

C. the policyholder may surrender the part of cash value representing net premiums paid into the contract tax-free

D. all choices listed

25. A 68-year-old retired teacher whose monthly pension distributions cover 95% of her living expenses is most exposed to which of the following investment risks?

A. Capital risk

B. Market risk

C. Inflation risk

D. Credit risk

26. Juan has a special cash account with $190,000 in securities and $310,000 in cash. He and his wife, also have a JTWROS account with securities worth $450,000 and $60,000 cash. What is the total SIPC coverage for these accounts?

A. $940,000

B. $1,000,000

C. $1,010,000

D. $500,000

27. A registered representative working for Broker-Dealer XYZ wants to start an investment account with Broker-Dealer PDQ. If both firms are FINRA members, which of the following correctly describes the steps that must be taken?

A. the account may not be opened

B. Broker-Dealer PDQ must notify XYZ in writing and send duplicate trade confirmations upon request

C. Broker-Dealer PDQ must obtain written permission from XYZ before opening the account

D. the account may be opened without further requirements

28. Doris contributed $60,000 into a non-qualified variable annuity at age 41. Nine years later Doris takes a withdrawal of $15,000 with the account at $85,000. Her tax liability is
A. Ordinary income tax on $15,000
B. Ordinary income tax on $15,000, plus a $1,500 penalty tax
C. None, as this represents a tax-free return of cost basis
D. Ordinary income tax on $25,000

29. An investor purchased a 5% bond @97 ½. $50 would, therefore, be
A. The bond's yield to maturity
B. The bond's nominal yield
C. The bond's current yield
D. The bond's effective yield

30. Which of the following investors profits if ABC common stock drops in price?
A. the owner of 1,000 shares of ABC
B. the owner of 5 ABC call options
C. the owner of 5 ABC put options
D. none of these choices

Answers

1. D, unlike with the Traditional IRA, a 72-year-old does not have to stop making contributions from earned income to a Roth IRA. But, contributions to a Roth are non-deductible.

2. C, bonds bought at a premium have current yields and yields to maturity that are lower than the stated nominal yield. Yield to maturity is lower than both current and nominal yield for a premium bond.

3. A, unlike the other three, sales charges are taken out of the investor's investment just one time.

4. B, as long as the rate is higher than AIR, the check goes up.

5. B, by investing a regular amount, the investor uses dollar cost averaging.

6. D, both the interest and principal payments on U.S. Treasuries are guaranteed by the U.S. Government.

7. C, a member firm can act in an agency or a principal capacity on any trade. When they act as a "dealer" they are taking the other side of the transaction with the customer, acting in a principal capacity.

8. A, if the customer has not named the security or the number of shares, the registered representative can only take it from there if the firm and he have discretion over the account.

9. B, a frozen account is one in which credit has been cut off for 90 days. All purchases require the full amount to be in the account prior to execution.

10. B, for capital appreciation investors purchase common stock, not bonds.

11. C, cash transactions > $10,000 on the same day require a Currency Transaction Report.

12. A, this is a matter for law enforcement, not securities regulators.

13. D, $3,000.

14. D, the firm's written supervisory procedures determine with whom a registered representative can borrow.

15. C, only closed-end fund shares trade among investors. Open-end fund shares are redeemed.

16. B, mutual funds offer no tax deferral.

17. D, universal life offers flexibility.

18. B, this is a direct transfer.

19. D, there is no maximum gift than can be given. Gifts above a certain amount may be taxable.

20. B, an annuity cannot be turned into a life insurance policy.

21. A, dividends plus interest minus expenses = net investment income. This is where dividend distributions to the shareholders of the fund come from.

22. D, a money purchase plan involves mandatory contributions from the employer.

23. C, reinvestments are taxable and are added to the investor's cost basis.

24. D, three true statements of insurance.

25. C, rising prices will make it tough to make ends meet.

26. A, only $250,000 of cash is covered, with each account covered up to $500,000 in total.

27. B, notify the employer and send duplicate documentation only upon their request.

28. B, the earnings are subject to taxation and--in this case--a 10% early withdrawal penalty.

29. B, this would be the income paid each year per bond, as named on the bond certificate.

30. C, put buyers profit if the under

Glossary

1035 Contract Exchange: a tax-free exchange of one annuity contract for another, one life insurance policy for another, or one life insurance policy for an annuity. The contracts do not have to be issued by the same company.

12b-1 Fee: annual fee deducted quarterly from a mutual fund's assets to cover distribution costs, e.g., selling, mailing, printing, advertising. An operating expense, unlike the sales charge that is deducted from the investor's check.

401(k) Plan: qualified defined contribution plan offering employer-matched contributions.

403(b): qualified plan for tax-exempt, non-profit organizations.

529 Plans: education savings plans offering tax-deferred growth and tax-free distributions at the federal level for qualified educational expenses. Prepaid tuition plans allow clients to purchase a certain number of tuition credits at today's prices to be used at a school within a specific state. 529 Savings Plans allow clients to contribute up to the current gift tax exclusion without paying gift taxes. Earnings grow tax-deferred and may be used for qualified education expenses (more than just tuition) later without federal taxation. States can tax the plans—so know the customer's situation!

72(t): a maneuver under IRS tax code allowing people to take money from retirement plans including annuities without paying penalties, even though they aren't 59½ yet.

75-5-10 Rule: diversification formula for a fund advertising itself as "diversified." 75% of the portfolio must have no more than 5% of assets invested in any one security, and no more than 10% of a company's outstanding shares may be owned.

A

A-shares: mutual fund shares sold with a front-end sales load/charge. Lower annual expenses than B- and C-shares.

ACATS: or Automated Customer Account Transfer Service, the system used to transfer customer assets among member firms.

Account Executive (AE): another name for a registered representative or agent.

Account Freeze: imposing a 90-day period during which a customer can enter purchase orders only if there is sufficient cash in the account due to violations of Regulation T. AKA "frozen account."

Account Statement: a document delivered to customers at least quarterly by a broker-dealer showing all existing securities positions and cash balances as well as all deposits, withdrawals, dividends and interest payments, and trading activity since the last statement.

Acceptance, Waiver, and Consent (AWC): method of resolving a disciplinary matter in which the respondent does not dispute the charges and waives his right to appeal the decision of the hearing panel.

Accredited Investors: large institutional investors, and individuals meeting certain income or net worth requirements allowing them to participate in, for example, a private placement under Reg D of the Securities Act of 1933, or hedge funds.

Accrued Interest: the interest that the buyer of a debt security owes the seller. Bond interest is payable only twice a year, and the buyer will receive the next full interest payment. Therefore, the buyer owes the sellers for every day of interest since the last payment up to the day before the transaction settles.

Accumulation Stage/Period: the period during which contributions are made to an annuity, at which time the investor holds "accumulation units."

Accumulation Units: what the purchaser of an annuity buys during the pay-in or accumulation phase, an accounting measure representing a proportional share of the separate account during the accumulation/deposit stage.

Active Management: a style of investing where the investor actively selects certain securities over other alternatives. Based on the premise that information is not immediately acted upon and that markets are not perfectly efficient.

Adjustable Rate Preferred Stock: preferred stock whose dividend is tied to another rate, often the rate paid on T-bills.

Adjusted Gross Income (AGI): earned income plus passive income, portfolio income, and capital gains. The amount upon which we pay income tax.

Administrator: (1) the securities regulator of a specific state, (2) a person or entity authorized by the courts to liquidate an estate.

ADR/ADS: American Depository Receipt/Share. A foreign stock on a domestic market. Toyota and Nokia are two examples of foreign companies whose ADRs trade on American stock markets denominated in dollars. Carry all the risks of owning stocks, plus "currency exchange risk."

Advertising: communications by a member firm directed at a general, uncontrolled audience, e.g., billboard, radio/TV/newspaper ads, website.

Affiliated Person: anyone in a position to influence decisions at a public corporation, including board members (directors), officers (CEO, CFO), and large shareholders (Warren Buffett at Coca-Cola or Wells Fargo).

After-tax Yield: the amount of interest income remaining after the investor pays taxes on it. For example, the after-tax yield on a 10% bond is 7% if the investor is in the 30% tax bracket.

Agency Issue (Agency Bond): a debt security issued by an agency authorized by the federal government but not directly backed by the federal government.

Agency Transaction: a securities transaction in which the broker-dealer acts as an agent for the buyer or seller, completing the transaction between the customer and another party.

Agent: an individual representing a broker-dealer or issuer in effecting/completing transactions in securities for compensation. What you will be after passing your exams and obtaining your securities license.

Agreement Among Underwriters: a document used by an underwriting syndicate bringing an issue of securities to the primary market. This document sets forth the terms under which each member of the syndicate will participate and details the duties and responsibilities of the syndicate manager.

Aggressive Growth: an investment objective involving higher-risk investing in higher-priced equities.

AIR: Assumed Interest Rate. Determined by an actuary, representing his best estimate of the monthly annualized rate of return from the separate account. Used to determine value of annuity units for annuities and death benefit for variable life contracts.

All or None: a type of underwriting in which the syndicate will cancel the offering if a sufficient dollar amount is not raised as opposed to being responsible for the unsold shares (as in a "firm commitment").

Alternative Minimum Tax: See AMT.

American Stock Exchange (AMEX): a private, not-for-profit corporation that handles roughly 20% of all securities trades in the U.S. One of the big secondary markets, along with NYSE, and the various NASDAQ markets.

AMT (Alternative Minimum Tax): tax computation that adds certain "tax preference items" back into adjusted gross income. Some municipal bond interest is treated as a "tax preference item" that can raise the investor's tax liability through the AMT.

Anti-Money Laundering (AML): required supervisory programs designed and implemented by FINRA-member firms according to what is appropriate for their business model, customers, and activities, etc.

Annual Compliance Review: a broker-dealer's mandatory annual compliance review process.

Annual Gift Tax Exclusion: annual amount that an individual may give to another person without having to pay gift taxes.

Annual Report: a formal statement issued by a corporation to the SEC and shareholders discussing the company's results of operations, challenges/risks facing the company, any lawsuits against the company, etc. Required by the Securities Exchange Act of 1934 and the Investment Company Act o 1940.

Annuitant: the person who receives an annuity contract's distribution.

Annuitize: the process of changing the annuity contract from the "pay-in" or accumulation phase to the "pay-out" or distribution phase. Defined benefit pension plans also generally offer their pensioners either a lump sum payment or the chance to annuitize.

Annuity: a contract between an individual and an insurance company that generally guarantees income for the rest of the individual's life in return for a lump-sum or periodic payment to the insurance company.

Annuity Units: what the annuitant holds during the pay-out phase. Value tied to AIR.

Anti-fraud Statute: legislation in federal and state securities law outlawing deception and manipulation in the offer or sale of securities. Violators subject to administrative penalties, civil action, and criminal prosecution.

Appreciation: the increase in an asset's value that is not subject to tax until realized.

Arbitrage: a word that has no business being mentioned on the Series 6. Arbitrage involves taking advantage of the disparity of two things. If you think GE will buy a small company, you can make a bet that GE's stock will temporarily drop and the small company's stock will skyrocket. Then, when you make your fantastic and fortuitous gain, you can explain to the SEC how you happened to make that bet.

Arbitration: settling a dispute without going to an actual court of law.

Arbitration Award: the decision rendered through FINRA Arbitration.

Ask, Asked: the higher price in a quote representing what the customer must pay/what the dealer is asking the customer to pay. Customers buy at the ASK because dealers sell to customers at the ASK price. Ask/asked is also called "offer/offered."

Asset Allocation: maintaining a percentage mix of equity, debt, and money market investments, based either on the investor's age (strategic) or market expectations (tactical).

Asset Allocation Fund: a mutual fund that focuses on a mix of equity, bond, and money market exposure, e.g., 50% equity, 45% bonds, 5% money market.

Asset-to-Debt: the ratio of assets to debts (3-to-1) that an open-end mutual fund must maintain when borrowing money.

Assets: something that a corporation or individual owns, e.g., cash, investments, accounts receivable, inventory, etc.

Associated Person: a registered representative or principal of a FINRA member firm.

Assumed Interest Rate: see AIR.

Auction Market: the NYSE, for example, where buyers and sellers simultaneously enter competitive prices. Sometimes called a "double auction" market because buying and selling occur at the same time, as opposed to Sotheby's, where only buyers are competing.

Authorized Stock: number of shares a company is authorized to issue by its corporate charter. Can be changed by a majority vote of the outstanding shares.

Automatic Reinvestment: a feature offered by mutual funds allowing investors to automatically reinvest dividend and capital gains distributions into more shares of the fund, without paying a sales charge.

Average Cost Basis: a method of figuring cost basis on securities for purposes of reporting capital gains and/or losses. The investor averages the cost for all purchases made in the stock, as opposed to identifying specific shares to the IRS when selling.

Award: The written determination of the arbitrator(s).

B

B-shares: mutual fund shares charging a load only when the investor redeems/sells the shares. Associated with "contingent deferred sales charges." B-shares have higher operating expenses than A-shares by way of a higher 12b-1 fee. Although the back-end load or "contingent deferred sales charges" decline over time, the higher 12b-1 fee usually makes B-shares appropriate only for investors who lack the ability to reach the first or second breakpoint offered on A-shares.

Back-end Load: a commission/sales fee charged when mutual fund or variable contracts are redeemed. The back-end load declines gradually, as described in the prospectus. Associated with B-shares.

Backdating: pre-dating a letter of intent for a mutual fund to include a prior purchase in the total amount stated in the letter of intent. LOIs may be backdated up to 90 calendar days.

Backing Away: a violation in which a market maker fails to honor a published firm quote to buy or sell a security at a stated price.

Balance Sheet: a financial statement of a corporation or individual showing financial condition (assets vs. liabilities) at a specific moment in time.

Balance Sheet Equation: Assets – Liabilities = Shareholders' Equity, or Assets = Liabilities + Shareholders' Equity.

Balanced Fund: a fund that maintains a mix of stocks and bonds at all times. Similar to an asset allocation fund but with a less rigid formula for its mix of assets.

Bank Secrecy Act (BSA): legislation that prevents financial institutions from being used as tools by criminals to hide or launder money earned through illegal activities. Financial institutions such as banks and broker-dealers must report currency transactions over $10,000 and must report suspicious activity to the Department of Treasury's Financial Crimes Enforcement Network (FinCEN).

Banker's Acceptance (BA): money-market security that facilitates importing/exporting. Issued at a discount from face-value. A secured loan.

Bar: the most severe sanction that FINRA can impose on an individual, effectively ending his/her career

Basis Points: a way of measuring bond yields or other percentages in the financial industry. Each basis point is 1% of 1%. Example: 2% = .0200 = 200 basis points. 20 basis points = .2% or 2/10ths of 1%.

Basis Quote: the price at which a debt security can be bought or sold, based on the yield. A bond purchased at a "5.50 basis" is trading at a price that makes the yield 5.5%.

Bear, Bearish: an investor who takes a position based on the belief that the market or a security will fall. Short sellers and buyers of puts are "bearish." They profit when stocks go down. Seriously.

Bear Market: a market for stock or bonds in which prices are falling and/or expected to fall.

Bearer Bond: an unregistered bond that pays principal to the bearer at maturity. Bonds have not been issued in this way for over two decades, but they still exist on the secondary market.

Beneficial Owner: for example, in an UGMA/UTMA account, the minor child, as opposed to the nominal owner—the custodian.

Beneficiary: the one who benefits. An insurance policy pays a benefit to the named beneficiary. IRAs and other retirement plans, including annuities, allow the owner to name a beneficiary who will receive the account value when the owner dies. A 529 plan names a beneficiary, who will use the money for educational expenses someday.

Best Efforts: a type of underwriting leaving the syndicate at no risk for unsold shares, and allowing them to keep the proceeds on the shares that were sold/subscribed to. Underwriters act as "agents," not principals, in a best efforts underwriting.

Beta: a way of measuring the volatility of a security or portfolio compared to the volatility of the overall market. A beta of more than 1 is associated with an investment or portfolio that is more volatile than the overall market. A beta of less than 1 is associated with an investment or portfolio that is less volatile than the overall market.

Beta Coefficient: another way of referring to "beta."

Bid: what a dealer is willing to pay to a customer who wants to sell. Customers sell at the bid, buy at the ask.

Blend Fund: an equity fund that invests in both growth and value stocks, e.g. Large Cap Blend or Small Cap Blend.

Blotter: a record of "original entry" showing "an itemized daily record at a broker-dealer of all purchases and sales of securities, all receipts and deliveries of securities (including certificate numbers), all receipts and disbursements of cash and all other debits and credits."

Blue Chip: stock in a well-established company with proven ability to pay dividends in good economic times and bad. Lower risk/reward ratio than other common stock.

Blue Sky: state securities law, tested on the Series 63 exam.

Board of Directors: the group elected by shareholders to run a mutual fund or a public company and establish corporate management policies.

Bond: a debt security issued by a corporation or governmental entity that promises to repay principal and pay interest either regularly or at maturity.

Bond Anticipation Note (BAN): a short-term municipal debt security backed by the proceeds of an upcoming bond issue. Often found in tax-exempt money market funds.

Bond Fund: a mutual fund with an objective of providing income while minimizing capital risk through a portfolio of—get this—bonds.

Bond Point: 1% of a bond's par value. 1 bond point = $10.

Bond Rating: an evaluation of a bond issue's chance of default published by companies such as Moody's, S&P, and Fitch.

Bonus Annuities: annuities with various features/enhancements added to the contract.

Book Entry: a security maintained as a computer record rather than a physical certificate. All U.S. Treasuries and many mutual funds are issued in this manner.

Branch Office: any location identified by any means to the public or customers as a location at which the member conducts an investment banking or securities business.

Breakpoint: a discounted sales charge or "volume discount" on mutual fund purchases offered on A-shares at various levels of investment.

Breakpoint Selling: preventing an investor from achieving a breakpoint. A violation.

Broad-based Index: an index such as the S&P 500 or the Value Line Composite Index that represents companies from many industries.

Broker: an individual or firm that charges a commission to execute securities buy and sell orders submitted by another individual or firm.

Broker Call Loan Rate: interest rate that broker-dealers pay when borrowing on behalf of margin customers.

BrokerCheck: service offered by FINRA in which information in the CRD system is made available to the public, allowing investors to verify the registration of firms and their agents as well as view arbitration awards and disciplinary actions against the individual or the broker-dealer.

Broker-Dealer: a person or firm in the business of completing transactions in securities for the accounts of others (broker) or its own account (dealer).

Brokered CD: a certificate of deposit sold by an intermediary and allowing investors to sell on a secondary market.

Bull, Bullish: an investor who takes a position based on the belief that the market or a security will rise. Buyers of stock and call options are bullish.

Bull Market: a market for stocks or bonds in which prices are rising and/or expected to rise.

Bulletin Board: OTC stocks too volatile and low-priced for NASDAQ.

Business Cycle: a progression of expansions, peaks, contractions, troughs, and recoveries for the overall (macro) economy.

Business Risk: the risk that the company whose stock or bond you own will not be successful as a business. Competition, poor management, obsolete products/services are all examples of business risk.

C

C-Shares: often called "level load" because of the high 12b-1 fee. Usually involve no front-end load, sometimes have a contingent deferred sales charge for 1 or 1.5 years. Appropriate for shorter-term investing only.

Call: (n.) a contract that gives the holder the right to buy something at a stated exercise price.

Call: (v.) to buy.

Call Premium: the price paid and received on a call option. Or, the amount above the par value paid by the issuer to call/retire a bond.

Call Protection: the period during which a security may not be called or bought by the issuer, usually lasting five years or more.

Call Provision: agreement between the issuer and the bondholders or preferred stockholders that gives the issuer the ability to repurchase the bonds or preferred stock on a specified date or dates before maturity.

Call Risk: the risk that interest rates will drop, forcing investors to sell their bonds back early to the issuer.

Callable: a security that may be purchased/called by the issuer as of a certain date, e.g., callable preferred, callable bonds. Generally pays a higher rate of return than non-callable securities, as it gives the issuer flexibility in financing.

Cap: the maximum amount than an equity indexed annuity's value can increase in any given year.

Capital: a fancy word for "money." When a corporation raises cash by offering stocks/bonds to investors on the primary market, we dignify the cash by calling it "capital."

Capital Appreciation: the rise in an asset's market price. The objective of a "growth stock investor."

Capital Gain: the amount by which the proceeds on the sale of a stock or bond exceed your cost basis. If you sell a stock for $22 and have a cost basis of $10, the capital gain or profit is $12.

Capital Gains Distribution: distribution from fund to investor based on net capital gains realized by the fund portfolio. Holding period determined by the fund and assumed to be long-term.

Capital Loss: loss incurred when selling an asset for less than the purchase price. Capital losses offset an investor's capital gains and can offset ordinary income to a certain amount.

Capital Preservation: investment objective that allows for no risk of capital loss and, secondarily, income that is consistent with the main goal of not losing money.

Capital Risk: the risk—presented by most investments—that the investor could lose some of all his invested principal.

Capital Structure: the make-up of a corporation's financing through equity (stock) and debt (bonds) securities.

Cash Account: an investment account in which the investor must pay for all purchases no later than 2 business days following regular way settlement. Not a margin account.

Cash Dividend: money paid to shareholders from a corporation's current earnings or accumulated profits.

Cash Equivalent: a security that can readily be converted to cash, e.g., T-bills, CDs, and money market funds.

Cash Settlement: same-day settlement of a trade requiring prior broker-dealer approval. Not the "regular way" of doing things.

Cash Value: the value of an insurance policy that may be "tapped" by the policyholder through a loan or a surrender.

Catch-Up Contribution: an increased contribution to a retirement account based on the account owner's age—usually 50+.

CDSC: See Contingent Deferred Sales Charge.

Central Registration Depository or CRD: a computerized system in which FINRA maintains the employment, qualification, and disciplinary histories of more than 600,000 securities industry professionals who deal with the public.

CEO: chief executive officer. Individual ultimately responsible for a corporation's results.

CFO: chief financial officer. Individual in charge of a corporation's financial activities.

Check-writing Privileges: a privilege offered by mutual funds, especially money market funds, by which investors can automatically redeem shares by writing checks.

Chinese Wall: the separation that is supposed to exist between the investment banking department and the traders and registered representatives to prevent insider trading violations.

Churning: excessive trading in terms of frequency and size of transactions designed to generate commissions without regard for the customer.

Closed-end Fund: an investment company that offers a fixed number of shares that are not redeemable. Shares are traded on the secondary market at a price that could be higher or lower than NAV (or even the same as NAV).

CMO: Collateralized Mortgage Obligation. A complicated debt security based on a pool of mortgages or a pool of mortgage-backed securities. Pays interest monthly but returns principal to one tranche at a time.

Code of Arbitration: FINRA method of resolving disputes (usually money) in the securities business. All decisions are final and binding on all parties.

Code of Procedure: FINRA system for enforcing member conduct rules.

Collateral Trust Certificate: a bond secured by a pledge of securities as collateral.

Combination Annuities: variable annuities in which some part of the payment is guaranteed by deposits in the general account.

Combination Privilege: allows investors to combine purchases of many funds within the mutual fund family to reach a breakpoint/reduced sales charge.

Commercial Paper: a short-term unsecured loan to a corporation. Issued at a discount from the face value. See "money market."

Commissions: why you're still reading this book, a service charge an agent earns for arranging a security purchase or sale.

Common Stock: the most "junior security," because it ranks last in line at liquidation. An equity or ownership position that usually allows the owner to vote on major corporate issues such as stock splits, mergers, acquisitions, authorizing more shares, etc.

Compliance Department: the principals and supervisors of a broker-dealer responsible for making sure the firm adheres to SEC, exchange, and SRO rules.

Conduct Rules: an SRO's rules for member conduct that, if violated, may lead to sanctions and fines.

Conduit Theory (Tax Treatment): a favorable tax treatment achieved if a company (REIT, mutual fund) distributes 90%+ of net income to the shareholders.

Confirmation: document stating the trade date, settlement date, and money due/owed for a securities purchase or sale. Delivered on or before the settlement date.

Constant Dollar Plan: a defensive investment strategy in which an investor tries to maintain a constant dollar amount in the account, meaning that securities are sold if the account value rises and purchased if it goes down.

Constructive Receipt: the date that the IRS considers an investor to have put his grubby little hands on a dividend, interest payment, retirement plan distribution, etc. For example, IRA funds are not taxable until "constructive receipt," which usually starts somewhere between age 59½ and 70½.

Consumer: for purposes of Regulation S-P, a prospect, someone interested in establishing some type of account.

Consumer Price Index (CPI): a measure of inflation/deflation for basic consumer goods and services. A rising CPI represents the greatest risk to most fixed-income investors.

Contested: the status FINRA lists when the respondent chooses to have a hearing over rule violations rather than using AWC or making an offer of settlement.

Contingent Deferred Sales Charge (CDSC): associated with B-shares, the sales charge is deducted from the investor's check when she redeems/sells her shares. The charge is deferred until she sells and is contingent upon when she sells—the sales charges decline over time, eventually disappearing after 7 years, at which point the B-shares become A-shares, to keep everything nice and simple.

Continuing Commissions: the practice of paying retired registered representatives and principals commissions on business written while still employed with the firm, e.g., 12b-1 fees on mutual funds and annuities.

Contraction: phase of the business cycle associated with general economic decline, recession, or depression.

Contractual Plan: a plan allowing the participant to gradually accumulate mutual fund shares by paying regular installments to a "plan company." Not legal in all states due to complexity of rules and high sales loads.

Contribution: the money you put into a retirement plan subject to the limits imposed by the plan.

Conversion/Exchange Privilege: a feature offered by many mutual funds whereby the investor may sell shares of one fund in the family and use the proceeds to buy another fund in the family at the NAV (avoiding the sales load). All gains/losses are recognized on the date of sale/conversion for tax purposes.

Conversion Ratio: the number of shares of common stock that the holder of a convertible bond or preferred stock would receive upon conversion. A bond "convertible at $50" has a conversion ratio of 20 (20 shares of stock per $1,000 par value).

Convertible Security: a preferred stock or corporate bond allowing the investor to use the par value to "buy" shares of the company's common stock at a set price.

Cooling Off Period: a minimum 20-day period that starts after the registration statement is filed. No sales or advertising allowed during this period, which lasts until the effective or release date.

Corporate Bond: a fixed-income security issued by a corporation as opposed to a government entity.

Corporate Bond Fund: a mutual fund investing in a portfolio of corporate bonds.

Corporation: the most common form of business organization, in which the business's total value is divided among shares of stock, each representing an ownership interest or share of profits.

Correspondence: under FINRA rules = any written (including electronic) communication that is distributed or made available to 25 or fewer retail investors within any 30 calendar-day period.

Cost Basis: the amount that has gone into an investment and has been taxed already. For stock, includes the price paid plus commissions. For a variable annuity, equals the after-tax contributions into the account. Investors pay tax only on amounts above their cost basis, and only when they sell or take "constructive receipt."

Coupon Rate: a.k.a. "nominal yield." The interest rate stated on a bond representing the percentage of the par value received by the investor each year. For example, a bond with a 5% "coupon rate" or "nominal yield" pays $50 per bond to the holder per year. Period.

Coverdell Educational Savings Account (CESA): tax-deferred educational savings account funded with after-tax dollars.

Covered Call: a position in which an investor generates premium income by selling the right to buy stock the investor already owns, and at a set price.

CPI: Consumer Price Index, a measure of inflation/deflation for basic consumer goods and services. A rising CPI represents the greatest risk to most fixed-income investors.

Credit Risk: a.k.a. "default" or "financial" risk. The risk that the issuer's credit rating will be downgraded, or that the issuer will default on a debt security.

Cumulative Preferred Stock: preferred stock where missed dividends go into arrears and must be paid before the issuer may pay dividends to other preferred stock and/or common stock.

Cumulative Voting: method of voting whereby the shareholder may take the total votes and split them up any way he chooses. Said to benefit minority over majority shareholders. Total votes are found by multiplying the number of shares owned by the number of seats up for election to the Board of Directors.

Currency Exchange Risk: the risk that the value of the U.S. dollar versus another currency will have a negative impact on businesses and investors.

Currency Transaction Report (CTR): a report that broker-dealers must file with the U.S. Treasury whenever customers deposit more than $10,000 cash-money on the same day.

Current Income: investment objective in which the investor seeks a regular, dependable stream of income, usually to pay regular expenses.

Current Yield: annual interest divided by market price of the bond. For example, an 8% bond purchased at $800 has a CY of 10%. $80/$800 = 10%.

CUSIP number: an identification number/code for a security.

Custodial Account: an investment account in which a custodian enters trades on behalf of the beneficial owner, who is usually a minor child.

Custodian: maintains custody of a mutual fund's securities and cash. Performs payable/receivable functions for portfolio purchases and sales. In an UGMA, the custodian is the adult named on the account who is responsible for the investment decisions and tax reporting.

Customer: for purposes of Regulation S-P, someone who has now opened a financial relationship with the firm.

Customer Identification Program: regulations requiring broker-dealers to verify customers through photo IDs, passports (for non-citizens), and a check against the OFAC list of suspected terrorists.

Customer Written Complaint: any grievance by a customer or any person authorized to act on behalf of the customer involving the activities of the member or a person associated with the member in connection with the solicitation or execution of any transaction or the disposition of securities or funds of that customer.

Cyclical Industry: a term of fundamental analysis for an industry that is sensitive to the business cycle. Includes: steel, automobiles, mining and construction equipment.

D

Dealer: a person who buys or sells securities for his/its own account, taking the other side of the trade. A dealer buys securities from and sells securities directly to a customer, while a broker merely arranges a trade between a customer and another party.

Death Benefit: the amount payable to the beneficiary of a life insurance (or annuity) contract, minus any outstanding loans and/or unpaid premiums.

Debenture: an unsecured corporate bond backed by the issuer's ability (or inability) to pay. No collateral.

Debt Security: a security representing a loan from an investor to an issuer. Offers an interest rate in return for the loan, not an ownership position.

Debt Service: the schedule for repayment of interest and principal on a debt security.

Declaration Date: the date the Board declares a dividend.

Default: when the issuer of the bond misses an interest or principal payment.

Default Decision: a decision reached by a disciplinary panel when the respondent refuses to cooperate and/or appear.

Default Risk: the risk that the issuer of the bond will stiff you. Measured by S&P and Moody's, with their fancy little lettering system (AAA, Aaa and on down the scale).

Defensive Industry: a company that can perform well even during bad economic times. For example, food and basic clothing represent two products purchased through both good and bad economic times; therefore, stocks of food and basic clothing companies would be "defensive" investments.

Defensive Strategy: a strategy in which maintaining a stable principal is more important than seeking high returns, as opposed to an aggressive strategy.

Deferred Annuity: an annuity that delays payments of income, installments, or a lump sum until the investor elects to receive it. Usually subject to surrender charges during this period.

Deferred Compensation Plan: a non-qualified business plan that defers some of the employee's compensation until retirement.

Deficiency Letter: SEC notification of additions or corrections that an issuer must make to a registration statement before the offering can be cleared for distribution.

Defined Benefit Pension Plan: a qualified corporate pension plan that, literally, defines the benefit payable to the retiree.

Defined Contribution Plan: a qualified corporate plan that defines the contribution made on behalf of the employee, e.g., profit sharing, 401(k).

Deflation: a general drop in the level of prices across the economy, usually connected to an economic slump.

Depression: a prolonged period of economic decline, more severe than a recession.

Designated Examining Authority: another name for an SRO or Self-Regulatory Organization, e.g., CBOE or FINRA

Developed Market: an international market that is more mature than an emerging market, e.g., Japan or Singapore.

Dilution: a reduction in the earnings per share of common stock, often due to convertible bonds or preferred stock being converted to common stock.

Direct Transfer: moving assets of one plan directly to the custodian of another plan.

Discount: the difference between the (lower) market price for a bond and the par value.

Discount Bond: any bond traded below the par value, e.g., @97.

Discount Rate: interest rate charged by the 12 Federal Reserve Banks to member banks who borrow from the FRB.

Discretion: authority given to someone other than the account owner to make trading decisions for the account.

Discretionary Account: a brokerage account in which the firm/registered representative may choose the asset/amount/activity without first speaking to the client.

Discretionary Authorization Form: form that grants discretion to the broker-dealer, allowing the firm/registered representative to enter trades without first discussing them with the client.

Distribution: the money you take out of a retirement plan.

Distribution Expenses: the cost of distributing/marketing a mutual fund, including selling, printing prospectuses and sales literature, advertising, and mailing prospectuses to new/potential clients. Covered by sales charges/12b-1fees.

Distribution Stage: the period during which an individual receives payments from an annuity.

Distributor: a.k.a. "sponsor," "underwriter," "wholesaler." A FINRA member firm that bears distribution costs of a fund upfront, profiting from the sales charges paid by the investors.

Diversification: purchasing securities from many different issuers, or industries or geographic regions to reduce "nonsystematic risk."

Diversified Company: a mutual fund that complies with an SEC rule so that no more than 5% of assets are invested in a specific stock or bond and so that the fund does not own more than 10% of any issuer's outstanding stock. Often called the "75-5-10 rule," where the 75 means that only 75% of the assets must be diversified this way just to keep things nice and simple.

Dividend: money paid from profits to holders of common and preferred stock whenever the Board of Directors is feeling especially generous.

Dividend Payout Ratio: the amount of dividends paid divided by the earnings per share. Stocks with high dividend payout ratios are typically found in "equity income" funds.

Dividend Yield: annual dividends divided by market price of the stock. Equivalent to current yield for a debt security.

Dividend/Income Distributions: distributions from a fund to the investors made from net investment income. Typically, may be reinvested at the NAV to avoid sales charge.

Dollar Cost Averaging: investing fixed dollar amounts regularly, regardless of share price. Usually results in a lower average cost compared to average of share prices, as investors' dollars buy majority of shares at lower prices.

Donor: a person who makes a gift of money or securities to another.

Dow Jones Industrial Average (DJIA): an index comprised of 30 large companies, weighted by share price. Often referred to simply as "the Dow."

Dual-Purpose Fund: a closed-end fund with two classes of stock: income shares and capital shares. The income shares receive dividends and interest, while the capital shares receive capital gains distributions.

Due Diligence: meeting between issuer and underwriters with the purpose of verifying information contained in a registration statement/prospectus

Duration: the weighted average of a bond's cash flows, expressed as a number, e.g., 10 or 12, and showing how sensitive the bond's market price is to a 1% rise in interest rates.

E

Earned Income: income derived from active participation in a business, including wages, salary, tips, commissions, and bonuses. Alimony received is also considered earned income. Earned income can be used toward an IRA contribution.

Earnings Per Share (EPS): the amount of earnings or "net income" available for each share of common stock. A major driver of the stock's price on the secondary market.

Education IRA: another name for the Coverdell Education Savings Account in which after-tax contributions may be made to pay qualified education expenses for the beneficiary.

Effective Date: a.k.a. "release date," date established by SEC as to when the underwriters may sell new securities to investors.

Elective Deferral: the amount chosen by the employee to be deducted from his paycheck and deposited into his 401(k) or SIMPLE account, for example.

Electronic Communications Networks (ECNs): electronic systems allowing for direct trading of securities in the so-called "fourth market."

Eligibility: a section of ERISA that outlines who is/is not eligible to participate in a qualified plan. Those 21 years old who have worked "full time" for one year (1,000 hours or more) are eligible to participate in the plan.

Emerging Market: the financial markets of a developing country. Generally, a small market with a short operating history, not as efficient or stable as developed markets. For example, Brazil, China, India.

Employer's Contribution: the amount contributed on behalf of an employee by the employer, often as a matching contribution to the employee's elective deferrals.

Equipment Trust Certificate: a corporate bond secured by a pledge of equipment, e.g., airplanes, railroad cars.

Equity: ownership, e.g., common and preferred stock in a public company.

Equity Fund: a mutual fund investing primarily in equity securities.

Equity Income Fund: a mutual fund that purchases common stocks whose issuers pay consistent and, perhaps, increasing dividends. The fund has less volatility than an equity fund with "growth" as an objective.

Equity Indexed Annuity (EIA): fixed annuity with a minimum guaranteed return plus participation in some of the upward movement of a specific index, usually the S&P 500.

Equity Securities: securities granting ownership to the investor, either common or preferred stock.

ERISA: the Employee Retirement Income Security Act of 1974 that governs the operation of most corporate pension and benefit plans.

Estate: a legal entity/person that represents all assets held by a deceased person before he died.

Estate Tax: a tax on estates over a certain amount, often called the "death tax" by those who don't like it.

ETF: "Exchange Traded Fund," a fund that trades on an exchange, typically an index fund tracking the S&P 500, the Dow Jones Industrial Average, etc. Unlike an open-end index fund, the ETF allows investors to sell short, trade throughout the day, and even purchase shares on margin.

Ex-Date: two days before the Record Date for corporate stock. The date upon which the buyer is not entitled to the upcoming dividend. Note that for mutual funds, this date is established by the Board of Directors, usually the day after the Record Date.

Excess Over Cost Basis: any amount received on a non-qualified variable annuity above the after-tax contribution into the account; the part that is taxable upon constructive receipt at ordinary income rates.

Exchange-listed Security: a security that has met listing requirements to trade on an exchange such as NYSE, AMEX, or NASDAQ.

Exchange Traded Fund: see ETF.

Exchanges: any electronic or physical marketplace where investors can buy and sell securities. For example, NASDAQ, NYSE, AMEX.

Exclusion Ratio: method of determining which part of an annuity payment is taxable, and which part represents the tax-free return of the annuitant's after-tax cost basis.

Executor: person named in the will charged with distributing assets to the beneficiaries of the estate.

Exempt Security: a security not required to be registered under the Securities Act of 1933. Still subject to anti-fraud rules; not subject to registration requirements, e.g., municipal bonds and bank stock.

Exempt Transaction: a transactional exemption from registration requirements based on the manner in which the security is offered and sold, e.g., private placements under Reg D.

Expansion: phase of the business cycle associated with increased activity.

Expense Ratio: a fund's expenses divided by/compared to average net assets. Represents operating efficiency of a mutual fund, where the lower the number the more efficient the fund.

Expenses: ongoing charges against the mutual fund portfolio to cover operational costs. AKA "operating expenses."

Expunged: to have a disclosure event removed from the respondent's record. Can only happen through a court order. Customer disputes and criminal convictions are subject to expungement.

Extension Risk: the risk to the holder of a mortgage-backed security that rising interest rates will cause principal to be received later than anticipated. As opposed to prepayment risk.

F

Face-Amount Certificate Company: a debt security bought at a lower price than the face-amount. An investment company.

Farm Credit System: organization of privately owned banks providing credit to farmers and mortgages on farm property.

FDIC (Federal Deposit Insurance Corporation): federal government agency that provides deposit insurance for member banks and prevents bank and "thrift" failures. Bank deposits are currently insured up to $250,000, a number that could have changed by the time you read this definition. A trip to your local bank will give you the updated number.

Federal Covered: a security or an investment adviser whose registration is handled exclusively by the federal government (SEC).

Federal Open Market Committee (FOMC): council of Federal Reserve officials that sets monetary policy based on economic data. The money supply is tightened to fight inflation, loosened to provide stimulus to a faltering economy.

Federal Reserve Board: a seven-member board directing the operations of the Federal Reserve System.

Federal Reserve System: the central bank system of the United States, with a primary responsibility to manage the flow of money and credit in this country.

Fed Funds Rate: interest rate charged on bank-to-bank loans. Subject to daily fluctuation.

Fees and Expenses: shareholder fees based on buying or selling fund shares plus the ongoing charges against the mutual fund portfolio including the management fee, 12b-1 fees, custodial and transfer agent fees, etc.

FHLMC: a.k.a. "Freddie Mac." Like big sister Fannie Mae, a quasi-agency, public company that purchases mortgages from lenders and sells mortgage-backed securities to investors. Stock is listed on NYSE.

Fiduciary: someone responsible for the financial affairs of someone else, e.g., custodian, trustee, or registered rep in a discretionary account.

Filing Date: the date that an issuer files a registration statement with the SEC for a new issue of securities.

Final Prospectus: document delivered with final confirmation of a new issue of securities detailing the price, delivery date, and underwriting spread.

FINRA (Financial Industry Regulatory Authority): the SRO formed when the NASD and the NYSE regulators merged.

Financial Risk: another name for "credit risk," or the risk that the issuer of a bond could default.

FinCEN: U.S. Treasury's "Financial Crimes Enforcement Network." Suspicious Activity Reports must be provided to FinCEN if a broker-dealer notices activity in accounts that appears suspicious or possibly related to fraud or money laundering activities.

Firm Commitment: an underwriting in which the underwriters agree to purchase all securities from an issuer, even the ones they failed to sell to investors. Involves acting in a "principal" capacity, unlike in "best efforts," "all or none," and "mini-max" offerings.

Firm Element: annual training program that member firms require of their registered representatives to satisfy FINRA rules for continuing education.

First-In-First-Out (FIFO): an accounting method used to value a company's inventory or to determine capital gains/losses on an investor's securities transactions.

First Market: the exchange market, e.g., NYSE or New York Stock Exchange.

Fiscal Policy: Congress and President. Tax and Spend.

Fixed-amount Settlement Option: payment option on an insurance contract in which a fixed amount is received over time until the account is depleted.

Fixed Annuity: an insurance product (not a security) in which the annuitant receives fixed dollar payments, usually for the rest of his or her life.

Fixed-income Security: a security promising a fixed rate of interest or dividends, e.g., bonds and preferred stock.

Fixed-period Settlement Option: payment option on an insurance contract in which the account is depleted over a fixed period of time, e.g., 5 years.

Flexible Premium: a premium that is flexible. Characteristic of "universal" insurance. Allows the policyholder to adjust the premiums and death benefit according to changing needs.

FNMA: a.k.a. "Fannie Mae." Like little brother Freddie Mac, Fannie buys mortgages from lenders and sells mortgage-backed securities to investors. A quasi-agency, a public company listed for trading on the NYSE.

FOMC: the Federal Reserve Board's Federal Open Market Committee. Sets short-term interest rates by setting discount rate, reserve requirement and buying/selling T-bills to/from primary dealers.

Form 1099-DIV: tax filing form showing dividends and capital gains distributed to an investor.

Form U4: registration form for agents and principals submitted to the CRD system.

Form U5: termination form for agents and principals submitted to the CRD system.

Form ADV: the registration form required of an investment adviser.

Form BD: the registration form required to form a broker-dealer.

Form N-1A: the registration form used by an investment company to register the company and its securities.

Forward Pricing: the method of valuing mutual fund shares, whereby a purchase or redemption order is executed at the next calculated price. Mutual fund shares are bought and sold at the next computed price, not yesterday's stale prices.

Fourth Market, INSTINET: an ECN (electronic communications network) used by institutional investors, bypassing the services of a traditional broker. Institutional = INSTINET.

Fractional Share: a portion of a whole share of stock. Mutual fund shares typically are issued as whole and fractional shares, e.g., 101.45 shares.

Fraud: using deceit to wrongfully take money/property from someone under false pretenses.

Free Credit Balance: the cash in a customer account that can be withdrawn.

Free-Look: period during which a contract- or policyholder may cancel and receive all sales charges paid.

Free-riding & Withholding: a violation in which underwriters fail to distribute all shares allocated in an offering of a "hot issue."

Front-end Load: a mutual fund commission or sales fee charged when shares are purchased (A-shares). The amount of the load is added to the NAV to determine the public offering price (POP).

Frozen Account: an account in which purchase orders will be accepted only if the cash is in the account due to the customer's failure to comply with Reg T.

Fund of Funds: a mutual fund holding shares of other mutual funds.

Funds of Hedge Funds: a mutual fund holding shares of hedge funds.

Funding: an ERISA guideline that stipulates, among other things, that retirement plan assets must be segregated from other corporate assets.

Fungible: interchangeable, e.g., $20 bills or shares of stock, where one is just as good as another.

Fully Registered Bonds: bonds that are fully registered. A physical certificate with the owner's name, and interest payable automatically by the paying agent (no coupons).

G

GDP: Gross Domestic Product, the sum total of all goods and services being produced by the economy. A positive GDP number is evidence of economic expansion.

General Account: where an insurance company invests net premiums to fund guaranteed, fixed payouts.

General Obligation Bond: a municipal bond that is backed by the issuer's full faith and credit or full taxing authority.

General Securities Representative: an agent who passed the Series 7 and may sell virtually any security, unlike a Series 6 holder, who sells mutual funds and variable contracts only.

Generic Advertising: communications with the public that promote securities as investments but not specific securities.

Gift: transferring property to someone else and expecting nothing in return, or selling something to someone for far less than its fair market value.

Gift Splitting: method of claiming that a gift over the annual gift tax exclusion is partly from the husband and partly from the wife. For example, a gift of $25,000 can be deemed a gift of $12,500 from Grandma and $12,500 from Grandpa to avoid gift taxes.

Gift Tax: a tax paid when a gift exceeds the current exclusion limit. For tax year 2016, the excess of a gift over $14,000 is taxable at gift tax rates.

Global Fund: a mutual fund investing in companies located and doing business all across the globe, including the U.S.

GNMA: a.k.a. "Ginnie Mae," nickname for Government National Mortgage Association. A government agency (not a public company) that buys insured mortgages from lenders, selling pass-through certificates to investors. Monthly payments to investors pay interest and pass through principal from a pool of mortgages. Recall that bonds pay interest and return principal only at maturity, while "pass throughs" pass through principal monthly. Thus, the clever name "pass through."

Grantor: the party who transfers assets into a trust.

Growth: investment objective that seeks "capital appreciation." Achieved through common stock, primarily.

Growth & Income Fund: a fund that purchases stocks for growth potential and for dividend income. Less volatile than pure growth funds due to the income that calms investors down when the ride becomes turbulent.

Growth Fund: mutual fund seeking stocks in companies expected to grow faster than the overall market and/or competitors.

Guaranteed Bond: bond that is issued with a promise by a party other than the issuer to maintain payments of interest and principal if the issuer cannot.

Guardian: a fiduciary who manages the financial affairs of a minor or a person declared mentally incompetent by a court of law.

Guardian Account: account established through a court order designating an adult as custodian for the affairs of a minor child or a mentally incompetent adult.

H

Hedge: to bet the other way. If you own stock, you can hedge by purchasing puts, which profit when the stock goes down.

Hedge Fund: a private investment partnership open to accredited investors only. Illiquid investments that generally must be held one or two years before selling. Typically charge a management fee plus the first 20% of capital gains in most cases.

High-yield: an investment whose income stream is very high. A high-yield bond is either issued by a shaky company or municipal government forced to offer high nominal yields, or it begins to trade at lower and lower prices on the secondary market as the credit quality or perceived credit strength of the issuer deteriorates.

High-yield Corporate Bond Fund: mutual fund investing in lower-rated corporate bonds.

High-yield Tax-exempt Fund: mutual fund investing in lower-rated municipal bonds.

Howey Decision: a U.S. Supreme Court decision that defined an "investment contract" as "an investment of money in a common enterprise where the investor will profit solely through the efforts of others."

Holding Company: a company organized to invest in other corporations, e.g., Berkshire-Hathaway, which holds large stakes in other companies such as Coca-Cola, See's Candy, Dairy Queen, and Wells Fargo.

Holding Period: the period during which a security was held for purposes of determining whether a capital gain or loss is long- or short-term.

HR-10: a reference to a Keogh plan.

Hypothecate: to pledge securities purchased in a margin account as collateral to secure the loan.

I

IDR: or "Industrial Development Revenue Bond," a revenue bond that builds a facility that the issuing municipality then leases to a corporation. The lease payments from the corporation back the interest and principal payments on the bonds.

Immediate Annuity: an insurance contract purchased with a single premium that starts to pay the annuitant immediately. Purchased by individuals who are afraid of outliving their retirement savings.

Income: investment objective that seeks current income, found by investing in fixed income, e.g., bonds, money market, preferred stock. An equity income fund buys stocks that pay dividends; less volatile than a growth & income fund or a pure growth fund.

Income Bond: a bond that will pay interest only if the issuer earns sufficient income and the Board of Directors declares the payment.

Income Statement: a financial statement showing a corporation's results of operations over the quarter or year. Shows revenue, all expenses/costs, and the profit or loss the company showed over the period. Found in the annual shareholder report among other places.

Index: a theoretical grouping of stocks, bonds, etc., that aids analysts who want to track something. The Consumer Price Index is a theoretical grouping or "basket" of things that consumers buy, used to track inflation. The Dow Jones Industrial Average is a theoretical grouping of 30 large-company stocks that analysts use to track the stock market. The NASDAQ 100 is an index or grouping of the 100 most important stocks trading on NASDAQ.

Index Fund: a passively managed mutual fund that mirrors an index, e.g., S&P 500.

Indication of Interest: an investor's expression of interest in purchasing a new issue of securities after reading the preliminary prospectus; not a commitment to buy.

Individual Account: an account at a member firm owned by an individual rather than a trust, business, or joint account.

Individual Retirement Account (IRA): also called an "individual retirement arrangement" to make sure it has at least two names. A tax-deferred account that generally allows any individual with earned income to contribute 100% of earned income up to the current maximum contribution allowed on a pre-tax basis that reduces the current tax liability and allows investment returns to compound.

Inflation: rising prices, as measured by the Consumer Price Index (CPI). Major risk to fixed-income investors (loss of purchasing power).

Inflation Risk: also called "constant dollar risk" or "purchasing power risk," it is the risk that inflation will erode the value of a fixed-income stream from a bond or preferred stock.

Initial Public Offering (IPO): a corporation's first sale of stock to public investors. By definition, a primary market transaction in which the issuer receives the proceeds.

Inside Information: material information about a corporation that has not yet been released to the public and would likely affect the price of the corporation's stock and/or bonds. Inside information may not be "disseminated" or acted upon.

Insider: for purpose of insider trading rules, an "insider" is anyone who has or has access to material non-public information. Officers (CEO, CFO), members of the Board of Directors, and investors owning > 10% of the company's outstanding shares are assumed to possess and have access to inside information. As fiduciaries to the shareholders, insiders may not use inside information to their benefit.

Insider Trading and Securities Fraud Enforcement Act (ITSFEA) of 1988: an Act of Congress that addresses insider trading and lists the penalties for violations of the Act. Insider traders may be penalized up to three times the amount of their profit or their loss avoided by using inside information.

Insurance: protection against loss of income due to death, disability, long-term care needs, etc.

Institutional Investor: not an individual. An institution is, for example, a pension fund, insurance company, or mutual fund. The large institutions are "accredited investors" who get to do things that retail (individual) investors often do not get to do.

Integration: stage of money laundering when the funds are invested in legitimate enterprises or investment vehicles.

Interpositioning: a violation in which an unnecessary third party is inserted into a transaction.

Interest Only Settlement Option: a settlement option in which the insurance company keeps the proceeds from the policy and invests it, promising the beneficiary a guaranteed minimum rate of interest.

Interest Rate Risk: the risk that interest rates will rise, pushing the market value of a fixed-income security down. Long-term bonds most susceptible.

Interest Rates: the cost of a commodity called money. To borrow money, borrowers pay a rate called an interest rate on top of the principal they will return at the end of the term. A one-year loan of $1,000 at 5% interest would have the borrower pay $50 on top of the $1,000 that will be returned at the end of the year.

Internal Revenue Code (IRC): tax laws for the U.S. that define, for example, maximum IRA contributions, or the "conduit tax theory" that mutual funds use when distributing 90% of net income to shareholders, etc.

Internal Revenue Service (IRS): an agency for the federal government that no one seems to like very much. Responsible for collecting federal taxes for the U.S. Treasury and for administering tax rules and regulations.

International Fund: a mutual fund investing in companies established outside the U.S.

Interstate Offering: an offering of securities in several states, requiring registration with the SEC.

Intrastate Offering: an offering of securities completed in the issuer's home state with investors who reside in that state, and, therefore, eligible for the Rule 147 Exemption to registration with the SEC. Intrastate offerings generally register with the state Administrator.

Inverse Relationship: when one goes up, the other goes down, and vice versa. Interest Rates and Yields are inversely related to Bond Prices. Your rate of speed is inversely related to your travel time to and from the office.

Investment Adviser: a business or professional that is compensated for advising others as to the value of or advisability of investing in securities. The entity that manages mutual funds/separate accounts for an asset-based fee. Financial planners are also advisers.

Investment Adviser Representative: a representative of an investment advisory firm receiving compensation for managing accounts or selling the services of the firm.

Investment Analysis Tool: an interactive technological tool that produces simulations and statistical analyses that present the likelihood of various investment outcomes if certain investments are made or certain investment strategies or styles are undertaken, thereby serving as an additional resource to investors in the evaluation of the potential risks and returns of investment choices.

Investment Banker: see "underwriter." A firm that raises capital for issuers on the primary market.

Investment Banking: the business of helping companies with mergers and acquisitions, performing IPOs and additional offerings. In other words, investment bankers raise capital for issuers not by loaning money (like a traditional bank) but by finding investors willing to contribute to the cause.

Investment Company: a company engaged in the business of pooling investors' money and trading in securities on their behalf. Examples include unit investment trusts (UITs), face-amount certificate companies, and management companies.

Investment Company Act of 1940: classified Investment Companies and set rules for registration and operation.

Investment Contract: a security, defined through Howey Decision, as "an investment of money whereby the investor profits solely through the efforts of others."

Investment Grade: a bond rated at least BBB by S&P or Baa by Moody's. The bond does not have severe default risk, so it is said to be appropriate for investors, as opposed to the speculators who buy non–investment grade bonds.

Investment Objective: any goal that an investor has including current income, capital appreciation (growth), capital preservation (safety), or speculation.

Investment Profile: what an agent must determine for each customer, defined by FINRA as, "a customer's investment profile includes, but is not limited to, the customer's age, other investments, financial situation and needs, tax status, investment objectives, investment experience, investment time horizon, liquidity needs, risk tolerance, and any other information the customer may disclose to the member or associated person in connection with such recommendation."

Investment Risk: any factor that can have a material negative effect on an investment, e.g. inflation or market risk.

Investment Style: an approach to investing, such as active, passive, or buy-and-hold.

IRA: Individual Retirement Account. A retirement account/arrangement for any individual with earned income. The Traditional IRA offers pre-tax contributions while the Roth IRA is funded with after-tax contributions.

Irrevocable Trust: a trust that may not be altered or revoked/canceled by the grantor. Because the trust is irrevocable, the grantor is no longer responsible for paying taxes on the income generated by the trust, and the assets do not count as part of the grantor's estate when he, you know, dies.

Issued Shares: the number of shares that have been issued by a corporation.

Issued Stock: the shares that have been issued to investors by the corporation at this time. Often a lower number than the number of shares authorized.

Issuer: any individual or entity who issues or proposes to issue any security. For example, the issuer of Google common stock is Google.

Issuing Securities: raising capital by offering securities to investors on the primary market.

J

Joint Account: investment account owned by more than one individual. Account owners sign a joint account agreement that stipulates which percentage of the assets is owned by each individual. Joint accounts are either "tenants in common" or "tenants with rights of survivorship." See "JTIC" and "JTWROS."

Joint with Last Survivor: a settlement/payout option on an annuity that requires the insurance company to make payments to the annuitants provided they are alive.

JTIC (Joint Tenants in Common): account where the assets of the deceased party pass to the deceased's estate, not the other account owner(s).

JTWROS (Joint Tenants With Rights Of Survivorship): account where the assets of the deceased party pass to the other account owner(s).

Junk Bond: a bond backed by a shaky issuer. It was either issued by an entity with shaky credit, or is now trading at a frightfully low price on the secondary market because the issuer's credit has suddenly or recently been downgraded. Since the price is low, given the low quality of the debt, the yield is high. High-yield and junk are synonymous.

K

K-1: a tax form required of people who own direct participation interests (limited partnership, S-corp).

Keogh: qualified retirement plan available to sole proprietorships.

Keynesian Economics: economic school of thought that advocates government intervention through fiscal policy as a way to stimulate demand for goods and services.

Know Your Customer: FINRA rule requiring member firms and associated persons to use reasonable diligence to determine a customer's investment profile before making recommendations to the customer.

L

Large Cap: a stock where the total value of the outstanding shares is large, generally greater than $10 billion. For example, GE, MSFT, IBM.

Last-In-First-Out: LIFO, an accounting method used for random withdrawals from an annuity. The IRS assumes that all withdrawals represent part of the taxable "excess over cost basis" first.

Layering: stage of money laundering when a confusing set of transactions is conducted to make it unclear where these funds originated.

Legislative Risk: the risk to an investor that laws will change and have a negative impact on an investment. For example, if municipal bonds lose their tax-exempt interest, their value would plummet.

Letter of Intent: LOI, a feature of many mutual funds whereby an investor may submit a letter or form expressing the intent to invest enough money over 13 months to achieve a breakpoint.

Level Load: an ongoing asset-based sales charge (12b-1 fee) associated with mutual fund C-shares. Appropriate for short-term investments only.

Leverage: using borrowed money to increase returns. Debt securities and margin accounts are associated with "leverage."

Liabilities: what an individual or corporation owes, e.g., credit card debt, bonds, mortgage balance, accounts payable.

Life-income Settlement Option: payment stream from an insurance contract in which the insurance company provides the beneficiary with a guaranteed income for the rest of his or her life by annuitizing the death benefit.

Life Only/Life Annuity: a payout option whereby the insurance/annuity company promises to make payments only for the rest of the annuitant's life.

Life With Joint and Last Survivor: a payout option whereby the insurance/annuity company promises to make payments to the annuitant for the rest of his life, then to the survivor for the rest of her life.

Life With Period Certain: a payout option whereby the insurance/annuity company promises to make payments to the annuitant for the rest of his life or a certain period of time, whichever is greater.

Life With Unit Refund: a payout option whereby the insurance/annuity company promises to make at least a certain number of payments to the annuitant or beneficiary.

Lifetime Gift Tax Credit: the maximum amount of gifts an individual may make over her lifetime before having to pay gift taxes. Deductible against the lifetime estate credit.

Limited Liability: an investor's ability to limit losses to no more than the amount invested. Holders of common stock and limited partnership interests enjoy "limited liability," which means they can only lose 100% of what they invest.

Limited Representative: what you'll be after passing the Series 6 and getting registered to represent your broker-dealer. You would be a "general securities representative" if you were crazy or bold enough to sit for the 6-hour, 250-question Series 7 exam.

Limited Trading Authorization: an authorization for someone other than the account owner to enter purchase and sale orders but make no withdrawals of cash or securities.

Liquid Net Worth: easily liquidated assets minus all liabilities.

Liquidation Priority: the priority of claims on a bankrupt entity's assets that places creditors (bondholders) ahead of stockholders and preferred stockholders ahead of common stockholders.

Liquidity: the ability to quickly convert an investment to cash and get a fair price. A home is not a liquid investment—100 shares of GE are extremely liquid. Mutual funds are very liquid, since the issuer must pay the NAV promptly. The most liquid investment imaginable is the money market mutual fund—just write checks and the fund redeems enough shares to cover it.

Liquidity Risk: the risk of not being able to quickly convert an asset to cash at a fair price.

Long: to buy or own.

Long-term Capital Gain: a profit realized when selling stock held for at least 12 months plus 1 day. Subject to lower capital gains tax rates than short-term gains.

Long-term Capital Loss: a loss realized when selling stock held for at least 12 months plus 1 day. Used to offset long-term capital gains.

Lump Sum Payment: a settlement/payout option for annuities or insurance where the annuitant or beneficiary receives a lump sum payment. Go figure.

M

Maloney Act: An amendment to the Securities Exchange Act of 1934 creating the NASD as the self-regulatory organization (SRO) for the over-the-counter market (OTC).

Management Company: one of the three types of Investment Companies, including both open-end and closed-end funds.

Management Fee: the percentage of assets charged to the mutual fund portfolio to cover the cost of portfolio management.

Manager's Fee: typically the smallest piece of the spread, paid to the managing underwriter for every share sold by the syndicate.

Margin: amount of equity contributed by a customer as a percentage of the current market value of the securities held in a margin account.

Marginal Tax Rate: the tax applied to the last dollar of income earned. The highest rate of tax applied to an investor's income in a progressive system.

Markdown: the difference between the highest bid price for a security and the price that a specific dealer pays an investor for her security.

Market Letter: a publication of a broker-dealer sent to clients or the public and discussing investing, financial markets, economic conditions, etc. Can be considered correspondence if sent to a limited number of clients; otherwise, considered retail communication and subject to pre-approval.

Market Maker: a dealer in the OTC market maintaining an inventory of a specific security and a firm Bid and Ask price good for a minimum of 100 shares. Acts as a "principal" on transactions, buying and selling for its/their own account.

Market Order: an order to buy or sell a security at the best available market price.

Market Risk: also called "systematic risk," the risk inherent to the entire market rather than a specific security. The risk that the stock market may suffer violent upheavals due to unpredictable events including natural disaster, war, disease, famine, credit crises, etc. Market risk can only be reduced by hedging with options or ETFs.

Marketability: the ease or difficulty an investor has when trying to sell a security for cash without losing his shirt. Thinly traded securities have poor marketability.

Markup: the difference between the lowest ask/offer price for a security and the price that a specific dealer charges.

Material Information: any fact that could reasonably affect an investor's decision to buy, sell, or hold a security. For example, profits and losses at the company, product liability lawsuits, the loss of key clients, etc.

Maturity Date: the date that a bond pays out the principal and interest payments cease. Also called "redemption."

Mediation: an alternative to FINRA arbitration proceedings.

Member Firm: a broker-dealer and/or underwriting firm that belongs to FINRA or another securities association (MSRB, CBOE).

Memorandum: a required document showing the key details of a transaction. A memorandum or order ticket must be created for all trades executed by a broker-dealer.

Mini-Max: a type of best efforts underwriting where the syndicate must sell a minimum amount and may sell up to a higher, maximum amount.

Minimum Death Benefit: the minimum death benefit payable to the insured, regardless of how lousy the separate account returns are in a variable policy.

Monetarist: an economist who believes that the economy can be managed by managing the money supply and, therefore, interest rates.

Monetary Policy: what the FRB implements through the discount rate, reserve requirement, and FOMC open market operations. Monetary policy tightens or loosens credit to affect short-term interest rates and, therefore, the economy.

Money Laundering: the illegal process of turning "dirty" money "clean." Hiding ill-gotten profits by disguising them as legitimate funds through a series of complex transactions.

Money Market: the short-term (1 year or less) debt security market. Examples include commercial paper, banker's acceptance, T-bills.

Money Market Mutual Fund: a highly liquid holding place for cash. Sometimes called "stable value" funds, as the share price is generally maintained at $1. The mutual funds invest in—surprisingly—money market securities.

Money Purchase: a retirement plan in which the employer must contribute a set percentage of the employee's salary.

Moody's Investors Service: one of the top three credit rating agencies for corporate and municipal bonds as well as stocks.

Mortality and Expense Risk Fee: expenses on variable contracts allowing the insurance company to offer death benefits and keep their expenses reasonable.

Mortality Guarantee: a promise from an insurance company to pay an annuitant no matter how long he lives, or to pay an insurance policyholder no matter how soon he dies.

Mortality Risk: the risk to the insurance company that the insured will die too soon or the annuitant will live too long.

Mortality Risk Fee: fee charged on a variable annuity allowing the insurance company to offer a death benefit and promise an income stream for life.

Mortgage-backed Security: a fixed-income security created with a pool of mortgages, e.g., GNMA.

Mortgage Bond: a corporate bond secured by a pledge of real estate as collateral.

Municipal Bond: a bond issued by a state, county, city, school district, etc., to build roads, schools, hospitals, etc., or simply to keep the government running long enough to hold another election.

Municipal Bond Fund: a mutual fund that invests in municipal bonds with an objective to maximize federally tax-exempt income.

Municipal Note: a short-term obligation of a city, state, school district, etc., backed by the anticipation of funds from revenues, taxes, or upcoming bond issues.

MSRB (Municipal Securities Rulemaking Board): the self-regulatory organization overseeing municipal securities dealers.

Mutual Fund: an investment company offering equity stakes in a portfolio that is usually managed actively and that always charges management fees and other expenses.

<u>N</u>

NASD (National Association of Securities Dealers): former name of the SRO empowered with the passage of the Maloney Act of 1938. Regulates its own members and enforces SEC rules and regulations. Now called FINRA after a merger with the regulators from the NYSE.

NASDAQ: National Association of Securities Dealers Automated Quotation system. The main component of the OTC market. Stocks that meet certain criteria are quoted throughout the day on NASDAQ, e.g., MSFT, ORCL, and INTC.

NASDAQ 100: an index comprised of the 100 largest stocks by market cap trading on NASDAQ.

National Adjudicatory Council: NAC, the first level of appeal for a party sanctioned under FINRA's Code of Procedure.

NAV: the net asset value of a mutual fund share. (Assets – Liabilities)/Outstanding Shares.

Negotiable: the characteristic of a security that allows an investor to sell or transfer ownership to another party. For example, savings bonds are not negotiable, while Treasury Bills are negotiable (able to be traded).

Negotiable CDs: large-denominated certificates of deposit that may be traded (negotiable) on a secondary market.

Negotiated Market: not an auction market, a market in which dealers/market makers negotiate prices on large blocks of securities.

Net Investment Income: the source of an investment company's dividend distributions to shareholders. It is calculated by taking the fund's dividends and interest collected on portfolio securities, minus the operating expenses. Funds using the "conduit tax theory" distribute at least 90% of net investment income to avoid paying taxes on the amount distributed to shareholders.

Net Worth: the difference between assets and liabilities. For example, the difference between the market value of a home and the mortgage balance still owed would represent the total net worth for many Americans. Other components would be checking, savings, and retirement accounts minus credit card debt. Add the pluses, subtract the minuses, and you have the individual's financial net worth.

New Account Form: the form that must be filled out for each new account opened with a broker-dealer. The form specifies, at a minimum, the name of the account owner, trading authorization, method of payment, and the type of investment securities that are appropriate for this specific account.

New Issue Market: the primary market, where securities are issued to investors with the proceeds going to the issuer of the securities. Initial public offerings (IPOs), for example, take place on the "new issue market."

NYSE: New York Stock Exchange, an auction market where buyers and sellers shout out competitive bid and asked/offered prices throughout the day.

No-load Fund: a mutual fund sold without a sales charge, but one which may charge an ongoing 12b-1 fee or "asset-based sales charge" up to .25% of net assets.

Nominal Owner: the named owner on the investment account. For example, the custodian in an UTMA account, versus the beneficial owner—the minor.

Nominal Yield: the interest rate paid by a bond or preferred stock. The investor receives this percentage of the par value each year, regardless of what the bond or preferred stock is trading for on the secondary market.

Non-accredited Investor: an investor who does not meet various SEC net worth and/or income requirements. For a Reg D private placement, accredited investors may participate, but only a limited number of non-accredited investors may purchase the issue.

Non-cumulative Preferred Stock: a type of preferred stock that does not must pay missed dividends (dividends in arrears).

Non-diversified Company: a mutual fund that doesn't meet the 75-5-10 rule, preferring to concentrate more heavily in certain issues.

Non-NASDAQ OTC: securities trading on the over-the-counter market that do not meet NASDAQ requirements. For example, the Pink Sheets.

Non-systematic Risk: the risk of holding any one specific stock or bond. Diversification spreads this risk among different issuers and different industries to minimize the impact of a bankruptcy or unexpected collapse of any one issuer.

Note: a short-term debt security.

Nolo Contendere: Latin for "no contest." Form U4 asks if the applicant has ever pled nolo contendere to any felony or to any misdemeanor relevant to the securities industry.

Numbered Account: an account identified only by a number or symbol, with the customer attesting to ownership in a separate document on file with the broker-dealer.

O

Obsolescence Risk: the risk to investors that the issuer's business will become dated and no longer relevant.

Odd Lot: an order for fewer than 100 shares of common stock or 5 bonds.

Offer: another name for "ask," or the price an investor must pay if he wants to buy a security from a dealer/market maker.

Offer of Settlement: a respondent's proposal to FINRA for sanctions and fines related to his violations of the rules.

Offer, Offer to Sell: any attempt to interest someone in buying a security.

Office of Foreign Asset Control (OFAC): office of the federal government that maintains a list of individuals and organizations viewed as a threat to the U.S.

Omitting Prospectus: an advertisement for a mutual fund that typically shows performance figures without providing (omitting) the full disclosure in the prospectus. Therefore, it must present caveats and encourage readers to read the prospectus and consider all the risks before investing in the fund.

Open-end Fund: an investment company that sells an unlimited number of shares to an unlimited number of investors on a continuous basis. Shares are redeemed by the company rather than traded OTC or on the exchanges.

Operating Expenses: expenses that a mutual fund deducts from the assets of the fund, including board of director salaries, custodial and transfer agent services, management fees, 12b-1 fees, etc.

Opportunity Cost: the return on an investment that must be foregone if the investor chooses an alternative.

Option: a derivative giving the holder the right to buy or sell something for a stated price up to expiration of the contract. Puts and calls.

Order Ticket: an electronic or paper document providing the key details of a transaction about to be entered by a broker-dealer.

OSJ: office of supervisory jurisdiction, a centralized office responsible for overseeing branch offices of a member firm.

OTC/Over-the-Counter: called a "negotiated market." Securities traded among dealers rather than on exchanges. Includes NASDAQ and Bulletin Board and Pink Sheets stocks, plus government, corporate, and municipal bonds.

Outstanding Shares: the number of shares a corporation has outstanding. Found by taking Issued shares minU.S. Treasury stock.

P

Par, Principal: the face amount of a bond payable at maturity. Also, the face amount of a preferred stock. Preferred = $100, Bond = $1,000.

Par Value: the face amount that a debt security will pay at maturity, e.g., $1,000. For preferred stock, the amount against which the dividend percentage is calculated, e.g., $100 par value.

Partial Surrender: life insurance policyholder cashes in part of the cash value. Excess over premiums is taxable.

Participating Preferred Stock: preferred stock whose dividend is often raised above the stated rate.

Participation: provision of ERISA requiring that all employees in a qualified retirement plan be covered within a reasonable length of time after being hired.

Pass-through Certificate: a mortgage-backed security (usually GNMA) that takes a pool of mortgages and passes through interest and principal monthly to an investor.

Passive Income: as opposed to "earned income," the income derived from rental properties, limited partnerships, or other enterprises in which the individual is not actively involved.

Passive Management: style of portfolio management using indexes based on a belief that markets are efficient and active management provides no value.

Payable (or Payment) Date: the date that the dividend check is paid to investors.

Payroll Deduction IRA: a voluntary retirement benefit in which the employer deposits an amount from the employee's paycheck into an IRA account.

P/E or Price-to-Earnings Ratio: the market price of a stock compared to the earnings per share. Stocks trading at high P/E ratios are "growth stocks," while those trading at low P/E ratios are "value stocks."

Peak: the phase of the business cycle between expansion (good times) and contraction (bad times).

Penny Stock Cold Calling Rules: rules to protect consumers receiving telemarketing pitches to buy risky stocks trading below $5 a share. Rules require special disclosure and investor signatures when selling penny stocks.

Pension Plan: a contract between an individual and an employer that provides for the distribution of benefits at retirement.

Performance Figures: total return for a mutual fund over 1, 5, and 10 years, and/or "life of fund." Only past performance may be indicated, and there must be a caveat that past performance does not guarantee future results.

Period Certain: a settlement option for an annuity that provides payments to the annuitant or his beneficiaries for a certain period of time, even if the annuitant dies before the period lapses.

Periodic Deferred Annuity: method of purchasing an annuity whereby the contract holder makes periodic payments into the contract. The pay-out phase must be deferred for all periodic payment plans.

Periodic-payment Annuity: annuity in which the annuitant makes contributions periodically, as he/she is able.

Permanent Insurance: life insurance other than "term."

Pink Sheets: a virtually unregulated part of the OTC market where thinly traded, volatile stocks change hands.

Placement: the stage of money laundering when funds are moved into the system.

Political Risk: the risk that a country's government will radically change policies or that the political climate will become hostile or counterproductive to business and financial markets.

POP: public offering price. For an IPO, this includes the spread to the underwriters. For a mutual fund, this includes any sales loads that go to the underwriter/distributor.

Portfolio: a batch of stocks, bonds, money market securities, or any combination thereof that an investor owns.

Power of Attorney: having the authority to make decisions on behalf of someone else, e.g., financial and health care decisions for someone ruled mentally incompetent.

Power of Substitution: a document that when signed by the security owner authorizes transfer of the certificate to another party.

Pre-emptive Right: the right of common stockholders to maintain their proportional ownership if the company offers more shares of stock.

Precious Metals Fund: a mutual fund focusing on mining companies extracting metals including gold, silver, copper, and platinum.

Preferred Stock: a fixed-income equity security whose stated dividends must be paid before common stock can receive any dividend payment. Also gets preference ahead of common stock in a liquidation (but behind all bonds and general creditors).

Preliminary Prospectus: a.k.a. "red herring." A prospectus that lacks the POP and the effective date. Used to solicit indications of interest.

Premium: the amount above the par value in a bond's market price. For example, a bond trading for $1,100 is trading at a $100 premium.

Premium Bond: a bond purchased for more than the par value, usually due to a drop in interest rates.

Prepaid Tuition Plan: a 529 Plan in which tuition credits to be used in the future are purchased at today's prices.

Prepayment Risk: the risk that the mortgages underlying a mortgage-backed security/pass-through will be paid off sooner than expected due to a drop in interest rates. Investors reinvest the principal at a lower rate going forward.

Preservation of Capital: an investment objective that places the emphasis on making sure the principal is not lost. Also called "safety."

Price-to-Earnings (P/E) Ratio: the market price of a stock compared to the earnings per share. Stocks trading at high P/E ratios are "growth stocks," while those trading at low P/E ratios are "value stocks."

Primary Market: where securities are issued to raise capital for the issuer.

Primary Offering: offering of securities in which the proceeds go to the issuer.

Prime Rate: interest rate charged to corporations with high credit ratings for unsecured loans.

Principal: (1) the face amount of a debt security, (2) a supervisor at a broker-dealer, (3) capital at risk in a transaction.

Principal-protected Fund: a mutual fund for people who want their principal protected. Involves holding the investment for several years, at which point the fund guarantees that the value of the investment will be equal to at least what the investor put in.

Private Placement: an exempt transaction under Reg D (Rule 506) of the Securities Act of 1933, allowing issuers to sell securities without registration to accredited investors, who agree to hold them fully paid for a stated time period before then selling them through Rule 144.

Private Securities Transaction: offering an investment opportunity not sponsored by the firm. Requires permission from the firm and any disclosure demanded; otherwise, a violation called "selling away."

Probate: the process of "proving the will" in open court to gather and distribute the assets of the deceased.

Profit Sharing: a defined contribution plan in which any contributions from the employer are discretionary and to which employees make no contributions.

Progressive Tax: a tax that increases as a percentage as the thing being taxed increases, including gift, estate, and income taxes. Not a flat tax.

Prospectus: a disclosure document that details a company's plans, history, officers, and risks of investment. It's the red herring plus the POP and the effective date.

Proxy Form: a form granting the power to vote according to a shareholder's instructions when the shareholder will not attend the meeting.

Proxy Statement: full disclosure document explaining all relevant information regarding an upcoming shareholder vote, filed with the SEC and delivered to shareholders of the issuer.

Public Appearance: addressing an audience on topics related to securities. Before speaking at a local Chamber of Commerce function, for example, registered representatives need prior principal approval.

Public Offering: the sale of an issue of common stock, either an IPO or an additional offer of shares.

Public Offering Price (POP): the price an investor pays for a mutual fund or an initial public offering. For a mutual fund = NAV + the sales charge.

Purchase Payment: payments made into an annuity contract.

Purchaser Representative: someone independent of the issuer in a private placement who can represent the needs of a non-accredited investor.

Purchasing Power Risk: also called "constant dollar" or "inflation" risk, the risk that a fixed payment will not be sufficient to keep up with rising inflation (as measured through the CPI).

Put (n.): a contract giving the owner the right to sell something at a stated exercise price.

Put (v.): to sell.

Q

Qualified Dividend: a dividend that qualifies for a lower tax rate vs. ordinary income. An idea that generally finds more favor among Republicans than Democrats.

Qualified Institutional Buyer: certain institutions and individuals with a large amount of assets who can engage in certain transactions that most investors are not eligible to participate in, e.g. purchasing stock acquired in a private placement before the holding period has elapsed through Rule 144a.

Qualified Plan: a retirement plan that qualifies for deductible contributions on behalf of employers and/or employees and covered by ERISA. For example, 401(k), defined benefit, Keogh. Must meet IRS approval, unlike more informal "non-qualified plans."

Quote, Quotation: a price that a dealer is willing to pay or accept for a security. A two-sided quote has both a bid and an asked/offer price.

R

Random Withdrawals: a settlement option in an annuity whereby the investor takes the value of the sub-accounts in two or more withdrawals, rather than one lump sum.

Ranking Entity: an entity that provides general information about investment companies to the public, independent of the investment company and its affiliates, and whose services are not procured by the investment company or any of its affiliates to assign the investment company a ranking. For example, Lipper.

Rating Service: e.g., S&P and Moody's; a company that assigns credit ratings to corporate and municipal bonds.

Real Estate Investment Trust (REIT): a corporation or trust that uses the pooled capital of investors to invest in ownership of either income property or mortgage loans. 90% of net income is paid out to shareholders.

Real Rate of Return: the rate of return minus the rate of inflation.

Realized Gain: the amount of the "profit" an investor earns when selling a security.

Recession: economic period associated with rising unemployment, falling interest rates, and falling gross domestic product.

Recommendation: a suggestion that the customer take action or refrain from taking action regarding a security or investment strategy.

Record Date: the date determined by the Board of Directors upon which the investor must be the holder "of record" to receive the upcoming dividend. Settlement of a trade must occur by the record date for the buyer to receive the dividend.

Red Herring: a.k.a. "preliminary prospectus." Contains essentially the same information that the final prospectus will contain, minus the POP and effective date.

Redeem: the act of selling back shares of a redeemable security to the issuer for its then-Net Asset Value.

Redeemable Security: a security that may be redeemed or presented to the issuer for payment.

Redemption: for mutual funds, redemption involves the sale of mutual fund shares back to the fund at the NAV (less any redemption fees, back-end loads). For bonds, the date that principal is returned to the investor, along with the final interest payment.

Redemption Fee: a charge to a mutual fund investor who sells her shares back to the fund much sooner than the fund would prefer.

Reg A: a laid-back and predictable form of island music. Also, an exempt transaction under the Securities Act of 1933 for smallferings of securities ($5 million issued in a 12-month period).

Reg D: an exempt transaction under the Securities Act of 1933 for private placements.

Reg T: established by the FRB as the amount of credit a broker-dealer may extend to a customer pledging a security as collateral for a margin loan. In a margin account, customers must put down ½ of the security's value, or at least $2,000.

Reg U: established by the FRB as the amount of credit a bank may extend to a broker-dealer or public customer pledging a security as collateral.

Registered As to Principal Only: a bond with only the principal registered. Interest coupons must be presented for payment.

Registered Principal: an associated person who supervises registered representatives and performs compliance activities for a member broker-dealer.

Registered Representative: an associated person of an investment banker or broker-dealer who effects transactions in securities for compensation.

Registrar: the party who audits the issuer's transfer agent.

Registration Statement: the legal document disclosing material information concerning an offering of a security and its issuer. Submitted to SEC under Securities Act of 1933.

Regressive Tax: a flat tax, e.g., gasoline, sales, excise taxes.

Regular Way Settlement: T + 3, trade date plus three business days. T + 1 for Treasury securities.

Regulated Investment Company: an investment company using the conduit tax theory by distributing 90% or more of net investment income to shareholders.

Regulation S-P: federal legislation designed to fight identity theft and to protect consumers and customers from having too much of their information shared with people they've never met.

Regulatory Element: a FINRA continuing education requirement that must be completed on your second registration anniversary and every third year thereafter.

Regulatory Risk: a.k.a. "legislative risk," the risk that a regulatory/legislative decision could have an adverse impact on an investment. For example, if tax rates are cut, municipal bonds lose their attractiveness.

Reinstatement Privilege: a feature of some mutual funds allowing investors to make withdrawals and then reinstate the money without paying another sales charge.

Reinvestment Risk: the risk that a fixed-income investor will not be able to reinvest interest payments or the par value at attractive interest rates. Happens when rates are falling.

REIT (Real Estate Investment Trust): a corporation or trust that uses the pooled capital of investors to invest in ownership of either income property or mortgage loans. 90% of net income is paid out to shareholders.

Release Date: a.k.a. "effective date," date established by the SEC as to when the underwriters may sell new securities to the buyers.

REMIC: real estate mortgage investment conduit. Another name for a CMO.

Reporting: section of ERISA requiring that participants receive regular reports on their accounts (at least quarterly).

Repurchase Agreement: an agreement in which one party sells something to the other and agrees to repurchase it for a higher price over the short-term.

Required Minimum Distribution (RMD): the required minimum distribution that must be taken from a retirement plan to avoid IRS penalties. Usually April 1 of the year following the individual's 70½th birthday.

Reserve Requirement: amount of money a bank must lock up in reserve, established by the FRB.

Residual Claim: the right of common stockholders to claim assets after the claims of all creditors and preferred stockholders have been satisfied.

Restricted Person: a person prohibited from buying an initial offering of equity securities.

Restricted Stock: stock held by an affiliated investor of the issuer, e.g., the CEO and his immediate family, or 10% shareholders.

Retail Investor: a customer who is not an institutional investor, e.g. an individual.

Revenue: the proceeds a company receives when selling products and services.

Revenue Bond: a municipal bond whose interest and principal payments are backed by the revenues generated from the project being built by the proceeds of the bonds. Toll roads, for example, are usually built with revenue bonds backed by the tolls collected.

Revocable Trust: a trust that can be altered or terminated by the grantor and, therefore, subjects the grantor to taxation on income while the grantor is alive and counts as part of the estate upon death.

Rights: short-term equity securities that allow the holder to buy new shares below the current market price.

Rights of Accumulation: feature of many mutual funds whereby a rise in account value is counted the same as new money for purposes of achieving a breakpoint.

Rights Offering: additional offer of stock accompanied by the opportunity for each shareholder to maintain his/her proportionate ownership in the company.

Risk-Averse: an investor for whom stable principal is most important.

Risk Tolerance: the ability to withstand wide fluctuations in investment values and even principal loss both financially and psychologically.

Rollover: moving retirement funds from a 401(k) to an IRA, or from one IRA to another. In a "60-day rollover," the check is cut to the individual, who must then send a check to the new custodian within 60 days to avoid early distribution penalties.

Roth IRA: individual retirement account funded with non-deductible (after-tax) contributions. All distributions are tax-free provided the individual is 59½ and has had the account at least five years.

Round Lot: the usual or normal unit of trading. 100 shares for common stock.

Rule 144: the rule under the Securities Act of 1933 under which affiliated investors report sales of the issuer's securities, subject to volume limits over a 90-day period.

Rule 147: exemption under the Securities Act of 1933 for intra-state offerings of securities.

S

Safety: an investment objective that seeks to avoid loss of principal first and foremost. Bank CDs, Treasury securities, and fixed annuities are generally suitable.

Sales Charge, Sales Load: a deduction from an investor's check that goes to the distributors/sellers of the fund. Deducted from investor's check, either when she buys (A-shares) or sells (B-shares).

Sales Literature: communications of a mutual fund designed to market and sell shares to investors, e.g. brochures, and websites.

Savings Bond: a U.S. Government debt security that is not "negotiable," meaning it can't be traded or pledged as collateral for a loan. Includes EE and HH series bonds.

Scheduled Premium: life insurance with established, scheduled premium payments, e.g., whole life, variable life. As opposed to "universal" insurance, which is "flexible premium."

Second Market: a "negotiated market" including NASDAQ and non-NASDAQ securities trading.

Secondary Offering/Distribution: a distribution of securities owned by major stockholders—not the issuer of the securities.

Secondary Market: where investors trade securities among themselves and proceeds do not go to the issuer.

Section 457 Plan: retirement plan for state and local government workers funded with pre-tax contributions, with similar rules as 403(b) and 401(k) plans.

Sector Fund: a specialized fund that concentrates heavily in a specific industry group, e.g., pharmaceutical or telecommunications. Higher risk/reward than funds invested in many industries.

Secured Bond: a corporate bond secured by collateral, e.g., mortgage bond, collateral trust certificate, equipment trust certificate.

Securities Act of 1933: an act of Congress that regulates the new-issue or primary market, requiring non-exempt issuers to register securities and provide full disclosure.

Securities and Exchange Commission: SEC, empowered by passage of Securities Exchange Act of 1934. A government body, the ultimate securities regulator.

Securities Exchange Act of 1934: prevents fraud in the securities markets. No security and no person exempt from anti-fraud regulations. Created/empowered the SEC. Requires broker-dealers, exchanges and securities associations to register with SEC. Requires public companies to report quarterly and annually to SEC.

Security: an investment of money subject to fluctuation in value and negotiable/marketable to other investors. Other than an insurance policy or fixed annuity, a security is any piece of securitized "paper" that can be traded for value.

Self-Regulatory Organization: SRO, e.g., FINRA. An organization given the power to regulate its members. Not government bodies like the SEC, which oversees the SROs.

Selling Away: a violation that occurs when a registered representative offers investment opportunities not sponsored by the firm.

Selling Concession: typically, the largest piece of the underwriting spread going to the firm credited with making the sale.

Selling Dividends: a violation where an investor is deceived into thinking that she must purchase a stock to receive an upcoming dividend.

Selling Group: certain broker-dealers with an agreement to act as selling agents for the syndicate (underwriters) with no capital at risk.

Semi-annual: twice per year, or "at the half year," literally. Note that "bi-annually" means "every two years." Bond interest is paid semi-annually. Mutual funds report to their shareholders semi-annually and annually. Nothing happens "bi-annually" as a general rule of thumb.

Semiannual Report: the detailed but unaudited report that mutual funds deliver to all existing shareholders mid-year.

Senior Security: a security that grants the holder a higher claim on the issuer's assets in the event of a liquidation/bankruptcy.

SEP-IRA: pre-tax retirement plan available to small businesses. Favors high-income employees (compared to SIMPLE). Only the employer contributes.

Separate Account: an account maintained by an insurance/annuity company that is separate from the company's general account. Used to invest clients' money for variable annuities and variable insurance contracts. Registered as an investment company under Investment Company Act of 1940.

Series EE bond: a nonmarketable, interest-bearing U.S. Government savings bond issued at a discount from the par value. Interest is exempt from state and local taxation.

Series HH bond: a nonmarketable, interest-bearing U.S. Government savings bond issued at par and purchased only by trading in Series EE bonds at maturity. Interest is exempt from state and local taxation.

Series I Bond: a savings bond issued by the U.S. Treasury that protects investors from inflation or purchasing power risk.

Settlement: completion of a securities transaction wherein payment has been made by the buyer and delivery has been made by the seller.

Settlement Date: the final date in the process of clearing and settling a trade on which monies due and securities are officially exchanged among both parties to the transaction.

Settlement Options: payout options on annuities and life insurance including life-only, life with period certain, and joint and last survivorship.

Share Identification: a method of calculating capital gains and losses by which the investor identifies which shares were sold, as opposed to using FIFO or average cost.

Short Sale: method of attempting to profit from a security whose price is expected to fall. Trader borrows certificates through a broker-dealer and sells them, with the obligation to replace them at a later date, hopefully at a lower price. Bearish position.

Short-term Capital Gain: a profit realized on a security held for 12 months or less.

Short-term Capital Loss: a loss realized on a security held for 12 months or less, deductible against Short-Term Capital Gains.

SIMPLE Plan: a retirement plan for businesses with no more than 100 employees that have no other retirement plan in place. Pre-tax contributions, fully taxable distributions. Both employer and employees may contribute.

Simple Trust: a trust that accumulates income and distributes it to the beneficiaries annually.

Simplified Arbitration: a method of resolving disputes involving a small amount of money (currently $50,000).

Single-payment Deferred Annuity: annuity purchased with a single payment wherein the individual defers the payout or "annuity" phase of the contract.

Single-payment Immediate Annuity: annuity purchased with a single payment wherein the individual goes immediately into the payout or "annuity" phase of the contract.

Sinking Fund: an account established by an issuing corporation or municipality to provide funds required to redeem a bond issue.

SIPC: Securities Investor Protection Corporation, a non-profit, non-government, industry-funded insurance corporation protecting investors against broker-dealer failure.

Small Cap: a stock where the total value of all outstanding shares is considered "small," typically between $50 million and $2 billion.

Sole Proprietor: business ownership structure that provides no separate legal entity between the business and the owner him- or herself. Leaves the business owner liable for lawsuits against the company and debts of the company.

Solvency: the ability of a corporation or municipality to meet its obligations as they come due.

Specialized Fund: a mutual fund specializing in a specific type of strategy, for example a sector fund, an asset allocation fund, or a fund that writes covered calls to increase portfolio returns.

S&P 500: a grouping of 500 large-cap companies representing the overall stock market, weighted by market capitalization.

Speculation: the highest-risk investment objective, in which the speculator makes a bold bet that an asset's value will rise.

Spousal Account: an IRA established for a non-working spouse.

Spread: generally, the difference between a dealer's purchase price and selling price, both for new offerings (underwriting spread) and secondary market quotes. For underwritings the spread is the difference between the proceeds to the issuer and the POP.

Spread Load: sales charges for a mutual fund contractual plan that permits a maximum charge of 20% in any one year and 9% over the life of the plan.

Stabilizing/Stabilization: the surprising practice by which an underwriting syndicate bids up the price of an IPO whose price is dropping in the secondary market.

Stable Value Fund: a money market mutual fund whose name implies that maintaining a stable Net Asset Value is the primary objective. NAV is typically maintained at $1 per-share.

Standby Offering: a firm commitment in a rights offering in which an underwriter will use any rights not subscribed to.

Standby Underwriting: a commitment by an underwriter to purchase any shares that are not subscribed to in a rights offering.

Statement of Additional Information, or SAI: a document with more detailed information than what's contained in the mutual fund prospectus.

Statute of Limitations: a time limit that, once reached, prevents criminal or civil action from being filed.

Statutory Disqualification: prohibiting a person from associating with an SRO due to disciplinary or criminal actions within the past 10 years, or due to filing a false or misleading application or report with a regulator.

Statutory Prospectus: the full prospectus for a mutual fund. Contains more information than the summary prospectus but far less than the SAI, or the shareholder reports.

Statutory Voting: method of voting whereby the shareholder may cast no more than the number of shares owned per candidate/item.

Stock: an ownership or equity position in a public company whose value is tied to the company's profits (if any) and dividend payouts (if any).

Stock Dividend: payment of a dividend in the form of more shares of stock; not a taxable event.

Stock Split: a change in the number of outstanding shares designed to change the price-per-share; not a taxable event.

Straight Life Annuity: a settlement option in which the annuity company pays the annuitant only provided he or she is alive. Also called "straight life" or "life only."

Straight Preferred: a.k.a. "non-cumulative preferred," a preferred stock whose missed dividends do not go into arrears.

Street Name: securities titled in the name of the broker-dealer for-benefit-of a customer.

STRIPS: Separate Trading of Registered Interest and Principal of Securities. A zero-coupon bond issued by the U.S. Treasury in which all interest income is received at maturity in the form of a higher (accreted) principal value. Avoids "reinvestment risk."

Subaccounts: investment options available within the separate account for variable contract holders.

Subchapter M: section of the Internal Revenue Code providing the "conduit tax treatment" used by REITs and mutual funds distributing 90% or more of net income to shareholders. A mutual fund using this method is technically a Regulated Investment Company under IRC Subchapter M.

Subordinated Debenture: corporate bond with a claim that is subordinated or "junior" to a debenture and/or general creditor.

Subscription Right(s): the securities used in additional offerings of stock to purchase available shares, usually at a slight discount.

Suitability: a determination by a registered representative that a security matches a customer's stated objectives and financial situation.

Summary Prospectus: the most abbreviated disclosure document used to offer and sell mutual funds. Contains clear instructions on how to also obtain the statutory (full) prospectus and the SAI.

Supervision: a system implemented by a broker-dealer to ensure that its employees and associated persons comply with federal and state securities law, and the rules and regulations of the SEC, exchanges, and SROs.

Surrender: to cash out an annuity or life insurance policy for its surrender value.

Suspicious Activity Report (SAR-SF): a report that broker-dealers must file with the Treasury department whenever they suspect that a customer or other party may be using investment accounts to further criminal activities.

Syndicate: a group of underwriters bringing a new issue to the primary market.

Systematic Risk: another name for "market risk," or the risk that an investment's value could drop due to an overall market panic or collapse.

Systematic Withdrawal Plans: method of taking money out of a mutual fund investment gradually.

T

T + 3: regular way settlement, trade date plus three business days.

T-bills: direct obligation of U.S. Government. Sold at discount, mature at face amount. Maximum maturity is 1 year.

T-bonds: direct obligation of U.S. Government. Pay semiannual interest. Quoted as % of par value plus 32nds. 10–30-year maturities.

T-notes: direct obligation of U.S. Government. Pay semiannual interested. Quoted as % of par value plus 32nds. 2–10-year maturities.

Target Fund: a mutual fund that shifts its allocation based on nearing an approximate date chosen by the shareholders for retirement.

Tax-advantaged Account: an account such as an IRA or annuity that provides special tax benefits to the account owner through tax deductions and/or tax-deferred growth.

Tax Anticipation Notes (TANs): short-term loans issued by municipalities and backed up by tax revenues.

Tax Credit: an amount that can be subtracted from the amount of taxes owed.

Tax-deferred: an account where all earnings remain untaxed until "constructive receipt."

Tax-equivalent Yield: the rate of return that a taxable bond must offer to equal the tax-exempt yield on a municipal bond. To calculate, take the municipal yield and divide that by (100% – investor's tax bracket).

Tax-exempt Bond: municipal bond whose interest is not subject to taxation by the federal government.

Tax-exempt Bond Fund: mutual fund investing in municipal bonds.

Tax-exempt Money Market Fund: mutual fund investing in short-term debt obligations of municipalities.

Tax Identification Number: a social security number or FEIN associated with an investment account.

Tax Preference Item: certain items that must be added back to an investor's income for purposes of AMT, including interest on certain municipal bonds.

Tax-Sheltered Annuity (TSA): an annuity funded with pre-tax (tax-deductible) contributions. Available to employees of non-profit organizations such as schools, hospitals, and church organizations.

Telemarketing: to market securities on behalf of a broker-dealer or issuer by telephone.

Telephone Consumer Protection Act of 1991: federal legislation restricting the activities of telemarketers, who generally may only call prospects between 8 a.m. and 9 p.m. in the prospect's time zone and must maintain a do-not-call list, also checking the national registry.

Tenants in Common: see Joint Tenants in Common, a joint account wherein the interest of the deceased owner reverts to his/her estate.

Tender Offer: an offer by the issuer of securities to repurchase the securities if the investors care to "tender" their securities for payment.

Term Life Insurance: form of temporary insurance that builds no cash value and must be renewed at a higher premium at the end of the term. Renting rather than buying insurance.

Third Market: exchange-listed stock traded OTC primarily by institutional investors.

Third-Party Account: account managed on behalf of a third party, e.g., trust or UGMA.

Time Horizon: the investor's anticipated holding period.

Timing Risk: the risk of purchasing an investment at a peak price not likely to be sustained or seen again. Timing risk can be reduced through dollar cost averaging, rather than investing in a stock with one purchase.

Tippee: the guy who listened.

Tipper: the guy who told the other guy the insider information.

Tombstone: an advertisement allowed during the cooling off period to announce an offer of securities, listing the issuer, the type of security, the underwriters, and directions for obtaining a prospectus.

Top-Heavy: a benefit plan, e.g. a 401(k), that provides more than 60% of the benefits to highly compensated employees, leading to tax problems for the employer.

Total Net Worth: assets minus liabilities.

Total Return: measuring growth in share price plus dividend and capital gains distributions.

Trade Confirmation: a printed document containing details of a securities transaction, e.g., price of the security, commissions, stock symbol, number of shares, registered rep code, trade date and settlement date, etc.

Trade Date: the date that a trade is executed.

Trading Authorization: a form granting another individual the authority to trade on behalf of the account owner. Either "limited" (buy/sell orders only) or "full" (buy/sell orders plus requests for checks/securities) authorization may be granted. Sometimes referred to as "power of attorney."

Tranche: a class of CMO. Principal is returned to one tranche at a time in a CMO.

Transfer Agent: issues and redeems certificates. Handles name changes, validates mutilated certificates. Distributes dividends, gains, and shareholder reports to mutual fund investors.

Transfer and Hold in Safekeeping: a buy order for securities in which securities are bought and transferred to the customer's name, but held by the broker-dealer.

Transfer and Ship: a buy order for securities in which securities are purchased and transferred to the customer's name, with the certificates sent to the customer.

Transfer on Death: individual account with a named beneficiary or beneficiaries in which assets are transferred directly to the named beneficiaries upon death of the account holder, avoiding the probate process.

Treasury Bill: see T-bill.

Treasury Bond: see T-bond.

Treasury Fund: a mutual fund investing in U.S. Treasury securities.

Treasury Note: see T-note.

Treasury Receipts: zero-coupon bonds created by broker-dealers backed by Treasury securities held in escrow. Not a direct obligation of U.S. Government.

Treasury Securities: securities guaranteed by U.S. Treasury, including T-bills, T-notes, T-bonds, and STRIPS.

Treasury Stock: shares that have been issued and repurchased by the corporation. Has nothing to do with the U.S. Treasury.

Treasury STRIPS: see STRIPS.

Trough: phase of the business cycle representing the "bottoming out" of a contraction, just before the next expansion/recovery.

Trust: a legal entity holding title to various assets.

Trust Account: a brokerage account opened in the name of a trustee.

Trust Agreement: the legal documents establishing and guiding a trust account.

Trust Indenture: a written agreement between an issuer and creditors wherein the terms of a debt security issue are set forth, e.g., interest rate, means of payment, maturity date, name of the trustee, etc.

Trust Indenture Act of 1939: corporate bond issues in excess of $5 million with maturities greater than 1 year must be issued with an indenture.

Trustee: a person legally appointed to act on a beneficiary's behalf.

TSA: Tax-Sheltered Annuity. A retirement vehicle for 403(b) and 501c3 organizations.

Turnover Rate: expresses the frequency of trading that a mutual fund portfolio engages in.

U

(Form) U4: registration form for agents and principals submitted to the CRD system.

(Form) U5: termination form for agents and principals submitted to the CRD system.

UGMA: Uniform Gifts to Minors Act. An account set up for the benefit of a minor, managed by a custodian.

UIT: Unit Investment Trust. A type of investment company where investments are selected, not traded/managed. No management fee is charged. Shares are redeemable.

Unauthorized Transaction: a violation in which an agent enters a transaction without talking to the customer about it.

Underwriter: see "investment banker." Just kidding. An underwriter or "investment banker" is a broker-dealer that distributes shares on the primary market.

Underwriting Spread: the profit to the syndicate. The difference between the proceeds to the issuer and the POP.

Unearned Income: income derived from investments and other sources not related to employment, e.g., savings account interest, dividends from stock, capital gains, and rental income. Alternatively, every dollar paid to every sitting member of the United States Congress.

Uniform Practice Code: how the FINRA promotes "cooperative effort," standardizing settlement dates, ex-dates, accrued interest calculations, etc.

Uniform Securities Act: a model act that state securities laws are based on. Designed to prevent fraud and maintain faith in capital markets through registration of securities, agents, broker-dealers, and investment advisers. Main purpose is to provide necessary protection to investors.

Unit of Beneficial Interest: what an investor in a Unit Investment Trust (UIT) owns.

Universal Life Insurance: a form of permanent insurance that offers flexibility in death benefit and both the amount of, and method of paying, premiums.

Unrealized Gain: the increase in the value of a security that has not yet been sold. Unrealized gains are not taxable.

Unsecured Bond: a debenture, or bond issued without specific collateral.

Unsolicited Order: an order placed after a customer tells the agent what he/she wants to buy or sell, not a recommended/solicited trade.

USA Patriot Act: federal government legislation requiring broker-dealers and other financial institutions to help the government monitor suspicious activity that could be tied to money laundering.

User Fees or User Charges: the revenues used to support municipal revenue bonds, e.g., tolls or parking charges.

UTMA: A custodial account for the benefit of a minor child.

V

Value: as in "value investing" or a "value fund," the practice of purchasing stock in companies whose share price is currently depressed. The value investor feels that the stock is trading below its "estimated intrinsic value" and, therefore, sees an opportunity to buy a good company for less than it's worth. Like a "fixer-upper" house in need of a little "TLC." With a few quick improvements, this property is going to be worth a lot more than people realize.

Variable Annuity: an annuity whose payment varies. Investments allocated to separate account as instructed by annuitant. Similar to investing in mutual funds, except that annuities offer tax deferral. No taxation until excess over cost basis is withdrawn.

Variable Contract: an annuity or insurance policy whose values are tied to the fluctuating stock and bond markets.

Variable Life Insurance: form of insurance where death benefit and cash value fluctuate according to fluctuations of the separate account.

Variable Universal Life Insurance: flexible-premium insurance with cash value and death benefit tied to the performance of the separate account.

Vesting: a schedule for determining at what point the employer's contributions become the property of the employee.

Viatical Settlement: the purchase of a life insurance policy wherein the investor buys the death benefit at a discount and profits as soon as the insured dies.

Volatility: the up and down movements of an investment that make investors dizzy and occasionally nauseated.

Voluntary Accumulation Plan: a mutual fund account into which the investor commits to depositing amounts of money on a regular basis.

W

Warrants: long-term equity securities giving the owner the right to purchase stock at a set price. Often attached as a "sweetener" that makes the other security more attractive.

Wash Sale: selling a security at a loss but then messing up by repurchasing it within 30 days and, therefore, not being able to use it to offset capital gains for that year.

Whole Life Insurance: form of permanent insurance with a guaranteed death benefit and minimum guaranteed cash value.

Will: a legal document expressing the decedent's wishes for distributing assets after her death to various beneficiaries.

Withdrawal Plan: a feature of most mutual funds that allows investors to liquidate their accounts over a fixed time period, or using a fixed-share or fixed-dollar amount.

Written Complaints: complaints against an agent or broker-dealer that are written in any form whatsoever.

Y

Yield: the income a security produces to the holder just for holding it.

Yield to Maturity: calculation of all interest payments plus/minus gain/loss on a bond if held to maturity.

Z

Zero-Coupon Bond: a bond sold at a deep discount to its gradually increasing par value.